HARD-TO-FIND PUBLISHERS AND THEIR ADDRESSES

1984 Edition

Alan Armstrong & Associates Ltd

FIRST EDITION PUBLISHED IN 1981

THIS SECOND EDITION PUBLISHED February 1984

by

ALAN ARMSTRONG & ASSOCIATES LTD.
2 ARKWRIGHT ROAD
READING RG2 0SQ ENGLAND
Tel : 0734 751855   Telex : 849937

© 1984 ALAN ARMSTRONG & ASSOCIATES LTD.

U.K. ISBN : 0 946291 06 3

- PUBLISHER'S INTRODUCTION -

This is the second edition of our directory *'5001 Hard to Find Publishers & Their Addresses'*. Before you read further we would hasten to point out that this edition, like the first, is :

        NOT Comprehensive
        NOT Editorially perfect
        NOT Strictly in alphabetical order
        NOT True to its title (a few of the publishers listed
                                    are very easy to find!)
        NOT The best thing since sliced bread.

BUT - IT IS A VERY USEFUL LIST OF NAMES AND ADDRESSES. There are well over 7,000 publishers with their full address and telephone and telex numbers where possible. It is an international list and in the main contains those publishers who produce books in English of U.K. or international interest. For example, you would not find the address of a Japanese publisher who produces books on Japanese folklore, but you would find the address of the Diamond Lead Company, who publish a directory of companies listed on the Tokyo Stock Exchange.

This book is designed to be used by librarians, booksellers, publishers, printers and anyone who has to track down the addresses of hard to find publishers. If it helps you just a few times it will have served its purpose and saved you many hours of research. If you find publishers that we have missed may we congratulate you and ask that you send details to us so that others may benefit from your research in the next edition.

In using the list you may see publishers whom you regard as not difficult to find. Be happy in your knowledge - many others new to libraries or bookselling may not find those publishers so easily.

Publishers are listed alphabetically by name. We have attempted to cross refer from initials or abbreviations to full name and vice versa, but it is always worth checking under all possibilities, because to make it perfect would have delayed publication and quadrupled the cost.

We do hope that you will find the list useful and that you will allow us to extend your thanks with ours to Julia Newman who spent innumerable hours researching, checking and double checking the addresses, and to Lesley Willoughby who had the unenviable task of typing the complete directory.

Alan Armstrong & Associates Ltd.
January 1984

THE PUBLISHERS OF THIS WORKBOOK ARE SPECIALIST BOOKSELLERS IN EDINBURGH, LONDON AND READING.

WE SUPPLY LIBRARIES IN MANY COUNTRIES WITH MEDICAL BOOKS, BUSINESS BOOKS, REFERENCE BOOKS, DIRECTORIES, ANNUALS, PAMPHLETS, TECHNICAL BOOKS, CONFERENCE PROCEEDINGS STANDARDS AND SO ON.

IF YOU THINK WE CAN HELP YOU

PLEASE TELL US!

IN LONDON	—	Brigid Macleod, Alan Armstrong & Associates Ltd., 72 Park Road, London NW1 4SH Tel: 01-723 3902 Telex: 297635
IN EDINBURGH	—	Philo Wood, Alan Armstrong & Associates Ltd., 6 Castle Street, Edinburgh EH2 3AT Tel: 031-226 4201 Telex: 72371
IN READING	—	Caroline Beech, Alan Armstrong & Associates Ltd., 2 Arkwright Road, Reading RG2 0SQ Tel: 0734 751855 Telex: 849937
IN READING (For Holders of a Library Licence)	—	Richard Armstrong, College Division, Alan Armstrong & Associates Ltd., 2 Arkwright Road, Reading RG2 0SQ Tel: 0734 751769 Telex: 849937

PLEASE CONTACT US BY NAME

A

A.A.A. - see American Accounting Association
AASHTO, National Press Building, Washington DC 26045, USA
AB Academic Publishers, PO Box 97, Berkhamsted, Herts HP4 2PX
ABC Hotel Guides, Oldhill, London Road, Dunstable, Beds. LU6 3EB Tel : 0582 604232/600036
ABC Travel Guides Ltd., World Timetable Centre, Dunstable, Beds. LU5 4HB Tel : 0582 600111
ABC World Airways Guide, 40 Bowling Green Lane, London EC1 Tel : 01.837 3636
ABM Publications Ltd., 6 Brodrick Road, London SW17 7DZ
ABP Ltd., 11 New Fetter Lane, London EC4P 4EE Tel : 01.583 9855 Telex : 263398
ABP/OMP Microforms - published by Chapman & Hall Ltd. distributed by Associated Book Publ.
ABT Assoc.Inc., 55 Wheeler Street, Cambridge, Massachusetts 02138, U.S.A.
ACAS, Cleland House, Page Street, London SW1P 4ND Tel : 01.222 4383
ACCA, 22 Bedford Square, London EC1B 3HS
ADAS, Great Westminster House, Horseferry Road, London SW1P 2AE Tel : 01.216 6311
AES Publications, 4 Steep Close, Green Street Green, Orpington, Kent BR6 6DS
AHM Publishing Corp.(U.S.) - distributed by Eurospan Ltd.
AIAA - see American Institute of Aeronautics & Astronautics
AIChE - see American Institute of Chemical Engineers
AICPA, 1211 Avenue of the Americas, NY 10836, USA
A.K.Books, 53 Great Sutton Street, London EC1V 0DQ Tel : 01.251 3783 distributed by Croom Helm
ALH Systems Ltd., Station Road, Westbury, Wilts. BA13 4TN Tel : 0373 864744
ALLM Books, 21 Beechcroft Road, Bushey, Watford, WD2 2JU Tel : 0923 30150
AMACOM - see American Management Association
AMS Press Inc., 56 East 13th Street, New York 10003, USA distributed by Eurospan Ltd.
AMSCO School Publications, 315 Hudson Street, New York 10013, USA
ANEP, Otto Vieth Verlag, Alfredstrasse 1, D 2000 Hamburg 76, Germany
ANSI - see American National Standards Institute
ANSLICS, The Library, Robert Gordon's Institute of Technology, St.Andrews Street, Aberdeen AB1 1HG
A.P.Financial Registers Ltd., 9 Courtleigh Gardens, London NW11 9JX Tel : 01.458 1607
AP Publications Ltd., 322 St.John Street, London EC1V 4QH Tel : 01.278 1102
APA - Associated Publishers, Amsterdam/Philo Press C.V. PO Box 1850, NL1000 Amsterdam, The Netherlands
APS - see American Phytopathological Society
A.R.C.Weed Research Organisation, Begbroke Hill, Yarnton, Oxford OX5 1PF Tel : 08675 3761
ASE - see Association for Science Education
A.S.E.E., Wix Hill House, West Horsley, Guildford, Surrey
A.S.H.R.A.E., United Engineering Centre, 345E 47th Street, New York 10017, USA
ASM - see American Society for Metals
A.S.M.E., 345 East 4th Street, New York 10017, USA (ASME Pressure Vessel Codes etc. available from Technical Help to Exporters (BSI) or London Information of Ascot)
ASTM - see American Society for Testing of Materials
AUEW, Little Green, Richmond, Surrey
AVI Technical Books, c/o TABS, 24 Red Lion Street, London WC1R 4PX
A&W Publ., c/o TABS, 24 Red Lion Street, London WC1R 4PX
A.W.Publications Ltd., 290a Hale Lane, Edgware, Middx. HA8 8NP
ABACUS Books Ltd., Abacus Press, Abacus House, Speldhurst Road, Tunbridge Wells, Kent TN4 0HU Telex : 95652 Tel : 0892 27237/29783
ABACUS Electronics plc, Kennet House, Pembroke Road, Newbury, Berks RG13 1BX Tel : 0635 33311
ABACUS Scrl, Via Villoresi 15, 20143 Milano, Italy Tel : 02 8322431 Telex : 311250
ABBA Consultants(Automation)Ltd., Maitland House, 35 Old Woking Road, West Byfleet, Surrey KT14 6LG Tel : 09325 49292
ABBEY Press, 16 Garden Court, Wheathampstead, Herts. 058283 2460
ABBEY Press, Fort Augustus, Invernessshire PH32 4DB Tel : 0320 6232
ABBEY Press, Sherborne (L.Coldwell Printing Ltd.), The Parade, Sherborne, Dorset Tel : 093 581 2367

ABELARD-Schuman Ltd., Furnival House, 14-18 High Holborn, London WC1V 6BX Tel : 01.242 5832
ABERDEEN Angus Cattle Society, Pedigree House, 6 Kings Place, Perth, Scotland PH2 8AD Tel : 0738 22477
ABERDEEN College of Education, Hilton Place, Aberdeen AB9 1FA Tel : 0224 42341
ABERDEEN Petroleum Publ.Ltd., 37 Huntly Street, Aberdeen AB1 1TH Tel : 0224 644725
ABERDEEN Post Office Directory Ltd., 21 Adelphi, Aberdeen AB1 2BL Tel : 0224 53292
ABERDEEN University Press Ltd., Farmers Hall, Aberdeen Ab9 2XT Tel : 0224 630724 Telex : 739477
ABINGDON Press, USA - distributed by SPCK, London
ABLEX Publishing Corp., Chancery House, 319 City Road, London EC1V 1LJ Tel : 01.837 3500 - distributed by IBD
ABRAHAMS (Norman), c/o N&N Associates of Regent Street, 6th Floor, Morley House, 320 Regent Street, London W1R 5HA Tel : 01.580 9702
ABRAMS(Harry N.)Inc. - distributed by New English Library
ABRASIVE Industries Association, 102 Gloucester Road, Hampton-on-Thames, Middx.TW12 2UJ Tel : 01.979 7396
ABSOLUTE Press, 14B Widcombe Crescent, Bath BA2 6AH Tel : 0225 316013
ABSON Books, Abson, Wick, Bristol BS15 5TT Tel : 027582 2446
ACADEMIC & Business Monographs Ltd., 6 Brodrick Road, London SW17 Tel : 01.672 9655
ACADEMIC & University Publishers Group, 1 Gower Street, London WC1 Tel : 01.580 3994 Telex : 82445
ACADEMIC Book Services, Oude Boteringestraat 22, Groningen PO Box 66, The Netherlands
ACADEMIC International, PO Box 555, Gulf Breeze, Florida 32561, USA
ACADEMIC Press (Inc.)London Ltd., 24-28 Oval Road, London NW1 7DX Tel : 01.267 4466 Telex : 25775
ACADEMIC Publications, Highfield, Danehill, Haywards Heath, W,Sussex RH17 7EX Tel : 0825 790214 Telex : 95246
ACADEMY Editions, 42 Leinster Gardens, London W2 Tel : 01.402 2141 Telex ; 896928
ACADEMY of Political Science, 2852 Broadway, New York 10025-0148, USA Tel : 212 866 6752
ACAIR Ltd., Unit 8a, 7 James Street, Stornoway, Scotland Tel : 0851 3020
ACANTHUS Books, Lanner, Redruth, Cornwall TR16 6BS Tel : 0209 217557
ACCESS Publishing, Workspace, 32 Sovereign Street, Leeds LS1 4BJ Tel : 0532 448580
ACCOUNTANCY, 56/66 Goswell Road, London EC1M 7AB Tel : 01.628 7060
ACCOUNTANTS Publishing Co.Ltd., 27 Queen Street, Edinburgh EH2 1LA Tel : 031.225 3687
ACE International, 8 St.John Street, Huntingdon, Cambs. PE18 6DD Tel : 0480 57595
ACHIEVEMENTS Ltd., Northgate, Canterbury, Kent CT1 1BA Tel : 0227 68664
ACORN Publications, 27 Bridge Street, Cambridge Tel : 0223 316833
ACROPOLIS Books - distributed in UK by Paul Maitland
ACTA Radiologica, Box 7449, S-10391 Stockholm, Sweden
ACTINIC Press Ltd. 129 St.John's Hill, London SW11 1TD Tel : 01.228 8091
ACTION Learning Associates, 83 Bilton Road, Rugby, Warwicks. CV22 7AS Tel : 0788 65787
ACTION Learning Trust, 45 Cardiff Road, Luton, Beds. LU1 1RQ Tel : 0582 414761
ACTION Research for the Crippled Child, Vincent House, Springfield Road, Horsham, W.Sussex Tel : 0403 64101
ACTION Resource Centre, Henrietta House, 9 Henrietta Place, London W1M 9AG Tel : 01.629 3826/7
ACTON Society Trust, Munro House, 9 Poland Street, London W1 Tel : 01.437 8954
ACUMEN-System Three, 125 New Bond Street, London W1Y 9AF Tel : 01.409 0147 Telex : 23341
AD Orientem Ltd., 2 Cumberland Gardens, St.Leonards-on-Sea, E.Sussex TN38 0QR Tel : 0424 427186
C.ADDENBROOKE, 10 Brechin Place, London SW7 Tel : 01.373 2508
ADDINGTON Press, Addington Palace, Croydon CR9 5AD Tel : 01.654 7676
ADDISON Wesley Publ.Co.Ltd., 53 Bedford Square, London WC1B 3DZ Tel : 01.631 1636

ADELAIDE Publishing Co.Ltd., 50 Bolton Street, Blackpool
    Tel : 0253 49144
Robert ADKINSON Ltd., 76 Old Compton Street, London W1V
    5PA Tel : 01.439 7086 Telex : 8952387
ADKINSON Parrish Ltd. (see BCP Publishing Ltd.) 49 Great
    Marlborough Street, London W1 Tel : 01.434 2617
ADLARD Coles Ltd. - imprint of Granada Publishing Ltd.
ADMINISTRATIVE Staff College - now Henley - The Management
    College
ADMERCA Ltd., Postfach 5, Arosastrasse 25, CH-8008 Zurich,
    Switzerland
ADMIRALTY Experiment Works, Haslar, Gosport, Hants. PO12
    2AG Tel : 0705 22351
ADMIRALTY Research Laboratory, Teddington, Middx.TW11
    0LN Tel : 01.977 3231
ADMIRALTY Tide Tables - distributed by J.D.Potter Ltd.,
    Admiralty Chart Agents, 145 Minories, London EC3
    Tel : 01.709 9076
ADSHEAD,Brian & Associates, 67 Bridge Street, Manchester
    Tel ; 061.832 2143
ADTECH Book Co.Ltd., 25 Victoria Street, London SW1H 0EX
    Tel : 01.222 0466
ADULT Literacy & Basic Skills Unit, Kingsbourne House, 229-
    231 High Holborn, London WC1V 7DA
    Tel : 01.405 4017
ADVANCE Books, Advance House, 101-109 Ladbroke Grove,
    London W11 1PG
ADVANCE Features, 34A High Street, Judges Terrace, East
    Grinstead Tel : 0342 28562
ADVANCED Computer Techniques Corp., 437 Madison Avenue,
    New York 10022, USA
ADVANCED Management Programmes Intl., 2 Seaforth Place,
    Buckingham Gate, London SW1 6JP Tel : 01.834 5764
ADVANCED Technology Marketing Ltd., PO Box 204, Coulson,
    Surrey CR3 1YB Tel : 07375 57496
ADVERTISING Agency Production Association, c/o W.S.Jones,
    Benton & Bowles, 197 Knightsbridge, London SW7
    Tel : 01.589 1444
ADVERTISING Association, Abford House, 15 Wilton Road,
    London SW1V 1NJ Tel : 01.828 2771
ADVERTISING Research Foundation Inc., 3 East 54th Street, New
    York 10022, USA Tel : 212 751 5656
ADVERTISING Standards Authority Ltd., Brook House, 2-16
    Torrington Place, London WC1E 7HN Tel : 01.580 5555
ADVICE Centre on Organisation of Industrial & Commercial
    Representation, 21 Tothill Street, London SW1
    Tel : 01.930 6711
ADVISORY Centre for Education (ACE)Ltd., 18 Victoria Park
    Square, London E2 9PF Tel : 01.980 4596
ADVISORY Committee on Pollution of the Sea, 60 New Oxford
    Street, London WC1A 1ES Tel : 01.580 3378/9
ADVISORY,Conciliation & Arbitration Service - see ACAS
ADVISORY Council for Adult & Continuing Education, 19B De
    Montfort Street,Leicester LE1 7GE Tel : 0533 542770
AERO Publishers Inc.,USA - distributed by Argus Books Ltd.
AERO Research Associates, PO Box 109, Great Neck, New York
    11022, USA Tel : 212 631 7886
AERONAUTICAL Quality Assurance Directorate, Headquarters -
    Government Offices, Kingston Byepass Road,
    Surbiton, Surrey KT6 5QP Tel : 01.398 4233
AFRICA-American Institute, 833 United Nations Plaza, New York
    10017, USA
AFRICA Bureau, 48 Grafton Way, London W1P 5LB
    Tel : 01.387 3182
AFRICA Buyer & Trader Publications, Wheatsheaf House, Sarmarite
    Street, London EC4 0AX Tel : 01.353 8397
AFRICA Christian Press, 49 Thornbury Road, Isleworth, Middx.
    TW7 RLE
AFRICA Journal Ltd., Kirkman House, 54A Tottenham Court Road,
    London W1P 0BT Tel : 01.637 9341
AFRICA Research Ltd., 18 Lower North Street, Exeter EX4 3EN
    Tel : 0392 76190
AFRICANA Publishing Co.,USA - distributed by Holmes & Meier
    Publ.Ltd.
AGE Concern(England), National Old People's Welfare Council, 60
    Pitcairn Road, Mitcham, Surrey CR4 3LL
    Tel : 01.640 5431
AGE Concern Greater London, 54 Knatchbull Road, London SE5 9QY
AGENDA Editions, 5 Cranbourne Court, Albert Bridge Rd,London
    SW11 4PE Tel : 01.228 0700
AGRA Europe(London)Ltd., 16 Lonsdale Gardens, Tunbridge Wells,
    Kent TN1 1PD Tel : 0892 33813 Telex : 95114
AGRICULTURAL Development & Advisory Service, Gt.Westminster
    House, Horseferry Road, London SW1P 2AE
    Tel : 01.216 6311
AGRICULTURAL Education Association, 5 Capel Close, Oxford
    OX2 7LA Tel : 0865 58654

AGRICULTURAL Press, Surrey House, 1 Throwley Way,
    Sutton, Surrey SM1 4OQ Tel : 01.643 8040
AGRICULTURAL Research Council, Headquarters, 160 Great
    Portland Street, London W1N 6DT Telex : 291218
    Tel : 01.580 6655
AGRICULTURAL Research Council, Food Research Institute,
    Colney Lane, Norwich NR4 7UA Tel : 0603 56122
AGRICULTURAL Research Council, Institute of Animal
    Physiology, Barbraham, Cambridge CB2 4AT
    Tel : 0223 832312
AGRICULTURAL Research Council, Meat Research Institute,
    Langford, Bristol BS18 7DY Tel : 0934 85 2661
AGRICULTURAL Research Council, Poultry Research Centre,
    Kings Building, West Mains Road, Edinburgh EH9
    3JS Tel : 031.667 4461
AGRICULTURAL Research Council, Weed Research Organisation
    Begbroke Hill, Yarnton, Oxford OX5 1PF
    Tel : 9185 3761
AGRICULTURE, Fisheries & Food, Ministry of, Directorate of
    Fisheries Research, Fisheries Laboratory, Pakefield
    Lowestoft, Suffolk NR33 0HT Tel : 0502 62244
AGRIDATA Ltd., 1B Harwood Row, London NW1 6SE
    Tel : 01.258 0470
AIKEN(Alex), 48 Merrycrest Avenue, Glasgow G46 6BJ
    Tel : 041.637 2438
AIMS of Industry Ltd.   ] now : Aims, the Free
AIMS for Freedom & Enterprise] Enterprise Organisation
AIMS, the Free Enterprise Organisation, 40 Doughty Street,
    London WC1N 2LF Tel : 01.405 5195
AIR Britain(Historians)Ltd., Stone Cottage, Great Sampford,
    Saffron Walden, Essex CB10 2RS Tel : 079986 323
AIR Data Publications, c/o Bookshelf, Wood Street, St.Annes-
    on-Sea, Lancs. Tel : 0253 728278
AIR Pollution Control, PO Box 2861, Pittsburgh, PA 15230
    USA
AIR Transport & Travel Industry Training Board - disbanded
AIRLIFE Publications(Shrewsbury)Ltd., 7 St.John's Hill,
    Shrewsbury SY1 1JE Tel : 0743 67858
AIRLIFT Distribution & Mail Order, Unit 5, 12 Market Road,
    London N7 9PW Tel : 01.609 3368
AIRLINE Publications, Noble Corner, Great West Street,
    Hounslow, Middx. Tel : 01.572 0225
AIRTOUR International, Elstree Aerodrome, Herts, WD6 3AW
    Tel : 01.953 4870
AJAX Publishing Co.(Sussex)Ltd., Rook Farm, Funtington,
    Sussex PO1 9LN Tel : 024 358 358 Telex : 86626
AKROS Publications, Albert House, 21 Cropwell Road,
    Radcliffe-on-Trent, Nottingham NG12 2FJ
    Tel : 06073 4802
AL Ahram Distribution Agency, Al Ahram Building, Al-Galaa
    Street, Cairo, Egypt Tel : 755500, 745666, 758333
    Telex : 92001, 92544
ALBATROSS - see W.W.Norton & Co.Ltd.
ALBION Scott Ltd., 45-51 York Road, Brentford, Middx. TW8
    0QP Tel : 01.560 3404 Telex : 291920
ALBYN Press, 214 Abbeymount, Edinburgh 8
    Tel : 031.661 9339
ALCOCK(R.C.)Ltd., 11 Regent Street, Cheltenham, Glos.
    GL50 1HJ Tel : 0242 25859
ALCOVE Press, 59 St.Martin's Lane, London WC2N 4JS
    Tel : 01.836 4194
ALDEN & Blackwell(Eton)Ltd., Eton College, Windsor, Berks
    SL4 DF Tel : 07535 63849
ALDEN Press Ltd., Osney Mead, Oxford OX2 0EF
    Tel : 0865 49071 Telex : 83636
ALDINE Publishing Co., 5295 Wasbach Avenue, Chicago, Ill.
    60605, USA Orders to - IBD
ALDRICH Chemical Co.Ltd., The Old Brickyard, New Road,
    Gllingham, Dorset SP8 4JL Tel : 07476 2211
ALDUS Books c/o TABS, 24 Red Lion Street, London WC1R
    4PX Tel : 01.242 0373
ALDWYCH Press Ltd., 3 Henrietta Street, London WC2E 8LU
    - distributed by Eurospan Ltd.
ALEXANDRINE Press, 51 Cornmarket Street, PO Box 15,
    Oxford OX1 3EB Tel : 0865 724627 Telex : 22914
ALFRED Publishing Co.Inc., 15335 Morrison Street, PO Box
    5964, Sherman Oaks, CA 91413, USA
    - distributed by TABS
ALL England Netball Association, Francis House, Francis
    Street, London SW1P 1DE Tel : 01.828 2176
ALL England Women's Hockey Association, 160 Great Portland
    Street, London W1N 5TB Tel : 01.636 0264
ALL Seasons Publ.Ltd., 13 Lower Green, Tettenhall,
    Wolverhampton Tel : 0902 758662
Ian ALLAN Ltd., Terminal House, Shepperton, Middx.TW17
    8AS Tel : 09322 28950 Telex : 929806

Philip ALLAN Publishers Ltd., Market Place, Deddington, Oxford OX5 4SE Tel : 0869 38652
George ALLEN & Unwin (Publ.)Ltd., 40 Museum Street, London WC1A 1LU Tel : 01.405 8577 Telex : 826261
J.A.ALLEN & Co.Ltd., 1 Lower Grosvenor Place, London SW1W 0EL Tel : 01.828 8855
Ralph ALLEN Press, 4-5 Milk Street, Bath Tel : 0225 61888
W.H.ALLEN & Co.Ltd., 44 Hill Street, London W1X 8LB Tel : 01.493 6777 Telex : 28117
ALLIANCE of Small Firms & Self-Employed People, 42 Vine Street, East Molesey, Surrey KT8 9LF Tel : 01.979 2293
ALLIED Brewery Traders' Association, 8 Ely Place, Holborn, London EC1N 6SE Tel : 01.404 0007
ALLISON & Busby Ltd., 6a Noel Street, London W1V 3RB Tel : 01.734 1498 Orders to - George Philip & Son
ALLMAN & Son (Publ.)Ltd. - imprint of Mills & Boon Ltd.
ALLOWAY Publishing, 39 Sandgate, Ayr, Scotland KA7 1BG Tel : 0292 89318
ALLYN & Bacon Ltd. 42 Colebrooke Row, London N1 8AF Tel : 01.354 2096 distributed by IBD
ALMARK Publishing Co.Ltd., c/o Albion Scott Ltd.
ALMQVIST & WIKSELL Intl., 108 Drottninggatan, PO Box 45150, S-10430 Stockholm, Sweden Tel : 23 79 90 Telex : 12430
ALNA Press & Castle Wynd Printers Ltd., East Mains Industrial Estate, Broxburn, W.Lothian Tel : 0506 853723
ALOES Books, 69 Lancaster Road, Lonon N4 Tel : 01.263 5413
ALPHA Books & Alphabet & Image, Church House, Half Moon Street, Sherbourne, Dorset DT9 3LN Tel : 093581 4944 Telex : 46534
ALPHA Commercial Enterprises, 22 The Precinct, Albion Parade Wall Heath, Birmingham Tel : 0384 293929
ALPINE Club, 74 South Audley Street, London W1
ALPINE Garden Society Publications, 282-284 Hoe Street, Walthamstow, London E17 9QD
ALSTON Books, Oulton Lodge, Oulton Broad, Lowestoft, Suffolk NR32 3PW Tel : 0502 65036
ALTERNATIVE Bookshop, 3 Langley Court, Covent Garden, London WC2E 9JY Tel : 01.240 1804
ALTERNATIVE Society - now The Foundation for Alternatives
ALTERNATIVE Technical Information Operations, c/o 145 Lovelace Road, Surbiton, Surrey
ALTON Book Distributors Ltd., 16 Newman Lane, Alton, Hants GU34 2PJ Tel : 0420 85822
ALUMINIUM Federation Ltd., Broadway House, Calthorpe Road, Five Ways, Birmingham B15 1TN
ALUMINIUM-Verlag GmbH, Konigsallee 30, 4 Dusseldorf 1, West Germany Tel : 0211 320821 Telex : 8587407
AMATEUR Athletic Association, Francis House, Francis Street, London SW1P 1DL Tel : 01.828 9326
AMATEUR Boxing Association, 70 Brompton Road, London SW3 1HA Tel : 01.584 9186/7
AMATEUR Collector Ltd., PO Box 242, Highgate, London N6 4LW Tel : 01.348 0296
AMATEUR Entomologists' Society, 355 Hounslow Road, Hanworth Feltham, Middx. TW13 5JH Tel : 01.672 4024
AMATEUR Swimming Association, Harold Fern House, Derby Square, Loughborough, Leics.LE11 0AL Tel : 0509 30431
AMATEUR Winemaker Publications Ltd., South Street, Andover, Hants. Tel : 0264 3177
AMATEUR Yacht Research Society, Woodacres, Hythe, Kent Tel : 0303 66456
AMBER Lane Press, 9 Middle Way, Oxford OX2 7LH
AMBER Lane Productions Ltd., Amber Lane Farmhouse, The Slack, Ashover, Derbyshire S45 0EB Tel : 0246 590499
AMBIT Books, 17 Priory Gardens, London N6 5QZ Tel : 01.340 3566
AMBIT International, 200 North Service Road, Brentwood, Essex CM14 4SG Tel : 0277 230909
AMBIT Publications Ltd., 6a College Green, Gloucester GL1 2LX Tel : 0452 417553
Charles AMBLER & Assocs.Ltd., 987 Clarkson Road South, Mississauga, Ontario, Canada L5J 2V8
AMBLESHIRE Ltd., 190 Church Road, Hove, Sussex Tel : 0273 722833
AMERICAN Academy of Arts & Science, 165 Allendale Street, Jamaica Plain Station, Boston, Mass.02130, USA
AMERICAN Accounting Association, 6535 Orange Avenue, Sarasota, Florida 33577, USA
AMERICAN Association for Cancer Research, 7701 Burholme Avenue, Fox Chase, Philadelphia, Penn.19111,USA

AMERICAN Association for Clinical Chemistry - distributed by Raven Press
AMERICAN Association for the Advancement of Science - distributed by Academic Press(Inc),London
AMERICAN Association of Advertising Agents, 100 Park Avenue, New York 10017, USA
AMERICAN Association of State Highway Transport Officials, 341 National Press Buildings, Washington DC 20004 USA
AMERICAN Bankers Association, 1120 Connecticut Avenue, Washington DC 20036, USA
AMERICAN Bureau of Shipping, ABS House, 1 Frying Pan Alley, London E1 7HR
AMERICAN Chamber of Commerce(U.K.), 75 Brook Street, London W1Y 2EB Tel : 01.493 0381
The AMERICAN Chemical Society, c/o The Chemical Society, Publications Sales Dept., Blackhorne Road, Letchworth, Herts.SG6 1HN
AMERICAN Concrete Institute, PO Box 19150, Detroit, Michigan 48219, USA
AMERICAN Conference of Government Industrial Hygienists, PO Box 1937, Cincinnatti, Ohio 45201, USA
AMERICAN Enterprise Institute for Public Policy Research, 1150 17th Street NW, Washington DC 20036, USA Tel : 202 862 5864 - distributed by TABS
AMERICAN Federation of Information Processing Societies - distributed by Tratsart(J.B.)Ltd.
AMERICAN Geographical Society, Broadway at 156th Street, New York 10032, USA
AMERICAN Hospital Association, 840 North Lake Shore Drive, Chicago, Illinois 60611, USA
AMERICAN Industrial Hygienists Association, 665 Miller Road, Akron, OH 44313, USA
AMERICAN Institute of Aeronautics & Astronautics, 555 West 57th Street, New York 10019, USA
AMERICAN Institute of Biological Sciences, 1401 Wilson Boulevard, Arlington, VA 22209, USA
AMERICAN Institute of Certified Public Accountants, 1211 Ave.of the Americas, New York 10034, USA
AMERICAN Institute of Chemical Engineers, 345 East 47th Street, New York 10017, USA
AMERICAN Institute of Steel Constructors, 1221 Ave.of the Americas, New York 10020, USA
AMERICAN Library & Educational Services (ALESCO), USA - distributed in the U.K. by TABS
AMERICAN Library Association, Book Publishing Division, 50 East Huron Street, Chicago, Ill.60611, USA - distributed by Eurospan Ltd.
AMERICAN Management Association - orders to IBD
AMERICAN Marketing Association, 250 South Wacker Drive, Chicago, Ill.60606, USA
AMERICAN Mathematical Society, PO Box 6248, Providence, RI 02940, USA
AMERICAN National Standards Institute - distributed by American Technical Publishers Ltd.
AMERICAN Nuclear Society, 555 North Kensington Avenue, La Grange Park, Ill.60525, USA Tel : 312 352 6611 Telex : 254 635
AMERICAN Petroleum Institute Publications, 2101 'L' Street NW, Washington DC 20037, USA
AMERICAN Pharmaceutical Association, 2215 Constitution Ave. NW, Washington DC 20037, USA Tel : 202 628 4410
AMERICAN Phytopathological Society, 3340 Pilot Knob Road, St.Paul, Minnesota 55121, USA Tel : 612 454 7250
AMERICAN Psychiatric Association, 1700 West NW, Washington DC 20009, USA
AMERICAN Psychological Association, 1200 17th Street NW, Washington DC 20036, USA
AMERICAN Public Health Association, 1015 18th Street NW, Washington DC 20037, USA
AMERICAN Railway Engineering Association, 2000 'L' Street NW, Washington DC 20036, USA
AMERICAN Society for Civil Engineers (ASCE) - orders to Thomas Telford Ltd.
AMERICAN Society for Heating, Refrigeration & Air Conditioning Engineers Inc., 345 East 47th Street, New York 10017, USA
AMERICAN Society for Information Science - orders to IBD
AMERICAN Society for Metals, Metals Park, OH44073, USA - distributed by American Technical Publishers Ltd.
AMERICAN Society for Microbiology, Fulfillment Centre, PO Box 1192 Birmingham, Alabama 35201, USA
AMERICAN Society for Quality Control, 230 West Wells Street, Milwaukee, Wisconsin 53203, USA

AMERICAN Society for Testing of Materials, 1916 Race Street, Philadelphia, PA 19103, USA Tel : 215 299 5585 Telex : 710 670 1037 - distributed by American Technical Publishers
AMERICAN Society of Agronomy, 677 South Segoe Road, Madison, Wisconsin 53711, USA
AMERICAN Society of Clinical Pathologists - distributed by Raven Press
AMERICAN Society of Hospital Pharmacists, 4630 Montgomery Avenue, Washington DC 20014, USA
AMERICAN Society of Information & Science, Knowledge Industry Publ.Inc., 2 Corporate Park Drive, White Plains, NY 10604, USA
AMERICAN Society of Mechanical Engineers, 345 E.47th Street, New York 10017, USA
AMERICAN Society of Non-Destructive Testing, 914 Chicago Avenue, Evanston, Ill.60202, USA Tel : 312 475 4600
AMERICAN Society of Petroleum Engineering, 6200 North Express Way, Dallas, Texas 75205, USA
AMERICAN Society of Photogrammetry, 210 Little Falls Street, Falls Church, VA 22046, USA Tel : 703 534 6617
AMERICAN Technical Publishers Ltd., 68a Wilbury Way, Hitchin, Herts. SG4 0TP Tel : 0462 31525 Telex : 825684
AMERICAN Technical Society, c/o Technical Press Ltd., Freeland, Oxford OX7 2AP Tel : 0993 881788
AMERICAN University Publishers' Group Ltd., 1 Gower Street, London WC1E 6HA Tel : 01.580 3994/5 Telex : 82445 - orders & distribution : IBD
AMERICAN Veterinary Publ.Inc., PO Box 111, Wheaton, Ill. 60187, USA
AMERICAN Water Works Association, 2 Park Avenue, New York 10016, USA
AMERICAN Welding Society, PO Box 351040, Miami, Florida 33135, USA
AMEX Electronic Components Ltd., 3 Blackhorse Lane, Stevenage Road, Hitchin, Herts.SG4 9EE Tel : 0462 52082
AMNESTY Intl.Publications, U.K.Distributors : British Section, 8-14 Southampton Street, London WC2E 7HF Tel : 01.836 5621/7788 Telex : 28502 International Distributors : 10 Southampton Street, London WC2E 7HF Tel : 01.836 7788 Telex : 28502
AN Foras Taluntais Publications, 19 Sandymount Avenue, Dublin 4, Ireland
AN Lef Kernewek, 93 Mount Pleasant Road, Camborne, Cornwall Tel : 0209 713417
ANALYSES Economiques et Sociales, Case Postale 60, CH-1025 St.Sulpice Road, Switzerland
ANALYTIC Press - distributed by IBD
ANBAR Publications Ltd., PO Box 23, Wembley, Middx.HA9 8DJ Tel : 01.902 4489 Telex ; 935779
ANCHOR Books - c/o TABS
ANDERSEN Press Ltd., 19-21 Conway Street, London W1P 6JD Tel : 01.380 0438 Telex : 261212
ANDERSON Keenan Publ.Ltd., 392 St.John Street, London EC1V 4NN Tel : 01.278 3371
ANDREAS & Co., South Snowdon Quay, Porthmadog, Gwynedd, N.Wales
ANDREW & Suter Ltd., Belmont Works, Belmont Hill, St.Albans, Herts. AL1 1RE
ANDREWS & McMEEL Inc., 4400 Johnson Drive, Fairway, KS66205 USA Tel : 913 362 1523
ANFORME Ltd., Pennine House, 4 Osborne Terrace, Newcastle upon Tyne NE2 1NE
ANGLO-German Foundation for the Study of Industrial Society, 17 Bloomsbury Square, London WC1A 2LP Tel : 01.404 3137
ANGLIA Mart-Foaldale Ltd., 9-19 St.Georges Street, Norwich, Norfolk Tel : 0603 24726
ANGLIANA(Norwich)Ltd., 44-48 Magdalen Street, Norwich, Norfolk Tel : 0603 619674
ANGLO-Israel Association, 9 Bentinck Street, London W1M 5RP Tel : 01.486 2300
ANGUS & Robertson(U.K.)Ltd., 16 Golden Square, London W1R 4BN Tel : 01.434 3767 Telex : 897284
ANGUS Books Ltd., 13-35 Bridge Street, Hemel Hempstead, Herts.HP1 1EE Tel : 0442 63841
ANGUS Hudson Ltd., Maxwell House, 74 Worship Street, London EC2A 2EN Tel : 01.377 4741 Telex : 885233
ANGUS Stewart Publications Ltd., The Old Rectory, Roughton, Norfolk NR11 8SU Tel : 026 376 626
ANIMA Graphics, 26 Cale Street, London SW3 Tel : 01.352 7694
ANIMAL Pharm, World Animal Health News, 18-20 Hill Rise, Richmond, Surrey TW10 6UA

ANIMYSTIC Publ., 66 Addison Road, Bromley, London Tel : 01.464 4863
ANN Arbor Paperbacks - c/o TABS
ANN Arbor Science Publ.Inc., Drawer 1425, Ann Arbor, Mich.48106, USA - distributed by Butterworth & Co.Ltd.
ANNAKIN Fine Arts Ltd., 13 Geneva Street, Peterborough, PE1 2RS Tel : 0733 44040
ANNUAIRE de France, Observatory House, Observatory Gardens, Kensington, London W8 7NS
ANNUAL Review Inc., 4139 El Camino Way, Palo Alto, Calif. 94306, USA Tel : 415 493 4400
Les ANSTEY, Round the Bend, Thixendale, Malton, Yorks.
ANSWERS(Research)Ltd., Algarve House, 140 Borden Lane, Sittingbourne, Kent, ME9 8HR
ANTI-Apartheid Movement, 89 Charlotte Street, London W1 Tel : 01.580 5311
ANTI-Common Market League, 52 Fulham High Street, London SW6 Tel : 01.736 7393
ANTI-Nuclear Campaign, PO Box 216, Sheffield S1 1BD Tel ; 0742 754691
ANTIOCH Press, Kent State University Press, Kent OH 44242 USA
ANTIQUARIAN Booksellers Association, 154 Buckingham Palace Road, London SW1W 9TZ Tel : 01.730 9273
ANTIQUE & General Advertising Ltd., Old Rectory, Hopton Castle, Craven Arms, Salop SY7 0QJ Tel : 054 74 356
ANTIQUE Collectors Club, 5 Church Street, Woodbridge, Suffolk Tel : 039 43 5501
ANTIQUE Finder, 5 Church Street, Woodbridge, Suffolk Tel : 039 43 5501
ANTIQUES Yearbooks, Chestergate House, Vauxhall Bridge Road, London SE1
ANTLER Press, Old Malt House, Upper Clatford, Hants. Tel : 0264 52530
Francis ANTONY Ltd., Trenance Mill, Blowing House Hill, St.Austell, Cornwall Tel : 0726 3476
ANVIL Books Ltd., 90 Lower Baggot Street, Dublin 2 Republic of Ireland Tel : 0001 762359
ANVIL Press Poetry, 69 King George Street, London SE10 8PX Tel : 01.858 2946
APPETRON Press Ltd. - no trace
APPLETON-Century-Crofts, 25 Van Zant Street, East Norwalk, CT 06855, USA - distributed by Prentice Hall/IBD
APPLETREE Press Ltd., 7 James Street South, Belfast BT2 7DL Tel : 0232 43074
APPLIED Science (Publ.)Ltd., 22 Ripple Side Commercial Estate, Ripple Road, Barking, Essex IG11 0SA Tel : 01.595 2121 Telex : 896950
APPLIED Skills for Management Ltd., 565 Fulham Road, London SW6 1ES Tel : 01.385 1992
APPLIED Technology Publications Ltd., 15 Coombe Road, New Malden, Surrey Tel : 01.949 3301
APPS, Steven - distributed by Wentworth Book Co.
AQUA International Publ.Ltd., Springfield House, The Parade, Oadby, Leicester Tel : 0533 718697
AQUARIAN Press Ltd., Denington Estate, Wellingborough, Northants. NN8 2RQ Tel : 0933 76031/4 - distributed by Thorsons Publ.Ltd.
AQUARIAN & Reprint Press - distributed by M.A.R.K. Book Distribution Ltd.
AQUILA/I.B.D., 11 Novi Lane, Leek, Staffs ST13 6NS
AQUILA Publishing Co.Ltd., 7 Banstead Road, Purley, Surrey CR2 3ER Tel : 01.668 5281 - distributed by J.B.Thomson, 12 Canal Terrace, Paisley, Renfrewshire PA1 2HS
ARAB Banking & Finance, MEED House, 21 St.John Street, London WC1N 2BP Tel : 01.404 5513 Telex : 27165
ARAB-British Chamber of Commerce, PO Box 4BL, 26a Albemarle Street, London W1A 4BL Tel : 01.629 1249
ARAB Consultants, 1a Ennismore Gardens Mews, London SW7 Tel : 01.589 4295/7980
ARAB Cultural Trust(Azure), 13a Hillgate Street, London W8 7SP Tel : 01.727 3131
ARAB Petroleum Research Centre, 7 Ave.Ingres, 75781 Paris, Cedex 161 France
ARAB Press Services, Flat 11, Karandokis Bldg., Nicosia, Cyprus
ARAB Publishing Co.Ltd., 107 Park Street, London W1Y 3FB Tel : 01.629 0892
ARAB Report & Memo, MEED Representative Office, 42 Ave. Hebes, 75116 Paris, France

ARAB Water World, PO Box 135121, Beirut, Lebanon
ARABIAN Information Ltd., 2 South Audley Street, London
    W1Y 5DQ Tel : 01.409 1525 Telex : 268663
ARABIAN Publications Ltd., 104 Great Russell Street, London
    WC1 Tel : 01.631 4272
The ARABIAN Yearbook, Neville House, Eden Street, Kingston-
    upon-Thames, Surrey KT1 1BY
Stanley ARASIM & Associates, 106 Galewood Road, Wilmington,
    DE 19803, USA
ARBORICULTURAL Association, Ampfield House, Ampfield,
    Romsey, Hants. SO5 9PA Tel : 0794 68717
    - see also A.B.Academic Publishers
ARC Welding Foundation, 22801 St.Clarra Junction, Cleveland,
    Ohio 44117, USA
ARCADE Recording Circuit, 23 Arcadian Gardens, London
    N22 5AG Tel : 01.888 7445
ARCADIAN Senes - see Hutchinson Publ.Group Ltd.
ARCADY Books Ltd., 2 Woodlands Road, Ashurst, Southampton,
    SO4 2AD Tel : 042 129 2601
ARCHITECTURAL Association, 34-36 Bedford Square, London
    WC1B 3ES Tel : 01.636 0974
ARCHITECTURAL Press Ltd., 9-13 Queen Anne's Gate, London
    SW1H 9BY Tel : 01.222 4333
ARCHITECTURE & Planning Publications Ltd. - ceased
    publishing 1983
ARCHIVE Press Ltd., 22 Belsize Park Gardens, London NW3
    4LH Tel : 01.722 6263 - distribution of military
    titles : Arms & Armour Press
ARCHON Books - orders to European Book Service, Hogeway
    Selaan 119, PO Box 124, Weesp, The Netherlands
ARCO Publications Ltd. - Prentice Hall/IBD
ARDIS/RLT, 2901 Heatherway, Ann Arbor, Michigan 48104, USA
AREA Trades Directory Ltd., Hillingdon House, 386-388 Kenton
    Road, Kenton, Harrow, Middx. HA3 9HA
    Tel : 01.907 8814/5
ARENA Publications Ltd., 325 Streatham High Road, London
    SW16 3NS Tel : 01.764 9889
ARGEE Publishers Ltd., 88 London Road, Leicester
    Tel : 0533 544335
ARGUS Books Ltd., PO Box 35, Wolsey House, Wolsey Road,
    Hemel Hempstead, Herts.HP2 4SS Tel : 0442 41221
ARGUS Communications, Plumpton House, Plumpton Road,
    Hoddesdon, Herts. EN11 0LB
ARGUS Distribution Ltd., 12-18 Paul Street, London EC2A 4JS
    Tel : 01.247 8233
L'ARGUS International, 18 Rue Cadet, 75009 Paris, France
ARIEL Press Ltd., 177 Clapham Manor Street, London SW4
    6DB Tel : 01.720 4967/4622
ARIS & Philips Ltd., Teddington House, Church Street,
    Warminster, Wilts. BH12 8PQ Tel : 0985 213409
    Telex : 449631
ARK Publishing, 130 City Road, London EC1 2NJ
    Tel : 01.250 1966 - orders to PO Box 38, Bristol,
    BS99 7NA Tel : 0272 771131
ARKLAY Publ., 64 Murray Place, Stirling FK8 2BX
ARKLETON Trust, Enstone, Oxford OX7 4HH Tel : 060872 255
ARLEN House Ltd., 2 Strand Road, Baldoyle, Dublin 13
    Tel : 0001 392520
ARLINGTON Books(Publ.)Ltd., 3 Clifford Street, London
    W1X 1RA Tel : 01.439 1688 - distributed by
    Biblios Publ.Distribution Services Ltd.
ARLINGTON House - see Crown Publ.Inc.
ARLINGTON Management Services Ltd., 87 Jermyn Street,
    London SW1Y 6JD Tel : 01.930 3638 Telex : 917835
ARLON House Publishing, Arlon House, Station Road, Kings
    Langley, Herts. 09277 68328
ARMADA Books, 14 St.James' Place, London SW1A 1PF
    Tel : 01.493 7070 - orders to Wm.Collins Sons & Co.
ARMS & Armour Press, 2-6 Hampstead High Street, London
    NW3 1QQ Tel : 01.794 7868 Telex : 896691
Alan ARMSTRONG & Assocs.Ltd., 2 Arkwright Road, Reading
    Berks RG2 0SQ Tel : 0734 751855/751769
    Telex : 849937
ARMSTRONG Publishing, 72 Park Road, London NW1 4SH
    Tel : 01.258 3740 Telex : 297635
Edward ARNOLD(Publ.)Ltd., 41 Bedford Square, London
    WC1B 3DP Tel : 01.637 7161 Telex : 847918
    - orders to Woodlands Park Avenue, Woodlands
    Park, Maidenhead, Berks. Tel : 062882 3104
E.J.ARNOLD & Son Ltd., Parkside Lane, Dewsbury Road,
    Leeds LS11 5TD
E.J.ARNOLD(Scotland)Ltd., Factory 18, 27-35 Napier Place,
    Ward Park North, Cumbernauld, Glasgow G68 6DN
Joseph ARNOLD & Co.Ltd., Church Bridge Works, Church,
    Lancs. Tel : 0254 382121 Telex : 635169

ARNOLD Services, 106 Runcorn Road, Moore, Warrington
    WA4 6UB Tel : 0925 74211 Telex : 667325
ARNOLD-WHEATON, Butterley Street, Leeds LS10 1AX
    Tel : 0532 442944 Telex : 556347
ARROW Books, 17-21 Conway Street, London W1P 6JD
    Tel : 01.387 2811 - distributed by Tiptree Book
    Services
J.W.ARROWSMITH Ltd., Winterstoke Road, Bristol BS3 2NT
    Tel : 0272 667545 Telex : 44246
ART Book Co.Ltd., 18 Endell Street, London WC2
    Tel : 01.836 7907
ART Guide Publ., 28 Colveill Road, London W11 2BS
    Tel : 01.229 4669
ART Needlework Industries Ltd., 7 St.Michael's Mansions,
    Ship Street, Oxford Tel : 0865 47556
ART Sales Index, Pond House, Weybridge, Surrey KT13 8SQ
    Tel : 0932 42678 Telex : 929476
ART Store (Kirkby Lonsdale)Ltd., 18 Main Street, Kirkby
    Lonsdale, Carnforth, Lancs. LA6 2AG
    Tel : 0468 71603
ART Trade Press Ltd., 9 Brockhampton Road, Havant, Hants.
    PO9 1NU Tel : 0705 484943
ARTECH Book Co., Artech House, 25 Victoria Street, London
    SW1H 0EX Tel : 01.222 0466 Telex : 885744
ARTECH House Inc. - distributed by Adtech Book Co.
ARTEMIS Press Ltd., Sedgwick Park, Horsham, W.Sussex
    RH13 6QH Tel : 040 376 369
ARTHRITIS & Rheumatism Council, 8-10 Charing Cross Road,
    London WC2H 0HN
James ARTHUR Book Co., 20 Walton Road, Tonbridge, Kent
    TN10 4EE Tel : 0732 358380
ARTIST Publ.Co.Ltd., 102 High Street, Tenterden, Kent
    TN30 6HT
ARTIST Reference, 90 George Lane, London E18
    Tel : 01.530 6145
ARTLOOK Books, 164-166 Beaufort Street, Perth 6000,
    W.Australia Tel : 328 9188 Telex : AA93191
ARTMUSIQUE Publ.Co.Ltd., 31 Perry Hill, London SE6 4LF
    Tel : 01.291 2076
ARTRAD Group of Companies, Hillingdon House, 368-388
    Kenton Road, Kenton, Harrow, Middx.HA3 9HA
    Tel : 01.907 8814/5
ARTS Council of Great Britain, 105 Piccadilly, London W1V
    0AU Tel : 01.629 9495
ARTUS Publ.Co.Ltd. - see Weidenfeld & Nicolson Ltd.
ARTWORKS Publicity & Publishing Ltd., Dryden Street,
    Kettering, Northants. Tel : 0536 520680
ASCENT Books Ltd., 22 Chewter Lane, Windlesham, Surrey
    GU20 6JP - distributed by George Philip & Son Ltd.
ASCENT Publications, 34 Elm Grove, London N8 9AH -
    distributed by Volturna Press
ASGARD Publ.Co.Ltd., 4A The Square, Petersfield, Hants.
    GU32 3HJ Tel : 0730 67131
ASH & Grant Ltd., 9 Henrietta Street, London WC2E 8PS
    Tel : 01.379 7169 - distributed by WHS Distrib.
Edwin ASHDOWN Ltd., c/o Music Sales Ltd. or William Elkin
    Music Services
ASHGROVE Press Ltd., 26 Gay Street, Bath, Avon BA1 2PD
    Tel : 0225 25539
ASHIRE Publ.Ltd., Mine & Quarry, 42 Gray's Inn Road,
    London WC1X 8LR Tel : 01.242 4553
ASHLEY Fields Music Ltd., 61 Frith Street, London W1V 5TA
    Tel : 01.734 7462/3
ASHMOLEAN Museum Oxford, Beaumont Street, Oxford OX1
    2PH Tel : 0865 511281
ASHRIDGE Management College, Berkhamsted, Herts.
    Tel : 044 284 3491
ASHTON & Denton Publ.Co.(C.I.)Ltd., 5 Burlington House,
    St.Saviours Road, St.Helier, Jersey, Channel
    Islands Tel : 0534 35461
ASIA Finance Publications - distributed by Kogan Page Ltd.
ASIA University Press, 228 Kew Gardens Road, Richmond,
    Surrey Tel : 01.940 9602
ASIAN Inst.Technology, PO Box 2754, Bangkok, Thailand
    - distributed by Thomas Telford Ltd.
ASIAN Productivity Organisation, Japan - distributed by
    Bowker & Co.Ltd.
ASKIN Publishers Ltd., 16 Ennismore Avenue, Chiswick,
    London W4 1SF Tel : 01.994 1314
ASLIB, 3 Belgrave Square, London SW1X 8RL
    Tel : 01.235 5050 Telex : 23667
ASLEX Publ.Co. 22-23 North Street, Guildford, Surrey
    Tel : 0483 60346
ASPHALT & Coated Macadam Association, 25 Lower Belgrave
    Street, London SW1W 0LS Tel : 01.730 0761

ASSIMIL Nelis Publ., 7 Russell Gardens, London NW11 9NJ
　　　Tel : 01.455 0716
ASSOCIATED Book Publ.(U.K.)Ltd., 11 New Fetter Lane,
　　　London EC4P 4EE Tel : 01.583 9855 Telex : 263398
　　　- orders to North Way, Andover, Hants. SP10 5BE
　　　Tel : 0264 62141 Telex : 47214
ASSOCIATED Business Press, Ludgate House, 107-111 Fleet
　　　Street, London EC4A 2AB Tel : 01.583 8888
　　　Telex : 262251 - distributed by Prentice-Hall/IBD
ASSOCIATED Business Programmes - now Associated Business
　　　Press
ASSOCIATED Catholic Publications Ltd., 33-39 Bowling Green
　　　Lane, London EC1R 0AB Tel : 01.278 7321
ASSOCIATED Newspapers Group Ltd., Carmelite House,
　　　Carmelite Street, London EC4Y 0JA Tel : 01.353 6000
ASSOCIATED Scientific Publ.Ltd. - distributed by Elsevier
　　　Science Publ.Ltd.
ASSOCIATED University Presses - c/o Golden Cockerel Press
The ASSOCIATION, Hermes House, St.John's Road, Tunbridge
　　　Wells, Kent TN4 9UZ Tel : 0892 26171
ASSOCIATION for Computing Machinery, 1133 Ave.of the
　　　Americas, New York 10036, USA
ASSOCIATION for Religious Education, Maplewood House,
　　　Boundstone Road, Rowledge, Farnham, Surrey
　　　GU10 4AT Tel : 025 125 3292
ASSOCIATION for Science Education, College Lane, Hatfield,
　　　Herts. AL10 9AA Tel : 07072 67411
ASSOCIATION for the Conservation of Energy, 39a Gloucester
　　　Place, London W1H 3PD Tel : 01.487 5544
ASSOCIATION of Applied Biologists, c/o National Vegetable
　　　Research Station, Wellesbourne, Warwick CV35 9EF
　　　Tel : 0789 840382
ASSOCIATION of Assistant Librarians - distributed by W.Dent,
　　　3 Kingsway, Harrowgate, N.Yorks. HA1 5NQ
　　　Tel : 0423 504322
ASSOCIATION of British Chambers of Commerce, 6-14 Dean
　　　Farrar Street, London SW1H 0DY Tel : 01.240 2340
　　　Telex : 888941
ASSOCIATION of British Generating Set Manufacturers Ltd.,
　　　Queensway House, 2 Queensway, Redhill, Surrey
　　　RH1 1QS Tel : 0737 68611
ASSOCIATION of British Manufacturers of Mineral Insulating
　　　Fibres, St.Pauls House, Edison Road, Bromley,
　　　Kent BR2 0EP Tel : 01.466 6719
ASSOCIATION of Certified Accountants, 29 Lincoln's Inn Fields,
　　　London WC2A 3EE Tel : 01.242 6855
ASSOCIATION of Colleges for Further & Higher Education,
　　　c/o Sheffield City Polytechnic, Pond Street, Sheffield
　　　S1 1WB Tel :0742 20911
ASSOCIATION of Commonwealth Universities, 36 Gordon Square,
　　　London WC1H 0PF Tel : 01.387 8572
ASSOCIATION of Community Health Councils for England &
　　　Wales, 362 Euston Road, London NW1 3BL
　　　Tel : 01.388 4814
ASSOCIATION Of Community Workers, Colombo St.Sports &
　　　Community Centre, Colombo, Blackfriars, London SE1
ASSOCIATION of Conference Executives, 8 St.John's Street,
　　　Huntingdon, Cambs. PE18 6BB Tel : 0480 57595
ASSOCIATION of Consulting Engineers, Alliance House, 12
　　　Caxton Street, London SW1H 0QL Tel : 01.222 6557
ASSOCIATION of Control Manufacturers, Leicester House, 8
　　　Leicester Street, London WC2H 7BN Tel : 01.437 0678
　　　Telex : 263536
ASSOCIATION of Cost Engineers, 33 Ovington Square,
　　　Kensington, London SW3 1LJ Tel : 0279 419975
ASSOCIATION of County Councils, Eaton House, 66a Eaton
　　　Square, London SW1W 9BH Tel : 01.235 5173
ASSOCIATION of Crossroads Care Attendant Schemes Ltd.,
　　　11 Whitehall Road, Rugby, Warwicks. CV21 3AQ
　　　Tel : 0788 61536
ASSOCIATION of Dispensing Opticians, 22 Nottingham Place,
　　　London W1M 4AT Tel : 01.935 7411
ASSOCIATION of Hydraulic Equipment Manufacturers,
　　　192 Vauxhall Bridge Road, London SW1
　　　Tel : 01.828 8128
ASSOCIATION of Illustrators, 17 Carlton House Terrace,
　　　London SW1Y 5BD
ASSOCIATION of Independent Contract Research Organisations,
　　　Bridge Works, Shoreham by Sea, Sussex BN4 5FG
　　　Tel : 07917 5611
ASSOCIATION of Independent Hospitals, 14 Fitzroy Square,
　　　London W1P 6AH Tel : 01.388 4921
ASSOCIATION of Iron & Steel Engineers, 3 Gateway Center,
　　　Suite 2350, Pittsburgh, Pa.15222, USA
ASSOCIATION of London Chief Librarians, Central Library,
　　　Katherine Street, Croydon, Surrey CR9 1ET

ASSOCIATION of Nurse Administrators, 13 Grosvenor Place,
　　　London SW1X 7EN Tel : 01.235 5258
ASSOCIATION of Official Analytical Chemists, 1111 N.19th
　　　Street, Suite 210, Arlington, VA 22209, USA
　　　Tel : 703 522 3032
ASSOCIATION of Optical Practitioners Ltd., Bridge House,
　　　233-234 Blackfriars Road, London SE1 8NW
　　　Tel : 01.261 9661
ASSOCIATION of Professional Engineers, 32 High Street,
　　　Bookham, Leatherhead, Surrey KT23 4AG
　　　Tel : 0372 56471
ASSOCIATION of Professional Executive, Clerical & Computer
　　　Staff, 22 Worple Road, London SW19 4DF
　　　Tel : 01.947 3131/6
ASSOCIATION of Professions for the Mentally Handicapped,
　　　126 Albert Street, London NW1 7NF
　　　Tel : 01.267 6111
ASSOCIATION of Public Health Inspectors - now Environmental
　　　Health Officers Association
ASSOCIATION of Railway Preservation Societies Ltd.,
　　　Sheringham Station, Norfolk Tel : 0263 822045
ASSOCIATION of Scientific, Technical & Managerial Staffs,
　　　10-26 Jamestown Road, Regent's Park, London NW1
ASSOCIATION Scientifique et Technique pour la Recherche en
　　　Information Documentative (ASTRID), Astrid
　　　Building, Koningham Astridlaan 89, B9000 Ghent,
　　　Belgium
ASSOCIATION of Short Circuit Testing Authorities Inc.,
　　　23-24 Market Place, Rugby, Warwicks.CV21 3DU
　　　Tel : 0788 78435
ASSOCIATION of Supervisory & Executive Engineers, Wix
　　　Hill House, West Hersley, Surrey
ASSOCIATION of Teachers of Management, Polytechnic of
　　　Central London, 35 Marylebone Road, London NW1
　　　5LS Tel : 01.486 5811 X259
ASSOCIATION of Teachers of Mathematics, Kings Chambers,
　　　Queen Street, Derby DE1 3DA Tel : 0332 46599
ASSOCIATION of University Radiation Protection Officers,
　　　Dept.of Chemistry, UWIST, King Edward VII Ave.,
　　　Cardiff CF1 3NU
ASSOCIATION of University Teachers, United House, 1
　　　Pembridge Road, London W11 3HJ Tel : 01.221 4370
ASSOCIATION Press, New York - distributed by TABS
ASSYST(U.K.)Computer Services Ltd., Armstrong House,
　　　Armstrong Road, Washington, Tyne & Wear NE37
　　　1LE Tel : 0632 460560
ASTESSEICHISCHE Apotheker, 9 Spitalgasse 31, 1094 Wien,
　　　Austria
ASTEX Publ.Co., Rooms 4, 3rd Floor Prudential Buildings,
　　　Epsom Road, Guildford, Surrey GU1 3JW
　　　Tel : 0483 60346/75674
ASTON Services, 200 Aston Brook Street, Birmingham B6 4SY
　　　Tel : 021.359 4647
ASTRAGAL Books - imprint of Architectural Press
Anthony ATHA Publ.Ltd., Hillmorton Road, Rugby, Warwicks.
　　　CV22 5AN Tel : 0788 72755
ATHENA Reproductions, 3 Windsor Arcade, Birmingham 2
　　　Tel : 021.236 2632
ATHENE Publ.Co.Ltd., Denington Estate, Wellingborough,
　　　Northants.NN8 2RQ Tel : 0933 76031
ATHERTON Press Inc., Lyon, Grant & Green Ltd., 22 South
　　　Audley Street, London W1P 1AA Tel : 01.629 2623
ATHLONE Press Ltd., 58 Russell Square, London WC1B 4HL
　　　Tel : 01.636 1301/2 Telex : 261507 - distributed
　　　by J.M.Dent & Sons Ltd.
ATHOL Books, 10 Athol Street, Belfast BT12 4GX
　　　Tel : 0232 25851
ATHOLL Press, 17 Regent Terrace, Edinburgh EH7
　　　Tel : 031.343 2386
ATLANTIC Books, 25 Scorrier Street, St.Day, Redruth,
　　　Cornwall TR16 5LH Tel : 0209 821016
ATLANTIS Publications, 71 Great Russell Street, London WC1B
　　　3BN Tel : 01.242 3457 Telex : 298246
ATLAS Book Sales Ltd., Atlas House, 61-71 Collier Street,
　　　London N1 9BE Tel : 01.837 9601 Telex:261396
ATLAS Publishing Co.Ltd., 334 Brixton Road, London SW9 7AG
　　　Tel : 01.733 4444
ATTERBURY & Justin, 29 Hurst Road, Sidcup, Kent DA15 9AE
ATTWOOD & Co.Ltd., 93-99 Gosnell Road, London EC1V 9QA
　　　Tel : 01.253 9355
AUBURN House Publ., USA - distributed by Eurospan Ltd.
AUDEL - distributed by IBD
AUDI-Market, Caixa Postal 2577, 20000 Rio de Janeiro, Brazil
　　　Tel : 021 223 9138
AUDIO Arts, 6 Briarwood Road, London SW4 9PX
　　　Tel : 01.720 9129

AUERBACH Publ.Inc., USA - some titles distributed by Van Nostrand Reinhold Co.Ltd. Computer Guides distributed by Heydon & Son Ltd.
AUGNER - imprint of Stainer & Bell Ltd.
AUGUSTINE Publ.Co., South View, Chawleigh, Chulmleigh, Devon EX18 7HL Tel : 076 98 540 - Britons Political titles distributed by Bloomfield Books, The Old Priory, Priory Walk, Sudbury, Suffolk Tel : 0787 76374
AURUM Press Ltd., 33 Museum Street, London WC1A 1LD Tel : 01.631 4596 Telex : 299557
AUSTICK'S Publications, Cookridge Chambers, 25 Cookridge Street, Leeds LS1 3AN Tel : 0532 455879
AUSTRALIAN Academy of Science, PO Box 783, Canberra City 2601, Australia Tel : 062 486011/475335
AUSTRALIAN Bureau of Mineral Research, PO Box 378, Canberra ACT 2601, Australia
AUSTRALIAN Federation of Modern Language Teachers Ass'n., 112 Surrey Street, Darlinghurst, NSW 2010, Australia
AUSTRALIAN Government Publishing Service, PO Box 84, Canberra ACT 2600, Australia
AUSTRALIAN Institute of Criminology, PO Box 28, Woden ACT 2606, Australia
AUSTRALIAN Institute of Petroleum Ltd., Wales Corner, 227 Collins Street, Melbourne, Victoria 3000, Australia Tel : 03 632756 Telex : 33421
AUSTRALIAN National University - distributed by Eurospan Ltd.
AUTOBOOKS Ltd., Bradford Road, East Ardsley, Wakefield, W.Yorks. WF3 2JN Tel : 0924 823971
AUTODATA Ltd., St.Peter's Road, Maidenhead, Berks SL6 7QU Tel : 0628 34321 Telex : 848314
AUTOMATIC Oil Tools Systems, Central Way, Walworth Ind. Estate, Andover, Hants. SP10 5BY Tel : 0264 65961 Telex : 47107
AUTOMATIC Vending Association of Britain, Bassett House, High Street, Banstead, Surrey SM7 2LZ Tel : 07373 57211
AUTOMOBILE Association, Fanum House, PO Box 50, Basingstoke, Hants. RG21 2EA Tel : 0256 20123 Telex : 858538 - Books & Guides distributed by Hutchinson Publ.Group Ltd., Maps & Atlases dist. by Geographia Ltd.
AVALON Books, Tudor Works, Tudor Street, Cardiff CF1 8UR Tel : 0222 28088
AVEBURY Publ.Co.Ltd., Olympic House, 63 Woodside Road, Amersham, Bucks HP6 5AA Tel : 02403 22121 - orders to : Distribution Centre, Blackhorse Road, Letchworth, Herts. SG6 1HN Tel : 04626 72555 Telex : 825372
AVEYARD Broadbent Ltd., Jessamine Leather Works, Spring Lane, Lees, Oldham Tel : 061 633 1126/7
AVIACHEM Marketing Ltd., 1 Court Downs Road, Beckenham, Kent BR3 2LL Tel : 01.658 6610
AVIATION Publications, Westport, Connecticut 06880, USA
F.C.AVIS, 25 Elliot Road, London NW4 3DS
AVON-Anglia Publications & Services, Annesley House, 21 Southside, Weston-super-Mare, Avon BS23 2QU Tel : 0934 31616
AUROM Press Ltd., c/o P.D.A.S.(Cowley)Ltd., Building 18, Denham Studio Estate, North Orbital Road, Denham, Bucks. Tel : 0895 4064
AWARD Publications Ltd., Spring House, Spring Place, London NW5 3BH Tel : 01.485 7747 Telex :296452
AXEL Springer Publ.Group, 58 Jermyn Street, London SW1Y 6PA Tel : 01.499 2994
AXHURST Ltd., 3 Roden Street, Ilford, Essex Tel : 01.514 0702
AXIS Viewdata, 21 Upper Brook Street, London W1 Tel : 01.629 5982
AYCLIFFE Press Ltd., 10 Pilton Street, Barnstaple, Devon EX31 1PE Tel : 0271 3301
AZTEC Corp., USA - c/o Patrick Stephens
AZURE, The Arab Cultural Trust, 13A Hillgate Street, London W8 7SP Tel : 01.727 3131

B

B&M Publications(London)Ltd., Victoria House, Birchfield Road, Birmingham Tel : 021.356 9901
BA Asia Ltd., Bank of America Tower, 20th Floor, 12 Harcourt Road , GPO Box 799, Hong Kong Tel : 5 2676666 Telex : 75679
BACIE - see British Association for Commercial & Industrial Education

BAS Overseas Publications Ltd., 48-50 Sheen Lane, London SW14 8LP Tel : 01.876 2131
BASF U.K.Ltd., Lady Lane, Hadleigh, Ipswich, Suffolk IP7 6BQ Tel : 0473 822531
B.B.Books, 1 Spring Bank, Salesbury, Blackburn BB1 9EU Tel : 0254 49128
BBC Monitoring Service Publications, Caversham Park, Reading Berks RG4 8TZ Tel : 0734 472742
BBC English by Radio & Television, Bush House, The Strand, POB 76, London WC2B 4PH Tel : 01.240 3456 Telex : 265781
BBC Publications, 144-152 Bermondsey Street, London SE1 3TH Tel : 01.407 6961 - trade orders & subscriptions
BBC Publications, 35 Marylebone High Street, London W1M 4AA Tel : 01.580 5577 - U.K.trade enquiries
BCA Publications, Akrem House, 82 Wellington Street, Thame, Oxon. OX9 3BF Tel : 084 421 2070
BCIRA, alvechurch, Birmingham B48 7QB
BCP Publ.Ltd., 3rd Floor, Berkshire House, 168 High Holborn London WC1V 7AA Tel : 01.379 6422
BCPC Publications, Shirley, Westfields, Cradley, Malvern, Worcs.WR13 5LP Tel : 088 684 362
BCW Publ.Ltd., 177a High Street, Ryde, Isle of Wight PO33 2HW Tel : 0983 67427 / 8 Farncombe Street, Farncombe Godalming, Surrey GU7 3AY
BDE International, Warwick Chambers, 14 Corporation Street, Birmingham B2 4RN Tel : 021.632 5654/5472
BED Business Books Ltd., Bridge House, Restmor Way, Wallington, Surrey SM6 7BY Tel : 01.647 1001/5
BFI Publishing, 81 Dean Street, London W1V 6AA Tel : 01.437 4355 Telex : 27674 - distributed by Biblios
BFM Exports Ltd., 30 Harcourt Street, London W1H 2AA Tel : 01.724 0857
BFP Books, Focus House, 497 Green Lanes, London N13 4BP Tel : 01.882 3315
BGA Business Services, 87 Jermyn Street, London SW1
BHRA Fluid Engineering, Cranfield, Bedford MK43 0AJ Tel : 0234 750422 Telex : 825059
BHRCA - see British Hotels, Restaurants & Caterers Ass'n.
BIM - see British Institute of Management
BIS Marketing Research Ltd., 199 Westminster Bridge Road, London SE1 7UT Tel : 01.633 0866 Telex : 8813024
BLAISE, 2 Sheraton Street, London W1V 4BH Tel : 01.636 1544
BMEG, 33 Alfred Place, London WC1E 7EN Tel : 01.636 5345
BML Business Meetings Ltd., 2 Station Road, Rickmansworth, Herts. WD3 1QP Tel : 09237 76363/4
BMR United Publ.Ltd., 245 Oxford Street, London W1R 1LF Tel : 01.734 4989
BNA Intl.Inc., 17 Dartmouth Street, London SW1H 9BL Tel : 01.222 8833 Telex : 262570
BNF Metals Technology Centre, Grove Laboratories, Denchworth Road, Wantage, Oxon.OX12 9BJ Tel : 02357 2992
BOC Ltd., Special Gases, PO Box 7, Manchester M17 1PP Tel : 061.794 4651
B.P.Educational Service, Britannic House, Moor Lane, London EC2Y 9BU Tel : 01.920 8985
BPA(Technology & Management)Ltd., Concept House, Deane Street, Dorking, Surrey RH4 2DR Tel : 0306 884522 Telex : 859424
BPCC, The Willows, 182 Beverley Road, Hessle, N.Humberside HV13 9AL Tel : 0482 648169
BPF, A7, Piccadilly, London W1V 6DN
BRAD - see British Rate & Data
B.S.A.Medical Sociology Group, Dept.of Sociology, University of Surrey, Guildford, Surrey
BSC Books Ltd., 33 Maiden Lane, Covent Garden, London WC2E 7JS Tel : 01.836 3341
B.S.I. - see British Standards Institution
B.S.O. - see Business Statistics Office
BSO Publications Ltd., 41 High Street, Wivenhoe, Nr. Colchester, Essex Tel : 020 622 5252
BSRIA, Old Bracknell Lane, Bracknell, Berks RG12 KAH
BSSM, 281 Heaton Road, Newcastle upon Tyne NE6 5PB Tel : 0632 655273
BSSRS - see British Society for Social Responsibility in Science
BWS Publishing Ltd., 4 Addison Bridge Place, Kensington, London W14 9BR Tel : 01.603 4567
B.Y.B.Ltd.(formerly Bottlers Yearbook Ltd.), 7 Higher Drive, Purley, Surrey CR2 2HP Tel : 01.668 7781
Bernard BABANI(Publ.)Ltd., The Grampians, Shepherds Bush Road, London W6 7NF Tel : 01.603 7296/2581
BABYLON Books, 69 Corporation Street, Manchester Tel : 061.834 8296
BACHMAN & Turner, Unit PP, Maidstone Industrial Estate, St.Peter Street, Maidstone, Kent ME16 0ST Tel : 0622 681034

BACK Issues Corp., 805 Mamaroneck Avenue, Mamaroneck, New York 10543, USA
BACK Pain Association, 31-33 Park Road, Teddington, Middx.
BADGEMORE Park Enterprises Ltd., Enterprise House, Badgemore Park, Henley-on-Thames, Oxon.RG9 4NR Tel : 04912 6633
BADGER Books, 37 Bridge Street, Evesham, Worcs. Tel : 0386 6071
BAG Brunner Verlag AG, Grossacherstrasse 88, Postfach, CH-8041 Zurich, Switzerland Tel : 482 84 74177
Samuel BAGSTER & Sons Ltd., 1 Bath Street, London EC1V 9LB Tel : 01.251 2925 Telex : 262364 / Unit 14, Trident Industrial Estate, Pindar Road, Hoddesdon, Herts EN11 0LD Tel : 0992 42033
BAHA'I Publishing Trust, 26a Melton Road, Oakham, Leics. LE15 6AY Tel : 0572 2780
BAHRAIN Business Directory, Columbia House, 69 Aldwych, London WC2
BAILEY Bros.& Swinfen Ltd., Warner House, Bowles Well Gardens, Folkestone, Kent CT19 6PH Tel : 0303 56501/8 Telex : 96328
BAILLIERE Tindall, 1 St.Anne's Road, Eastbourne BN21 3UN Tel : 0323 638221 Telex : 877503
BAINES Derek, 8 Brock Road, Langley Green, Crawley, W.Sussex RH11 7PP
G.G.BAKER & Associates, PO Box 20, Godalming, Surrey GU8 4AJ Tel : 04868 6653
Howard BARKER Press Ltd., 27a Arterberry Road, Wimbledon, London SW20 8AF Tel : 01.947 5482
John BAKER Publishers Ltd., 35 Bedford Row, London WC1R 4JH - distributed by A&C Black Ltd.
Michael BALFOUR Ltd., 3 Wedgwood Mews, Greele Street, London W1V 5LW Tel : 01.437 1558 Telex : 28905
BALFOUR Publications, c/o Photo Precision Ltd., Caxton Road, St.Ives, Huntingdon PE17 4LS Tel : 0480 64364
A.A.BALKEMA, Postbus 1675, Rotterdam, The Netherlands
John BALL Publ.Ltd., Topic House, Alfred Street North, Nottingham Tel : 0602 51202
BALLANTINE Books Inc. (division of Random House Inc.) 201 E.50th Street, New York 10022, USA
BALLINGER Publ.Co., USA - c/o Harper & Row Ltd.
BAMFORTH & Co.Ltd., Station Road, Holmfirth, W.Yorks Tel : 048 489 3107
BANBURY Historical Society, Banbury Museum, 8 Horsefair, Banbury, Oxon. OX16 0AA
BANCROFT & Co.(Publ.) - now Purnell Books
BANK of England, Threadneedle Street, London EC2R 8AH Tel : 01.601 4444
BANKER Research Unit, Financial Times, Minster House, Arthur Street, London EC4R 9AX Tel : 01.623 1211
BANKERN Publ.Co., 210 South Street, Boston, MA 02111,USA
BANNER of Truth Trust, 3 Murrayfield Road, Edinburgh EH12 6EL Tel : 031.337 7310
BANTAM Books Ltd., Century House, 61-63 Uxbridge Road, Ealing, London W5 5SA Tel : 01.579 2652 Telex : 267974 Trade counter - PO Box 17, Wellingborough, Northants.NN8 4BU Tel : 0933 225761 Telex : 311306
BAPTIST Publications, Baptist Church House, 4 Southampton Row, London WC1B 4AB Tel : 01.405 9803
BARBADOS Export Promotion Corp., Harbour Road, Bridgetown St.Michael, Barbados
BARBOUR (B.McCall), 28 George IV Bridge, Edinburgh EH1 1ES Tel : 031.225 4816
BARBOUR Index, New Lodge, Drift Road, Windsor, Berks SL4 4RQ Tel : 0344 4121
BARCLAY Mail Sates, Dept.BM, 200 Madison Avenue, 15th Floor, New York, USA
BARDO Publ.Co., 69 Cuxton Road, Strood, Kent Tel : 0634 727124
BARKELEY Book Co.Ltd., 36 Lattimore Road, St.Albans, Herts AL1 3XP Tel : 05827 60039
Arthur BARKER Ltd. - imprint of Weidenfeld & Nicolson Ltd.
BARKER & Howard Ltd., Barker House, 106-110 Watney Street, London E1 2QE Tel : 01.790 5081/2
BARMERLEA Book Sales Ltd., 64 Cricklewood Broadway, London NW2 3DL Tel : 01.450 7711/2
A.S.BARNES, USA - c/o Tantivy Press
Paul BARNETT, 84 Wykes Road, Exeter, Devon Tel : 0392 74524
BARNETT Norford Ltd., Standard House, 16-22 Epworth Street, London EC2A 4SX Tel : 01.628 7651
BARNSLEY Chronicle Ltd., 47 Church Street, Barnsley, S.Yorks S70 2AS Tel : 0226 43131
BARON Jay Ltd., Faraday Road, Prince Rock, Plymouth, Devon Tel : 0752 662096
BARON Publishing - imprint of Antique Collectors Club

BARR Brown Intl.Ltd., 17 Exchange Road, Watford, Herts. WD1 7EB
BARRACUDA Books, Radclive Hall, Radclive, Buckingham Tel : 02802 4441/2
BARRETT Book Co., 388 Summer Street, Stamford, CT06901 USA
BARRIE & Jenkins Ltd., 3 Fitzroy Square, London W1P 6JD Tel : 01.387 2888 Telex : 21373 - see Hutchinson Publ.Group
BARRON's Educational Series Inc., 113 Crossways Park Drive, Woodbury, New York 11797, USA
BARTAMS Books Ltd., PO Box 17, Wellingborough, Northants.
J.BARTHOLOMEW & Son Ltd., 12 Duncan Street, Edinburgh EH9 1TA Tel : 031.667 9341 Telex : 728134
BARTON (D.Bradford) Ltd., Trethellan House, St.Aubyn's Road, Truro, Cornwall TR1 2DU Tel : 0872 76737
BARTON Publ.Ltd., 8 Buckland Road, Yeovil, Somerset BA21 5EA Tel : 0935 6272/20477
BASIC Books Inc. Publ. - see Harper & Row Ltd.
BASIC Skills Unit, 18 Brooklands Avenue, Cambridge CB2 2HN Tel : 0223 316644
Jossey BASS Inc., c/o J.M.Dent & Son Ltd., Dunhams Lane, Letchworth, Herts. SG6 1LF
BATH University Press, Bath University, Claverton Down, Bath BA2 7AY Tel : 0225 6941
B.T.BATSFORD Ltd., 4 Fitzharding Street, London W1H 0AH Tel : 01.486 8484 - orders to PO Box 4, Braintree, Essex CM7 7QY Tel : 0376 21276
BATTELLE Press, Dept.PPA, 505 King Avenue, Columbus, Ohio 43201, USA Tel : 614 424 6393 Telex : 24-5454
BATTENBERG Verlag München, Prinzregentenstrasse 79, 8000 München 80, Germany Tel : 089 4702066/67
BAY Books, 16 Golden Square, London W1R 4BN Tel : 01.437 9602 Telex : 897284
BAY Tree Books, Hollins, Balmaclellan, Castle Douglas, Kirkcudbrightshire DG7 3QH
BAYARD Books - see Business Books Ltd.
BAYFAIR Publ., Bridge End House, New Road, Robin H Bay, Middlesbrough Tel : 0947 880335
Ernest BAYLY, 19 Glendale Road, Bournemouth BH6 4JA
BAYWOOD Publ.Co.Inc., PO Box 609, Farmingdale, New York 11735, USA
BEACON Press Inc. - distributed by Harper & Row Ltd.
BEACON Publishing, Jubilee House, Billing Brook Road, Weston Favell, Northampton NN3 4NW Tel : 0604 407288
BEACONSFIELD Publ.Ltd., 20 Chiltern Hills Road, Beaconsfield, Bucks HP9 1PL Tel : 04946 2118
David BEAMAN Publications, 52 Worcester Street, Wolverhampton Tel : 0902 23311
BEAMORE Ltd., Printing House, Longfield Road, Tunbridge Wells Tel : 0892 39628
Ruth BEAN Publishers, Victoria Farmhouse, Carlton, Beds. MK42 7LP Tel : 0234 720356
Derek BEATTIE, PO Box 29, Twickenham, Middx.TW1 3BN Tel : 01.891 3513
BEAUTY Books Ltd., PO Box 25, Arundel, W.Sussex BN18 0SW Telex : 87323
BEAVER Books, Astronaut House, Hounslow Road, Feltham, Middx. Tel : 01.890 1480
BEAVERBROOK Newspapers Ltd. - now Express Newspapers Ltd.
Saul BECK, 757 Third Avenue, New York 10017, USA
BECKNELL Books, PO Box 21, Kings Lynn, Norfolk PE30 2QP Tel : 0553 61328
BEDFORD Books Ltd. - stock taken over by Gordon Fraser Gallery Ltd.
BEDFORD College, Regent's Park, London NW1 4NS Tel : 01.486 4400
BEDFORD Square Press National Council for Voluntary Organisations, 26 Bedford Square, London WC1B 3HU Tel : 01.636 4066 - distributed by Macdonald & Evans
BEE Books New & Old, Tappingwall Farm, Burrowbridge, Bridgwater, Somerset TA7 0RY Tel : 082 369 781
BEE Jay, Skye View, Strath, Gairloch, Ross-shire IV21 2DB Tel : 0445 2220
W.A.BEECHING, Flat 45, The Albany, Manor Road, Bournemouth BH1 3EJ Tel : 0202 25567
BEECHAM Research Laboratories, Beecham House, Great West Road, Brentford, Middx.
BEECRAFT Ltd., 13 Althorp Road, London SW17 / High Trees Dean Lane, Merstham, Surrey RH1 3AH Tel : 07375 53111
BEEKAY Publ.Ltd., 103 Worcesters Avenue, Enfield, Middx. EN1 4ND Tel : 01.366 7679

BEEKMAN Pubs.Inc., PO Box 888, Woodstock, New York 12498, USA
BEE's Business Guides - see Malcolm Stewart Books Ltd.
Richard BELL, 23 Kingswood Close, Englefield Green, Egham, Surrey Tel : 0784 2055
BELL & Howell Ltd., Alperton House, Bridgewater Road, Wembley, Middx.HA0 1EG Tel : 01.902 8812 Telex : 261378
BELL & Hyman Ltd., Denmark House, 37-39 Queen Elizabeth Street, London SE1 1QB Tel : 01.407 5237 Telex : 886245
G.BELL & Sons Ltd. - now Bell & Hyman Ltd.
BELL Yard Press, 24 Hatton Wall, London EC1N 8JH
BELLBRIGHT Investments Ltd., 204 Longbridge Road, Barking, Essex Tel : 01.591 5952
BELLDRAKE Ltd., Adler House, Tavistock Square, London WC1H 9HN Tel : 01.387 1066
BELLEROPHON Books, California, USA - distributed by Kingswood Educational Services
BELLONA Publications - see Argus Books Ltd.
BELLOWER Ltd., 12 Whittlesford Road, Little Shelford Cambridge Tel : 0223 842853
BELTON Books - imprint of Stainer & Bell Ltd.
BEMROSE Publ.Ltd., 90-91 Great Russell Street, London WC1B 3PY Tel : 01.631 4141 - orders to J.M.Dent
BEN Uri Art Society, 21 Dean Street, London W1V 6NE
Raymond BENARDOUT, 5 William Street, Knightsbridge, London SW7X 9HL Tel : 01.235 3360 Telex : 25247/666387
Matthew BENDER & Co.Inc., 31 Dollis Park, London N3 1HJ Tel : 01.794 1617
Bo BENGTSSON, Ab Inmar, Hus 767, 430 90 Öckerö, Sweden
BENJAMIN/CUMMINGS Publ.Co.Inc. - distributed by Addison-Wesley Publ.Ltd.
W.A.BENJAMIN Inc., USA - now Benjamin/Cummings Publ. Co.Inc.
Michael BENN & Assocs. Ltd., PO Box 5, Wetherby, Yorks. LS23 7EH Tel : 0937 844524
BENN Brothers Ltd., Sovereign Way, Tonbridge, Kent TN9 1RW Tel : 0732 364422
BENN Electronics Publications, PO Box 28, Luton, Beds. LU1 2NT Tel : 0582 417438 Telex : 826314
Ernest BENN Ltd., Sovereign Way, Tonbridge, Kent TN9 1RW Tel : 0732 362468 Telex : 27844 - distributed by A&C Black
BENN Publications Ltd., Sovereign Way, Tonbridge, Kent TN9 1RW Tel : 0732 364422 Telex : 95132
E.W.BENTLEY, Northside, Crosspark Hill, Oakford, Tiverton, Devon
BENTLEY Films Ltd., PO Box 22, Pudsey, W.Yorks LS28 5NB
BENWELL Community Project, 85-87 Adelaide Terrace, Benwell, Newcastle upon Tyne NE4 8BB Tel : 0632 31210
BEREAN Publishing Trust, 52a Wilson Street, London EC2A 2ER
BERG Publishers Ltd., 24 Binswood Avenue, Leamington Spa, Warwicks. Tel : 0926 29470
BERGENWAY, 20 Webster Street, Derby Tel : 0332 368232
Roland BERGER & Partner GmbH, Truderinger Strasse 13, 8000 Munich 80, W.Germany Tel : 089 41761 Telex : 0522761
BERGSTRÖM & Boyle Books Ltd., 31 Foubert's Place, London W1V 1HE Tel : 01.437 4825
BERKELEY Publishers, 9 Warwick Court, London WC1R 5DJ
BERKSWELL Publishing Co.Ltd., 24-26 Blackfriars Lane, London EC4V 6ER Tel : 01.794 6221
BERLINER Research Center Inc., Danbury, Conn.06810, USA Tel : 203 744 2333 Telex : 969658
BERLITZ Travel Guides, c/o Cassell Ltd., 1 Vincent Square, London SW1P 2PN
BERMONT Books Inc. - distributed by Prentice-Hall
BERTIE Ramifications Ltd., 125 Abingdon Road, Standlake, Oxford OX8 7QN
BERTRAM Books Ltd., The Nest, Rosary Road, Norwich NR1 94H Tel : 0603 26277/614095
BESTSELLER Publications Ltd., 24-28 Friern Park, North Finchley, London N12 9DA Tel : 01.446 4461 Telex : 22303
BETON Verlag, Düsseldorfer Strasse 8, Postfach 450, D-4000 Düsseldorf 11, Germany Tel : 0211 571068/69
BETTER Books, 15A Chelsea Road, Lower Weston, Bath BA1 3DU Tel : 0225 28010
BETTISCOMBE Press, Bettiscombe, Bridport, Dorset Tel : 03086 239/278
BETWEEN The Lines, 7 Albany Street, Edinburgh EH1 Tel : 031.557 4280

J.M.BEVERIDGE & Assocs.Inc., 691 South 31st Street, Richmond, CA94804, USA
BEWICK Publications Ltd., E Floor, Milburn House, Newcastle upon Tyne NE1 1LF Tel : 0632 610078
BIBLE & Medical Missionary Fellowship, 352 Kennington Road London SE11 4LF Tel : 01.735 8227/8
BIBLE Club Movement, Prospect Hall, Prospect Place, Weston-super-Mare, Avon BS23 1RW Tel : 0934 413484
BIBLE Fellowship Union, 11 Lyncroft Gardens, Hounslow, Middx. Tel : 01.894 6498
BIBLE Reading Fellowship, St.Michael's House, 2 Elizabeth Street, London SW1W 9RQ Tel : 01.730 9181/2
The BIBLIOGRAPHICAL Society, c/o Hon.Sec., Mrs M.Foot, British Library, Reference Division, Great Russell Street, London WC1B 3DG
BIBLIOPHILE Books, Unit 4, St.Annes Trading Estate, St. Anne's Street, London E14 7HJ
BIBLIOS Publishers Distribution Services Ltd., Glenside Industrial Estate, Star Road, Partridge Green, Horsham, W.Sussex RH13 8LD Tel : 0403 710971
BIG-O Publishing, 13-19 Stroud Road, Gloucester GL1 5AA Tel : 0452 417305 Telex : 437289 Trade counter - 228 Fulham Road, London SW10 9NB Tel : 01.352 2251
BIGGAR & Co.Publ.Ltd., Suite One, Little Oaks, Mersham, Nr.Ashford, Kent Tel : 0233 72636
BILLBOARD Ltd., 7 Carnaby Street, London W1 Tel : 01.437 9411 - distributed by Argus Books
BILINGUAL Books Inc., 511 Eastlake Ave.E, Seattle, Washington 98109, USA Tel : 206 624 5344
BINDER Hamlyn Fry & Co., 8 St.Bride Street, London EC4A 4DA
P.F.BINGHAM, Claire House, Bridge Street, Leatherhead, Surrey Tel : 0372 76133
Clive BINGLEY Ltd. - distributed by Library Association Publishing
BINSTED Publications, Hanover House, 77 Cliddesden Road, Basingstoke, Hants. RG21 3EY Tel : 025679 5711
BIOCHEMICAL Society, Book Depot, PO Box 32, Commerce Way, Colchester, Essex CO2 8HP Tel : 0206 46351/2/3
BIODETERIORATION Information Centre, 80 Coleshill Street, Birmingham B4 7PF Tel : 021.359 3611
BIOENERGY Council, Suite 825A, 16-25 Eye Street NW, Washington DC 20006, USA
BIOMEDICAL Publications - distributed by J.Wiley & Sons
BIOMETRIKA, University College London, Gower Street, London WC1 Tel : 01.387 7050
Anthony BIRD Publications Ltd., Strettington House, Strettington, Chichester, W.Sussex PO18 1LA Tel : 0243 775930
BIRKHÄUSEN, CH-4010 Basel, PO Box 34, Elisabethenstrasse 19, Basel, Switzerland - distributed by Global Book Resources Ltd.
BIRKNER & Co., Wichmannstrasse 4, 2000 Hamburg 52, Postfach 520662, Germany
BIRMINGHAM Museums & Art Gallery, Chamberlain Square, Birmingham B3 3DH Tel : 021.235 4051
BIRMINGHAM Post & Mail Ltd., 28 Colmore Circus, Queensway Birmingham B8 6AX Tel : 021.236 3366
BIRMINGHAM Public Libraries, Central Library, Paradise Circus, Birmingham B3 3HQ Tel : 021.235 3392
P.J.BISH & J.A.BAKER, Honeypot Cottage, Beehive Lane, Binfield, Berks RG12 4TX Tel : 0344 21527
BISHOPSGATE Press Ltd., 37 Union Street, London SE1 1SE Tel : 01.403 6544
BLACK Cat Books - c/o TABS
BLACK Knight Press, 15 Woodlands Road, Cookley, Kidderminster, Worcs.
A&C BLACK Ltd., 35 Bedford Row, London WC1R 4JH Tel : 01.242 0946 Telex : 21792
BLACK Pig Press, Carreg Fawr, Porthyhyd, Llanwrda, Dyfed
BLACK Raven Press, Flat 2, 17 Sheffield Terrace, London W8 7NQ Tel : 01.727 7439
BLACK Sparrow Press, PO Box 3993, Santa Barbara, CA93105 USA
BLACKIE Publishing Group, Wesler Cleddens Road, Bishopbriggs, Glasgow G64 2NZ Tel : 041.772 2311 - trade orders to J.M.Dent(Distribution)Ltd.
BLACKSTAFF Press Ltd., 3 Galway Park, Dundonald, Belfast BT16 0AN Tel : 02318 7161/2
BLACKTHORN Publications, 44 Moat Farm Road, Northolt, Middx.UB5 5DR Tel : 01.845 4106
Basil BLACKWELL Publisher, 108 Cowley Road, Oxford OX4 1JF Tel : 0865 722146

Derrick BLACKWELL Ltd., 81 Great Gardens Road,
    Hornchurch, Essex RM11 2BA Tel : 04024 3287
BLACKWELL Scientific Publ.Ltd., 8 John Street, London
    WC1N 2ES Tel : 01.404 4101 - orders to Osney
    Mead, Oxford OX2 0EL Tel : 0865 40201
    Telex : 83118 / 9 Forrest Road, Edinburgh EH1
    2QH Tel : 031.225 4234
James BLACKWOOD & Co.Ltd., 32-34 Bridge Road East,
    Welwyn Garden City, Herts. AL7 1HY
    Tel : 07073 25061
William BLACKWOOD & Sons Ltd., 32 Thistle Street,
    Edinburgh EH2 1HA Tel : 031.225 3411/2/3
BLAKES Holidays Ltd., Wroxham, Norwich NR12 8DH
    Tel : 060 53 2141/5 Telex : 97114
Thomas BLAND & Sons, 21-22 New Row, St.Martins Lane,
    London WC2N 4LA Tel : 01.836 9122
BLANDFORD Press Ltd., Link House, West Street, Poole,
    Dorset BH15 1LL Tel : 0202 671171 /
    Robert Rogers House, New Orchard, Poole, Dorset
    BH15 1LU
BLAY'S Guides Ltd., Churchfield Road, Chalfont St.Peter,
    Bucks. SL9 9EW Tel : 07538 84417
BLAZE Fine Arts Ltd., 204A London Road, East Grinstead
    Tel : 0342 27941
E.& W.BLEASDALE, 13 Starling Road, Radcliffe, Manchester
    M26 OLW Tel : 061.764 1654
BLEASDALE Computer Systems Ltd., 7 Church Path, Merton
    Park, London SW19 Tel : 01.540 8611
BLERMANN, Kuhnardt Breckmann, Helmstedtec Strasse 151,
    D3300 Braunschweig, W.Germany
Geoffrey Bles Ltd., Barlavington Farm House, Barlavington,
    Petworth, W.Sussex Tel : 079 87 349 - distributed
    by George Philip & Son Ltd.
BLITZ Publications Ltd., Penrallt Riding Stables, Llanrhychwyn,
    Trefriw, Llanrwst, N.Wales Tel : 0492 640063
BLOND & Briggs, Dataday House, 8 Alexandra Road, London
    SW19 7JZ Tel : 01.946 9188 Telex : 928536
BLOODAXE Books, PO Box 1SN, Newcastle upon Tyne NE99
    1SN Tel : 0632 739703
Roy BLOOM Ltd., 81 Goswell Road, London EC1
    Tel : 01.251 4345/6 Telex : 24224
BLOOMFIELD Books, The Old Priory, Priory Walk, Sudbury,
    Suffolk Tel : 0787 76374
BLUE Light Publications, 10 Lefroy Road, London W12
BLUEBELL Railway Ltd., Sheffield Park Station, Nr.Uckfield
    E.Sussex TN22 3QL Tel : 082 572 2370
BLYTMAN International, 195 Dry Creek Road, PO Box 788,
    Healdsbury, CA 95448, USA
BOARD of Deputies of British Jews, Woburn House, Upper
    Woburn Place, London WC1H 0EP Tel : 01.387 3952
BOARD of the Inland Revenue, Somerset House, Strand, London
    WC2R 1LB
BOAT Technology Intl.& Gear Test, 147 Moorgreen Road, West
    End, Hants. Tel : 04218 4243
BOBBS Merrill Co.Inc - distributed by Eurospan Ltd.
The BODLEIAN Library, Oxford OX1 3BG Tel : 0865 44675
    Telex : 83656
BODLEY Head, 9 Bow Street, Covent Garden, London WC2E
    7AL Tel : 01.379 6637 Telex : 299080
BOFOERS Publ.Ltd., Edgbaston House, 83 Broad Street,
    Birmingham Tel : 021.632 4097
BOGHANDEL, 3 Klarcboderne, DK1001 Copenhagen, Denmark
BLKFÖRLAGET Braböcker/Forlagsaktiebolaget Wiken, Södra
    Vägen, S-26300 Höganäs, Sweden Tel : 042 39000
    Telex : 72643
BOLSOVER Press Ltd., 109 Bolsover Street, London W1
    Tel : 01.631 0723
BONDWAY Publ.Co.Ltd., 6 Cobbett Close, Pound Hill,
    Crawley, Surrey Tel : 0293 882817
BONIM Books, USA - distributed by George Prior Ltd.
Richard de BOO Ltd., 70 Richmond Street East, Toronto,
    Ontario M5C 2M8, Canada
BOOK Centre Ltd., Southport PR9 9YF Tel : 0704 24331
    Telex : 67457
BOOK Club Associates, Smith/Doubleday House, 87 Newman St.
    London W1P 4EN Tel : 01.637 0341 Telex : 24359
BOOK Guild Ltd., Dial House, 221 High Street, Lewes, Sussex
    BN7 2AE Tel : 0273 890171
BOOK People, 2940 7th Avenue, Berkeley, CA94710, USA
BOOK Production Consultants Ltd., 7 Brooklands Avenue,
    Cambridge Tel : 0223 61762
BOOK Promotion Services Ltd., Well House, Ewhurst Road,
    Cranleigh, Guildford Tel : 0483 272858
BOOK Publishers Representative Association, 154 Buckingham
    Palace Road, London SW1W 9TZ

BOOK Sales Ltd., 78 Newman Street, London W1P 3LA
    Tel : 01.636 9033 Telex : 21892 - orders to Book
    Sales Ltd., c/o Music Sales, Newmarket Road,
    Bury St.Edmunds, Suffolk
BOOKLAND & Co.Ltd., 1 Stanley Street, Chester CH1 2NJ
    Tel : 0244 24394
BOOKMARKS, 265 Seven Sisters Road, London N4 2DE
BOOK-Point Ltd., 78 Milton Trading Estate, Abingdon, Oxon.
    OX14 4TD Tel : 0235 834146 Telex : 837091
BOOKS Canada - now Canada Books International - distributed
    by European Book Service
BOOKS for Children, Park House, Dollar Street, Cirencester
    Glos. GL7 2AN Tel : 0285 76081
BOOKS for Europe Ltd., Sovereign Way, Tonbridge, Kent
    TN9 1RW
BOOKS from India (U.K.)Ltd., 45 Museum Street, London
    WC1B 3BQ Tel : 01.405 7226
BOOKS of Wessex Ltd., 82 Priory Bridge Road, Taunton,
    Somerset TA1 1PZ Tel : 0823 3904
BOOKSELLERS Association of Great Britain & Ireland, 154
    Buckingham Palace Road, London SW1W 9TZ
    Tel : 01.730 8214
BOOKSTALL Publications, 241 Henbury Road, Bristol 10
BOOKWISE Service Ltd., Langham Trading Estate, Catteshall
    Lane, Godalming, Surrey GU7 1NG
    Tel : 04868 4152
BOOKWORM Publ.Co., PO Box 3037, Ontario, CA 91761, USA
BOOLE Press Ltd., PO Box 5, 51 Sandycove Road, Dun
    Laoghaire, Co.Dublin, Ireland
BOOSEY & Hawkes Music Publ.Ltd., The Hyde, Edgware Road
    London NW9 6JN Tel : 01.205 3861 Telex : 8952811
David BOOTH (Publ.)Ltd., 6 Kings Avenue, London SW4 8BD
    Tel : 01.720 2309 Telex : 261507
BOOZ Allen & Hamilton, 101 Park Avenue, New York 10178,
    USA Tel : 212 697 1900 Telex : 620196
BORDEN Publ.Co., 1855 West Main Street, Albambia, CA91801,
    USA
BOREAS Publ.House, 63 Ninian Road, Cardiff CF2 5EL
    Tel : 0222 492017
BORNFMAN & Cohen Publications, 12 Telach Tikera Road,
    Tel Aviv, PO Box IL09, Israel
BOROUGH Directories Ltd., 171 Fordwych Road, London NW2
    Tel : 01.452 9440
BORROWDALE Press, 22 St.Andrews Close, Thorpe St.Andrew
    Norwich NR7 0RJ
BORTHWICK Institute of Historical Research, St.Anthony's
    Hall, Peasholme Green, York YO1 2PW
    Tel : 0904 59861 X274
BOSSINEY Books, Land's End, St.Teath, Bodmin, Cornwall
    Tel : 0840 213401
BOSWORTH & Co.Ltd., 14-18 Heddon Street, Regent Street,
    London W1R 8DP Tel : 01.734 4961/0475
BOTTIN, 28 Rue du Docteur Finlay, 75738 Paris Cedex 15,
    France Tel : (1) 578 61 66 Telex : 204286F
BOTTLERS Yearbook - now BYB Ltd.
BOURNEMOUTH Local Studies Publications, Teachers' Centre,
    Lowther Road, Bournemouth
BOURNVILLE Village Trust, Estate Office, Oak Tree Lane,
    Birmingham B30 1UB Tel : 021.472 3831
BOW Publications Ltd., 240 High Holborn, London WC1V 7DT
    Tel : 01.405 0878
BOWERDEAN Press, 15 Blackfriars Lane, London EC4V 6ER
    Tel : 01.248 4793
BOWES & Bowes Publishers, 9 Bow Street, London WC2E 7AL
    Tel : 01.836 9081
BOWKER & Bertram Ltd., Whitewalls, Harbour Way, Bosham,
    Chichester, W.Sussex PO18 8QH
BOWKER Publishing Co., Erasmus House, PO Box 5, Epping
    Essex CM16 4BU Tel : 0376 77333 Telex : 81410
BOWLEY Publications Ltd., PO Box No.1, St.Mary's, Isles of
    Scilly
BOWYER Hyslop Publ.Ltd., Alendale House, Hexham Road,
    Newcastle upon Tyne
Marion BOYARS Publ.Ltd., 18 Brewer Street, London W1R
    4AS Tel : 01.439 7827 - distributed by George
    Philip & Son Ltd.
BOYDELL & Brewer Ltd., PO Box 9, Woodbridge, Suffolk
    IP12 3DF Tel : 044 971 497 / 0394 411320
BOZO Publications, PO Box BMBozo, London WC1N 3XX
A.C.BRABY Pty.Ltd., PO Box 731, Durban 4000, South Africa
De BARRY Bracewell-Milnes, 26 Lancaster Court, Banstead,
    Surrey SM7 1RR
BRACKNELL Development Corporation, Farley Hall, Bracknell,
    Berks RG12 5EU Tel : 0344 3161

BRADDA Books Ltd., Educational Books, 3c Glebe Road, Letchworth, Herts. SG6 1DS Tel : 046 26 4499
BRADFORD Chamber of Commerce, Commerce House, Cheapside, Bradford BD1 4JZ Tel : 0274 28166/9
Barton D.BRADFORD Ltd., Trethellan House, St.Aubyns Road, Truro, Cornwall Tel : 0872 76737
BRADFORD University Press, University of Bradford, Bradford, W.Yorks, BD7 1DP Tel : 0274 33466 Telex : 51309
BRADFORDS Directory, PO Box 276, Fairfax, Virginia 22036 USA
Joseph BRADSHAW, 1 Westhill Road, Blackdown, Leamington Spa CV32 6RA
BRADT Enterprises, Overmead, Monument Lane, Chalfont St. Peter, Bucks SL9 0HY Tel : 02407 3865 - orders to 41 Nortoft Road, Chalfont St.Peter, Bucks SL9 0LA Tel : 02407 3478
Robert BRADY - distributed by IBD
BRAITHWAITE & Taylor, PO Box 400, Havelock Terrace, London SW8 4AU Tel : 01.622 1262
BRAMLEY Books, Bramley, Basingstoke, Hants. RG26 5AT Tel : 025 686 510
BRANCH & Mobile Libraries Group, Library Association, 11 Cryon View, Gloweth, Truro, Cornwall TR1 3JT
BRAND Brothers & Co., 32 Southborough Road, London E9 7EF Tel : 01.986 2833
BRANDON Systems Press Inc - distributed by Input Two-Nine Ltd.
Christian BRANN Ltd., Phoenix Way, Cirencester, Glos.GL7 1RY Tel : 0285 5944 Telex : 43473
BRANT Wright Associates Ltd., PO Box 22, 22a Bank Street, Ashford, Kent TN23 1DN Tel : 0233 21262
BRASSEY's Publishers Ltd., 10 Upper Berkeley Street, London W1H 7PE Tel ; 01.486 2637 Telex : 27578 - orders to Croom Helm
BREAKTHRU Publications(Poetry), c/o Ken Geering, 38 Penn Crescent, Haywards Heath, W.Sussex RH16 3HN Tel : 0444 412961
BRENNAN Publications, 3 College Place, Derby Tel : 0332 368127
BRENTANON, 37 Ave. de l'Opera, 75002 Paris, France
BRENTHAM Press, 137 Fowler's Walk, London W5 1BQ Tel : 01.997 7401
BREWHOUSE Private Press, Wymondham, Melton Mowbray, Leics. LE14 2AZ Tel : 057 284 274
BREWING Publications, 42 Portman Square, London W1H 0BB
BREYSTAND Ltd., Cross Street Chambers, Cross Street, Wakfield Tel : 0924 382782
The BRICK Development Association, Woodside House, Winkfield Windsor, Berks SL4 2DX Tel : 0344 5651
BRIDGES, 85 Stijkvierted, 2543 De Madin, Utrecht, The Netherlands
BRIGHAM Young University Press, 209 University Press Building, Provo, Utah 84601, USA - distributed by IBD
BRIGHTON Polytechnic School of Librarianship, Falmer, Brighton BN1 9PH
BRIGHTSTART Books - imprint of Souvenir Press
E.J.BRILL, 41 Museum Street, London WC1A 1LX Tel : 01.405 5482
BRIMAX Books, 347U Cherry Hinton Road, Cambridge CB1 4DH Tel : 0223 44914/5 Telex : 817625
BRISTOL & Avon Archaeological Research Group, c/o City Museum, Queens Road, Bristol BS8 1RL Tel : 0272 299771 X227
BRISTOL & Gloucester Archaeological Society, 9 Pembroke Road, Bristol BS8 3AU Tel : 0272 36751
BRISTOL Broadsides, 27 Clerkenwell Close, London EC1R 0AT Tel : 01.251 4976
BRISTOL City Museum & Art Gallery, Queens Road, Bristol BS8 1RL Tel : 0272 299771
BRISTOL Classical Press, 72 Park Row, Bristol, Avon Tel : 0272 214187
BRISTOL Polytechnic, Coldharbour Lane, Frenchay, Bristol BS16 1QY Tel : 0272 656261 X208
BRISTOL Technical Publications Ltd., St.Stephens House, Station Road, Filton, Bristol Tel : 0272 699036
BRITANNIA Trust Management Ltd., 3 London Wall Buildings, London Wall, London EC2M 5QL
The BRITISH Academy, 20-21 Cornwall Terrace, Regent's Park London NW1 4QP
BRITISH Admiralty-Chart Publications, General Maps Section, MOD Room 0172, Whitehall Main Building, Whitehall, London SW1
BRITISH Aerosol Manufacturers Association, Alembic House 93 Albert Embankment, London SE1 7TU Tel : 01.582 1115
BRITISH Aerospace Ltd., Six Hills Way, Stevenage, Herts SG1 2DA
BRITISH Agencies for Adoption & Fostering, 11 Southwark Street London SE1 1RQ Tel : 01.407 8800

BRITISH Agricultural Export Council, 35 Belgrave Square, London SW1X 8QN Tel : 01.244 9819
BRITISH Agricultural History Society, Museum of English Rural Life, Whiteknights, Reading, Berks RG6 2AG
BRITISH Agrochemicals Association, Alembic House, 93 Albert Embankment, London SE1 7TU Tel : 01.735 8471/2
BRITISH Airports Authority, 2 Buckingham Gate, London SW1E 6JZ
BRITISH Airways Board, Speedbird House, Heathrow Airport Hounslow, Middx. TW6 2JA Tel : 01.759 5511
BRITISH Amateur Athletic Board, Francis House, Francis Street, London SW1P 1DL
BRITISH American Research Association, 1 Gough Square London EC4A 3DE Tel : 01.353 6371
BRITISH & Foreign Bible Society, 146 Queen Victoria Street London EC4V 4BX Tel : 01.248 4751
BRITISH & Irish Communist Organisation - distributed by Athol Books
BRITISH Antarctic Survey, Madingley Road, Cambridge CB3 0ET Tel : 0223 61188 - orders to Distribution Centre, Blackhorse Road, Letchworth, Herts
BRITISH Archaeological Reports, 122 Banbury Road, Oxford OX2 7BP Tel : 0865 50254
BRITISH Association of Commercial & Industrial Education (BACIE), 16 Park Crescent, London W1N 4AP Tel : 01.636 5351
BRITISH Association for the Advancement of Science, Fortress House, 23 Savile Row, London W1X 1AB Tel : 01.734 6010
BRITISH Association of Conference Towns, 6 Falsgrave Road Scarborough Tel : 0723 68735
BRITISH Association of Picture Libraries & Agencies, 46 Addison Avenue, London W11 4QP Tel : 01.603 8811
BRITISH Association of Ski Instructors, Hazel Bain, Grampian Road, Aviemore, Inverness-shire, Scotland PH22 1RP
BRITISH Astronomical Association, Burlington House, Piccadilly London W1V 0NL Tel : 01.734 4145
BRITISH Birds Ltd., Fountains, Park Lane, Blunham, Bedford MK44 3NJ
BRITISH Business Schools Librarians Group - Post Experience Courses in Management - new title 'Management Training Directory' - distributed by Alan Armstrong & Assocs.Ltd., 72 Park Road, London NW1 4SH Tel : 01.723 3902 Telex :
BRITISH Calibration Service, National Physical Laboratory, Teddington, Middx.TW11 0LW Tel : 01.977 3222
BRITISH Canoe Union, Flexel House, 45-47 High Street, Addlestone, Weybridge, Surrey KT15 1JV Tel :0932 41341
BRITISH Carbonization Research Association, Wingerworth, Chesterfield, Derbyshire S42 6JS Tel : 0246 76821
BRITISH Carpet Manufacturers Association, 26 St.James's Square, London SW1Y 4JH Tel : 01.839 2145
BRITISH Cast Iron Research Association, Alvechurch, Birmingham B48 7QB Tel : 0527 66414
BRITISH Cave Research Association, Queens Road, Penkhull, Stoke-on-Trent ST4 7LQ Tel : 0782 45431 Telex : 36228
BRITISH Ceramic Plant & Machinery Manufacturers Association, PO Box 87, Weybridge, Surrey KT13 9JS Tel : 09322 28597/8
BRITISH Ceramic Research Association, Queens Road, Penkhull, Stoke-on-Trent ST4 7LQ Tel : 0782 45431
BRITISH Chess Magazine Ltd., 9 Market Street, St.Leonards-on-Sea, E.Sussex TN38 0DQ Tel : 0424 424009
BRITISH Compressed Air Society, Leicester House, 8 Leicester Street, London WC2H 7BL
BRITISH Computer Society, 13 Mansfield Street, London W1M 0BP Tel : 01.637 0471 - distributed by Heyden & Sons Ltd.
BRITISH Constructional Steelwork Association Ltd., 92-96 Vauxhall Bridge Road, London SW1V 2RL Tel : 01.834 1713
BRITISH Consultants Bureau, 1 Westminster Palace Gardens, Artillery Row, London SW1P 1RJ Tel : 01.222 3651
BRITISH Copyright Council, 29-33 Berners Street, London W1P 3DB Tel : 01.930 1911
BRITISH Council, Publications Dept., 65 Davies Street, London W1Y 2AA Tel : 01.499 8011 - some titles distributed by Longman Group Ltd.
BRITISH Council of Churches, Edinburgh House, 2 Eaton Gate London SW1W 9BL Tel : 01.730 9611 Telex : 916504
BRITISH Council of Productivity Associations, 8 Southampton Row, London WC1B 4AQ Tel : 01.405 1023

BRITISH Crop Protection Council - now BCPC Publications
BRITISH Dental Association - see British Medical Association
BRITISH Diabetic Association, 10 Queen Anne Street, London
    W1M 0BD Tel : 01.323 1531
BRITISH Direct Marketing Association, 1 New Oxford Street,
    London WC1A 1NQ Tel : 01.242 2254 Telex : 23549
BRITISH Electrical & Allied Manufacturers Association Ltd.
    (BEAMA), Leicester House, 8 Leicester Street,
    London WC2H 7BN Tel : 01.437 0678 Telex : 263536
BRITISH Engine Insurance Ltd., Longridge House, Manchester
    M60 4DT Tel : 061.833 9282
BRITISH Entomological & Natural History Society, c/o The
    Alpine Club, 74 South Audley Street, London W1
BRITISH Esperanto Association Ltd., 140 Holland Park Avenue,
    London W11 4UF Tel : 01.727 7821
BRITISH European Associated Publishers Ltd., BEAP House,
    106 Hammersmith Grove, London W6 7HB
    Tel : 01.748 8783
BRITISH Export Houses Association, 69 Cannon Street, London
    EC4N 5AB Tel : 01.248 4444
BRITISH Film Institute, 81 Dean Street, London W1V 6AA
    Tel : 01.437 4355 Telex : 27674 - distributed by IBD
BRITISH Food Manufacturing Industries Research Association,
    Randalls Road, Leatherhead, Surrey KT22 7RY
    Tel : 0372 376761
BRITISH Franchise Association, Grove House, 628 London Road,
    Colnbrook, Slough, Berks SL3 8QH Tel : 02812 4909
BRITISH Gas Corporation, 59 Bryanston Street, London W1A 2AZ
    Tel : 01.723 7030
BRITISH Geotechnical Society, Institution of Civil Engineers,
    Great George Street, Westminster, London SW1P 3AA
    Tel : 01.839 3611
BRITISH Glass Industry Research Association, Northumberland
    Road, Sheffield S10 2VA Tel : 0742 686201
BRITISH Grassland Society, Grassland Research Institute, Hurley,
    Maidenhead, Berks SL6 5LR Tel : 062882 3626/3631
BRITISH Herbal Medicine Association, Lane House, Cowling,
    Keighley, W.Yorks BD22 0LX Tel : 0535 34487
BRITISH Homing World, 26 High Street, Welshpool Tel : 0938 2360
BRITISH Horse Society, British Equestrian Centre, Stoneleigh,
    Kenilworth, Warwicks. CU8 2LR Tel : 0203 52241
BRITISH Hotels Restaurants & Caterers Association, 40 Duke
    Street, London W1M 6HR Tel : 01.499 6641
    Telex : 296619
BRITISH Humanist Association, 13 Prince of Wales Terrace,
    London W8 5PG Tel : 01.937 2341
BRITISH Hydromechanics Research Association, Cranfield,
    Bedford MK43 0AJ Tel : 0234 750422
BRITISH Independent Grocers' Association, 17 Farnborough
    Street, Farnborough, Hants. GU14 8AG
    Tel : 0252 515001/2
BRITISH Industrial Biological Research Association, Woodman-
    sterne Road, Carshalton, Surrey SM5 4DS
    Tel : 01.643 4411
BRITISH Industrial & Scientific Film Association Ltd., 26
    D'Arblow Street, London W1N 3FH Tel : 01.439 8442
BRITISH Industrial Truck Association, Buckhurst Hill, Ascot
    Berks SL5 7RP Tel : 0990 23800 Telex : 848048
BRITISH Institute of Management, Management House, Parker
    Street, London WC2B 5PT Tel : 01.405 3456 -
    distributed by Professional Publ.
BRITISH Institute of Mental Handicap, Wolverhampton Road,
    Kidderminster, Worcs.DY10 3PP Tel : 0562 850251
BRITISH Institute of Non-Destructive Testing, 1 Spencer
    Parade, Northampton Tel : 0604 30124
BRITISH Institute of Radiology, 32 Welbeck Street, London
    W1M 7PG Tel : 01.935 6237
BRITISH Institute of Recorded Sound, 29 Exhibition Road,
    London SW7 Tel : 01.589 6603
BRITISH Journal of Industrial Relations, Houghton Street,
    Aldwych, London WC2A 2AE
BRITISH Journal of Radiology, 36 Portland Place, London
    W1N 3DG Tel : 01.580 4189/4085
BRITISH Leather Manufacturers Research Association,
    Milton Park, Egham, Surrey TW20 9UQ
    Tel : 078 43 3086
BRITISH Library Bibliographic Services Division, 2 Sheraton
    Street, London W1V 4BH Tel : 01.636 1544
    Telex : 21462
BRITISH Library - BLAISE, 2 Sheraton Street, London W1V
    4BH Tel : 01.636 1544 Telex : 21462
The BRITISH Library Board, 2 Sheraton Street, London
    W1V 4BH Tel : 01.636 1544
The BRITISH Library, British Education Index, Store Street,
    London WC1E 7DG Tel : 01.636 1544

The BRITISH Library, British National Bibliography, Store
    Street, London WC1E 7DG Tel : 01.636 1544
The BRITISH Library Department of Manuscripts, Great
    Russell Street, London WC1B 3DG Tel : 01.636 1544
The BRITISH Library Department of Oriental Manuscripts &
    Printed Books, Great Russell Street, London WC1B
    3DG Tel : 01.636 1544
The BRITISH Library Department of Printed Books, Great
    Russell Street, London WC1B 3DG Tel : 01.636 1544
The BRITISH Library Lending Division, Publications Section,
    Boston Spa, Wetherby, W.Yorks. LS23 7BQ
    Tel : 0937 843434 Telex : 557381
The BRITISH Library Newspaper Library, Colindale Avenue,
    London NW9 5HE Tel : 01.205 4788
The BRITISH Library Press & Publications Section, 2 Sheraton
    Street, London W1V 4BH Tel : 01.636 1544
The BRITISH Library Reference Division, Great Russell Street,
    London WC1B 3DG Tel : 01.636 1544
The BRITISH Library, Research & Development Department,
    Sheraton House, Great Chapel Street, London W1V
    4BH Tel : 01.636 1544
The BRITISH Library Science Reference Library, 25
    Southampton Buildings, London WC2A 1AW
    Tel : 01.405 8721
The BRITISH Library U.K.Marc Tape Service, Store Street
    London WC1E 7DG Tel : 01.636 1544
BRITISH Management Data Foundation, 29 St.James's Street,
    London SW1A 1HB Tel : 01.839 2789/930 1385
BRITISH Market Research Bureau Ltd., 53 The Mall, Ealing
    London W5 3TE Tel : 01.567 3060 Telex : 935526
BRITISH Medical Association, BMA House, Tavistock Square
    London WC1H 9JR Tel : 01.387 4499 Telex : 265929
BRITISH Medical Bulletin, 65 Davies Street, London W1Y 2AA
BRITISH Museum(Natural History), Cromwell Road, London
    SW7 5BD Tel : 01.589 6323 X386
BRITISH Museum Publications Ltd., 46 Bloomsbury Street,
    London WC1B 3QQ Tel : 01.323 1234 - books
    distributed by Thames & Hudson Ltd.
BRITISH National Bibliography Ltd.(Council of the) - now
    British Library Bibliographic Services Division
BRITISH National Committee, International Chamber of Commerce
    103 New Oxford Street, London WC1A 1QB
    Tel : 01.240 5588
BRITISH National Film Catalogue, 127 Charing Cross Road
    London WC2H 0EA Tel : 01.437 4355 Telex : 27624
BRITISH-North America Research Association, 1 Gough Square
    London EC4A 3DE Tel : 01.353 6371
BRITISH Nuclear Energy Society - distributed by Thomas
    Telford Ltd.
BRITISH Nuclear Fuels Ltd., Risley, Warrington WA3 6AS
    Tel : 0925 35953 X3359
BRITISH Nutrition Foundation, 15 Belgrave Square, London
    SW1X 8PS Tel : 01.235 4904
BRITISH Ornithologists' Union, c/o Zoological Society of London
    Regent's Park, London NW1 4RY Tel : 01.586 4443
BRITISH Overseas Trade Board, 1 Victoria Street, London
    SW1H 0ET Tel : 01.215 3031 / Ludgate Hill,
    London EC4M 7HU
BRITISH Paper & Board Industry Federation, 3 Plough Place,
    Fetter Lane, London EC4A 1AL Tel : 01.353 5222
    Telex : 24854
BRITISH Parking Association, 17 The Croft, Chiswell Green,
    St.Albans, Herts. AL2 3AR Tel : 0727 57206
BRITISH Petroleum Co.Ltd., BP Educational Service, Britannic
    House, Moor Lane, London EC2Y 9BU
    Tel : 01.920 6100/8985 - orders to PO Box 5,
    Wetherby, W.Yorks LS23 7EH Tel : 0937 843477
BRITISH Philatelic Federation Ltd., 1 Whitehall Place, London
    SW1A 2HE Tel : 01.930 5254
BRITISH Phonographic Industry Ltd., Roxburghe House,
    273-287 Regent Street, London W1R 8BN
    Tel : 01.629 8642
BRITISH Plastics Federation, 5 Belgrave Square, London
    SW1X 8PH Tel : 01.235 9888 Telex : 8951528
BRITISH Ports Association, 35 Queen Square, London WC1N
    3AR Tel : 01.278 6995/8
BRITISH Postgraduate Medical Federation (University of
    London), Central Office, 33 Millman Street, London
    WC1N 3EJ Tel : 01.831 6222
BRITISH Printing Industries Federation, 11 Bedford Row,
    London WC1R 4DX
BRITISH Property Federation, 35 Catherine Place, London
    SW1E 6DY Tel : 01.828 0111
BRITISH Psychological Society, St.Andrews House, 48 Princess
    Road East, Leicester LE1 7DR

BRITISH Publishing Co.Ltd., Brunswick Square, Gloucester GL1 1UQ Tel : 0452 418191/2
BRITISH Pump Manufacturers Association, 37 Castle Street, Guildford, Surrey GU1 3UQ Tel : 0483 37997/8 - distributed by Trade & Technical Press
BRITISH Quarrying & Slag Association Ltd., Carolyn House, Dingwall Road, Croydon CR0 9XF Tel : 01.680 7850
BRITISH Radio Equipment Manufacturers Association, 31 Soho Square, London W1V 5DG Tel : 01.734 7471 Telex : 27869
BRITISH Railways Board, Euston Square, PO Box 100, London NW1 2DZ Tel : 01.262 3232 Telex : 24678
BRITISH Rate & Data, 76 Oxford Street, London W1N 0HH Tel : 01.434 2233 - distributed by McLean-Hunter Ltd.
BRITISH Ready Mixed Concrete Association, Shepperton House, Green Lane, Shepperton, Middx. TW17 8DN Tel : 09322 43232
BRITISH Records Association, Master's Court, The Charterhouse, Charterhouse Square, London EC1M 6AU Tel : 01.253 0436
BRITISH Red Cross Society, 4 Grosvenor Crescent, London SW1X 7EJ Tel : 01.235 5454 Telex : 918657
BRITISH Relais Routiers, 354 Fulham Road, London SW10 9UH Tel : 01.351 3522
BRITISH Road Federation Ltd., Cowdray House, 6 Portugal Street, London WC2A 2HG Tel : 01.242 1285
BRITISH Rubber Manufacturers Association Ltd., 90-91 Tottenham Court Road, London W1P 0BR Tel : 01.580 2794
BRITISH Safety Council, National Safety Centre, Chancellor's Road, London W6 9RS Tel : 01.741 1231/2371
BRITISH Ship Research Association, Wallsend Research Station, Wallsend, Tyne & Wear NE28 6UY Tel : 0632 625242
BRITISH Small Animal Veterinary Association, Grove Lodge Veterinary Hospital, Upper Brighton Road, Worthing, Sussex BN14 9DL Tel : 0903 34866
BRITISH Society for Middle Eastern Studies, 68 Woodstock Road, Oxford OX2 6JF Tel : 0865 59651
BRITISH Society for Social Responsibility in Science, 9 Poland Street, London W1V 3DG Tel : 01.437 2728
BRITISH Society for the Promotion of Vegetable Research, National Vegetable Research Station, Wellesbourne, Warwick. CV35 9EF Tel : 0789 840382
BRITISH Standards Institution, 101 Pentonville Road, London N1 9ND Tel : 01.837 8801 Telex : 23218
BRITISH Standards Institution, Linford Wood, Milton Keynes MK14 6LE Tel : 0908 320033/320066
BRITISH Steel Corporation, Information Services, 9 Albert Embankment, London SE1 7SN
BRITISH Sub Aqua Club, 16 Upper Woburn Place, London WC1H 0QW Tel : 01.387 9302
BRITISH Sulphur Corp.Ltd., Parnell House, 25 Wilton Road, London SW1V 1NH Tel : 01.828 5571 Telex : 918918
BRITISH Technology Group, 101 Newington Causeway, London SE1 6BU Tel : 01.403 6666 Telex : 894397
BRITISH Telecommunications, British Telecom Research Labs. Martlesham Heath, Ipswich IP5 7RE Tel : 0473 644538
BRITISH Theatre Institute, 30-36 Clareville Street, London SW7 5AW
BRITISH Tourist Authority, Queens House, 64 St.James Street, London SW1A 1NF Tel : 01.629 9191 - orders to 4 Bromells Road, London SW4 0BJ Tel : 01.622 3256
BRITISH Toy & Hobby Manufacturers Association, 80 Camberwell Road, London SE5 0EG Tel : 01.701 7271
BRITISH Trampoline Federation Ltd., 152a College Road, Harrow Middx. HA1 1VH Tel : 01.863 7278
BRITISH Travel Guide, 64 St.James Street, London SW1A 1NF
BRITISH Universities Film Council, 55 Greek Street, London W1V 5LR Tel : 01.734 3687/8
BRITISH Waterways Board, Melbury House, Melbury Terrace, London NW1 6JX Tel : 01.262 6711 Telex : 263605
BROADCAST, 11a Wardour Street, London W1V 3TD Tel : 01.439 9756
BROADCASTING Support Services, PO Box 7, London W3 6XJ
BROADLEYS Publ.Co., The Bothy, Broadleys, Widdington, Essex Tel : 0799 40922
BROADOAK Press(Heathfield)Ltd., Ragstones, Broadoak, Heathfield, E.Sussex TN21 8UD Tel : 04352 2012
BROCKHAMPTON Press - now Hodder & Stoughton Children's Books
James BRODIE Ltd., 15 Queen Square, Bath BA1 2HW Tel : 0225 22110
Irwin BROH & Associates Inc., 1001 East Touhy Avenue, Des Plaines, Illinois 60018, USA Tel : 312 297 7515
BRONEMAN & Cohen Publ.Ltd., 12 Derech Petach-Tikra, PO Box 1109, Tel Aviv 61010, Israel

BROOKINGS Institution, 1775 Massachusetts Avenue NW, Washington DC 20036, USA - distributed by Marston Book Services
BROOKLANDS Books, Holmerise, Seven Hills Road, Cobham, Surrey Tel : 093 26 5051
Lewis BROOKS Ltd., 52 Manchester Street, London W1M 6DR Tel : 01.935 3441 Telex : 24817
BROOMHEAD Publications, 74 Fore Street, Heavitree, Exeter Devon Tel : 0392 74095
BROOMHILLS Publishing, 23 Park Street, Old Hatfield, Herts AL9 5AT Tel : 07072 63399
BROOMSLEIGH Press - see Fudge & Co.Ltd.
BROWN Knight & Truscott, 11-12 Bury Street, London EC3A 5AP Tel : 01.623 2296
BROWN, Son & Ferguson Ltd., 4-10 Darnley Street, Glasgow G41 2SD Tel : 041.429 1234
BROWN University Press - distributed by IBD
BROWN Watson (Division of General Book Distributors Ltd.) 43-44 Great Windmill Street, London W1V 7PA Tel : 01.734 7394/7 Telex : 21996 - distributed by Tiptree Book Services Ltd.
BROWN Watson(Leicester)Ltd., 55a London Road, Leicester LE1 0PE Tel : 0533 545008 Telex : 341401
BROWN's Geological Information Service Ltd., 160 North Gower Street, London NW1 2ND Tel : 01.387 0610
BRUCE Publishing Co., USA - distributed by Collier Macmillan
BRUEL & Kjaer(U.K.)Ltd., Cross Lances Road, Hounslow, Middx. TW3 2AE Tel : 01.570 7774
BRUNEL Industrial Services Bureau, Brunel University, Kingston Lane, Uxbridge, Middx. Tel : 0895 39234
BRUNEL Institute of Organisation & Social Studies, Brunel University, Uxbridge, Middx. UB8 3PH Tel : 0895 56461
BRUNEL University, Uxbridge, Middx. UB8 3PH
BRUNNER/MAZEL Inc. - distributed by Raven Press
R.H.BRUSKIN Assoc., 303 George Street, New Brunswick, NJ 08903, USA Tel : 201 249 1800
M.E.BRYAN, 469 Walshaw Road, Bury, Lancs. Tel : 061.764 3608
BUCHHANDLER Vereinigung GmbH, Grosser Hirschgraben 17/21, Postfach 2404, 6000 Frankfurt am Main 1, West Germany
BUCHHANDLUNG Walther König, Breite Strasse 93, 5000 Köln1, Germany
BUCKINGHAM Press, Rostherne Hall Close, Maids Morton, Buckingham MK18 1RH Tel : 02802 3931
BUCKLEY Press Ltd., The Butts, Half Acre, Brentford, Middx. TW8 8BN Tel : 01.568 8441 Telex : 25657
BUCKMASTER & Moore, The Stock Exchange, London EC2P 2JT. Tel : 01.588 2868
BUDDHIST Society, 58 Eccleston Square, London SW1V 1PH Tel : 01.828 1313
BUFFALO Forge & Co., 490 Broadway, Buffalo, New York 14204, USA
BUFF's Publishing Co.Ltd., 5 New Square, London WC2A 3RP
BUIDHEANN-Foillseachaidh Nan Eilean An Iar, 63 Kenneth Street, Stornoway, Isle of Lewis Tel : 0851 3244
The BUILDER, PO Box 87, 1-3 Pemberton Row, Red Lion Court Fleet Street, London EC4P 4HL Tel : 01.353 2300 Telex : 25212
The BUILDERS Group, Box 135, 4 Catherine Street, London WC2B 5JN
BUILDING & Contract Journals Ltd. - see IPC Building & Contract Journals Ltd.
BUILDING Industry Careers Service, 82 New Cavendish Street London W1M 8AD
BUILDING Maintenance Cost Information Service Ltd., 85-87 Clarence Street, Kingston-upon-Thames, Surrey KT1 1RB Tel : 01.546 7555
BUILDING Management & Marketing Consultancy, 1-3 Pemberton Row, Fleet Street, London EC4P 4HL Tel : 01.353 2300 Telex : 25212
BUILDING Materials Market Research, 7 St.Peters Place, Brighton, Sussex Tel : 0273 680041
BUILDING Products, 1 Grover Walk, Corringham, Stanford-le-Hope Tel : 0375 41007
BUILDING Publishers Ltd., PO Box 87, 1-3 Pemberton Row, Red Lion Court, Fleet Street, London EC4P 4HL Tel : 01.353 2300
BUILDING Research Establishment, Garston, Watford, Herts. WD2 7JR Tel : 09273 76612 Telex : 923220
BUILDING Research Institute, Keldnaholt, Reykjavih, Iceland
BUILDING Services Research & Information Association, Old Bracknell Lane, Bracknell, Berks RG12 4AH Tel : 0344 25071

BUILDING Societies Association, 34 Park Street, London W1Y
    3PF Tel : 01.629 7233
BUILDING Societies Institute - now Chartered Building Societies
    Institute
BUILDING Statistical Services, 120 Glenthorne Road, London
    W6 0LP Tel : 01.582 5155
BULLMAN Publ.Co.Ltd., 20 Church Green East, Redditch,
    West Midlands Tel : 0527 60005
BUNCH Books Ltd., 14 Rathbone Place, London W1
    Tel : 01.631 1433
Market Research BURDA GmbH, Postfach 1230, 7600 Offenburg
    West Germany Tel : 0781 8401 Telex : 5280041
BURDETT Workbooks, 137 Torbay Road, Harrow, Middx.
    Tel : 01.422 6445
BUREAU de Recherches Geologiques et Minieres, 6-8 Rue
    Chasseloup-laubet, 75015 Paris, France
BUREAU of Business Practices Inc., 24 Rope Ferry Road,
    Waterford, Connecticut 06385, USA - distributed
    by IBD
BUREAU of Hygiene & Tropical Diseases, Keppel Street, London
    WC1E 7HT Tel : 01.636 8636
BUREAU of Mineral Resources, PO Box 378, Canberra City
    ACT 2601, Australia
BUREAU of National Affairs Inc., Distribution & Customer
    Service Center, 9401 Decoverly Hall Road,
    Rockville, MD 20850, USA Tel : 301 258 1033
BURGESS Publ.Co., 7108 Ohms Lane, Minneapolis, Minnesota
    55435, USA
BURKE Publ.Co.Ltd., The Barn, Northgate, Beccles, Suffolk
    WR34 9AX Tel : 0502 713239
BURKE's Peerage, 1 Hay Hill, London W1X 7LF Tel : 01.409 1583
Graham BURN, 122 Derwent Road, Linslade, Leighton Buzzard
    Beds.LU7 7XT Tel : 0525 376390
BURNS & Harris Ltd., 14 Long Wynd, Marketgait, Dundee
    DD1 1QS Tel : 0382 22591/3
BURNS & Oates Ltd., Wellwood, North Farm Road, Tunbridge
    Wells, Kent TN2 3DR Tel : 0892 44037/8
John S.BURNS & Sons, 25 Finlas Street, Possilpark, Glasgow
    G22 5DS Tel : 041.336 8678/9
BURR-Brown Intl.Ltd., 17 Exchange Road, Watford, Herts
    WD1 7EB Tel : 0923 33837
E.J.BURROW & Co.Ltd., Publicity House, Streatham Hill,
    London SW2 4TR Tel : 01.674 1222
BURRUP Mathieson & Co.Ltd., Crane House, Lavington Street,
    London SE1 0NX Tel : 01.928 8911
BUSINESS & Finance Publ.(Scotland)Ltd., 14 Great King Street
    Edinburgh EH3 Tel : 031.556 6344
BUSINESS & Market Research, The Court, Buxton Road, High
    Lane, Stockport, Cheshire SK6 8DX Tel : 06632 3983
BUSINESS & Research Associates, 1 Buxton Road West, Disley,
    Stockport, Cheshire SK12 2AF Tel : 06632 5202
BUSINESS Books, 24 Highbury Crescent, London N5 1RX
    Tel : 01.359 3711 Telex : 21373 - distributed by
    Tiptree Book Service Ltd.
BUSINESS Communications Co.Inc., 9 Viaduct Road, PO Box
    2070C, Stamford, CT06906, USA Tel : 203 325 2208
BUSINESS Connections, 25-31 Wellington Street, London WC2E
    7DW Tel : 01.240 2861
BUSINESS Decisions Ltd., 24-30 Great Titchfield Street, London
    W1P 7AD Tel : 01.580 9636
BUSINESS Dictionaries Ltd. - see Sells Publications Ltd.
BUSINESS Equipment Association, 109 Kings Way, London
    WC2B 6PU
BUSINESS Graduate Association, 74 St.James Street, London
    SW1 Tel : 01.930 9368
BUSINESS in Yorkshire, Commerce House, New North Road,
    Huddersfield Tel : 0484 513482
BUSINESS Information Press, Alan Armstrong & Assocs.Ltd.
    2 Arkwright Road, Reading, Berks RG2 0SQ
    Tel : 0734 751855 Telex : 849937
BUSINESS Information Service, 2 Tan House Brae, Culross,
    Dunfermline, Fife KY12 8HX Tel : 0383 880476
BUSINESS International S.A., 12-14 Chemin Rieu, CH 1208
    Geneva, Switzerland Tel : 022 47 53 55
BUSINESS Monitors - a statistical series from the Dept.of Trade
    & Industry - annual subscriptions available from
    HMSO
BUSINESS News Publ.Co., PO Box 6000, Birmingham, Mich.
    48012, USA
BUSINESS Publications Ltd., Audit House, 260 Field End Road
    Eastcote, Ruislip, Middx.HA4 9LT
BUSINESS Publications Ltd., 75-77 Ashgrove Road, Ashley
    Down, Bristol BS7 9LW Tel : 0272 514828 -
    distributed by European Book Service
BUSINESS Publishers Inc. - distributed by J.Wiley & Sons Ltd.
BUSINESS Ratios - see ICC Business Ratios

BUSINESS Research Services, 27 Antrobus Road, London
    W4 5HY Tel : 01.994 4147
BUSINESS Statistics Office, Cardiff Road, Newport, Gwent
    NPT 1XG Tel : 0633 56111 X2973 Telex : 497121
    - most titles distributed by HMSO
BUSINESS Surveys Ltd., PO Box 21, Dorking, Surrey
    RH5 4EE Tel : 0306 887857
BUSINESS Trend Analysts, 2171 Jericho Turnpike, Commack
    NY 11725, USA Tel : 516 462 5454
BUSINESS West Publishers Ltd., Golf Course Lane, Filton,
    Bristol, Avon Tel : 0272 791122
BUSINESS World, 35 St.John's Road, Huddersfield, Yorks.
    Tel : 0484 46837
BUTLER Cox & Partners Ltd., Morley House, 26-30 Holborn
    Viaduct, London EC1A 2BP Tel : 01.583 9381
    Telex : 8813717
BUTTERWORTH & Co.(Publ.)Ltd., 88 Kingsway, London
    WC2B 6AB Tel : 01.405 6900 - orders to Borough
    Green, Sevenoaks, Kent TN15 8PH
    Tel : 0732 884567 Telex : 95678
BUTTERWORTH Scientific Ltd., Westbury House, Bury Street,
    Guildford, Surrey Tel : 0483 31261

C

C&D Partners, 145-147 High Street, Kelvedon, Essex
    Tel : 0376 70391
CAB - see Commonwealth Agricultural Bureaux
CAF Publications Ltd., 48 Pembury Road, Tonbridge, Kent
    TN9 2JD Tel : 0732 356323
CAFD (Campaign for Academic Freedom & Democracy), 27
    Clerkenwell Close, London EC1R 0AT
    Tel : 01.251 4976
CAM Publishing, Hartspring, 17 King Harry Lane, St.Albans
    Herts. Tel : 0727 54365
CBD Research Ltd., 154 High Street, Beckenham, Kent BR3
    1EA Tel : 01.650 7745
CBI - see Confederation of British Industry
CBI Publishing Co.Inc., 286 Congress Street, Boston, Mass.
    02210, USA Tel : 617 426 2224 Telex : 940949
CBMPE, 170 Great Portland Street, London W1N 6DU
CCH Editions Ltd., 21-22 Grosvenor Street, London W1X 9FE
    Tel : 01.491 1322
CCJ Ltd., Ely House, 37 Dover Street, London W1X 4HQ
    Tel : 01.499 4688/01.493 5061 Telex : 24224 ref.
    3545
CCM Distribution Centre, 8 Trident Way, Brent Road,
    Southall, Middx. Tel : 01.571 2291
CCSA, 1 Cambridge Terrace, London NW1 4JL
C.D's Graphic, Basement Flat, 56 Bath Road, Cheltenham,
    Glos. Tel : 0242 518781
C.E.Publications Ltd., C.E.Office, Ashley Lane, Lymington,
    Hants. Tel : 0590 75947
C.H.G.Travel Publications, Waterside House, West Common,
    Gerrards Cross, Bucks. Tel : 02813 82124
CHW Roles & Assocs.Ltd., CBMPE, Centronic House, King
    Henry's Drive, New Addington, Croydon, Surrey
    CR9 0BG Tel : 0689 48221/2
C.I.A.Publications, Alembic House, 93 Albert Embankment,
    London SE1
C.I.O.Publishing, Church House, Dean's Yard, Westminster,
    London SW1P 3NZ Tel : 01.222 9011 Telex : 916010
    - some titles distributed by Bailey Bros.& Swinfen
C.I.S. - see Counter Information Services
CISSY(Campaign to Impede Sex Stereotyping in the Young),
    27 Clerkenwell Close, London EC1R 0AT
    Tel : 01.251 4976
C.I.T.Financial Services, 6050 Madison Avenue, NY 10032, USA
CIT Research Ltd., Circus House, 21 Great Tichfield Street,
    London W1P 7FD
CITB(Construction Industry Training Board), London Road,
    Norbury, London SW16
CLAIM - see Centre for Library & Information Management
CML Publications, Ashurst Lodge, Ashurst, Southampton,
    SO4 2AA Tel : 042 129 3223
CND Publications, 27 Clerkenwell Close, London EC1R 0AT
    Tel : 01.251 4976
C.O.M.E.T., 33 Bury Street, London SW1Y 6AX
    Tel : 01.839 1170 Telex : 912881
COPAT(Committee on Poverty & the Arms Trade), 27 Clerken-
    well Close, London EC1R 0AT Tel : 01.251 4976
COSIRA, Queens House, Fish Row, Salisbury, Wilts.SP1 1EX
    Tel ; 0722 24411

CPAG(Child Poverty Action Group), 27 Clerkenwell Close, London EC1R 0AT Tel : 01.251 4976
CRAC(Careers Research & Advisory Centre Ltd.) - distributed by Hobsons Press Ltd.
CRC Press Inc., 2255 Palm Beach Lakes Blvd., West Palm Beach, Florida 33409, USA / 18901 Cranwood Parkway, Cleveland, Ohio 44128, USA - distributed by Blackwell Scientific Publ.Ltd.
CS Publications Ltd., McMillan House, 54 Cheam Common Road, Worcester Park, Surrey KT4 8RJ Tel : 01.330 3911 Telex : 8953141
CSE Books, 25 Horsell Road, London N5 1XL - distributed by Publications Distribution Cooperative
CSG Press, 6110 Executive Blvd., Suite 250-6, Rockville MD20852, USA
CSIRO, 314 Albert Street, East Melbourne, Victoria 3002, Australia - agent in U.K.: British Museum(Natural History)
CSS International(U.K.)Ltd., 232-242 Vauxhall Bridge Road, London SW1V 1AU Tel : 01.834 2223
CTN Enterprises Ltd., 53 Christchurch Avenue, North Finchley London N12 0DH Tel : 01.445 6344/5
C.U.Y.B., Directory of Software, 430 Holdenhurst Road, Bournemouth, Dorset BH8 9AA Tel : 0202 301130
CADIG Liaison Centre, Liaison Officer, Reference & Technical Library, Bayley Lane, Coventry CV1 5RG Tel : 0203 25555 Telex : 31469
CADOGAN Books Ltd., 15 Pont Street, London SW1X 9EH Tel : 01.235 3851
CAEDMON of Whitby, 9 John Street, Whitby, N.Yorks YO21 3ET Tel : 0947 604646
CAFFREY Smith Publ.Co. - orders to Caffrey Saunders & Co. Ltd., Station House, Darkes Lane, Potters Bar, Herts.EN6 1AT Tel : 0707 50055
CAHNERS Publishers, 221 Edunibus Avenue, Boston, Mass. USA - distributed by Proost en Branot nv
CAITHNESS Books, 3 Mears Place, Thurso, Caithness Tel : 0847 2556
CAKE & Biscuit Alliance Ltd., 127-131 Westmorland House, Regent Street, London W1
CALDER & Boyers Ltd. - now divided into John Calder & Marion Boyars
John CALDER (Publ.)Ltd., 18 Brewer Street, London W1R 4AS Tel : 01.734 3786 - distributed by George Philip & Son Ltd.
CALIBAN Books, 73 College Place, London NW1 Tel : 01.380 0704
CALLANDER Robin, Haughend, Finzean, Feughside, Aberdeen Tel : 033 045 264
CALLUND & Co.Ltd., 15-17 King Street, St.James's, London SW1Y 6QU Tel : 01.839 3316/7
John CALMANN & Cooper Ltd., 71 Great Russell Street, London WC1B 3BN Tel : 01.831 6351 Telex : 298246
CALMANN-Levy, 3 Rue Auber, 75009 Paris, France Tel : 742 38 33
CALYPSO Publications, 2 Gatcombe Road, London N19 4PT
CAM Books, 13 Oakrits, Meldreth, Royston, Herts.
CAMBRIAN Chemicals, Suffolk House, George Street, Croydon CR9 3QL Tel : 01.686 3961
CAMBRIDGE Agricultural Marketing Services Ltd., The Stag, Cornish Hall End, Finchingfield, Essex Tel : 079986 291
CAMBRIDGE Aids to Learning Ltd., 24 Occupation Road, Cambridge Tel : 0223 69664
CAMBRIDGE Economic Policy Group, Dept.of Applied Economics, Sidgewick Avenue, Cambridge CB2 9DE Tel : 0223 358933/44
CAMBRIDGE Information & Research Services Ltd. - now Energy Publications(Cambridge)
CAMBRIDGE Institute of Education, Shaftesbury Road, Cambridge CB2 2BX Tel : 0223 69631
CAMBRIDGE Learning Enterprises, Unit B Rivermill Site, St. Ives, Huntingdon, Cambs.PE17 4BR Tel : 0480 67446
CAMBRIDGE Medical Books, 26 Tenison Avenue, Cambridge CB1 2DY Tel : 0223 60093
CAMBRIDGE University Press, The Edinburgh Building, Shaftesbury Road, Cambridge CB2 2RU Tel : 0223 312393
CAMBRIDGESHIRE & Isle of Ely Naturalists' Trust, 1 Brookside Cambridge CB2 1JF
CAMBRIDGESHIRE Times Group, First Drove,Fengate, Peterborouh
CAMDEN History Society Publications, c/o 28 Willoughby Road London NW3 1SA Tel : 01.794 2752
CAMDEN Publ.Co.Ltd., 323 Upper Street, London N1 2XQ Tel : 01.226 3445

CAMPAIGN for Justice in Divorce, PO Box 164, Aylesbury, Bucks HP17 8XQ
CAMPAIGN for Nuclear Disarmament, 11 Goodwin Street, London N4 3HQ Tel : 01.263 5673
CAMPAIGN for Press Freedom, 27 Clerkenwell Close, London EC1R 0AT Tel : 01.251 4976
CAMPAIGN for Real Ale, 34 Alma Road, St.Albans, Herts AL1 3BW - distributed by Dent
CAMPBELL Davies Publ.Ltd., 13 London Road, Bromley,Kent Tel : 01.464 0236
CAMPDEN Food Preservation Research Association, Chipping Campden, Glos. GL55 6LD Tel : 0386 840319 Telex : 337017
CAMPING Club of G.B.& Ireland Ltd., 11 Lower Grosvenor Place, London SW1W 0EY Tel : 01.828 1012/7
David CAMPTON, 35 Liberty Road, Glenfield, Leicester Tel : 0533 873951
CANADA Books International, 1 Bedford Road, London N2 9DB Tel : 01.444 5237/9 - distributed by IBD
CANADIAN Newspaper Services Intl.Ltd., 55 Edlington Ave. East, Toronto, Ontario M4P 1G8, Canada
CANADIAN Women's Education Press, 313-280 B Floor St.West Toronto, Ontario, M5S 1W1, Canada
CANDOUR Publ.Co., Forest House, Liss Forest, Hants GU33 7DD Tel : 073 082 2109
CANINE Press Ltd., 7 Greenwichs Street, London SE10 Tel : 01.858 0380
CANINE Publications, 50 George Street, Portsmouth PO1 5QZ Tel : 0705 825039
CANNING Publications Inc., 925 Anza Avenue, Vista, California 92083, USA Tel : 714 724 3233/5900
CANNON, PO Box 2610, Santa Fe, NM 87501, USA
CANONGATE Publ.Ltd., 17 Jeffrey Street, Edinburgh EH1 1DR Tel : 031.556 0023
CANOVA Press Ltd., 2-4 Abbeymount, Edinburgh EH8 8JH Tel : 031.661 9339
Jonathan CAPE Ltd., 30 Bedford Square, London WC1B 3EL Tel : 01.636 3344 Telex : 299080
CAPITAL Planning Information, 6 Castle Street, Edinburgh EH2 3AT Tel : 031.226 4367
CAPPELEN, Kirkegt 15, Oslo 1, Norway Tel : 02 33 62 80
CAPSTAN Press Ltd., Queen Street Chambers, Queen Street Exeter, Devon EX4 3RW Tel : 0392 214422
CAPTAN Assocs.Inc., 218 Stuyvesant Avenue, Lyndhurst NJ 07071, USA Tel : 201 935 6231
CARCANET Press, Corn Exchange, Manchester M4 3BQ Tel : 061.834 8730 - distributed by Noonan Hurst Ltd.
CARDIFF University Industry Centre, PO Box 78, Cardiff CF1 1XL Tel : 0222 44211 X2645
CAREERS Consultants Ltd., 12-14 Hill Rise, Richmond Hill, Richmond, Surrey TW10 6UA Tel : 01.940 5668
CAREERS Publications, 76 Dean Street, London W1A 1BU Tel : 01.439 4242
CAREERS Research & Advisory Centre Ltd. - distributed by Hobsons Press Ltd.
CAREY Reprinters Ltd., 58 Carey Street, London WC2A 2JB Tel : 01.242 5778
CARGO Systems, McMillan House, 54 Cheam Common Road, Worcester Park, Surrey KT4 8RJ Tel : 01.330 3911
CARLTON Bury(Lloyds)Ltd.,Lime Street, London EC3M 7HA Tel : 01.623 7100 Telex : 987321
CARNEGIE Endowment for Intl.Peace, 345 East 46th Street, New York 10017, USA
CAROLINA Biological Supply Company, Burlington, North Carolina 27215, USA Tel : 919 584 0381 Telex : 574354
J.L.CARR Publisher, 27 Milldale Road, Kettering, Northants. Tel : 0536 4995
Louie CARR, 41 Woodfield Court, Queens Road, Edgerton, Huddersfield HD2 2AR
CARRAIG Books, 25 Newton Avenue, Blackrock, Co.Dublin, Rep.of Ireland Tel : 0001 882575
CARRICK James, 21 Soho Square, London W1V 5FD Tel : 01.734 7171 Tel : 21879
CARROLLTON Press, 43 Harbour Road, Inverness Tel : 0463 33445
CARSON & Comerford Ltd., Stage House, 47 Bermondsey Street, London SE1 3XT Tel : 01.403 1818
CARTER Industrial Products, Bedhill Road, Birmingham B25
CARTER Midgley & Co., The Paddocks, Mill Lane, Rodmell, Lewes, Sussex Tel : 079 16 5943
CASA Editrice Felice le Monnier, Casella Postale 202, 50100 Firenze, Italy
CASDEC Ltd., 11 Windermere Avenue, Garden Farm Estate, Chester le Street, Durham DH2 3DU Tel : 0385 882906

CASE Clearing House of G.B.& Ireland, Cranfield Inst.of
    Technology, Cranfield, Bedford MK43 0AL
    Tel : 0234 750903
CASH & Carry Publ.Services, 12-18 High Road, London N2
CASE Law Ltd., 2 York Cottages, Elm Grove Road, Cobham,
    Surrey   Tel : 01.266 7008 - orders to Gateway,
    Crewe CW1 1YN   Tel : 0270 587028
Frank CASS & Co.Ltd., Gainsborough House, 11 Gainsborough
    Road, London E11 1RS   Tel : 01.530 4226 -
    distributed by MacDonald & Evans Ltd., 10 Woburn
    Walls, London WC1   Tel : 01.387 7340
CASSANDRA Publications, 3 Horbury Mews, London W11 3NL
    Tel : 01.727 9391
CASSELL Ltd., 1 Vincent Squre, London SW1P 2PN
    Tel : 01.630 7881   Telex : 28648
Bruno CASSIRER(Publ.)Ltd., 31 Portland Road, Oxford OX2 7EZ
    Tel : 0865 59180 - distributed by Faber & Faber Ltd.
J.CASSON, 15 Lawrence Street, London SW3   Tel : 01.352 7077
CASTLE Books, Westhill Road, Blackdown, Leamington Spa CV32
    6RA   Tel : 0926 28370
CASTLE Cary Press, Castle Cary, Somerset   Tel : 0963 50357
CASTLE House Publications, Castle House, 27 London Road,
    Tunbridge Wells, Kent TN1 1BX   Tel : 0892 39606
The CASTLE Museum, York YO1 1RY   Tel : 0904 53611
CASTLELAW Press, West Linton, Peebleshire   Tel : 09686 450
CASUALTIES Union, 1 Grosvenor Crescent, London SW1X 7EE
    Tel : 01.235 5366
CATALYTICA Assocs.Inc., 3255 Scott Boulevard, Suite 7E
    Santa Clara, California 95051, USA
CATFORD Link, 53 Silvermere Road, London SE6
    Tel : 01.690 0961
CATHOLIC Institute for International Relations, 22 Coleman
    Fields, London N1 7AF   Tel : 01.354 0883
CATHOLIC Truth Society, 38-40 Eccleston Square, London SW1V
    1PD   Tel : 01.834 4392 - Bookshop : 25 Ashley Place
    London SW1P 1LT   Tel : 01.834 1363
CAUSTON Publishing, Brookwood Avenue, Eastleigh, Hants.
    SO5 5YB   Tel : 0703 619711
CAUTION Magazine, 15 St.Georges Road, Cheltenham, Glos.
    Tel : 0242 36336
Godfrey CAVE Associates Ltd., 42 Bloomsbury Street, London
    WC1B 3QJ   Tel : 01.636 9177
Paul CAVE Publ.Ltd., 74 Bedford Place, Southampton, Hants.
    SO1 2DF   Tel : 0703 333457/23591
CAVERSHAM Publ.Co.Ltd., 96a Queens Road, Reading, Berks
    Tel : 0734 580925
CAXTON Publ.Ltd., Holywell Houwe, 72-90 Worship Street,
    London EC2A 2HR   Tel : 01.247 8492   Telex : 886048
    - orders to PO Box 14, Gatehouse Road, Aylesbury
    Bucks   Tel : 0296 24596
CEDAR Books Co., 30516 South East 392nd Street, Enumdaw,
    WN98022, USA
CEGOS Industrial Marketing GmbH, Altenbergstrasse 26,
    4 Dusseldorf, West Germany   Tel : 87 53 53
    Telex : 25076
CELDIS Ltd., 37 Loverock Road, Reading, Berks. RG3 1ED
    Tel : 0734 586191
CELEBRATION Publishing, 57 Dorchester Road, Lytchett Minster,
    Poole, Dorset BH16 6JE   Tel : 0202 623651
CELTIC Educational(Services)Ltd., Celtic House, 18 St.James
    Gardens, Swansea SA1 6AE   Tel : 0792 56205
CELTIC Revision Aids, 30-32 Gray's Inn Road, London WV1X
    8JL   Tel : 01.405 2087/01.242 4562
CELTION Publishing - now Rainbow/Celtion Books
CEMENT & Concrete Association, Wexham Springs, Slough,
    Berks SL3 6PL   Tel : 02816 2727
CENCRASTUS(Magazine), 5 Buccleuch Place, Edinburgh EH8
    Tel : 031.667 6800
CENTAUR Press Ltd., Fontwell, Arundel, W.Sussex BN18 0TA
    Tel : 024 368 3302
CENTER for Intl.Education & Research in Accounting, 320
    Commerce & Business Administration West, Box 109,
    Univ.of Illinois at Urbana-Champaign, 1206 South
    Sixth Street, Champaign, IL 61820-6271, USA
CENTRAL Asian Research Centre, 8 Wakley Street, London
    EC1   Tel : 01.278 9441
CENTRAL Association of Beekeepers, 8 Gloucester Gardens,
    Ilford, Essex IG1 3NJ   Tel : 01.554 1243
CENTRAL Books Ltd., 14 The Leathermarket, London SE1 3ER
    Tel : 01.407 5447 - orders to 37 Gray's Inn Road,
    London WC1X 8PS   Tel : 01.242 6166/9
CENTRAL Bureau for Educational Visits & Exchanges, Seymour
    Mews House, Seymour Mews, London W1H 9PE
    Tel : 01.486 5101
CENTRAL Bureau for Educational Visits & Exchanges, 3
    Bruntsfield Crescent, Edinburgh EH10 4HD
    Tel : 031.447 8024
CENTRAL Bureau for Educational Visits & Exchanges, 16
    Malone Road, Belfast BT9 5BN   Tel : 0232 66418/9
CENTRAL Bureau of Statistics, Holland - distributed by
    Netherland State Printers, Christoffel Plantijn-
    straat, The Hague, The Netherlands
CENTRAL Council for the Disabled, 34 Eccleston Square,
    London SW1V 1PE
CENTRAL Electricity Generating Board, Sudbury House,
    15 Newgate Street, London EC1A 7AU
    Tel : 01.248 1202
CENTRAL Institute for Nutrition & Food Research, Urechtseweg
    48-Zeist, The Netherlands   Tel : 03404 18411
CENTRAL Office of Information, Hercules Road, London SE1
    7DU   Tel : 01.643 5363 X28
CENTRAL Services Unit, Crawford House, Precinct Centre,
    Oxford Road, Manchester M13 9EP
    Tel : 061.273 6464/5   Telex : 666635
CENTRAL Statistical Office, Cabinet Office, Great George
    Street, London SW1P 3AQ - most publications
    distributed by HMSO
CENTRAL Veterinary Laboratories, New Haw, Weybridge,
    Surrey
CENTRE d'Etude des Revenus et des Couts, 3 Bvd.de Latour-
    Maubourg, 75007 Paris, France   Tel : 555 4281
CENTRE d'Etude du Commerce et de la Distribution, 19 Rue
    de Calais, 75009 Paris, France   Tel : 281 9133
CENTRE d'Etudes Industrielles, 4 Chemin de Conches, 1231
    Conches, Geneva, Switzerland
CENTRE for Agricultural Strategy, 2 Earley Gate, Univ.of
    Reading, Reading, Berks RG6 2AU
CENTRE for Alternative Technology - see National Centre for
    Alternative Technology
CENTRE for Applied Research in Education - distributed by
    IBD/Prentice-Hall
CENTRE for Banking & Intl.Finance, City University,
    Northampton Square, London EC1
CENTRE for European Agricultural Studies, Wye College,
    Ashford, Kent TN25 5AH   Tel : 0233 812181
CENTRE for Information on Language Teaching & Research,
    20 Carlton House Terrace, London SW1Y 5AP
    Tel : 01.839 2626
CENTRE for Interfirm Comparison, 25 Bloomsbury Square,
    London WC1A 2PJ   Tel : 01.637 8406
CENTRE for International Studies, Univ.of Pittsburgh,
    218 Oakland Avenue, Pittsburgh PA15260, USA
CENTRE for Library & Information Management, Loughborough
    University, Dept.of Library & Information Studies,
    Loughborough, Leics.LE11 3TU   Tel : 0509 63171
    X312   Telex : 34319
CENTRE for Overseas Pest Research, Publications Dept.,
    College House, Wrights Lane, London W8 5SJ
    Tel : 01.937 8191
CENTRE for Policy on Ageing, Nuffield Lodge, Regent's Park
    London NW1 4RS   Tel : 01.586 9844/9
CENTRE for Policy Studies, 8 Wilfred Street, London SW1E 6PL
    Tel : 01.828 1176
CENTRE for Science & Mathematics Education, Chelsea College
    University of London, Bridges Place, London SW6
    4HR   Tel : 01.736 3401
CENTRE for the Study of Human Learning, Brunel University,
    Uxbridge, Middx.UB8 3PH   Tel : 0895 37188
CENTRE for the Study of Public Policy, Univ.of Strathclyde
    McCance Building, 16 Richmond Street, Glasgow
    G1 1XQ   Tel : 041.552 4400
CENTRE for Socio-Legal Studies, Wolfson College, Oxford
    OX2 6UD   Tel : 0865 52967/9
CENTRE for World Development Education, 128 Buckingham
    Palace Road, London SW1W 9SH   Tel : 01.730 8332/3
CENTRE Francaise la Corrosion (CEFRACOR), 28 Rue St.
    Dominique, Paris, France
CENTRE of the Studies of Education in Changing Societies,
    Nuffie, 27 Molenstraat, The Hague, The Netherlands
CENTRE on Environment for the Handicapped, 126 Albert Street
    London NW1 7NF
CENTURION Publications International - see New Opportunity
    Press Ltd.
CENTURY Publishing Co.Ltd., 76 Old Compton Street, London
    W1V 5PA   Tel : 01.439 9416   Telex : 8954665
CEOLFRITH Press, 27 Stockton Road, Sunderland SR2 7AQ
    Tel : 0783 43976
CERAMIC Book Company, St.John's & Chepstow Roads, Newport
    Gwent NPT 8GW   Tel : 0633 274266
CERBERUS Publ.Ltd., Wildcrest,Sunning Avenue,Sunningdale
    Berks
CERCLE de la Librairie, 5 High Street, Beckenham, Kent
    BR3 1AZ   Tel : 01.658 0286

CEREBUS,PH Canada - distributed by IBD
CERPI SPA, Via Vittor Pisami 31, 20124 Milano, Italy
    Tel : 2 345 2076
The CERTIFIED Accountants Educational Trust, PO Box 244
    London WC2A 3EE Tel : 01.242 6855
CERVED SpA, Corso Stati Uniti 14, Padora, Italy
    Tel : 049 760733 Telex : 430433
CESARA Publications, Huntingdon Castle,Clonegal,Enniscorthy,
    Rep.of Ireland
CHADWYCK-Healey Ltd., 20 Newmarket Road, Cambridge CB5
    8DT Tel : 0223 311479
CHALLENGE Books, 6 Koloff Court, Woodridge, IL60515, USA
W&R CHAMBERS Ltd., 11 Thistle Street, Edinburgh EH2 1DG
    Tel : 031.225 4463 Telex : 727967
CHAMELEON, 27 Clerkenwell Close, London EC1R 0AT
    Tel : 01.251 4976
CHANCEREL Publ.Ltd., 40 Tavistock Street, London WC2E 7PB
    Tel : 01.240 2811
S.CHAND & Co.Ltd.,New Delhi, India - distributed by Asian
    Book Service, 69 Great Russell Street, London WC1
CHANDLER & Sharp Publ.Inc., 11a Commercial Blvd., Novato
    CA94947, USA
R.H.CHANDLER Ltd., PO Box 55, Braintree, Essex CM7 6JT
    Tel : 0376 20857
CHANDLER Publications Ltd., 2 South Street, Totnes, Devon
    Tel : 0803 864668
CHANNEL Press Ltd., Elsinore House, Buckingham Street,
    Aylesbury, Bucks HP20 2NQ Tel : 0296 88411
CHANNING Weinberg, 950 Third Avenue, New York 10022,USA
    Tel : 212 753 8922
CHANSITOR Publ.Ltd., 3 Creed Lane, London EC4V 5BR
    Tel : 01.248 6085
CHANTAL Wine Publ.Ltd., 3 Berwick Street, London W1G 1GW
    - distributed by New English Library
CHANTRY Press(Wakefield)Ltd., 2 Cheapside, Wakefield, Yorks.
    Tel : 0924 376836
CHAPELFIELDS Press, PO Box 104, Coventry CV5 8NE
CHAPMAN & Hall Ltd. - see Associated Book Publishers(U.K.)
    Ltd.
H.V.CHAPMAN Ltd., Box 8, 29th Floor, 1 Dundas Street West,
    Toronto, Ontario M5G 1Z3, Canada
Geoffrey CHAPMAN Publ/Johnson & Bacon Ltd., c/o Collier
    Macmillan, 35 Red Lion Square, London WC1R 4SG
    Tel : 01.831 6100 - orders to Cassell Ltd.
CHAPPELL & Co.Ltd. - now Chappell Music Ltd., 50 New Bond
    Street, London W1A 2BR Tel : 01.629 7600
    Telex : 268403 - distributed by TBL Book Service
CHARITIES Aid Foundation, 48 Pembury Road, Tonbridge, Kent
    TN9 2JD Tel : 0732 356323
Alain CHARLES Publ.Ltd., Alain Charles House, 27 Wilfred Street,
    London SW1E 6PR Tel : 01.828 6107 Telex : 297166
CHARLES Press Publ.Inc., USA - distributed by Prentice Hall
CHARLOTTE Press Publ., 5 Charlotte Square, Newcastle upon
    Tyne NE1 4XF Tel : 0632 22634
CHARNWOOD Publ.Co.Ltd., Vaughan Street, Coalville, Leicester
    Tel : 0530 32288
CHARTERED Building Societies Institute, Fanhams Hall, Ware,
    Herts. Tel : 0920 5051
CHARTERED Institute of Arbitrators, 75 Cannon Street, London
    EC4N 5BH Tel : 01.236 8761/2
CHARTERED Institute of Building, Englemere, Kings Ride, Ascot
    Berks SL5 8BJ Tel : 0990 23355
CHARTERED Institute of Loss Adjusters, Manfield House, 376
    Strand, London WC2R 0LR Tel : 01.240 1496
CHARTERED Institute of Patent Agents, Staple Inn Buildings,
    High Holborn, London WC1V 7PZ Tel : 01.405 9450
CHARTERED Institute of Public Finance & Accountancy,
    1 Buckingham Place, London SW1E 6HS
    Tel : 01.828 7661
CHARTERED Institute of Secretaries,(C.I.S.), 221 Seven Sisters
    Road, London N4 2DA Tel : 01.263 4441
CHARTERED Institution of Building Services, Delta House, 222
    Balham High Road, London SW12 9BS Tel : 01.675 5211
CHARTSEARCH Ltd., 11-12 Blomfield Street, London EC2M 7AY
CHARTWELL Press - ceased publishing 1980
CHARTWELL-Bratt(Publ.& Training)Ltd., Old Orchard, Bickley
    Road, Bickley, Bromley, Kent BR1 2NE
    Tel : 01.467 1956 Telex : 8952171
CHASE Trade Information Corporation, 1 World Trade Center, New
    York 10048, USA Tel : 212 432 8071
CHATHAM House Papers, Royal Inst.of International Affairs,
    Chatham House, 10 St.James's Square, London SW1Y
    4LE Tel : 01.930 2233
CHATTO & Windus Ltd., 40 William IV Street, London WC2N 4DF
    Tel : 01.379 6637 Telex : 299080 - distributed by
    Chatto, Bodley Head & Cape Services Ltd.

CHAUCER Publ.Co.Ltd., Newlands House, 3 Hazelgrove Road
    Haywards Heath, W.Sussex RH16 3PH
    Tel : 0444 459911
CHELFAM Publ.& Distribution Co.Ltd., Finance House, 27 Queen
    Street, Barnstaple, Devon
CHELSEA House Publ., USA - distributed by Bowker
CHELTENHAM Technical Publ.Ltd., Montpellier House, Suffolk
    Place, Cheltenham, Glos. Tel : 0242 519119
    Telex : 437198
CHEM Systems Intl.Ltd., 28 St.James's Square, London SW1Y
    4JH Tel : 01.839 4652 Telex : 916636
CHEMICAL Abstracts, 1155 16th Street NW, Washington DC
    USA
CHEMICAL & Allied Products ITB, Staines House, 158-162
    High Street, Staines, Middx.TW18 4AT
    Tel : 0784 51366
CHEMICAL Business Development Co.Inc., 70 Park Street,
    Montclair, NJ 07042, USA Tel : 201 746 8840
CHEMICAL Data Services, Quadrant House, The Quadrant
    Sutton, Surrey SM2 5AS Tel : 01.661 3500
    Telex : 892084
CHEMICAL Daily Co.Ltd., 19-16 Shibaura 3-Chome, Minato-ku
    Tokyo 108, Japan
CHEMICAL Economic Services, PO Box 468, Princeton, NJ8540
    USA
CHEMICAL Engineering Reprints, 1221 Ave of the Americas
    New York 10020, USA
CHEMICAL Industries Association, 93 Albert Embankment
    London SE1 7TU Tel : 01.735 3001 Telex : 916672
CHEMICAL Info.Services Ltd., PO Box 61, Oceanside, NY11572
    USA
CHEMICAL Insight, 64 West Grove, Greenwich, London SE10
    8QT Tel : 01.852 5526
CHEMICAL Publ.Co.Inc., 200 Park Ave.South, New York
    10003, USA - distributed by TABS
CHEMICAL Rubber Co., 2255 Palm Beach Lakes Boulevard,
    West Palm Beach, Florida 33409, USA - distributed
    by Blackwell Scientific Publ.
CHEMICAL Services, PO Box 178, Mountain Lakes, NJ 07046,
    USA
The CHEMICAL Society, Burlington House, London W1V 0BN
    Tel : 01.734 9864 Telex : 268001 - orders to
    The Distribution Centre, Blackhorse Road,
    Letchworth, Herts. SG6 1HN Tel : 046 26 72555
    Telex : 825372
CHEMICON Surveys Ltd., 2 Downing Court, Grenville Street,
    London WC1N 1LX Tel : 01.837 5779 Telex : 27950
CHESHIRE Publ.Co.Ltd., 346 St.Kilda Road, Melbourne,
    Vic.3004, Australia
The CHESS Player Ltd., 12 Burton Avenue, Carlton, Nottingham
    NG4 1PT Tel : 0602 87 1891 / 37 Stoney Street,
    Nottingham NG1 1LS Tel : 0602 51200
CHEST, Heart & Stroke Association, Tavistock House North,
    Tavistock Square, London WC1H 9JE
    Tel : 01.387 3012/4
CHESTER House Publications - distributed by Methodist Publ.
    House
CHESTERFIELD Colleges of Art & Technology, Infirmary Road
    Chesterfield, Derbyshire
CHICAGO Group Inc., 744 N.Wells Street, Chicago, Ill.60610,
    USA Tel : 312 751 0303
Francis CHICHESTER(Map Publ.)Ltd., 9 St.James's Place
    London SW1A 1PE Tel : 01.493 0931/2
CHILD Poverty Action Group, 1 Macklin Street, Drury Lane
    London WC2 5NH TEl : 01.242 3225/9149
CHILDREN's Illustrated Classics - imprint of J.M.Dent & Son Ltd.
CHILDREN's Legal Centre Ltd., 2 Malden Road, London NW5
    3HR Tel : 01.267 6392
CHILDS Play (Intl.)Ltd., Restrop Manor, Purton, Swindon,
    Wilts. SN5 9LW Tel : 0793 770389 Telex : 449391
    / 153 High Street, Wootton Bassett, Swindon, Wilts.
    Tel ; 0793 850901
CHILTERN Educational & T-S Services, PO Box 241, Gerrards
    Cross, Bucks SL9 8PA Tel : 02813 84136
CHILTON International, 14 Bath Road, Swindon, Wilts.
    Tel : 0793 611102
CHINA Phone Book Co., GPO Box 11581, Hong Kong
The CHINA Society, 31B Torrington Square, London WC1
    Tel : 01.636 7985
Cedric CHIVERS Ltd., Portway, Bath BA1 3NF
    Tel : 0225 23201/3
CHIVERS Press, 93-100 Locksbrook Road, Bath BA1 3HB
    Tel : 0225 316872 Telex : 449897
J.F.CHOWN & Co.Ltd., 108 Cannon Street, London EC4N 6EU
    Tel : 01.626 6031/5

CHRISTADELPHIAN Magazine & Publ.Association Ltd., 404
    Shaftmoor Lane, Hall Green, Birmingham B28 8SZ
    Tel : 021.777 6328/6324
CHRISTIAN Association of Business Executives, 114 Mount
    Street, London W1Y 6AH Tel : 01.491 7596
CHRISTIAN Community Press - distributed by Floris Books
CHRISTIAN Focus Publ.Ltd., Geanies House, Fearn, Tain,
    Rosshire, IV20 1TW Tel : 086287 541
CHRISTIAN Journals Ltd., c/o Book Distribution(N.I.)Ltd.,
    Boucher Road, Belfast BT12 6HR Tel : 0232 662218
CHRISTIAN Literature Crusade, The Dean, Alresford, Hants.
    SO24 9BJ Tel : 096 273 3142
CHRISTIAN Medical Fellowship, 157 Waterloo Road, London SE1
    8XN Tel : 01.928 4694
CHRISTIANS Against Racism & Fascism, St.James Vicarage,
    Highfield Street, Coalville, Leicester
L.CHRISTIE, 129 Franciscan Road, Tooting, London SW17 8DT
    Tel : 01.672 4024
CHRISTIE's Wine Publications, 8 King Street, St.James's,
    London SW1Y 6QT Tel : 01.839 9060
CHROMATOGRAPHY Sew Ltd., Cars Lang Industrial Estate,
    Hoylake, Wirral, Merseyside
CHURCH Book Room Press Ltd. - now Vine Books Ltd.
CHURCH Information Office, Warner House, Folkestone, Kent
    CT19 6PH Tel : 0303 56501
CHURCH Literature Association, 7 Fufton Street, Westminster
    London SW1P 3QN Tel : 01.222 6952
CHURCH Missionary Society, 157 Waterloo Road, London SE1
    8UU Tel : 01.928 8681
CHURCH Pastoral-Aid Society, Falcon Books, Falcon Court,
    32 Fleet Street, London EC4Y 1DB - Falcon Books
    taken over by Kingsway Publications Ltd.
CHURCH of Christ Publications(Berean Press) - ceased
    publishing 1980 - enquiries to Tavistock Bookshop
CHURCHILL Livingstone, Robert Stevenson House, 1-3 Baxter's
    Place, Leith Walk, Edinburgh EH1 3AF
    Tel : 031.556 2424 Telex : 727511 - distributed by
    Longman Group Ltd.
CHURCHILL Press Ltd. - distributed by Ken Dickson Ltd.
CIBA Foundation, 41 Portland Place, London W1N 4BN
    Tel : 01.636 9456 Telex : 27950
CICADA Press, 27 Clerkenwell Close, London EC1R 0AT
    Tel : 01.251 4976
CICERONE Press, Harmoney Hall, Milnthorpe, Cumbria CA7 7QE
CIDER Press - now Books of Wessex Ltd.
CIENFUEGOS Press Ltd., Over the Water, Sanday, Orkney
    KW17 2BL Tel : 08575 369 - distributed by Southern
    Distribution, 27 Clerkenwell Close, London EC1R
    0AT Tel : 01.251 4976
CILLINGHAM(Publ.), 4 Credit Will, London NW6 7UP
CIRCLE of State Librarians, c/o Main Library, Q4 Building,
    Royal Aircraft Establishment, Farnborough, Hants.
CIRCLE Press, 22 Sydney Road, Guildford, Surrey GU1 3LL
    Tel : 0483 504843
CIRCLETT Publ.Co.Ltd., 93 Fyide Road, Preston, Lancs.
    Tel : 0772 55160
CITADEL Press Inc., USA - distributed by LSP Books Ltd.
CITY & Guilds of London Institute, 76 Portland Place, London
    W1N 4AA Tel : 01.580 3050
CITY Financial Business Publ.Ltd., Orient House, 42-45 New
    Broad Street, London EC2M 1QY
    Tel : 01.628 3040/0898 Telex : 8953086/8811725
CITY Financial Insurance Publ.Ltd., 20-24 Ropemaker Street,
    London EC2Y 9AS Tel : 01.588 4274/7 Telex : 8811725
CITY Financial Services, 6050 Madison Avenue, NY 10022, USA
CITY of London Polytechnic, 117 Houndsditch, London EC3 /
    Calcutta House Precinct, Old Castle Street, London
    E1 7NI Tel : 01.283 1030
CITY of London Weekly Ltd.(City Press), Fairfax House,
    Colchester, Essex CO1 1RJ Tel : 0206 45121
    Telex ; 98517
CITY Press Ltd., Fairfax House, Colchester, Essex CO1 1RJ
    Tel : 0206 45121 Telex : 98517
CITY Research Associates Ltd., 5 Carthusian Street, London EC1M
    6EB Tel : 01.251 4549 Telex : 21792 ref.3625
CITY University Business School, Frobisher Crescent, Barbicon
    London EC2Y 8HB Tel : 01.920 0111
CITY University, Centre for Arts & Related Studies - see John
    Offord Publications
CIVIC Trust, 17 Carlton House Terrace, London SW1Y 5AW
    Tel : 01.930 0914
CIVIC Trust for the North West, c/o Environmental Institute,
    Greaves School, Bolton Road, Swinton, Manchester
    M27 2UX Tel : 061.794 9314
CIVIL Aviation Authority, Greville House, 37 Gratton Road,
    Cheltenham, Glos. GL50 2BN Tel : 0242 35151
    Telex : 27464

CIVIL Service Commission, Civil Service Dept., Alencon Link,
    Basingstoke, Hants.RG21 1JB Tel : 0256 29222
CIVIL Service Department, Careers Information Division,
    Alencon Link, Basingstoke, Hants.RG21 1JB
    Tel : 0256 29222
John CLARE Books, c/o P.D.A.S.(Cowley)Ltd., Unit 6,
    2 Derby Road, Greenford, Middx.UB6 8UJ
    Tel : 01.575 5756
CLARENDON Press - see Oxford University Press
CLARK Boardman Co.Ltd., 435 Hudson Street, New York
    10014, USA - distributed by Sweet & Maxwell
T.&T.CLARK Ltd., 36 George Street, Edinburgh EH2 2LQ
    Tel : 031.225 4703
James CLARKE & Co., 7 All Saints Passage, Cambridge CB2
    3LS Tel : 0223 350865 Telex : 817570
Anthony CLARKE Books, 16 Garden Court, Wheathampstead
    Herts.AL4 8RE Tel : 058 283 2460 - orders to
    27 Brewhouse Hill, Wheathampstead, Herts AL4 8RF
H.CLARKSON & Co.Ltd., 12 Camomile Street, London EC3A
    7BP Tel : 01.283 8955
E.W.CLASSEY Ltd., PO Box 93, Faringdon, Oxon.SN7 7DR
CLASSIC Albums Ltd., 49 Vincent Court, Bell Lane, London
    NW4 2AW Tel : 01.203 3254
CLASSIC Publ.Ltd., Recorder House, 91 Church Street,
    London N16 Tel : 01.254 7231
CLASSICAL Music, 52a Floral Street, London WC2E 9DA
    Tel : 01.836 2385
CLAY Pipe Development Association Ltd., Drayton House,
    30 Gordon Street, London WC1H 0AN
    Tel : 01.388 0025
CLEAR, Calm & Company, Tan Bank Annexe, Wellington,
    Telford, Shropshire Tel : 0952 52469
CLEARWAY Publ.Co.Ltd., Unit 19, Nechetts House, Dartmouth
    Street, Birmingham 7 Tel ; 021.359 2495
CLEMATIS Press Ltd., 18 Old Church Street, London SW3
    5DQ Tel : 01.352 8755 - distributed by Wentworth
    Book Co.Ltd.
CLEMENT(Publ.)Ltd., 6 Stanbrook House, Orchard Grove,
    Orpington, Kent BR6 0SR
CLEVELAND Museum - distributed by IBD
CLIFTON Books, New England House, New England Street
    Brighton, Sussex
CLIFTON Data Research, 21 Culver Road, St.Albans, Herts.
    Tel : 0727 5838
Barry R.CLIFTON Ltd., 21 Culver Road, St.Albans, Herts.
    Tel : 0727 5838
CLIMBERS' Club, c/o A.H.Jones, 42 Corring Way, London W5
    Tel : 01.997 9640 - distributed by Cordee
CLINICA, World Medical Device News, 18a Hill Street,
    Richmond, Surrey TW9 1TN Tel : 01.948 5034
    Telex : 8951042
CLIO Press Ltd., 55 St.Thomas Street, Oxford OX1 1JG
    Tel : 0865 250333 Telex : 83130
The CLIQUE (Stoate & Bishop Ltd.), St.James Square,
    Cheltenham GL50 3PU Tel : 0242 36741
CLOTHING & Footwear Institute, Albert Road, Hendon, London
    NW4 2JS Tel : 01.203 0191
CLOTHING Export Council of G.B., 26-28 Sackville Street
    London W1X 2QT Tel : 01.434 1881
CLOTHING Industry Productivity Resources Agency, Wira
    House, Clayton Wood Rise, Leeds LS16 6RF
    Tel ; 0532 741526
CLOVER Press, High Street, Dulberton, Somerset
CLOVER Publications, 8 Ashby Drive, Caldecote, Biggleswade
    Beds.SG18 9DJ Tel : 0767 315566
COAL Outlook, 1730 K Street NW, Suite 713, Washington DC
    20006, USA Tel : 202 783 2660
William CLOWES Publ.Ltd., 31 Newgate, Beccles, Suffolk
    NR34 9QE Tel : 0502 714656 - orders to 14 Commerce
    Way, Whitehall Road Industrial Estate, Colchester
    Essex Tel : 0206 73012
CLUB Leabhar, PO Box 1, Portree, Isle of Skye, IV1 9BT
CLYDE Surveys Ltd., Reform Road, Maidenhead, Berks
    SL6 8BU Tel : 0628 21371 Telex : 847352
COACH Publ.House Ltd., Parsons Farm, Kerves Lane,
    Southwater, W.Sussex Tel : 0403 730022
COATES Sewing Group, 50 Bothwell Street, Glasgow G2 5PA
    Tel : 041.221 8711 Telex : 77711
COBDEN Trust, 27 Clerkenwell Close, London EC1R 0AT
    Tel : 01.251 4976
COBURGH Publications, 91 Cranwich Road, London N16 5JA
COBWEBS Press Ltd. - now Regal Print Co.
COLES Publ.Co.Ltd., Canada - distributed by McGraw-Hill
    Book Co.(U.K.)Ltd.
COLLEGE Course Guides - c/o TABS
COLLEGE of Estate Management, Whiteknights, Reading,
    Berks RG6 2AW Tel : 0734 861101

COLLEGE of Law, Braboeuf Manor, St.Catherines, Guildford, Surrey   Tel : 0483 76711
COLLEGE of Librarianship, Llanbadarn Fawr, Aberystwyth, Dyfed SY23 3AS   Tel : 0970 3181
COLLEGE of Management, Library, Dunchurch, Rugby, Warwicks. CV22 6QW
COLLEGE of Radiographers, 14 Upper Wimpole Street, London W1M 8BN
COLLEGE Placement Council Inc., PO Box 2263, Bethlehem PA18001, USA
COLLEGIATE Music Publications Ltd., 12-14 Mortimer Street, London W1N 8EL   Tel : 01.580 2827
COLLET's Holdings Ltd., Denington Estate, Wellingborough Northants.NN8 2QT   Tel : 0933 224351   Telex : 31165
COLLIER Macmillan Ltd., Stockley Close, Stockley Road, West Drayton, Middx.UB7 9BE   Tel : 08954 40651   Telex : 28648
P.F.COLLIER Publ.Co., 18a Park Street, Bristol, Avon.   Tel : 0272 214498
COLLIERY Guardian, Queensway House, 2 Queensway, Redhill, Surrey   Tel : 0737 68611
COLLINGRIDGE Books Ltd. - see Hamlyn Publ.Group Ltd.
Rex COLLINGS Ltd., 6 Paddington Street, London W1M 3LA   Tel : 01.487 4201   Telex : 337340 - distributed by Noonan Hurst
William COLLINS Sons & Co.Ltd., PO Box, Glasgow G4 0NB   Tel : 041.772 3200   Telex : 77 8107 / 8 Grafton Street London W1X 3LA
COLORADO Associated University Press, 1338 Grandview Avenue, Box 480, University of Colorado, Boulder, Colorado 80309, USA
COLOUR & Play Books - imprint of Helicon Press
COLOUR Library Intl.Ltd., 86 Epsom Road, Guildford, Surrey GU1 2BX   Tel : 0483 579191   Telex : 859182
COLT Associates, 8 New Row, London WC2N 4LH   Tel : 01.836 4550   Telex : 21120
COLUMBIA University Press, 136 South Broad Way, Irvington New York 10533, USA
COLUMBUS Books/Bookshelf, 24 Red Lion Street, London WC1R 4PX   Tel : 01.242 8136   Telex : 28257
COLUSCO Ltd., 122 Shaftesbury Avenue, London W1V 8HA
An COMANN Gaidhealach, Abertarff House, Church Street, Inverness IV1 1EU
An COMANN Gaidhealach:Roinn nan Eilean Siar, 91 Cromwall Street, Stornoway, Isle of Lewis
COMBINED Service Publ.Ltd., PO Box 4, Farnborough, Hants. GU14 7LR   Tel : 0252 515891   Telex : 858808
COMEDIA Publ.Co.Ltd., 9 Poland Street, London W1V 3DG   Tel : 01.439 2059
COMET, 33 Bury Street, London SW1Y 6AX
COMMERCE Clearing House Inc., 5 Charterhouse Buildings, Goswell Road, London EC1   Tel : 01.251 0837
COMMERCIAL Information Co.(N.I.)Ltd., 116 University Street Belfast   Tel : 0232 224697
COMMERCIAL Publ.Co., 4 St.John's Terrace, London W10
COMMERCIAL Research Services, 21 Sunnymead Road, Nailsea Bristol BS19 1ER   Tel : 0272 853041
COMMERCIAL Shearing Inc., PO Box 239 Youngstown, Ohio 44501, USA
COMMERCIAL Union Risk Management Ltd., PO Box 240, St.Helens, 1 Undershaft, London EC3P 3DQ   Tel : 01.283 7500 X2463
COMMISSION for Racial Equality, Elliot House, 10-12 Allington Street, London SW1E 5EH   Tel : 01.828 7022
COMMISSION for the New Towns, Farley Hall, Bracknell, Berks RG12 5EU   Tel : 0344 3161
COMMISSION of the European Communities, 200 Rue de la Loi, 1049 Brussels, Belgium
COMMITTEE for Middle East Trade, 33 Bury Street, St.James's, London SW1 6AX   Tel : 01.839 1170
COMMITTEE of Directors of Polytechnics, 309 Regent Street, London W1R 7PE   Tel : 01.637 9939
COMMITTEE of London Clearing Bankers, 10 Lombard Street, London EC3V 9AP
COMMITTEE of Vice Chancellors & Principals of the Universities of U.K., 29 Tavistock Square, London WC1H 9EZ   Tel : 01.387 0256
COMMITTEE on Industrial Ventilation, PO Box 16153, Lansing, Michigan 48901, USA
COMMITTEE on Invisible Exports, 7th Floor, The Stock Exchange, London EC2N 1HH   Tel : 01.628 3161
COMMODITIES Research Unit Ltd., Consolidated Research, 31 Mount Pleasant, London WC1X 0AD   Tel : 01.278 0414   Telex : 264008
COMMODITY Research Bureau Inc., 1 Liberty Playa, 47th Floor, New York 10006, USA

COMMODITY Research Unit, 26 Red Lion Square, London WC1   Tel : 01.242 9462
COMMON Ground Filmstrips - distributed by Longman Group Ltd.
COMMONS Preservation Society, 166 Shaftesbury Avenue, London WC2H 8JH
COMMONWEALTH Agricultural Bureaux, Farnham House, Farnham Royal, Slough, Berks SG2 3BN   Tel : 02814 2662
COMMONWEALTH Bureau of Agricultural Economics, Dartington House, Little Clarendon Street, Oxford OX1 2HH   Tel : 0865 59829
COMMONWEALTH Bureau of Animal Health, Central Veterinary Laboratory, New Haw, Weybridge, Surrey   Tel : 09323 42826
COMMONWEALTH Bureau of Dairy Science & Technology, Lane End House, Shinfield, Reading, Berks RG2 9BB   Tel : 0734 883895   Telex : 847204
COMMONWEALTH Bureau of Horticulture & Plantation Crops, East Malling Research Station, Maidstone, Kent ME19 6BJ   Tel : 0732 843833
COMMONWEALTH Bureau of Nutrition, Rowett Research Inst., Bucksburn, Aberdeen AB2 9SB   Tel : 0224 712162
COMMONWEALTH Bureau of Pastures & Field Crops, Grassland Research Institute, Hurley, Maidenhead, Berks SL6 5LR   Tel : 062 882 3457
COMMONWEALTH Bureau of Plant Breeding & Genetics, Pembroke Street, Cambridge CB2 3DX   Tel : 0223 358381 - orders to Commonwealth Agricultural Bureaux
COMMONWEALTH Bureau of Soils, Rothamsted Experimental Station, Harpenden, Herts AL5 2JQ   Tel : 058 27 63133
COMMONWEALTH Forestry Institute, South Parks Road, Oxford OX1 3RB   Tel : 0865 511431   Telex : 53147
COMMONWEALTH Institute, Kensington High Street, London W8 6NQ   Tel : 01.602 3252
COMMONWEALTH Institute of Helminthology, The White House 103 St.Peters Street, St.Albans, Herts.AL1 3EW   Tel : 0727 52126
COMMONWEALTH Mycological Institute, Kew, Surrey   Tel : 01.940 4086
COMMONWEALTH Secretariat, Marlborough House, Pall Mall, London SW1Y 5HX   Tel : 01.839 3411   Telex : 27678
COMMONWORK Trust, Bore Place, Bough Beech, Edenbridge, Kent
COMMONWORD Writers Workshop, 27 Clerkenwell Close, London EC1R 0AT   Tel : 01.251 4976
COMMUNICATION Channels Inc., 6285 Barfield Road, Atlanta Georgia 30328, USA
COMMUNICATIONS Information Systems, Regal House, Lower Road, Chorleywood, Rickmansworth, Herts.WD3 5LQ   Tel : 0927 84119
COMMUNICATIONS Management, PO Box 15, Fleet, Hants. GU13 9XP   Tel : 025 14 28778
COMMUNIST Party of G.B., 16 King Street, London WC2E 8HY   Tel : 01.831 2151 - distributed by Central Book Ltd.
COMMUNITY Action, PO Box 665, London SW1X 8DZ   Tel : 01.251 3008
COMMUNITY Development Project, Home Office Room 1007, 50 Queen Anne's Gate, London SW1H 9AT
COMMUNITY Media Ltd., 22 Gay Street, Bath, Avon   Tel : 0225 333400
COMMUNITY Project Development, C.P.D.Co.Ltd., Finance House, 27 Queen Street, Barnstaple, Devon   Tel : 0271 71057
COMMUNITY Projects Foundation, 60 Highbury Grove, London N5 2AG
COMPANY Communications Centre Ltd., c/o Derek Beattie Distribution, PO Box 29, Twickenham, Middx.TW1 3BN
COMPRINT Ltd., 177 Hagden Lane, Watford, Herts.WD1 8LW   Tel : 0923 34543
COMPTON Russell Ltd. - now Michael Russell(Publ.)Ltd.
COMPUTER Aid for Management Ltd., 32-36 Great Portland Street, London W1N 5AD   Tel : 01.637 3691
COMPUTER Aided Design Centre, Madingley Road, Cambridge CB3 0HB   Tel : 0223 314848
COMPUTER Bookshop, 30 Lincoln Road, Olton, Birmingham B27 6PA   Tel : 021.707 7544
COMPUTER Economics Ltd., 51 Portland Road, Kingston-upon-Thames, Surrey KT1 2SH   Tel : 01.549 8726/8
COMPUTER Guides Ltd., EMAP Business & Computer Publ., 5th Floor, Petersham House, 57a Hatton Garden, London EC1N 8JD   Tel : 01.242 6552/6
COMPUTER Microfilm Intl.Corp., 2020 14th Street North, Arlington, Virginia 22201, USA

COMPUTER Research Press, Abacus House, Speldhurst Road, Tunbridge Wells, Kent TN4 0HU
COMPUTER Solutions Ltd., Treway House, Hanworth Lane, Chertsey, Surrey KT16 9LA Tel : 09328 65292
COMPUTER Users Yearbook - see Computing Publications Ltd.
COMPUTERBITS Ltd., PO Box 13, Yeovil, Somerset Tel : 0935 26522
COMPUTING Publications Ltd., 53-55 Frith Street, London W1A 2HG Tel : 01.323 3211
COMPUTING Services Association Ltd., 5th Floor, Hanover House, 73-74 High Holborn, London WC1V 6LE Tel : 01.405 2171/3161
CONCEPT Inc., 2224 Skyline Drive, Fortworth, Texas 76114, USA
CONCERTINA Publications, 2nd Floor, 19 Broad Court, London WC2 Tel : 01.836 1758
CONCORD Films Council, 201 Felixstowe Road, Ipswich, Suffolk IP3 9BJ Tel : 0473 76012
CONCORDIA Publ.House Ltd., The Garden House, Hothorpe Hall, Theddingworth, Lutterworth, Leics.LE17 6QX
CONCRETE Association, Wexham Springs, Wexham, Slough, Berks.
CONDE Nast Publications Ltd., Vogue House, Hanover Square, London W1R 0AD Tel : 01.499 9080 Telex : 27338
CONDOR Books - imprint of Souvenir Press Ltd.
CONFEDERATION of British Industry, Centre Point, 103 New Oxford Street, London WC1 Tel : 01.379 7400 Telex : 21332
CONFERENCE & Exposition Management Co.Inc., PO Box 844, Greenwich, Connecticut 06830, USA
CONFERENCE Blue Book - now Spectrum Publishing
The CONFERENCE Board, 845 Third Avenue, New York 10002, USA Tel : 212 759 0900 / Ave.Louise 326, Btc48 B1030 Brussels, Belgium
CONFERENCE Communication, Monks Hill, Tilford, Farnham, Surrey GU10 2AJ Tel : 02518 2066 Telex : 858623
CONGREGATIONAL Federation, 12 Canal Street, Nottingham NG1 7EH Tel : 0602 51569
CONGREGATIONAL Union of Scotland, Hillhead Centre, 1 University Avenue, Glasgow G12 8NN Tel : 041.339 6711
CONGRESSIONAL Quarterly Inc., 1414 22nd Street NW, Washington DC 20037, USA Tel : 202 887 8500
CONNOISSEUR, The Chester Gate House, Vauxahll Bridge Road, London SW1V 1HF Tel : 01.834 2331
Joseph CONRAD Society(U.K.), 113 West Street, Farnham, Surrey GU9 7HH Tel : 02513 5135 - orders to Churstons, Mill Lane, Felbridge, E.Grinstead, West Sussex Tel : 0342 24921
CONRAN Octopus - c/o Octopus Publ.Group
CONSERVATION Foundation, Washington, USA - distributed by Bowker
CONSERVATIVE Central Office, 32 Smith Square, London SW1P 3HH   Tel : 01.222 9000
CONSERVATIVE Group in Europe, Europe House Club, 1a Whitehall Place, London SW1A 2HA Tel : 01.839 6622
CONSERVATIVE Political Centre   ] 32 Smith Square,
CONSERVATIVE & Unionist Central Office] London SW1P 3HH
CONSIGLO Nazionale Delle Ricerche, 00100 Roma, Piazzale Aldo Moro 7, Rome, Italy Tel : 4993 255
CONSOLIDATED Goldfields Ltd., 49 Moorgate, London EC2R 6BQ
CONSTABLE & Co.Ltd., 10 Orange Street, London WC2H 7EG Tel : 01.930 0801/7 - distributed by Tiptree Book Services Ltd.
CONSTAPLE Travel Publishers, Imperial House, Harley Place, Bristol 8, Avon Tel : 0272 735380
CONSTRADO, NLA Tower, Addiscombe Road, Croydon, Surrey CR9 3JH Tel : 01.688 2688 Telex : 946372
CONSTRUCTION Industry Computing Association, Guildhall Place Cambridge CB2 3QQ Tel : 0223 311246
CONSTRUCTION Industry Research & Information Association, (CIRIA), 6 Storey's Gate, London SW1P 3AU Tel : 01.222 8891
CONSTRUCTION Industry Training Board, Publications, Radnor House, London Road, London SW16 4ZZ
CONSTRUCTION Markets, 120 Glenthorne Road, London W6 0LP Tel : 01.741 4957
CONSTRUCTION Press - c/o Longman Group Ltd.
CONSTRUCTION Safety Assocation of Ontario, 74 Victoria Street Toronto, Ontario M5C 2As, Canada
CONSTRUCTION Specification Institute, 1150 17th Street NW, Suite 300, Washington DC 20036, USA
CONSULTEX SA, CH-1261 Bogis-Bossey/VD, Switzerland Tel : 022 761145 Telex : 422500
CONSUMER Pulse Inc., 6 San Rafael Street, Barrio Kapitolyo, Pasig Metro, Manila, Philippines Tel : 693 8705 Telex : 7423100

CONSUMER Association, 14 Buckingham Street, London WC2N 6DS Tel : 01.839 1222 Telex : 918197 - distributed by Hodder & Stoughton Ltd.
CONTACT - imprint of Weidenfeld & Nicolson
CONTAK Publications, 29 White Horse Lane, London E1 Tel : 01.790 6288
CONTEMPORARY Books Inc., 180 North Michigan Avenue, Chicago, Ill.60601, USA Tel : 312 782 9181 - distributed by Feffer & Simon Inc.
CONTEXT Publishing, Greyfriars House, Henton, Oxford Tel : 0844 51508 - distributed by Biblios Distribution
CONTINENTAL Railway Circle, 25 Woodcock Dell Avenue, Kenton, Harrow, Middx.HA3 0PW
CONTINUA Publ.Ltd., Estover Road, Plymouth P26 1PZ Tel : 0752 705251
CONVENTURE Books, Box 4YH, London W1 - distributed by Wentworth Book Co.
CONWAY Maritime Press Ltd., 24 Bride Lane, Fleet Street, London EC4Y 8DR Tel : 01.583 2412
CONWAY Perkins Publ.Ltd., 33 Albion Place, Maidstone, Kent Tel :0622 55245
COO Press, 19 Doughty Street, London WC1N 2PT Tel : 01.405 7562
Frank COOK Travel Guides, 8 Wykeham Court, Old Perry Street, Chislehurst, Kent BR7 6PN Tel : 01.467 5049 - distributed by Seymour Press
Thomas COOK Ltd., Timetable Publishing Office, PO Box 36, Peterborough, PE3 6SB
COOLING Water Association, 74 Queensway, London W2 3RW
COOMBE Springs Press Ltd., Moorcote, Ellingstring, Masham, Nr.Rippon, N.Yorks. HG4 4PL Tel : 0677 60282
Leo COOPER, 54 Poland Street, London W1V 3DF Tel : 01.437 2075 Telex : 8954961
COOPER Square Publ.Inc., 59, 4th Avenue, New York 10003 USA
COOPERATIVE Development Agency, 20 Albert Embankment London SE1 7TJ Tel : 01.211 5492
COOPERATIVE Union Ltd., Holyoake House, Hanover Street, Manchester M60 0AS Tel : 061.832 4300
COOPERATIVE Wholesale Ltd., PO Box 53, New Century House Manchester M60 4ES Tel : 061.834 1212 X6084
COPPER Development Association, Orchard House, Matton Lane Potters Bar, Herts. Tel : 0707 50815
COPPLESTONE(Trewin)Publ.Ltd., Advance House, 101-109 Ladbroke Grove, London W11 1PG Tel : 01.229 8861 Telex : 25766
CORBITT & Hunter, POB 1LW, 5 St.Nicholas Buildings, Newcastle-upon-Tyne Tel : 0632 21036/21784 - orders to J.H.Corbitt Ltd., 105 Clayton Street Newcastle-upon-Tyne NE1 5PZ Tel : 0632 24356
CORDEE, 249 Knighton Church Road, Leicester LE2 3JQ Tel : 0533 709353
CORGI Books Ltd., Century House, 61-63 Uxbridge Road, .London W5 5SA Tel : 01.579 2652 Telex : 267974 - orders to PO Box 17, Wellingborough, Northants. NN8 4BU Tel : 0933 225761 Telex : 311306
CORK University Press, University College, Cork, Rep.of Ireland Tel : Cork 26871
CORNELL University Press, PO Box 1000 Ithaca, New York 14853, USA - distributed by IBD
CORNERSTONE Library, New York, USA - distributed by Silco Books Ltd.
CORNHILL Publications Ltd., 4-7 Nottingham Court, Short's Gardens, London WC2H 9AY Tel : 01.240 1515
CORNISH Life Magazine, Belmont House, Green Lane, Redruth Cornwall Tel : 0209 215273
CORNWALL Books - imprint of Golden Cockerel Press
CORONDAY Ltd., Marston Court, 102 Manor Road, Wallington Surrey
CORONET & Knight Books, Mill Road, Dunton Green, Sevenoaks Kent TN13 2YE Tel : 0732 450111 Telex : 95122
L.CORPER-Mordannt & Co., Pitman House, Parker Street London WC2B 5PB
CORPORATE Development Consultants, Vale House 13 High Street, Thornbury, Bristol BS12 2AR
CORPORATE Development Laboratory, British Steel Corporation - now British Steel Corporation, Sheffield Labs.
CORPORATE Publ.Ltd., 26 Parkway, London NW1 7AH Tel : 01.485 0975
CORPORATION of London, Guildhall, London EC2P 2EJ Tel : 01.606 3030 - Information Centre : St.Paul's Churchyard, London EC4M 8BX Tel : 01.606 3030
CORUUS Publ.Ltd., Upper King Street, Royston, Herts Tel : 0763 41265

COSMETIC Toiletry & Fragrance Association, 1110 Vermont Avenue NW, Suite 800, Washington DC 20005, USA
COSTANTE Basin Ajansi, Peykhane Cad.No.14, Cemberlitaz, Istanbul, Turkey
D.J.COSTELLO(Publ.)Ltd., 43 High Street, Tunbridge Wells Kent TN1 1XU Tel : 0892 45355
COTSWOLD Life Ltd., Alma House, Rodney Road, Cheltenham Glos. Tel : 0242 33165
COTTON Silk & Man Made Fibres Research Association(Shirley Institute), Didsbury, Manchester M20 8RX Tel : 061.445 8141
COUCHMEAD Communications Ltd., 153 High Street, London SE20 Tel : 01.778 1102
COUNCIL for British Archaeology, 112 Kennington Road, London SE11 6RE Tel : 01.582 0494
COUNCIL for Education Technology for the U.K., 3 Devonshire Street, London W1N 2BA Tel : 01.580 7553
COUNCIL for Environmental Education, School of Education, University of Reading, London Road, Reading, Berks RG1 5AQ
COUNCIL for Postgraduate Medical Education in England & Wales, 7 Marylebone Road, London NW1 5HH Tel : 01.323 1289
COUNCIL for Professions Supplementary to Medicine, Park House 184 Kennington Park Road, London SE11 4BU Tel : 01.582 0866
COUNCIL for Science & Society, 3-4 St.Andrews Hill, London EC4V 5BY Tel : 01.236 0032
COUNCIL for Small Industries in Rural Areas, 141 Castle Street, Salisbury, Wilts. SP1 3TB Tel : 0722 6255
COUNCIL for the Education & Training of Health Visitors, Clifton House, Euston Road, London NW1 2RS Tel : 01.387 3456 X45
COUNCIL of Christians & Jews, 48 Onslow Gardens, London SW7 3PX Tel : 01.589 8854/5
COUNCIL of Economic Priorities Inc.(C.E.P.), 84, 5th Avenue, New York 10011, USA
COUNCIL of Engineering Institutions, 2 Little Smith Street, Westminster, London SW1P 3DL Tel : 01.222 3912
COUNCIL of Europe, 67006 Strasbourg Cedex, France
COUNCIL of Law Reporting for England & Wales, 3 Stone Buildings, Lincoln's Inn, London WC2A 3XN Tel : 01.242 6471/2
COUNCIL of the Stock Exchange, London EC2N 1HP Tel : 01.588 2355 Telex : 886557
COUNCILS & Education Press Ltd., c/o Longman Group Ltd., 5 Bentinck Street, London W1M 5RN Tel : 01.935 0121 - orders to Longman Group Journals Division, 43-45 Annandale Street, Edinburgh EH7 4AT
COUNTER Information Services, 9 Poland Street, London W1 Tel : 01.439 3764/6541
COUNTER Intelligence Service, 52 Shaftesbury Avenue, London W1 Tel : 01.734 8862
COUNTRY Landowners' Association, 16 Belgrave Square, London SW1X 8PQ Tel : 01.235 0511
COUNTRY Life Books, 84-88 The Centre, Feltham, Middx. Tel : 01.844 1177 Telex : 918327
COUNTRYGOERF Books, The School House, 12 Market Street, Buxton, Derbyshire SK17 6LD Tel : 0298 2958
COUNTRYSIDE Books, 3 Catherine Road, Newbury, Berks. Tel : 0635 43816
COUNTRYSIDE Commission for Scotland, Battleby, Redgorton, Perth, Scotland Tel : 0738 27921
COUNTRYSIDE Publ.Ltd., School Lane, Brinscall, Lancs. Tel : 0254 831172
COUNTY Guide Publications, 19 Baldock Road, Letchworth, Herts.SG6 3JX Tel : 046 26 2229
COUNTY Publishing Co., 28 Lurke Street, Bedford, Beds. Tel : 0234 40938
COUNTY Surveyors' Society, Northampton House, Northampton NN1 2HZ Tel : 0604 34833 Telex : 312516
COURCAN Ltd., 194 West Drayton Road, Hillingdon, Middx. Tel : 08954 48444
COURONNE Publ.Ltd., 182-188 Corn Exchange Buildings, Fennel Street, Manchester Tel : 061.834 5883
COURPRINT Ltd., 157 Hayden Lane, Watford, Herts.WD1 8LW Tel : 0923 32308
COURT & Judicial Publ., PO Box 39, Henley-on-Thames, Oxon. RG9 5UA
COVENANT Publ.Co.Ltd., 6 Buckingham Gate, London SW1E 6JP Tel : 01.834 7222/3
COVENT Garden Press, 80 Long Acre, London WC2E 9NG Tel : 01.240 0336
COVENTRY & District Employers Association, 18 Davenport Road, Coventry CV5 6PX Tel : 0203 74333
COVENTRY Women's Education Group, 27 Clerkenwell Close, London EC1R 0AT Tel : 01.251 4976

COVENTRY Workshop, 27 Clerkenwell Close, London EC1R 0AT Tel : 01.251 4976
COVENTURE Ltd. - c/o Thorsons Publ.Ltd.
COVERDALE House Publ.Ltd., Lottbridge Drive, Eastbourne E.Sussex BN23 6NT
The COVERDALE Organisation, 53 Homefield Road, Seaford Sussex BN25 3DX
CRAFTS Advisory Committee, 28 Haymarket, London SW1Y 4SU Tel : 01.839 8000
CRAFTS Council, 12 Waterloo Place, London SW1Y 4AU Tel : 01.930 4811
CRAFTSMAN's Directory, Brook House, Mint Street, Godalming Surrey GU7 1HE Tel : 04868 22184
CRAIG Publications, 313 Romford Road, London E7 Tel : 01.555 7780
CRAIN Communications Inc., 740 Rusk Street, Chicago, Ill. 60611, USA
J.B.CRAMER & Co.Ltd., 99 St.Martins Lane, London WC2N 4AZ Tel : 01.240 1612
CRAMER Electronics, Hawke House, Green Street, Sunbury on Thames, Middx. Tel : 09327 85577
CRANE Ltd., 194 High Street, Chippin, Ongar, Essex
CRANFIELD Institute of Technology, Cranfield, Bedford MK43 0AL Tel : 0234 750111
CRANFIELD School of Management, Cranfield, Bedford MK43 0AL Tel : 0234 751122
CRANFIELD Unit for Precision Engineering, Cranfield, Bedford MK43 0AL Tel : 0234 750111
CRANLEY Publications, 5 Chapel Street, Woking, Surrey GU21 1DZ Tel : 04862 22398
CRANWELL Publ.Co.Ltd., 419a Queen Street, Auckland, New Zealand
CRAWFORD Publ.Ltd., 25 St.James Street, London SW1A 1HG Tel :01.839 7000 Telex : 919555
CREAGH-Osborne & Partners, 6 Station Street, Lymington, Hants. Tel : 0590 74832
CREATIONS Editions Productions Publicitaires, 1 Place d'Estienne d'Orves, 75009 Paris, France Tel : (1) 280 67 62 Telex : 210311F
CREATIVE Business Ltd., 7 Weal Street, London WC2H 9PW Tel : 01.836 2821
CREATIVE Computing, 27 Andrew Close, Stoke Golding, Nuneaton CV13 6EL
CREATIVE Handbook Ltd., 3th Floor, 100 St.Martins Lane, London WC2
CREATIVE Strategies Intl., Banda House, Cambridge Grove, London W6 0LN Tel : 01.741 4767 Telex : 939844
CREMATION Society of G.B., Woodcut House, Ashford Road, Hollingbourne, Maidstone, Kent ME17 1XH Tel :0622 38034/37877
CRESCENT Books, 27 Clerkenwell Close, London EC1R 0AT Tel : 01.251 4976
CRESSET Press, c/o WBR Distributors Ltd., 45-49 Gorst Road, North Acton, London NW10
CRESSRELLES Publ.Co.Ltd., 311 Worcester Road, Malvern Worcs.WR14 1AN Tel : 06845 65045
CRICKETERS' Who's Who Ltd., Masons Yard, 34 High Street London SW19 5BU
The CRIME Club - see Wm.Collins Sons & Co.Ltd.
R.A.CRITCHLEY, 9 Sea Avenue, Rustington, Sussex BN16 2DQ Tel : 09062 6575
Bernard CROFT/Antony Melville, 5 Comeragh Mews, Comeragh Road, London W14 Tel : 01.385 0342
CROFT Publ.Co.Ltd., Unit 4, Sewell Street, London E13 Tel : 01.471 8221
Paul H.CROMPTON Ltd., 638 Fulham Road, London SW6 Tel : 01.788 9130 - distributed by IBD
CROMWELL Publ., 3 Cromwell Terrace, St.Ives, Cambs. PE17 4JE Tel : 0480 64974
CRONER Publ.Ltd., Croner House, 173 Kingston Road, New Malden, Surrey KT3 3SS Tel : 01.942 8966 Telex : 267778
CROOM Helm Ltd., Provident House, Burrell Row, Beckenham Kent BR3 1AT Tel : 01.658 7813/01.650 6061
CROSBY Lockwood & Staples, c/o Granada, Technical Division
CROWN Agents, AO5 Branch, 5th Floor New Wing, 4 Millbank London SW1P 3JD
CROWN Publ.Inc., 1 Park Avenue, New York 10016, USA Tel : 212 532 9200 Telex : 427195
CROWOOD Press, Crowood House, Ramsbury, Marlborough, Wilts. Tel : 0672 20242
CRUISING Association, Ivory House, St.Katherine Dock, London E1 9AT
CRUSE-The National Organisation for the Widowed & their Children, Cruse House, 126 Steen Road, Richmond Surrey TW9 1UR Tel : 01.940 4818/9047

CUISENAIRE Co.Ltd., 40 Silver Street, Reading, Berks RG1 2SU Tel : 0734 83101
William CULROSS & Son Ltd., Coupar Angus, Perthshire PH13 9DF Tel : 08282 266
CUMMINS Daventry, Royal Oak Way South, Daventry, Northants. NN11 5NU Tel : 03272 4400 Telex : 58643
CUMULATIVE Index Co., 1172 Commonwealth Avenue, Boston, Mass.02184, USA
CUPID Press, 2 Quay Street, Woodbridge, Suffolk Tel : 03943 7414
CURLEW Publ., Colton House, Burnsall, Skipton, N.Yorks BD23 6BN Tel : 075 672 248
CURLEY's Directories Ltd., 49 Woodfield Avenue, Wembley, Middx.HA0 3NP Tel : 01.904 1000
CURLON Press Ltd. - c/o Book Point Ltd.
CURRENT Publications Ltd., GPO Box 9848, 504 Enterprise Building, 238 Queens Road Central, Hong Kong
CURWEN Press Ltd., 9 North Street, Plaistow, London E13 9HJ Tel : 01.472 1466
CURZON Press Ltd., 42 Gray's Inn Road, London WC2 Tel : 01.405 5416 - distributed by Biblios Distrib.
CUSTOMER Satisfaction Research Institute, 4901 College Boulevard, Suite 107, Leawood Manor, Shawnee Mission, Kansas 66211, USA Tel : 913 381 8209
CUSTOMS Corporation Council, 40 Rue Washington, 1050 Brussels, Belgium
CYCLOGRAPHIC Publ., PO Box 20, Great Missenden, Bucks HP16 0HU Tel : 01.404 4202
CYNGOR Gwlad Gwynedd, Cai Llechi, Caernarton, Gwynedd

D

D.A.F.S.A., 125 Rue Montmartre, Paris 75002, France Tel : 233 2123
D.A.T.A.International, 16 Victoria Road, Romford, Essex Tel : 0708 46447
DBI, c/o Arms & Armour Press, 2-6 Hampstead High Street, London NW3 1QQ Tel : 01.794 7868
DHEW Publ., Washington DC 20201, U.S.A. / 5600 Fishers Lane, Rockville, MD20857, USA
D.K.Agencies, 313-74-D Inderlok, Old Rohtak Road, Delhi 110035, India
DMS Inc., 29-31 Station Road, Henley-on-Thames, Oxon.RG9 1AT Tel : 0491 5880 Telex : 848672
D.P.Press Ltd., St.Julians, Sevenoaks, Kent TN15 0RX Tel : 0732 58261
DP Publications, 12 Romsey Road, Eastleigh, Hants. SO5 4AL Tel : 0703 642649
DA Capo Press, 3 Henrietta Street, London WC2E 8LU Tel : 01.240 0856
DABOR Science Publ., 130 Gazza Blvd., Farmingtabs, New York 11735, USA
Peter DAFFON Assocs.Ltd., 30 Marsh Road, Pinner, Middx. HA5 5NQ Tel : 01.868 5499
DAGON Books - imprint of Studio Publ.(Ipswich) Ltd.
DAGRA NV, Verrijn Stuartweg 60, PO Box 171, 1110 BC Diemen The Netherlands
DAILY Express Books - see Express Newspapers Ltd.
DAILY Mail - see Associated Newspapers Group Ltd.
DAILY Mirror Books - now Mirror Books Ltd.
DAILY Telegraph - see Day Publishing
DALESMAN Publ.Co.Ltd., Clapham, Lancs. LA2 8EB Tel : 04685 225
DALLAS Museum of Fine Art (Fleetbooks) - c/o TABS
Terence DALTON Ltd., Water Street, Lavenham, Sudbury, Suffolk Tel : 0787 247572
DALTON Watson Ltd., 76 Wardour Street, London W1V 4AN Tel : 01.734 7710
DANCE Books Ltd., 9 Cecil Court, London WC2N 4EZ Tel : 01.836 2314
DANCING Times Ltd., 18 Hand Court, London WC1V 6JF Tel : 01.405 1414/5
G.P.DANGER, 121D St.Georges Drive, London SW1V 4DA Tel : 01.834 5622
C.W.DANIEL Ltd., 1 Church Path, Saffron Walden, Essex CB10 1JP Tel : 0799 21909
DANSK Media Komite, Norgesmindevej 15, DK-2900 Hellerup Denmark Tel : 01 61 17 20
Alan DARBY Publ.Ltd., 8 Stourbridge Road, Bromsgrove, Birmingham Tel : 0527 71979
DARK Peak Ltd., 336 Abbey Lane, Sheffield S8 0BY Tel : 0742 586587
DART Publ., 21 Sandquay Road, Dartmouth, Devon Tel ; 080 43 3225

DARTINGTON Press, Dartington Hall-Central Offices, Skinners Bridge, Dartington, Totnes, Devon TQ9 6JE Tel : 0803 862271
DARTNELL Corp., B/B 100, PO Box 60267, Chicago, Ill. 60660, USA - distributed by IBD
DARTON Longman & Todd Ltd., 89 Lillie Road, London SW6 1UD Tel : 01.385 2341
DATA Publications Ltd., 45 Yeading Avenue, Rayners Lane, Harrow, Middx.HA2 9RL Tel : 01.868 4851
DATA Research Group, Bridge House, Great Missenden, Bucks Tel : 02406 4271 Telex : 837663
DATA Script Ltd., 30 South Street, Bishops Stortford, Herts. Tel : 0279 56203
DATA Transcripts Euro-Data Analysts, 7 Priors, Ashtead Surrey KT21 2QE Tel : 037 22 5714 Telex : 262284
DATABANK SpA, Via dei Piatti 11, 20123 Milan, Italy Tel : 02 809556
DATABASE(H.K.)Ltd., 2109 Alexandra House, Hong Kong Tel : 5 25 11 54
DATAQUEST Inc., 19055 Pruneridge Avenue, Cupertino CA95014, USA Tel : 408 725 1200 Telex : 171973
DAVID & Charles(Holdings)Ltd., Brunel House, Brunel Road Newton Abbot, Devon TQ12 2DW Tel : 0626 61121 Telex : 42904
DAVIDSON Pearce Berry & Spottiswoode Ltd., 67 Brompton Road, London SW3 1EF Tel : 01.589 4595
Christopher DAVIES(Publ.)Ltd., 52 Mansel Street, Swansea SA1 5EL
Peter DAVIES Ltd., 10 Upper Grosvenor Street, London W1X 9PA Tel : 01.493 4141 Telex : 8954961 - orders to Windmill Press, Kingswood, Tadworth, Surrey KT20 6TG
Alexander DAVIS Publications Ltd., 43 South Hill Road Hemel Hempstead, Herts.HP1 1JB Tel : 0442 61802
DAVIS & Moughton Ltd. - in liquidation 1980
F.A.DAVIS Co., USA - c/o Blackwell Scientific Publ.
DAVIS Publications Inc., 50 Portland Street, Worcester Mass.01608, USA Tel : 617 754 7201
DAVIS-Poynter Ltd., 11 Bolt Court, Fleet Street, London EC4 Tel : 01.353 7831/9362
DAVISON Publ.Ltd., 54 Elgin Avenue, London W9 2HA Tel : 01.289 7623
DAWSON Research & Marketing Services Ltd., 3586 Henderson Hiway, Winnipeg, Manitoba, R3C 2E7, Canada Tel : 204 338 0712
DAY Publishing, The Daily Telegraph, 135 Fleet Street, London EC4P 4BL Tel : 01.353 4242 X3590
DE CLIVIO Press, Usterstr.126, Postfach 8600 Dübendorf Switzerland
Walter DE Gruyter, Berlin - distributed by Global Book Resources
Robert E.DE La Rue Assocs., PO Box 2370, Santa Clara, CA95055, USA Tel : 408 243 2040
DEAN & Son Ltd., 2nd Floor, 52-54 Southwark Street, London SE1 1UA Tel : 01.407 6682/3
DEBELI Press, 15 Willenhall Road, London SE18 6TY
DEBENHAM Tewson & Chinnocks, Bancroft House, Paternoster Square, London EC4P 4ET Tel : 01.236 1520 Telex : 883749
DEBRETT's Peerage(Publ.)Ltd., 73-77 Britannia Road, London SW6 Tel : 01.736 6524/6
DECISION Models Ltd., 186 Westcombe Hill, Blackheath, London SE3 7DH Tel : 01.852 6098
DECISION Research Ltd., Box 2, Docking, Kings Lynn, Norfolk PE31 8QR
DECORATING Contractor Annual Directory, Elm Bank, Walton Lane, Shepperton, Middx.TW17 8LQ Tel : 093 22 43592
DEEMAR Co.Ltd., 6th Floor, Anglo-Thai Building, 64 Silom Road, Box 2732, Bangkok, Thailand Tel : 234 4520 Telex : 87258
DEFENCE Research Information Centre, Station Square House, St.Mary Cray, Orpington, Kent BR5 3RG
DEFENSE & Aerospace Marketing Services Inc., 100 Northfield Street, Greenwich, Connecticut 06830, USA Tel : 203 661 7800 / 31 Station Road, Henley-on-Thames, Oxon. RG9 1AT Tel : 04912 5880
DEFENSE Manufacturers' Association, 136 High Street, Guildford, Surrey GU1 3HL Tel : 0483 35355
Marcel DEKKER AG, Elisabethenstrasse 19, Postfach 34, 4010 Basel, Switzerland Tel : 061 23 10 30 Telex : 63475
DEKKER & Nordemann/Van Stockum, Ox Voorburgival 239, Amsterdam, The Netherlands

DELFT University Press, Mijnbouwplein 11, 2628RT Delft,
    The Netherlands Tel : 015 783254
DELMAR Publ.Co. - distributed by Van Nostrand Reinhold
DELPHI Marketing Services Inc., 400 East 89th Street, New York
    10018, USA Tel : 212 534 4868
DELTA Books Ltd., Box 4, Worthing, Sussex Tel : 0903 48446
DELTA International Co., 101 Cedar Lane, Teaneck, NJ 07666,
    USA Tel : 201 836 0762   Telex : 135307
DEMOLITION Industry Conciliation Board, 141 London Road,
    Leicester LE2 1EP
Michael W.DEMPSEY, 27 John Adam Street, London WC2N 6HX
    Tel : 01.930 6387
DENDROFLORA, Postbus 133, 2770 AC Boskoop, The Netherlands
DENHOLM House Press (NCEC), Robert Denholm House, Nutfield
    Redhill, Surrey RH1 4HW Tel : 0737 2411
Richard DENNIS, 144 Kensington Church Street, London W8 4BN
    Tel : 01.727 2061
DENNY Publ.Ltd., 2 Carthusian Street, London EC1M 6ED
    Tel : 01.253 5421
J.M.DENT & Sons Ltd., Aldine House, 33 Welbeck Street, London
    W1M 8LX Tel : 01.486 7233 Telex : 8954130
    - orders to J.M.Dent & Sons (Distribution)Ltd.
J.M.DENT & Sons(Distribution)Ltd., Dunhams Lane, Letchworth,
    Herts.SG6 1LF Tel :0462 266241 Telex : 825751
DEPARTMENT of Agriculture & Fisheries for Scotland, Marine
    Laboratory Library, PO Box 101, Victoria Road,
    Aberdeen,AB9 8DB Tel : 0224 876544
DEPARTMENT of Applied Economics, University of Cambridge,
    Sidgewick Avenue, Cambridge CB3 9DE
    Tel : 0223 58944
DEPARTMENT of Employment, 8 St.James' Square, London
    SW1Y 4JB Tel : 01.214 6000
DEPARTMENT of Energy, Thames House South, Millbank, London
    SW1P 4QJ Tel : 01.211 3394
DEPARTMENT of the Environment, 2 Marsham Street, London
    SW1P 3EB Tel : 01.212 3434
DEPARTMENT of Industry, Business Statistics Office, Cardiff
    Road, Newport, Gwent NP2 1XG Tel : 0633 56111
DEPARTMENT of Industry, Technology Reports Centre,Orpington
    Kent BR5 3RF Tel : 0689 32111
DWPARTMENTS of Industry & Trade, Library, 1 Victoria Street
    London SW1H 0ET Tel : 01.215 7877 Telex : 8811074/5
DERBYSHIRE Countryside Ltd., Lodge Lane, Derby DE1 3HE
    Tel : 0332 47087
DERWENT Publ.Ltd., Rochdale House 128 Theobald Road, London
    WC1X 8BP Tel : 01.242 5823/6
DESIGN & Art Direction Ltd., Nash House, Carlton Terrace,
    London SW1 Tel : 01.839 2964
DESIGN & Industries Association, c/o Nell Chamberlain, 17 Lawn
    Crescent, Kew Gardens, Surrey Tel : 01.940 4925
DESIGN Council Publications, The Design Council, 28 Haymarket
    London SW17 4SU Tel : 01.839 8000 Telex : 8812963
DET Norske Veritas, Veritas House, 112 Station Road, Sidcup
    Kent DA15 7DU Tel : 01.302 6234
Andre DEUTSCH Ltd., 105 Great Russell Street, London WC1B
    3LJ Tel : 01.580 2746 Telex : 21792 - orders to
    The Windmill Press
DEUTSCHES Hydrographisches, Bertrand Noch, 2000 Hamburg 4,
    West Germany
DEVELOPMENT Commission, 11 Cowley Street, London SW1P
    3NA Tel : 01.222 9134
DEVELOPMENT Corporation for Wales, Pearl Assurance House,
    Greyfriars Road, Cardiff CF1 3AG
DEVELOPPEMENT Construction, 31 Ter.Rue Louise-Michel, 92300
    Levallois-Perret, France Tel : 758 5360
DEVON & Cornwall Record Society, 7 The Close, Exeter EX1 1EZ
DEVONSHIRE Association for the Advancement of Science,
    Literature & Art, 7 The Close, Exeter EX1 1EZ
DEVOTO, Reid & Co.Ltd., 8 Bryanston Square, London W1
    Tel : 01.262 9043
DEWIT Publications, 915 15th Street NW, Suite 600, Washington
    DC 20005, USA Tel : 202 783 6060
DEWITT Co.Inc., 3650 Dresser Street, Houston, Texas 77002,
    USA Tel : 713 652 0576 Telex : 762854
DIADEM Book/Cordee, 249 Knighton Church Road, Leicester
    Tel : 0533 709353
DIAMOND Lead Co.Ltd., 4-2 Kasumigaseki 1 Chome, Chiyoda-ku,
    Tokyo 100, Japan Tel : 03 5046794
K.DICKENSON(Distribution), Building 18, Denham Studio Estate,
    North Orbital Road, Denham, Bucks.
    Tel : 0895 4064
Keith DICKSON Publ.Ltd., 30 Parkhill Road, Hemel Hempstead,
    Herts. Tel : 0442 50522
Ken DICKSON (Marketing)Ltd., 14 Crossways, Silwood Road,
    Sunninghill, Ascot, Berks SL5 0PY Tel : 0990 25421
DICKSON Price Publ.Ltd., PO Box 88, Gravesend, Kent DA13 9PR
    Tel : 047 483 3732

DIDACTIC Ltd., Gatwick House, Horley, Surrey RH6 9SU
    Tel : 029 34 5353
DIDIER (Librairie Marcel) - distributed by European School-
    Books Ltd.
DIDOT Bottin, 28 Rue du Docteur Finlay, 75738 Paris Cedex
    15, France
DIEBOLD Europe S.A., Sutherland House, 5-6 Argyll Street,
    London W1V 1AD Tel : 01.734 6911
    Telex : 266407
DIESEL & Gas Turbine Worldwide Catalogue, 13555 Bishops
    Court, Brookfield, Wisconsin 53005, USA
DIGITAL Equipment Co.Ltd., Fountain House, The Butts
    Centre, Reading, Berks RG1 7QN
    Tel : 0734 583555 Telex : 848327/8
DILITHIUM Press Inc. - distributed by Computer Research
    Press
DINOSAUR Publ.Ltd., Beechcroft House, Over, Cambridge
    CB4 5NE Tel : 0954 30324
Robert DINWIDDIE & Co.Ltd., 102-104 Irish Street,
    Dumfries Tel : 0387 52489
DIPLOMA Press Ltd., Ludgate House, 107-111 Fleet Street,
    London EC4 2AB Tel : 01.583 8888
DIPLOMATIC & Consular Yearbook, 11-13 Cricklewood Lane
    London NW2 1ET Tel : 01.450 9322
DIPLOMATIC Press & Publ.Co., 44-46 South Ealing Road
    Ealing, London W5 Tel : 01.959 4837
The DIRECTOR Publications Ltd., 116 Pall Mall, London
    SW1Y 5ED Tel : 01.839 1233
DIRECTORY Enquirers, 18 Trouville Road, London SW4 8PL
DIRECTORY of Conventions, 633 3rd Avenue, New York
    10017, USA
DIRECTORY of Social Change, 9 Mansfield Place, London NW3
    1HS
DIRECTORY of Training, Enterprise House, Badgemore Park
    Henley-on-Thames, Oxon. RG9 4NR
    Tel : 0491 6633
DIROSAB, Vasterakern 11, S-80226 Gavle, Sweden
    Tel : 026 119489 Telex : 81040
DISABILITY Press, 21 Davenham Avenue, Northwood, Middx.
    HA6 3HW
DISABLED Living Foundation, 346 Kensington High Street,
    London W14 8NS Tel : 01.602 2491
DISCLOSURES Ltd., 36 Crescent Road, Tunbridge Wells,
    Kent TN1 2LZ Tel : 0892 26397
DISCOVERY Guide Ltd., 35 Galsgate, Barnd Castle,
    Middlesbrough Tel : 0833 40638
DISK/Trend Report, 1224 Arbor Court, Mountain View,
    CA 94040, USA Tel : 415 961 6209 Telex : 172029
DISTRIBUTED Systems Ltd., 70 Borough High Street, London
    SE1 1XF Tel : 01.403 1568
DISTRIBUTION & Management Services Ltd., Sheldon Way,
    New Hythe Lane, Larkfield, Maidstone, Kent
    Tel : 0622 78648 Telex : 965514
DISTROPA Ltd., 3 Henrietta Street, London WC2E 8LT
    Tel : 01.240 1003/0856
DITTON Associates, 4 Portman Mews South, London W1H 9AU
    Tel : 01.629 0762
DIWAN Press, 81a Upper St.Giles Street, Norwich NR2 1AB
    Tel : 0603 23337
J.Arthur DIXON, Forest Side, Newport, Isle of Wight
    Tel : 0983 523381 Telex : 86188
DOANE-Western Agricultural Service Inc., 8900 Manchester
    Road, St.Louis, MO 63144, USA
    Tel : 314 968 1000 Telex : 447698
DOBSON Books Ltd., Brancepeth Castle, Durham DH7 8DF
    Tel : 0385 780628
DR.William's Trust, 14 Gordon Square, London WC1H 0AG
    Tel : 01.387 3727
La DOCUMENTATION Française, 29-31 Quai Voltaire, 75340
    Paris, Cedex 07, France
M.Jonathan DODD, Dodd, Mead & Co., 79 Madison Avenue,
    New York 10016, USA Tel : 212 685 6464
DODGE Corp. - division of McGraw-Hill Book Co.
R.J.DODD Publ.Ltd., Gladiator House, Gladiator Street,
    London SE23 Tel : 01.690 8288
DOD's Parliamentary Companion Ltd., Elm Cottage, Chilsham
    Lane, Herstmonceux, Hailsham, E.Sussex BN27
    4QQ Tel : 0323 832250
DODWELL Marketing Consultants, CPO Box 297, Tokyo, Japan
    Tel : 584 2351 Telex : J23790
DOG World Ltd., Clergy House, Churchyard, Ashford, Kent
    TN23 1QW Tel : 0233 22389
DOLMEN Press Ltd., North Richmond Industrial Estate, North
    Richmond Street, Dublin Tel : 0001 740324
DOLPHIN Book Co.Ltd., 58 Hurst Lane, Cumnor, Oxford OX2
    9PR - distributed by Dolphin Book Co.(Tredwr)
    Ltd.

DOLPHIN Book Co.(Tredwr)Ltd., Tredwr, Llangranog,
    Llandyssul, Dyfed SA44 6BA Tel : 023 978 404
DOLPHIN Books - c/o TABS
DOLPHIN Press - distributed by Blandford Press Ltd.
DOMUS, c/o London Art Bookshop, 8 Holland Street, Kensington
    London
John DONALD(Publ.)Ltd., 138 St.Stephen Street, Edinburgh
    EH3 5AA Tel : 031.225 1146
DONNINGTON Press, Aldermaston Court, Aldermaston, Reading
    Berks RG7 4PW Tel : 073 521 2241 - distributed by
    Cassell & Co.Ltd.
DORLING Kindersley Ltd., 9 Henrietta Street, London WC2E
    8PS Tel : 01.240 5151 Telex : 8954527
The DORNEY Press, 1818 Ridge Road, Homewood, OH 60430, USA
    - distributed by Irwin
DORSET Natural History & Archaeological Society, c/o County
    Museum, Dorchester, Dorset DT1 1XA Tel : 0305 2735
DORSET Publ.Co., Knock-na-Cre, Milborne Port, Sherborne,
    Dorset DT9 5HJ Tel : 0963 32583
DORSEY Press(Irwin) - c/o TABS
DOUBLEDAY & Co.Inc., 100 Wigmore Street, London W1H 9DR
    Tel : 01.935 1269 Telex : 264676 - distributed by
    TABS
Henry DOUBLEDAY Research Association, 27 Clerkenwell Close,
    London EC1R 0AT Tel : 01.251 4976
DOVECOTE Press, Stanbridge, Wimborne, Dorset BH21 4JD
    Tel : 0258 840549
DOVER Publications, New York, USA - distributed by Constable
    & Co.Ltd.
DOW Jones/Irwin - c/o TABS
DOWDEN, Hutchinson & Ross - distributed by Academic Press
DRAGON's World Ltd., High Street, Limpsfield, Surrey RH8
    9DY Tel : 08833 5044 Telex : 95631 - orders to
    Phin Publ.Ltd.
DRAKE Educational Assoc.Ltd., 212 Whitchurch Road, Cardiff
    Tel : 0222 29414
DRAKE Publ.Inc. - distributed by TABS
Richard DREW Publ.Ltd., 20 Park Circus, Glasgow G3 6BE
    Tel : 041.333 9341
H.P.Drewey Shipping Publ.Ltd., 34 Brook Street, Mayfair
    London W1Y 2LL Tel : 01.629 5366
DRIVE Publications, Berkeley Square House, Berkeley Square
    London W1X 5PD - distributed by Hodder &
    Stoughton Ltd.
DROP Forging Research Association, Shepherd Street, Sheffield
    S3 7BA Tel : 0742 27463
DRUG Business Research Co.Ltd., 1-25-2 Koishikawa, Bunkyo-ku
    Tokyo 112, Japan
DRUG Intelligence Publ.Inc., 1241 Broadway, Hamilton, Ill.
    62341, USA Tel : 217 847 2504
DRUGES of Today, Apartado de Correos 540, Barcelona, Spain
DRYAD Press, PO Box 38, Northgates, Leicester LE1 9BU
    Tel : 0533 50405
DRYDEN Press, USA - distributed by Holt-Saunders Ltd.
DRYDENS Printers Ltd., Brent Crescent, North Circular Road,
    London NW10 7XU Tel : 01.965 2631
DUBLIN University Press, 17 Gilford Road, Sandymount, Dublin
    4, Rep.of Ireland Tel : 0001 694422
DUCIMUS Books Ltd., De Worde House, 283 Lonsdale Road,
    Barnes, London SW13 9QW Tel : 01.878 2454
G.DUCKWORTH & Co.Ltd., The Old Piano Factory, 43
    Gloucester Crescent, London NW1 7DY
    Tel : 01.485 3484
James DUFFY & Co.Ltd., 21 Shaw Street, Dublin 2, Rep.of
    Ireland Tel : 0001 778115
Robert DUGDALE, c/o Corpus Christi College, Oxford OX1 4JF
    Tel.enquiries to : Henry Hardy 0865 56767 X256
DUGDALE Society, The Shakespeare Centre, Stratford-upon-
    Avon, Warwicks. CV37 6QW Tel : 0789 4016
DUKE University Press - distributed by IBD
DUN & Bradstreet, 6-8 Bonhill Street, London EC2A 4BU
    Tel : 01.247 4377
DUN Donneldley Publ.Corp., 666 5th Avenue, New York 10019
    USA
DUNCAN Publishing, 3 Colin Gardens, Hendon, London NW9
    6EL Tel : 01.205 4186
DUNCKER & Humblot, Deutsch-schaferweg 9, Postfach 40 329
    1000 Berlin 41, West Germany
DUNDALGAN Press(W.Tempest) Ltd., Francis Street, Dundalk
    County Louth, Rep.of Ireland Tel : Dundalk 34013
DUNDURN Press, PO Box 245, Station F, Toronto, Ontario
    Canada M4Y 2L5 Tel : 416 368 9390
Martin DUNITZ Ltd., 154 Camden High Street, London NW1 0NE
    Tel : 01.482 2202 Telex : 296307
Jonathan DUNN & Co., 19 Cambrian Place, Swansea
    Tel : 0792 474881

DUNROD Press, 8 Brown's Road, Newtownabbey, Co.Antrim
    BT36 8RN Tel : 023 13 2362
DUO Publ.Ltd., 1 Hermes Street, London N1
    Tel : 01.837 7931 Telex : 24892 - distributed by
    Mitchell Beazley Marketing Ltd.
DUPONT(U.K.)Ltd., Wedgwood Way, Stevenage, Herts.SG1
    4QN Tel : 0438 734000 Telex : 825591
DUSTBOOKS, Box 100, Paradise, CA94969, USA
DUTCK EIASM, Place Stephanne 20, 1050 Brussels, Belgium
E.P.DUTTON & Co.Inc., 201 Park Ave.South, New York
    10003, USA Telex 125836 - some distribution by
    TABS, some by WHS Distribution, some Phaidon
    Press Ltd.
DYLLANSOW Truran, Trewolsta, Trewirgie, Redruth, Cornwall
    Tel : 0209 216796
DYMAY, PO Box 310, Menlo Park, CA94025, USA
DYTECNA Ltd., Spring Lane, Malvern Link Malvern, West
    Midlands Tel : 06845 2255

E

ECI Services, 88-90 Gray's Inn Road, London WC1X 8AA
EIMJ Mining Services, PO Box 459, Heightstorm, NJ08500,USA
E.M.Courses, 4 Mapledale Avenue, Croydon CR0 5TA
    Tel : 01.654 4659
EMA U.K.Office, 9 Ashton Road, Nuneaton, Warwicks.
EMAP Business & Computer Publications, Durrant House, 8
    Herbal Hill, London EC1R 5JB Tel : 01.278 6556
EMC Doc., PO Box 190, Arlington, Virginia 22210, USA
EMI Music Publ.Ltd., 138 Charing Cross Road, London WC2H
    0LD Tel : 01.836 6699 - distributed by Noonan
    Hurst Ltd.
EMJOC Press, Garden House, Welbury, Northallerton, N.Yorks
    DL6 2SE Tel : 060 982 501
EMKA, 9770 Kruiskoutenn, Belgium
EOSYS, Clove House, The Broadway, Farnham Common, Slough
    Berks SL2 3PQ Tel : 02814 5123 Telex : 849826
EP Microform Ltd., Main Street, East Ardsley, Wakefield WF3
    2AT Tel : 0924 825700
EP Publishing Ltd., Bradford Road, East Ardsley, Wakefield
    W.Yorks WF3 2JN Tel : 0924 823971 Telex : 51458
E.P.O.C. - see Equal Pay & Opportunity Campaign
EPRI - see Electric Power Research Institute
ERA Technology Ltd., Cleeve Road, Leatherhead, Surrey KT22
    7SA Tel : 0372 374151 Telex : 264045
E.R.D.Publ.Ltd., 10 Sarlsdown Road, Exmouth, Devon EX8 1AN
    Tel : 039 52 72769
ERIS Publications, Braeside, Clarach Road, Borth, Aberystwyth
    Dyfed Tel : 097 081 267
E.S.Publications, 46-50 Coombe Road, New Malden, Surrey KT3
    4QH Tel : 01.949 5621
ESA Creative Learning Ltd., PO Box 22, Pinnacles, Harlow,
    Essex CM19 5AY Tel : 0279 21131 Telex : 82189
ESAB, PO Box 8850, Gothenberg 8, Sweden
ESC Publ.Ltd., 25 Beaumont Street, Oxford OX1 2NP
    Tel : 0865 512281 Telex : 83147
ESL (Publ.)Ltd., 14 Suffolk House, 265 Banbury Road, Oxford
ESOMAR, European Society for Opinion & Marketing Research,
    Raadhuisstraat 15, Amsterdam, The Netherlands
EAGLE Publ.Co., 63b Lansdowne Place, Hove, E.Sussex BN3
    1FL Tel : 0273 773174 Telex : 87323
EAGLEMOSS Publ. - now Managing Your Own Business Ltd.
EALING Publ.Ltd., 73a High Street, Maidenhead, Berks SL6
    1JX
EARLS Court Publ.Ltd., 129-130 Shepherds Bush Centre,
    London W12 Tel : 01.749 3097
EARTH Resources Research, 27 Clerkenwell Close, London
    EC1R 0AT Tel : 01.251 4976
EASON & Son Ltd., 80 Middle Abbey Street, PO Box 810,
    Dublin1 Tel : 0001 733811 Telex : 24286 -
    distributed by Colin Smythe Ltd.
EAST African Literature Bureau, c/o Text Book Centre, PO
    Box 47540, Nairobi
EAST & West Library - distributed by B.Horwitz Publ.Co.
EAST Anglian Magazine Ltd., 6 Great Colman Street, Ipswich
    IP4 2AE Tel : 0473 56291/2
EAST Asian Executive Reports, 1115 Mass Avenue NW No.16,
    Washington DC 20005, USA Tel : 202 289 3900
    Telex : 440462
EAST Malling Research Station, East Malling, Maidstone, Kent
    ME19 6BJ Tel : 0732 843833
EAST Midlands Regional Management Centre, c/o Trent
    Polytechnic, Burton Street, Nottingham NG1 4BU

EAST of Scotland College of Agriculture, The Edinburgh School of Agriculture, West Mains Road, Edinburgh EH9 3JG Tel : 031.667 1041
EAST Sussex County Council, County Library, 44 St.Anne's Crescent, Lewes, E.Sussex BN7 1SQ Tel : 07916 5400 Telex : 877515
EAST-WEST Publ.(U.K.)Ltd., Gloucester Mansions, Cambridge Circus, London WC2H 8HD Tel : 01.240 1152
EAST Yorks Local History Society, Beverley Library, Champney Road, Beverley, N.Humberside HU17 9BQ Tel : 0482 867108
EASTERN Counties Newspapers Ltd., Prospect House, Raven Road, Norwich NR1 1RE Tel : 0603 28311
EBURY Press, 44 Bedford Square, London WC1B 3DU Tel : 01.323 3200 Telex : 21322
ECCENTRIC Music, 139a Sloane Street, London SW1 Tel : 01.730 9958
ECLIPSE Publ.Ltd., 286 Kilburn High Road, London NW6 Tel : 01.328 6633
ECONOMIC Forecasters Publ.Ltd., c/o Palantype Organisation Ltd., 4 North News, London WC1 Tel : 01.242 3460
ECONOMIC Forecasting Unit, London Business School, Sussex Place, London NW1 Tel : 01.262 5050 - distributed by Gower Publ.Co.Ltd.
ECONOMIC Information Systems Inc., 310 Madison Avenue, New York 10017, USA
ECONOMIC Research Consultants Inc., 1429 Murray Bay, Houston, Texas 77080, USA Tel : 713 464 4859 Teles : 8813715
ECONOMIC Research Institute, Stockholm School of Economics, Seavägen 65, Box 6501, 11383 Stockholm, Sweden Tel : 08 736 01 20
The ECONOMICS Association, Temple Lodge, South Street, Ditchling, Sussex BN6 8UQ Tel : 079 18 5911
ECONOMIST Intelligence Unit Ltd., Spencer House, 27 St.James's Place, London SW1A 1NT Tel : 01.493 6711
ECONOMIST Newspaper Ltd., 25 St.James's Street, London SW1A 1HG Tel : 01.839 7000 Telex : 24344
ECONOMSKA Politika, Borba NPDE, 11000 Besgrad, TRG Marksa Engelsa, Jugoslavia
ECONTEL Ltd. - now World Economics Ltd.
ECON-Verlag, PO Box 9229, D-4000 Dusseldorf, Germany
EDACS Data Ltd., Beacon House, 15a Christchurch Road, Bournemouth, Dorset BH1 3LJ
EDDISON Press Ltd., 58 North Hill, Colchester, Essex CO1 1PX Tel : 0206 44526 - distributed by Melrose Press Ltd.
EDDISON Sadd & Partners Ltd., 2 Julian Court, Julian Hill, Harrow-on-the-Hill, Middx.HA1 3NF Tel : 01.422 7087
EDIAFRIE la Documentation Africaine, 57 Ave.d'Lena, 75783 Paris Cedex 16, France Tel : 553 14 47
EDINBURGH University Press, 22 George Square, Edinburgh EH8 9LF Tel : 031.667 1011 Telex : 727442 / 17a West Cross Causeway, Edinburgh
EDINBURGH University Student Publications Board, 1 Buccleuch Place, Edinburgh EH8 9AL Tel : 031.667 5718/9278
EDIRES France S.A., 15 Avenue Victor Hugo, 75116 Paris France Tel : 525 70 42
EDISON Technical Services, 5324 Wakfield Road, Bethesda, MD 20016, USA Tel : 301 654 1515 Telex : 898408
EDITIO Cantor, Postfach 1310, 7960 Aulendorf, W.Germany
EDITIONS Atelier 74 UK, 109-110 Bolsover Street, London W1P 7HF Tel : 01.636 5265
EDITIONS Berlitz - distributed by Johnston Bacon Publ.
Les EDITIONS de Physique, Zone Industrielle de Courtaboeuf, B.P.112, 91944 Les Ulis Cedex, France Tel : 907 36 88
EDITIONS Delta - distributed by Bowker
Les EDITIONS d'Organisation, 5 Rue Rousselet, 75007 Paris France Tel : 567 18 40
EDITIONS Jacques Lafitte, 12 Rue de l'Arcade, 75008 Paris France Tel : 265 98 82
EDITIONS Technic, 27 Rue Ginoux, 75737 Paris, Cedex 15, France
EDITORIAL Escudo de Oro, Ala Palaudaries 26, Barcelona 4, Spain
EDITORIAL Service Company - c/o TABS
EDITRICE Bibliografica - distributed by Bowker
EDIZIONI Caldeerini, 40139 Boldgna, Via Emilia Levante 31, Casella Postale 2202, Italy
B.EDSALL & Co.Ltd., 124 Belgrave Road, London SW1V 2BL Tel : 01.834 0717
EDUCATION & Technical Publ., 140 Sylvan Avenue, Englewood Cliff, New Jersey 07832, USA
EDUCATIONAL & Business Services(Sheffield)Ltd., 32 Stradbroke Road, Sheffield S13 8LS Tel : 0742 390841
EDUCATIONAL Company of Ireland Ltd., PO Box 43a, Ballymount Road, Walkinstown, Dublin 12, Rep.of Ireland Tel : 0001 500611 Telex : 5864
EDUCATIONAL Explorers Ltd., 40 Silver Street, Reading, Berks RG1 2SU Tel : 0734 83101/4
EDUCATIONAL Foundation for Visual Aids, National Audio-Visual Aids Centre, Paxton Place, Gipsy Road, London SE27 9SR
EDUCATIONAL Supply Association Ltd. - now ESA Creative Learning Ltd.
EDUCATIONAL Systems Ltd., Waverley Road, Yate, Bristol BS17 5RB Tel : 0434 316774
EEL Pie Publishing, The Boathouse, Ranelagh Drive, Twickenham, Middx.TW1 1QZ - distribution : 43/47 Broadwick Street, London W1 Tel : 01.434 1011
EGGERT Economic Enterprises Inc., PO Box 1569, Sedona Arizona 86336, USA Tel : 602 282 4882
EGGS Authority, Union House, Eridge Road, Tunbridge Wells Kent TN4 8HF Tel : 0892 33987
EGMONT-Methuen, 11 New Fetter Lane, London EC4P 4EE Tel : 01.583 9855 - distributed by ABP Ltd.
EGON Publ.Ltd., Meeting House Lane, Church Street, Baldock Herts.SG7 5BP Tel : 0462 894498
EGON Ronay Organisation Ltd. - see Ronay(Egon) Org.Ltd.
EGYPT Exploration Society, 3 Doughty Mews, London WC1N 2PG Tel : 01.242 1880 - Pharaonic titles distributed by Aris & Phillips Ltd.
ELECTORAL Reform Society, 6 Chancel Street, Blackfriars, London SE1 0UX Tel : 01.928 9407/8 Telex:8812703
ELECTRIC Power Research Institute, 3412 Hillview Avenue, PO Box 10412, Palo Alto, CA94303, USA Tel : 415 855 2411
ELECTRIC Railway Society, 17 Catherine Drive, Sutton Coldfield, W.Midlands B73 6AX Tel : 021.354 8332
ELECTRICAL Contractors' Association, ESCA House, 34 Palace Court, London W2 4HY Tel : 01.229 1266
ELECTRICAL Contractors' Association of Scotland, 23 Heriot Row, Edinburgh EH3 6EW Tel : 031.225 7221/3
ELECTRICAL Engineering, Massons Institute of Technology, Cambridge, MA02142, USA
ELECTRICAL Quality Assurance Directorate, Aquila, Golf Road, Bromley, Kent BR1 2JB Tel : 01.467 2600
ELECTRICAL Research Association Ltd. - now ERA Technology Ltd.
ELECTRICITY Consumers Council, Brook House, 2-16 Torrington Place, London WC1E 7LL Tel : 01.636 5703
ELECTRICITY Council, 30 Millbank, London SW1P 4RD Tel : 01.834 2333 X380
ELECTROCHEMICAL Publ.Ltd., 29 Barns Street, Ayr, Scotland KA7 1XB Tel : 0292 263281
ELECTROCHEMICAL Society Inc., PO Box 2071, Princeton, NJ08540, USA
ELECTRONIC Engineering Publ.Ltd., 106 High Street, Stevenage, Herts Tel : 0438 727371
ELECTRONIC Trends Publ., 10080 N.Wolfe Road, Suite 372 Cupertino, CA95014, USA Tel : 408 996 7401
ELECTRO Optical Research Co., 2029 Century Park East, Suite 422, Los Angeles, CA90067, USA Tel : 213 277 7422
Paul ELEK Ltd. - see Granada Publ.Ltd.
ELEKTOR Publ.Ltd., Elektor House, 10 Longport Street, Canterbury CT1 1PE Tel : 0227 54430/54439 Telex : 965504
ELEMENT Books Ltd., The Old Brewery, Tisbury, Salisbury Wilts. SP3 6NH Tel : 0747 870747
William ELKIN Music Services, Station Road Industrial Estate, Salhouse, Norwich, Norfolk NR13 6NY
ELLIOT Right Way Books, Brighton Road, Lower Kingswood Tadworth, Surrey KT20 6TD Tel : 0737 2202
ELLIOTT Publ., Merchants House, Barley Market Street, Tavistock, Devon
Aidan ELLIS Publ.Ltd., Cobb House, Nuffield, Henley-on-Thames, Oxon.RG9 5RU Tel : 0491 641496 - distributed by J.M.Dent & Sons Ltd.
ELM Publications, Seaton House, Kings Ripton, Cambs.PE17 2NJ Tel : 04873 238
ELM Tree Books, 57-59 Long Acre, London WC2E 9JZ Tel : 01.836 7733 Telex : 298265
ELMDON Publ., Elmdon, Saffron Walden, Essex CB11 4NH Tel : 076 383 359
ELMFIELD Press - distributed by Severn House Publ.Ltd.
ELRON Press Ltd., 20 Garrick Street, London WC2E 8BS Tel : 01.836 0670/0771
ELSEVIER Biomedical Press, 66 Hills Road, Cambridge Tel : 0223 315961

ELSEVIER International Bulletins, Mayfield House, 256 Banbury Road, Oxford OX2 7DH   Tel : 0865 512242
ELSEVIER-Phaidon, Littlegate House, St.Ebbe's Street, Oxford OX1 1SQ   Tel : 0865 46681   Telex : 83308
ELSEVIER Scientific Publ.Co., PO Box 211, 1000 AE Amsterdam, The Netherlands   Tel : (0) 20 5803 911   Telex : 18582
ELVENDON Press, 33 Elvendon Road, Goring-on-Thames, Reading, Berks RG8 0DP   Tel : 0491 873227
ELVITICA Edizioni S.A., PO Box 694, CH-6830 Chiasso, Switzerland   Tel : 091 435056   Telex : 842116
EMBANKMENT Press Ltd., Crown House, 60 North Circular Road, London NW10 0QS   Tel : 01.965 1667   Telex : 8956552
EMERALD Valley Publ.Co., 2715 Terrace View Drive, Eugene, Oregon 97405, USA
EMERSON Rowat Information Services, Braeside, Clarach Road, Borth, Dyfed   Tel : 09708 267
EMMA (Printers & Publishers), Arden House, Sunny Point, Walton-on-Naze, Essex CO14 8LD   Tel : 025 56 4748
EMMASGLEN Ltd., Enholmes Hall, Patrington, Hull HU12 0PR   Tel : 0964 30033
EMPLOYEE Attitude Surveys, Granville Chambers, 2 Radford Street, Stone, Staffs.ST15 8DA   Tel : 078583 242617
EMPLOYEE Benefits in Europe, 15-17 King Street, St.James's, London SW1Y 8QU   Tel : 01.839 3316/7
EMPLOYMENT Relations Ltd., 62 Hills Road, Cambridge   Tel : 0223 315944   (formerly Industrial Relations Training Resource Centre)
ENCYCLOPAEDIA Britannica Intl.Ltd., Mappin House, 156-162 Oxford Street, London W1N 0HJ   Tel : 01.637 3371   Telex : 23866
ENCYCLOPAEDIA of Japan - distributed by IBD
ENCYCLOPAEDIC Press Ltd., 115 Salisbury Road, London NW6 6RJ   Tel : 01.624 5008
ENERGY Consultancy, 24 Elm Close, Bedford MK41 8BZ   Tel : 0234 62677
ENERGY Economics Research Ltd., 7-9 Queen Victoria Street, Reading, Berks RG1 1SY   Tel : 0734 587689   Telex : 849021
ENERGY in Buildings, 20 Gloucester Place, Cheltenham, Glos.   Tel : 0242 42752
ENERGY Mines & Resources, 580 Booin Street, Ottawa, Ontario K1A 0E4, Canada
ENERGY Publications(Cambridge), PO Box 147, Cambridge CB1 1NY   Tel : 0763 83615/6 - distributed by Bowker
ENERGY Reports Ltd., 1 Founders Court, Lothbury, London EC2R 7DB
ENERGY Systems Laboratory, The Royal Institute of Technology S-10044 Stockholm 70, Sweden   Tel : 08 787 7000
ENGINEERING & Mining Journal - see Mc-Graw Hill Publ.Co.(USA)
ENGINEERING Employers' Federation, Broadway House, Tothill Street, London SW1H 9NQ
ENGINEERING Equipment Users Association, 14 Belgrave Square, London SW1X 5PB   Tel : 01.235 5316/7
ENGINEERING Index Inc. - distributed by Henry Thompson Ltd.
ENGINEERING Industry Training Board, PO Box 176, 54 Clarendon Road, Watford WD1 1LB   Tel : 0923 38441
ENGINEERING Press, PO Box 1142, San Jose, CA 95108, USA
ENGINEERING Societies Library, 345 East 47th Street, New York 10017, USA
ENGINEERS Joint Council, 345 East 47th Street, New York 10017, USA
ENGLISH Bowling Association, 2a Iddesleigh Road, Bournemouth BH3 7JR   Tel : 0202 22233
ENGLISH Electric Company - see G.E.C.
ENGLISH Folk Dance & Song Society, Cecil Sharp House, 2 Regent's Park Road, London NW1 7AY   Tel : 01.485 2206
ENGLISH Golf Union, 12a Denmark Street, Wokingham, Berks RG11 2BE   Tel : 0734 781952
ENGLISH Language Teaching Development Unit Ltd., 23 Market Square, Bicester, Oxon.OX6 7BR   Tel : 08692 45255
ENGLISH Life Publ.Ltd., Lodge Lane, Derby DE1 3HE   Tel : 0332 47087
ENGLISH Table Tennis Association, 21 Claremount, Hastings, E.Sussex TN34 1HA   Tel : 0424 433121
ENGLISH Tourist Board, 4 Grosvenor Gardens, London SW1W 0DU   Tel : 01.730 3400
ENGLISH Universities Press Ltd. - now Hodder & Stoughton Ltd.
ENIGMA Books - see Severn House
ENITHARMON Press, 22 Huntingdon Road, London N2 9DU   Tel : 01.883 8764
ENTERPRISE Books, 8 Westholme Road, Didsbury, Manchester M20 9QY   Tel : 061.445 0358
Dept.of the ENVIRONMENT, 2 Marsham Street, London SW1F 3EB
ENVIRONMENTAL Control Consultancy Services Ltd., 32 Bell Street, Romsey, Hants. SO5 8GW   Tel : 0794 516556   Telex : 477719

ENVIRONMENTAL Data Services Ltd., Orchard House, 14 Great Smith Street, London SW1P 3BU   Tel 01.222 3684
ENVIRONMENTAL Health Officers Association, 19 Grosvenor Place, London SW1X 7HU   Tel : 01.235 5158/9
ENVO Publ.Co.Inc., PO Box 2326, Lehigh Valley, PA18001 USA
EPWORTH Press - see Methodist Publishing House
EQUAL Opportunities Commission, Overseas House, Quay Street Manchester M3 3HN   Tel : 061.833 9244
EQUAL Pay & Opportunity Campaign, 59 Canonbury Park North, London N1
EQUESTRIAN Management Consultants, Wothersome Grange, Bramham, Wetherby, Yorks.LS23 6LY   Tel : 0532 892267
EQUINOX(Oxford)Ltd., Mayfield House, 256 Banbury Road Oxford OX2 7DH   Tel : 0865 511151   Telex : 837484
EQUIPMENT for the Disabled, 2 Foredown Drive, Portslade, Sussex BN4 2BB
ERIC Reproduct Services, PO Box 190, Arlington, Virginia 22210, USA
Lawrence ERLBAUM - distributed by IBD
Wilhelm ERNST & Sohn, Hohenzollerndamm 170, 1000 Berlin 31 Germany
ESSENTIAL Oil Association of USA Inc., 60 East 42nd Street, New York 10017, USA
ESSETTE Fürlag Distributors A.B., Fack 175, 02 Järfäua Sweden
ESSEX Electronics Centre, University of Essex, Colchester Essex CO4 3SQ   Tel : 0206 44144 X2267
C.ESSEX Music Co.Ltd., 78 Newman Street, London W1P 3LA   Tel : 01.636 9033   Telex : 21892 - distributed by Music Sales Ltd.
ESSEX Sociology of Literature Publ.Co., 27 Clerkenwell Close London EC1R 0AT   Tel : 01.251 4976
ESSEX Telegraph Press, Chidwell Works, Magdalen Street, Colchester, Essex CO1 2JZ
ESSO Petroleum Co.Ltd., Victoria Street, London SW1 - distributed by Hobsons Press Ltd.
ESTATE Publications, 22a High Street, Tenterden, Kent TN30 6AP   Tel : 05806 4225
ESTATES Gazette Ltd., 151 Wardour Street, London W1V 4BN   Tel : 01.437 0141
ETHROGRAPHICA Ltd., 19 Westbourne Road, London N7 8AN   Tel : 01.607 4074
EURASIA Distributors, 114 Chertsey Road, Twickenham, Middx.   Tel : 01.948 0114
EUREDITIONS, Circle House South, 65-67 Wembley Hill Road Wembley, Middx.HA9 8DP   Tel : 01.903 6455   Telex : 923421
EUROBOOK Ltd., 49 Uxbridge Road, London W5 5SA   Tel : 01.840 4411   Telex : 934610
EURODATA Foundation, Broad Street House, 55 Old Broad Street, London EC2M 1RX   Tel : 01.638 3021
EUROFI Ltd., The Old Rectory, Northill, Nr.Biggleswade, Beds.SG18 9AH   Tel : 0767 27680
EUROFINANCE, 9 Avenue Hoche, 75008 Paris, France   Tel : 766 0400
EUROFOOD, 60 Kingley Street, London W1R 5LH   Tel : 01.734 8373
EUROLEC - see David Rayner Publisher
EUROMONEY Publ.Ltd., Nestor House, Playhouse Yard, London EC4V 5EX   Tel : 01.236 3288
EUROMONITOR Publ.Ltd., PO Box 26, 18 Doughty Street, London WC1N 2PN   Tel : 01.242 0042   Telex : 21120
EUROPA Publ.Ltd., 18 Bedford Square, London WC1B 3JN   Tel : 01.580 8236/8
EUROPANEL, 22 Rue de l'Athénée, Casa Postale 280, 1211 Genève 12, Switzerland   Tel : 022 47 8687   Telex : 289530
EUROPE Export Edition GmbH, Postfach 4034, Berliner Allee 8, D6100 Darmstadt, W.Germany   Tel : 06151 33411 13   Telex : 419257
EUROPEAN Association of Exploration, 30 Carel Van Bylandtlaan The Hague, The Netherlands
EUROPEAN Association of Teachers, 20 Brookfield, Highgate West Hill, London N6 6AS   Tel : 01.340 9136
EUROPEAN Book Service, Flevolaan 36-38, PO Box 124, 1380 AC Weesp, The Netherlands   Tel : 02940 14459   Telex : 17025
EUROPEAN Business Publications, 34 Middleton Road, London E8 4BS   Tel : 01.254 7187
EUROPEAN Centre for Study & Information on Multinational Corporations, Belgium - replaced by European Institute for Research & Information on Multinationals (IRM), 29 Boulevard Bourdon, F75004 Paris, France

EUROPEAN Centre of Public Enterprises, Rivermill House, 152 Grosvenor Road, London SW1V 3JL Tel : 01.821 1444
EUROPEAN Chemical Market Research Association - distributed by B.P.Chemicals(U.K.)Ltd.
EUROPEAN Communications Consultants, 30-31 Islington Green, London N1 8BJ
EUROPEAN Communities, Commission of, Press & Information Office, 20 Kensington Palace Gardens, London W8 4QQ Tel : 01.727 8090 - distributed by HMSO
EUROPEAN Council of International Schools, 18 Lavant Street, Petersfield, Hants. GU32 3EW
EUROPEAN Data & Research Ltd., Outer Temple, 222 The Strand London WC2 1BA Tel : 01.353 4513
EUROPEAN Democratic Group, 2 Queen Anne's Gate, London SW1
EUROPEAN Directories, 23 City Road, London EC1Y 1AA Tel : 01.588 2698
EUROPEAN Engineering Services, Rotunda Buildings, Montpelier Exchange, Cheltenham, Glos. Tel : 0242 28045
EUROPEAN Federation of Chemical Engineering, Tsladari St.34 Amoroussion, Greece
EUROPEAN Illustration, 12 Carlton House Terrace, London SW1Y 5AH Tel : 01.839 2464
EUROPEAN Industrial Forecasting Ltd., 18 Doughty Street, London WC1N 2LJ Tel : 01.242 1982
EUROPEAN Industrial Relations Review, Eclipse Publ.Ltd., 170 Finchley Road, London NW3 Tel : 01.794 455418
EUROPEAN Institute for Advanced Studies in Management, Place Stephanie 20, B-1050 Brussels, Belgium Tel : 511 91 16
EUROPEAN Institute for Research & Information on Multinationals, 29 Boulevard Bourdon, F75004 Paris, France Tel : 244 2510
EUROPEAN Law Centre Ltd., 4 Bloomsbury Square, London WC1A 2RL Tel : 01.404 4300
EUROPEAN Marketing Association, EMA Membership Secretariat 9 Aston Road, Nuneaton, Warwicks.
EUROPEAN Nuclear Society, Bärenplatz 2, PO Box 2613, CH-3001 Berne, Switzerland Tel : 031 22 03 82 Telex : 33528
EUROPEAN Parliament, 2 Queen Anne's Gate, London SW1
EUROPEAN Research Associates(Economic Consultancy), Bd.Clovis 39, 1040 Brussels, Belgium
EUROPEAN Research Consultants Ltd., PO Box 115, 41 Russell Square, London WC1B 5DL Tel : 01.637 8316 Telex : 24224
EUROPEAN School Books Ltd., 122 Bath Road, Cheltenham, Glos. GL53 7LW Tel : 0242 45252 Telex : 43658
EUROPEAN Society for Opinion & Marketing Research, Raadhuisstraat 15, Amsterdam, The Netherlands
EUROPEAN Study Conference Ltd., Kirby House, 31 High Street Uppingham, Rutland LE15 9PY Tel : 057282 2711
EUROPEAN Teratology Society, Hudsons Hill, Wethersfield, Essex
EUROPLATE, 18 Tudor Road, Crosby, Liverpool 23
EUROPOTENTIALS Press, 12 Lambs Conduit Passage, Red Lion Square, London WC1R 4HR Tel : 01.493 8319
EUROSKETCH, 1 Commercial Road, Eastbourne, E.Sussex BN21 3XD
EUROSPAN Ltd., 3 Henrietta Street, London WC2E 8LU Tel : 01.240 0856 - distributed by IBD
EUROTRADE Service Centre, 5 Chantry Hurst, Woodcote Estate Epsom, Surrey KT18 7BN Tel ; 03727 23321
EVAN Steadman Services Ltd., 34-36 Higha Street, Saffron Walden, Essex CB10 1EP Tel : 0799 22612
EVANGELICAL Press & Services Ltd., PO Box 5, Welwyn, Herts.AL6 9NU Tel : 043 871 7025 - orders to Blossomgate, Ripon, N.Yorks HG4 2AJ Tel : 0765 2362
EVANS Brothers Ltd., Montague House, Russell Square, London WC1B 5BX Tel : 01.637 1466 Telex : 8811713 - distributed by Distribution & Management Services Ltd.
Hugh EVELYN Ltd., 53 Charlbert Street, London NW8 6JN Tel : 01.586 5108 - distributed by Godfrey Cave Assoc.
EVEREST Books Ltd., 4 Valentine Place, London SE1 8QH Tel : 01.261 1536
EVERGREEN Books - c/o TABS
EVERGREEN Lives Ltd., 5 Conplan House, Nork Way, Banstead SM7 1PB Tel : 07373 54353
EXCERPTA Medica, PO Box 211, 1000 AE Amsterdam, The Netherlands Tel : (0) 20 5803 911 Telex : 18582
EXE Publ.Co., 209 Exeter Road, Exmouth, Devon Tel : 03952 3647
EXECUTIVE Grapevine Publ.Ltd., 79 Manor Way, Blackheath, London SE3 9XG Tel : 01.318 4462/1148
EXHIBITION & Conferences Yearbook - see York Publ.Co.
EXLEY Publ.Ltd., 12 Ye Corner, Chalk Hill, Watford, Herts. WD1 4BS Tel : 0923 50505 Telex : 261234 - distributed by Noonan Hurst Ltd.
EXMOOR Press, Dulverton, Somerset Tel : 064 383 268/423
The EXPATRIATE, 89 Portland Road, London W11 4LN
EXPERIMENTAL Cartography Unit, Holbrook House, Station Road, Swindon, Wilts. SN1 1DE
EXPERIMENTAL Learning Method Inc., 39819 Plymouth Road, Plymouth, Michigan, USA
EXPORT Finance Publ.Ltd., 309 Seddon House, Barbican London EC2Y 8BX
EXPOSITION Press Inc., 325 Rabro Dr., Box 2120, Smithtown New York 11787, USA
EXPRESS Books, 121 Fleet Street, London EC4P 4JT Tel : 01.353 8000
L'EXPRESS Edition International, 78 Rue Olivier de Serres, 75739 Paris, Cedex 15, France
EXPRESS Logic Ltd., Foley Estate, Hereford HR1 2SJ Tel : 0432 4516
EXPRESS Newspapers plc, 121-128 Fleet Street, London EC4P 4JT Tel : 01.353 8000 Telex : 21841
EXTEL Statistical Services Ltd., 37-45 Paul Street, London EC2A 4DB Tel : 01.253 3400 Telex : 262687
EYRE & Spottiswoode(Publ.)Ltd. - see ABP Ltd.
EYROLLES, 61 Boulevard Saint-Germain, 75240 Paris, Cedex 05, France

F

F&S Publications - c/o TABS
F.A.O.(Food & Agriculture Organisation), Via Della Terme Di Caracalla, I-00100 Rome, Italy Tel : Rome 57971 - distributed by HMSO
FID - see International Federation for Documentation
FMB Publications Ltd., PO Box 45, Richmond, Surrey TW10 6UA Tel : 01.948 6187 Telex : 296022
FMT Editions, Spring House, Mill Lane, Broxbourne, Herts. Tel : 0992 465783
F.T.Business Publications, Greystoke Place, Fetter Lane, London EC4A 1ND Tel : 01.405 6969
FABER & Faber Ltd., 3 Queen Square, London WC1N 3AU Tel : 01.278 6881 Telex : 299633 - orders to Burnt Mill, Elizabeth Way, Harlow, Essex CM20 2HX Tel : 0279 21352/3
FABIAN Society, 11 Dartmouth Street, London SW1H 9BN Tel : 01.222 8877
FABRIC Care Research Association, Forest House Laboratories Knaresborough Road, Harrogate, N.Yorks HG2 7LZ Tel : 0423 883201
FACE to Face, 124 Union Street, Aberdeen Tel : 0224 56838
FACHVERLAG Schiele und Schön, Markgrafenstr.11, D-1000 Berlin 61, West Germany Tel : 030 251 6029
FACTEL Ltd., 297-299 High Street, Cheltenham, Glos. Tel : 0242 515004
FACTS on File Inc. - orders to Clio Press Ltd., Woodside House Hinksey Hill, Oxford OX1 5BE Tel : 0865 735001
FACULTY of Environmental Studies, N.E.London Polytechnic, Forest Road, London E17 4JB
FAIRCHILD Publications, 7 East 12th Street, New York 10003 USA Tel : 212 741 4280
FAIRMONT Press Inc. - distributed by Van Nostrand Reinhold
FAIRPLAY Intl.Shipping Weekly, 1 Pudding Lane, London EC3R 8AA Tel : 01.248 8000
FAIRPLAY Publ.Ltd., 52-54 Southwark Street, London SE1 1UJ Tel : 01.403 3164 Telex : 884595
FAITH Press Ltd. - ceased publishing 1979 - some titles distributed by Powage Press, 17 Wing Road, Leighton Buzzard, Beds.LU7 7NQ Tel : 0525 373527
FALCON Audio Visual Aids, Falcon Court, 32 Fleet Street, London EC4Y 1DB
FALLING Wall Press, 79 Richmond Road, Montpelier, Bristol BS6 5EP Tel : 0272 422116
C.J.FALLON Ltd., Lucan Road, Palmerstown, Dublin 20, Rep. of Ireland Tel : 0001 365777
FALMER Press Ltd., 4 John Street, London WC1N 2ET Tel : 01.405 2237/9 Telex : 858540
FALMOUTH Guide Ltd., Information Bureau, The Moor, Falmouth, Cornwall Tel : 0326 318618
FAMEDRAM Publ.Ltd., Gartocharn, Alexandria, Dumbartonshire G83 8RT Tel : 038 983 340
FAMILY Rights Group, 6 Manor Gardens, Holloway Road, London N7 6LA Tel : 01.272 4231
FAMILY Welfare Association, 501-505 Kingsland Road, Dalston London E8 4AU Tel : 01.254 6251
FAR Eastern Economic Review Ltd., 218 Feltham Road, Ashford Middx. Tel : 01.622 0325

FAR Eastern Economic Review Ltd., Circulation Dept., GPO Box 47, Hong Kong
FARM Buildings Information Centre, National Agricultural Centre, Stoneleigh, Kenilworth, Warwicks.CV8 2LG Tel : 0203 22345
FARM Holiday Guides Ltd., 18 High Street, Paisley, Renfrewshire PA1 2BX Tel : 041.887 0428/9
FARM Shop & Pick your Own Association, Hunger Lane, Mugginton, Derby DE6 4PL Tel : 033 528 515
FARMING Press Ltd., Wharfedale Road, Ipswich IP1 4LG Tel : 0473 43011
FARNELL Electronic Components Ltd., Canal Road, Leeds LS12 2TU Tel : 0532 636311
FARNHAM Book Distributors - now Alton Book Distributors
FARNSWORTH Publ.Co.Inc., 78 Randall Avenue, Rickville Centre New York 11570, USA
FARRAR Straus & Giroux, 19 Union Square West, New York 10003, USA Tel : 212 741 6900 Telex : 667428
FARRINGDON Publ.Co.Ltd., Petershill House, Distaff Lane, London EC4V 4BL Tel : 01.248 4962
The FARSET Co-operative Press, 27 Clerkenwell Close, London EC1R 0AT Tel : 01.251 4976
FAWCETT World Library, 67 West 44th Street, New York 10026 USA
FEARON Publ.Inc. - distributed by Book Centre Ltd.
FEDERAL Aviation Administration, Dept.of Transportation, Office of Aviation Policy, Washington DC20591, USA
FEDERAL Energy Administration, National Energy Information Center, Technical Services Division, Washington DC20461, USA
FEDERAL Publ.Pte.Ltd., Times Jurong, 2 Jurong Port Road Singapore 2261 Tel : 2658855
FEDERAL Reserve Bank of New York, Public Information Dept. 23 Liberty Street, New York 10045, USA
FEDERAL Reserve System, Washington DC20551, USA
FEDERAL Trust for Education & Research, 12a Maddox Street, London W1R 9PL Tel : 01.492 0727/9
FEDERATION Nationale des Logis de France, 25 Rue Jean Mermoz 75009 Paris, France
FEDERATION of Alcoholic Rehabilitation Establishments, 3 Grosvenor Crescent, London SW1X 7EE Tel : 01.235 0609/0600
FEDERATION of American Societies for Experimental Biology, 9650 Rockville Pike, Bethesda, MD20014, USA
FEDERATION of Civil Engineering Contractors, 7 South Parade Leeds LS1 5PX Tel : 0532 451294
FEDERATION of Civil Engineering Contractors(Scottish Section), Empire House, 131 West Nile Street, Glasgow G1 2RX
FEDERATION of Family History Societies, 96 Beaumont Street, Milehouse, Plymouth PL2 3AQ Tel : 0752 55149
FEDERATION of Master Builders, 33 John Street, London WC1N 2BB Tel : 01.242 7033
FEDERATION of the U.K.Milk Marketing Board, Thames Ditton Surrey KT7 0EL Tel : 01.398 4101
FEEDBACK Instruments Ltd., Park Road, Crowborough, Sussex TN6 2QR
FEFFER & Simons (Netherlands)B.V., Rijnkade 170, PO Box 112, 1382 GT Weesp, The Netherlands Tel : 02940 10051 Telex : 15141
FEFFER & Simons/TABS Education Division, 8 High Street, Arundel W.Sussex BN18 9AB - distributed by Feffer & Simons (Netherlands)B.V.
FELLOWSHIP of Reconciliation, 9 Coombe Road, New Malden, Surrey KT3 4QA Tel : 01.942 6521/2
FEMINIST Books, 27 Clerkenwell Close, London EC1R 0AT Tel : 01.251 4976
FEMINIST Intl.(Japan), 27 Clerkenwell Close, London EC1R 0AT Tel : 01.251 4976
FERNHILL House Ltd., 303 Park Avenue South, New York 10010, USA
FERNSWAY Publ., 14 Fernsway, Bainbridge Holme Road, Sunderland, Tyne & Wear SR3 1YS
FERRARY Publ.Ltd., The Cedars, Appledore Road, Tentenden, Kent TN30 7DJ Tel : 05806 3949
FERRY Book Co., c/o 19 King Street, Richmond, Surrey Tel : 01.940 4916/01.948 4922
FERTILIZER Economic Studies Ltd., 150 Buckingham Palace Road, London SW1W 9TR Tel : 01.730 8817 Telex : 291743
FFYNNON Press, PO Box 13, Crosby, Liverpool L23 6WA
FIELD Enterprises Educational Corporation - now World Book - Childcraft Intl.Inc.
Francis J.FIELD Ltd., Aero Philatelic Publ., Sutton Coldfield W.Midlands B73 6BJ Tel : 021.354 1748

Arthur FIELDHOUSE Ltd., Advertiser Press Ltd., Premier Works, Paddock Head, Huddersfield HD3 4ES Tel : 0484 20444
Allen FIGGIS & Co.Ltd., The Mall, Donnybrook, Dublin 4 Rep.of Ireland Tel : 0001 760471
F.N.FILBY, 15 Cavendish Gardens, Cranbrook, Ilford, Essex IG1 3EA
FINANCIAL Analysis Group Ltd. - now Jordan & Sons Ltd.
FINANCIAL Executives Research Foundation Inc., 10 Madison Avenue, PO Box 1938, Morristown, NJ07960, USA
FINANCIAL Intelligence, 49-51 The Avenue, London W13 8JR Tel : 01.997 8214
FINANCIAL Publ.Co., USA - distributed by Routledge Kegan Paul
FINANCIAL Research & Publ.Ltd., 28-29 Chancery Lane, London WC2 Tel : 01.405 6724/5
FINANCIAL Techniques Ltd. - now called Templegate Press Ltd.
FINANCIAL Times Business Publ.Ltd., Greystoke Place, Fetter Lane, London EC4A 1ND Tel : 01.405 6969 Telex : 883694
FINANCIAL Times Publications, Minster House, Arthur Street London EC4R 9AX Tel : 01.623 1211 Telex: 8814734 - yearbooks now published by Longman Directories Division, Harlow
FINANCIAL Training Publ.Ltd., Avenue House, 131 Holland Park Avenue, London W11 4UT Tel : 01.603 4688
FINAX Publications - now Tax Management International
FIND/SVP, 500 5th Avenue, New York 10110, USA Tel : 212 354 2424
FINDHORN Publications, The Park, Forres, Morayshire IV36 0TZ Tel : 03093 582
FINDLAY Press, Franks Hall, Horton Kirby, Dartford DA4 9LL Tel : 0322 77755
FINE Books Ltd., 115 Bayham Street, London NW1 Tel : 01.267 1331
FINISHING Publ.Ltd., 28 High Street, Teddington, Middx. TW11 8EW Tel : 01.943 2610
FIRE Horse Associates, 14 Barn Street, Haverfordwest, Dyfed SA61 1TG Tel : 0437 66219
FIRE Protection Association, Aldermary House, Queen Street London EC4N 1TJ Tel : 01.248 5222 X255
FIRE Research Station, Melrose Avenue, Boreham Wood, Herts.
FIRECREST Publ.Ltd., 93-100 Locksbrook Road, Bath BA1 3HB Tel : 0225 331945 Telex : 449897
FIRST Ave Publ.Co., 29 Barns Street, Ayr, Scotland KA7 1XB
FIRST Computer Handbook, 10a Chandos Street, London W1M 9DE Tel : 01.223 1976
Robert S.FIRST Inc., 707 Westchester Avenue, White Plains, New York 10604, USA Tel : 914 949 4248 Telex : 131414
FISCAL Publications, 84 Liverpool Road, Cadishead, Manchester Tel : 061.775 0557
Gustav FISCHER Verlag, Postfach 720143, D-7000 Stuttgart 72 W.Germany - orders to IBD, represented by Global Book Resources Ltd.
FISHING News Books Ltd., 1 Long Garden Walk, Farnham, Surrey Tel : 0252 726868
FITYHENNY & Whiteside Ltd., 150 Lesmill Road, Don Mills, Ontario M3B 2T5, Canada
FLAME Books, 9 Kensington Park Gardens, London W11 Tel : 01.727 6941
FLEEMAN Consultants Ltd., 34-36 Streetly Lane, Four Oaks Sutton Coldfield, W.Midlands B74 4TU Tel : 021.308 0800
FLEET Planning Ltd., Church House, Solihull Road, Hampton-in-Arden, Solihull B92 0EX
FLEETBOOKS - c/o TABS
FLEETBOOKS S.A., c/o Rijnkade 170, PO Box 112, 1382 GT Weesp, The Netherlands Tel : 02940 10051 Telex : 15141
FLORAL Press, Sovereign Way, Tonbridge, Kent TN9 1RW Tel : 0732 362468
FLORAPRINT Ltd., Park Road, Calverton, Nottingham NG14 6LL Tel : 0602 652991 Telex : 377233
FLORIS Books, 21 Napier Road, Edinburgh EH10 5AZ Tel : 031.337 2372
FLOUR Milling & Baking Research Association, Chorleywood, Rickmansworth, Herts.WD3 5SH Tel : 092 78 4111
FOCAL Press Books - see Butterworth & Co.Ltd.
FOCUS on Information Ltd., 186 Westcombe Hill, Blackheath London SE3 7DH Tel : 01.852 6098
FOCUS Publications, 9 Priors Road, Windsor, Berks SL4 4PD Tel : 07535 61386
FOCUS Research Systems, 342 N.Main Street, West Hertford CT06117, USA Tel : 203 561 1047

FOILSEACHAIN An Rialtais - see Ireland Stationery Office, Dublin
FOENS Publishers, Airton Road, Tallaght, County Dublin, Rep.
    of Ireland Tel : 0001 515311
FOLIO Press, 202 Great Suffolk Street, London SE1 1PR
    Tel : 01.407 7411
FOLIO Society, 202 Great Suffolk Street, London SE1 1PR
    Tel : 01.407 7411
FOLLETT Intl.Sales Corp., 1000 West Washington Blvd., Chicago
    Ill.60607, USA
FOLLOW-Your-Finger Books, 42 The Ridgeway, Radlett, Herts.
    Tel : 09276 7696
FONTANA Paperbacks, 14 St.James's Place, London SW1A 1PS
    Tel : 01.493 7070
FOOD & Agriculture Organisation(FAO), Via Della Terme di
    Caracalla, I-00100 Rome, Italy Tel : Rome 57971
    - distributed by HMSO
FOOD Manufacturers Federation, 6 Catherine Street, London
    WC2B 5JJ Tel : 01.836 2460
FOOD Marketing Institute, 1750 K.Street NW, Washington
    DC 20006, USA Tel : 202 452 8444
FOOD Trade Press Ltd., 29 High Street, Green Street Green,
    Orpington, Kent BR6 6LS Tel : 0689 53070
FOOTPATH Publications, Adstock Cottage, Adstock, Buckingham
    MK18 2HZ Tel : 029671 2993
FORBES Publ.Ltd., Redan House, Redan Place, London W2 4SB
    Tel : 01.229 9322
FORD Foundation, PO Box 1919, New York 10001, USA
FORD Sidevalve Owners Club, Yvon Precieux, 12 Firs Close
    London SE23 1BB
FORECAST Associates Inc., 52 Sugar Hollow, Danbury, CT06810
    USA Tel : 203 743 0212
FOREIGN Affairs Publ.Co.Ltd., Church House, 139 Petersham
    Road, Richmond, Surrey TW10 7AA Tel : 01.948 4833
FORENSIC Science Society, Clarke House, 18a Mount Parade,
    Harrogate, N.Yorks HG1 1BX Tel : 0423 56068
FOREST Press Inc., USA - distributed by Don Gresswell Ltd.
FOREST Publ.Co., Doverhay Knap, Porlock, Minehead, Somerset
    TA24 8LL Tel : 0643 862432
FORESTRY Commission, 231 Corstorphine Road, Edinburgh EH12
    7AT Tel : 031.334 0363
FORMAT Books, 23 Jeffreys Street, London NW1 Tel : 01.267 8537
FORWARD Publicity Ltd., Falcon House, 20-22 Belmont Road
    Wallington, Surrey SM6 8TA Tel : 01.669 8131/5
FOULAG, Skelbackgade No.4, DK1717, Copenhagen, Denmark
G.T.FOULIS & Co.Ltd., Sparkford, Yeovil, Somerset BA22 7JJ
    Tel : 0963 40635 Telex : 46212
W.FOULSHAM & Co.Ltd., Yeovil Road, Slough, Berks SL1 4JH
    Tel : 0753 26769/38637
FOUNDATION for Alternatives, Rookery North, Adderbury, Oxon.
    Tel : 0295 810706
FOUNDATION for Business Responsibilities, 40 Doughty Street,
    London WC1N 2LF Tel : 01.405 5195
FOUNDATIONAL Book Co.Ltd., 29 Pinfold Road, Streatham,
    London SW16 2SL Tel : 01.584 1053
FOUNTAIN Press, 65 Victoria Street, Windsor, Berks SL4 1EH
    Tel : 07535 56959
FOUR Courts Press Ltd., 3 Serpentine Avenue, Dublin 4
    Tel : 0001 688236
FOUR Seasons Publ., The Stables, Monxton, Nr.Andover, Hants.
    SP11 8AT Tel : 026471 215/6
FOURLANCE Books Ltd., 140 High Street, West Wickham, Kent
    BR4 0LZ Tel : 01.777 5691/3781
F.FOURNIES & Assocs.Ltd., 129 Edgewood Drive, Bridgewater,
    NJ08807, USA Tel : 201 526 2442
L.N.FOWLER & Co.Ltd., 1201-3 High Road, Chadwell Heath,
    Romford, Essex RM6 4DH Tel : 01.597 2491/2
FOWLER-Wright Books Ltd., Leominster, Hereford
    Tel : 0568 4561
FOXBORO Yoxall, Redhill, Surrey RH1 2HL Tel : 0737 65000
FOXWOOD Publ.Ltd., Acorn Typesetting & Litho Ltd., 635 River
    Gardens, North Feltham Trading Estate, Feltham,
    Middx.TW14 0RW Tel : 01.890 2610 Telex : 21451
FOYE Books, 42 Rectory Lane, Bracknell, Berks RG12 4BP
    Tel : 0734 3409
W.&G.FOYLE Ltd., 119-125 Charing Cross Road, London WC2H
    0EB Tel : 01.437 0216 Telex : 261107
FRANCHISE Development Services Ltd., Castle House, Castle
    Meadow, Norwich NR2 1PJ Tel : 0603 20301
    Telex : 97267
FRANCO Angeli, Viale Monzla 106, CP4294, I-20127, Milan, Italy
FRANEY & Co.Ltd., 2-3 Burgon Street, London EC4V 5DP
    Tel : 01.236 0855
FRANKLIN Watts, 1 Vere Street, London W1M 0AD
    Tel : 01.493 8557 - orders to J.M.Dent & Sons Ltd.
Gordon FRASER Books, Eastcotts Road, Bedford MK42 0JX
    Tel : 0234 56531

FREE Enterprise Organisation, 40 Doughty Street, London
    WC1N 2LF Tel : 01.405 5195
FREE Press, USA - c/o Collier Macmillan Publ.Ltd., Stockley
    Close, West Drayton, Middx.UB7 9BE
FREEDOM Press(in Angel Alley), 84B Whitechapel High Street
    London E1 7AX Tel : 01.247 9249
FREELAND Press Ltd., Freeland, Oxford OX7 2AP
    Tel : 0993 881788
H.FREEMAN & Co.(Music Publ.), 138-140 Charing Cross Road
    London WC2H 0LD Tel : 01.836 6699
W.H.FREEMAN & Co.Ltd., 20 Beaumont Street, Oxford OX1 2NQ
    Tel : 0865 726975 Telex : 83677 - distributed by
    Marston Book Services
FREER Gallery - distributed by IBD
FREIGHT Information Service Ltd., adelphi Chambers,
    Houghton Street, Southport, Merseyside PR9 0NZ
    Tel : 0704 38515
FRENCH Books, c/o LN Rex Port, 21 Rue Froideraux, 75014
    Paris, France
Samuel FRENCH Ltd., 26 Southampton Street, Strand, London
    WC2E 7JE Tel : 01.836 7513
FRESHWATER Biological Association, The Ferry House,
    Ambleside, Cumbria LA22 0LP Tel : 09662 2468
L.FREWIN Publ.Ltd. - now Wisphouse Ltd.
J.FRIEDMANN Publ.Ltd., 4 Perrins Lane, Hampstead, London
    NW3 1QY Tel : 01.379 3248 - distributed by Kogan
    Page Ltd.
FRIENDLY Publ.Intl.Inc., 2 St.John's Lane, London EC1
    Tel : 01.253 0230
FRIENDS of the Earth, 9 Poland Street, London W1V 3DG
    Tel : 01.434 1684
FRIENDS Home Service Committee - now Quaker Home Service
    Friends House, Euston Road, London NW1 2BJ
    Tel : 01.387 3601
FRIENDS Press, 27 Clerkenwell Close, London EC1R 0AT
    Tel : 01.251 4976
FROEBEL Educational Institute, Templeton, 118 Priory Lane
    London SW15 5JW
FROMMERS Guides - orders to Roger Lascelles, 3 Holland Park
    Mansions, London W14 8DY Tel : 01.603 8489
FROST & Sullivan Ltd., 104-112 Marylebone Lane, London
    W1M 5FU Tel : 01.486 8377
FUDGE & Co.Ltd., 115 Old Street, London EC1V 9JR
FUEL & Metallurgical Journals Ltd., 2 Queensway, Redhill,
    Surrey RH1 1QS Tel : 0737 68611
FULL Moon Press, Westhope, Herts. Tel : 043271 465
FULLER D'Arch Smith Ltd., 30 Baker Street, London W1
    Tel : 01.722 0063
FULMER Research Institute Ltd., Stoke Poges, Slough, Berks
    SL2 4QD Tel : 02816 2181
FUNDEX Ltd., Greystoke Place, Fetter Lane, London EC4
    Tel : 01.405 6969
FUR & Feather, Idle, Bradford BD10 8NL Tel ; 0274 612111
FURNITURE Industry Research Association, Maxwell Road
    Stevenage, Herts SG1 2EW Tel : 0438 3433
FUTURA Publ.Ltd., 110 Warner Road, Camberwell, London
    SE5 7HQ Tel : 01.737 2431
The FUTURES Group, 76 Eastern Boulevard, Glastonbury
    CT06033, USA Tel : 203 633 3501

G

G.E.C.Measurements, St.Leonards Works, Stafford
G.E.C.Power Engineering Ltd., Estates Division Library,
    Cambridge Road, Whetstone, Leicester LE8 3LH
GIE, 11 Rue Hamelin, 75783 Paris, Cedex 16, France
GIRA Group, 1249 Collex, Geneva, Switzerland
    Tel : 022 74 10 10 Telex : 27556
GIRA(U.K.), Adam & Eve Court, 142 Oxford Street, London
    W1N 9DL Tel : 01.580 7412 Telex : 23449
GIRAL S.A., 7 Place Longemalle, 1204 Geneva, Switzerland
    Tel : 022 28 03 33 Telex : 289870
GKN Contractors, PO Box 19, Redditch, Worcs.
GLC - see Greater London Council
G.M.C.Publ.Ltd., Parklands House, Keymer Road, Burgess
    Hill, Sussex RH15 0BA Tel : 044 46 45267
GML Corporation, 594 Marrett Road, Lexington, Mass.02173
    USA Tel : 617 861 0515
GABERBOCCHUS Press Ltd., c/o De Harmonie, Singel 390
    Amsterdam 1016AJ, The Netherlands
    Tel : 020 245 181
GAGE Publ.Ltd., Information Services, 164 Commander Blvd.
    Agincourt, Ontario M1S 3C7, Canada

GAIRM Publications, 29 Waterloo Street, Glasgow G2 6BZ
   Tel : 041.221 1971
GALAHAD Books - c/o TABS
GALE Research Co., U.S.Book Tower, Detroit, Michigan 48226
   USA
GALILEE Books(Doubleday) - c/o TABS
GALL & Inglis Ltd., 62 Buckstone Terrace, Edinburgh EH10 6RQ
   Tel : 031.445 1466
GALLEON Publ.Ltd., 61 Howell Road, Exeter, Devon
   Tel : 0392 31045
GALLERY Press, Peter Fallon, 19 Oakdown Road, Dublin 14
   Ireland Tel : 0001 985161
GALLERY Press, 75 Kings Road, New Haw, Weybridge, Surrey
   KT15 3HQ
GALLERY Press, Neston, Leemans/Seel House, Leighton Road,
   Neston, South Wirral Tel : 051 336 5281
GALLIARD Ltd. - now Stainer & Bell Ltd.
GALLOWAY & Porter, 30 Sidney Street, Cambridge CB2 3HS
   Tel : 0223 67876
GALLUP Organization, 53 Bank Street, Princeton, NJ08540, USA
   Tel : 609 924 9600
The GALPIN Society, 5 The Avenue, Alderley Edge, Cheshire
   SK9 7NJ
GAMBIT, USA - see Houghton Mifflin
GAME Conservancy, Fordingbridge, Hants.SP6 1EF
   Tel : 0425 52381
GARDENER Press - distributed by IBD
GARDENERS' Sunday Organisation, c/o Mrs K.Collett, White
   Witches, Claygate Road, Dorking, Surrey
   Tel : 0306 884053
GARDNER Press, 319 City Road, London EC1V 1LJ
   Tel : 01.837 3500
GARDNER Publ.Inc., 6600 Clough Pike, Cincinnati, Ohio 45244
   USA Tel : 513 231 8020
GARLAND Publ., 136 Madison Avenue, New York 10016, USA
   - U.K.Office : Mrs H.Hockliffe, Ashburn, The Green
   Horsted Keynes, W.Sussex RH17 7AW
   Tel : 0825 790772
GARLANDFOLD Ltd., 115 Friern Barnet Road, London N11 3EU
   Tel : 01.368 1661 Telex : 8955909
J.GARNET Miller Ltd., 129 St.John's Hill, London SW11
   Tel : 01.228 8091
GARNSTONE Press Ltd., Barlavington Farm House, Nr.Petworth
   W.Sussex Tel : 07987 349 - distributed by George
   Philip & Son Ltd.
GARTHDEE Writers Co-operative, 27 Clerkenwell Close, London
   EC1R 0AT Tel : 01.251 4976
Warren GASH, c/o 247 Molesey Avenue, West Molesey, Surrey
GASTECH Exhibitions Ltd., 2 Station Road, Rickmansworth,Herts
   WD3 1QP Tel : 09237 76363/4
GATEWAY Books, 37 Upper Addison Gardens, London W14 8AJ
   Tel : 01.603 6619
GAVIN Press, 36 Fore Street, Evershot, Dorchester, Dorset
   DT2 0JW
GAY Men's Press, PO Box 247, London N15 6RW Tel : 01.800 5861
GEE & Co., Alhambra House, 27-33 Charing Cross Road, London
   WC2H 0AU Tel : 01.930 3951
GEMEINSCHAFTSVERLAG GmbH, Spreestrasse 9, POB 110509,
   6100 Darmstadt 11, Germany Tel : 06151 334 26/27
GEMINI Book Distribution Ltd., Vale Road, Tonbridge, Kent
   TN9 1TB Tel : 0732 359387
GEMINI Publ.Ltd., Fairfax House, Causton Road, Colchester,
   Essex Tel : 0206 40003
GENERAL Council of British Shipping, 30-32 St.Mary Axe
   London EC3A 8ET Tel : 01.283 2922/01.626 8131
GENERAL Dental Council, 37 Wimpole Street, London W1M 8DQ
   Tel : 01.486 2171
GENERAL Electric Co., 120 Erie Boulevard, Room 800,
   Schenectady, NY 12305, USA
GENERAL Gramophone Publ.Ltd., 177-179 Kenton Road, Harrow
   Middx.HA3 0HA Tel : 01.907 4476 Telex : 298721
GENERAL Learning Corp., 250 James Street, Morristown, NJ
   07960, USA - distributed by IBD
GENERAL Medical Council, 44 Hallam Street, London W1N 6AE
   Tel : 01.580 7642
GENERAL Optical Council, 41 Harley Street, London W1N 2DJ
   Tel : 01.580 3898
GENESIS Publ.Ltd., 45 Stoke Road, Guildford, Surrey GU1 4HT
   Tel : 0483 37431
GENTRY Books Ltd., 15 Pont Street, London SW1X 9EH
   Tel : 01.235 3851
GEO Abstracts Ltd., University of East Anglia, Norwich, Norfolk
   NR4 7TJ Tel : 0603 26327
GEO Books, Regency House, 34 Duke Street, Norwich NR3 3AP
   Tel : 0603 26327

GEOGRAPHERS A-Z Map Co.Ltd., Vestry Road, Sevenoaks,
   Kent TN14 5EP Tel : 0732 51152/55383 / 28 Gray's
   Inn Road, London WC1X 8HX Tel : 01.242 9246/
   01.405 7322
GEOGRAPHIA Ltd., 17-21 Conway Street, London W1P 5HL
   Tel : 01.387 2811 - Tiptree Book Services Ltd.
The GEOGRAPHICAL Association, 343 Fulwood Road, Sheffield
   S10 3BP Tel : 0742 661666
GEOGRAPHICAL Field Group, c/o Dept.of Geography, Univ.
   of Nottingham, University Park, Nottingham NG7
   2RD Tel : 0602 56101
GEOGRAPHICAL Publ.Ltd., The Keep, Berkhamsted, Herts
   HP4 1HQ Tel : 04427 2981
GEOLOGICAL Society, Burlington House, Piccadilly, London
   W1V 0JU
GEOLOGICAL Survey of India, 29 Jawaharlal Nehru Road,
   Calcutta 700 016, India
GEOMETRICA Press Ltd., 21 Nassington Road, London NW3
   2TX
GEOPHYSICAL Directory Co.Ltd., 2200 Welch Avenue,
   Houston, Texas 77019, USA
GEORGESON & Co., Wall Street Plaza, New York 10005, USA
GEORGIA State University, 33 Gilmer Street SE, Atlanta
   GA 30303, USA Tel : 404 658 2622
GEOSYSTEMS, PO Box 1024, Westminster, London SW1P 2JL
   Tel : 01.222 7305 Telex : 915771
GEOTHERMAL World Corporation, 5762 Firebird Court,
   Mission Oaks, Camarillo, CA93010, USA
GERMAN Chamber of Industry & Commerce, 12-13 Suffolk Street
   St.James's, London SW1Y 4HG Tel : 01.930 7251
   Telex : 919442
GERMAN Hydrographic Institute, Bernhard-Nochtstr.78,
   2000 Hamburg-4, W.Germany
Francis GERRARD (Publ.), Bloomsbury House, 89 Stockport
   Road, Hyde, Cheshire SK14 5QU
   Tel : 061.368 2000/4469
GERRARD Publications - now taken over by Frederick Warne
   (Publ.)Ltd.
GEWIPLAN GmbH, Frederick-Ebert-Anlage 38, D-6000 Frankfurt
   am Main 1, W.Germany Tel : 0611 740471
   Telex : 412998
GEYER-McAllister Intl.Inc., 27-28 George Street, Richmond
   on Thames, Surrey TW9 1HY Tel : 01.940 73668
Stanley GIBBONS(Publ.)Ltd., 391 Strand, London WC2R 0LX
   Tel : 01.836 8444 Telex : 28883 / Stangib House,
   Sarehole Road, Birmingham B28 8EE
   Tel : 021.777 7255
Robert GIBSON & Sons, Glasgow, Ltd., 16-17 Fitzroy Place
   Glasgow G3 7SF Tel : 041.248 5674
E.A.GIBSON Shipbrokers Ltd., PO Box 278, Remington House
   61-65 Holborn Viaduct, London EC1P 1HP
   Tel : 01.236 4222
John GIFFORD Ltd., 119-125 Charing Cross Road, London
   WC2H 0EB Tel : 01.437 0216
GILBERTSON & Page Ltd., Corry's, Roestock Lane, Colney
   Heath, St.Albans, Herts.AL4 0QW
   Tel : 0727 22614
GILL & Macmillan Ltd., Goldenbridge Industrial Estate,
   Inchicore, Dublin 8, Ireland Tel : 0001 783 288/
   0001 715 182
George GILL & Sons Ltd., 59-61 Norman Road, St.Leonards
   on Sea, E.Sussex Tel : 0424 428561
GINN & Co.Ltd., Prebendal House, Parson's Fee, Aylesbury
   Bucks. HP20 2QZ Tel : 0296 88411
GIRL Guides Association, Trading Service, Atlantic Street,
   Broadheath, Altrincham, Cheshire WA14 5EQ
   Tel : 061.941 2237
Mary GLASGOW Publ.Ltd., 140 Kensington Church Street,
   London W8 4BN Tel : 01.229 9531 / Brookhampton
   Lane, Kineton, Warwick CV35 0JB
   Tel : 0926 640606
GLASGOW Post Office Directory Association - gone away 1980
GLASS & Glazing Federation, 6 Mount Row, London W1Y 6DY
   Tel : 01.409 0545
GLASS Manufacturers Federation, 19 Portland Place, London
   W1N 4BH Tel : 01.580 6952
Christopher J.GLAZEBROOK, 294 Birchfield Road East,
   Northampton NN3 2SY Tel : 0604 47750
GLEN Rossal House, Westthorpe Lane, Byfield, Daventry,
   Northants.NN11 6XB Tel : 0327 60598
GLENCOE Press, USA - distributed by Collier Macmillan Ltd.
GLENGARRY Publ.Ltd., Burnside, Invergarry, Inverness-
   shire PH35 4HR Tel : 080 92 216
GLENIFFER Press, 11 Low Road, Castlehead, Paisley PA2
   6AQ Tel : 041.889 9579

GLOBAL Book Resources Ltd., 109 Great Russell Street, London
  WC1B 3NA Tel : 01.580 2633 - distributed by IBD
GLOBAL Engineering, 3301 W.McArthur Boulevard, Santa Ana,
  CA 92704, USA
GLOBE Book Services Ltd., Brunel Road, Houndmills,
  Basingstoke, Hants.RG21 2XS Tel : 0256 26222
  Telex : 858493
GLOBE Publ.Ltd., 139a Connaught Avenue, Frinton-on-Sea,
  Essex CO13 9PS Tel : 025 56 4225
GLOBEFIELD Press, Globefield, Exeter, Devon EX3 0HA
  Tel : 0392 875095
GLOSSARY of Scottish Building, 24 George Street, Glasgow
  G2 1EF Tel : 041.221 1466/7
GLYDENDL, 3 Blare Boderm, DK-1001 Copenhagen, Denmark
GLYN Summers Books, Marshall Hall Mills, Elland Lane, Elland
  W.Yorks HX5 9DU Tel : 0422 71585
GNOSTIC Concepts Inc., 2710 Sand Hill Road, Menlo Park
  CA 94025, USA Tel : 415 854 4672 Telex : 3731164
Charles E.GOAD Ltd., 18a Salisbury Square, Old Hatfield
  Herts.AL9 5BE Tel : 070 72 71171
David R.GODINE Publ.Inc., 306 Dartmouth Street, Boston,
  Mass.02116, USA Tel : 617 536 0761
George GODWIN - see Longman Group
David GOLD & Son(Holdings)Ltd., 15-17a Rich Industrial Estate
  Crimscott Street, London SE1 Tel : 01.237 4334/7
Julian GOLD Ltd., 73 Church Street, Hartlepool, Middlesbrough
  Tel : 0429 31922
GOLD Star Publ.Ltd., Gadoline House, 2 Godstone Road,
  Whyteleafe, Surrey Tel : 01.660 0102/6
  Telex : 946628
GOLDEN Age Postcard Books, 28 St.Peters Road, Malvern,
  Worcs. WR14 1QS Tel : 068 45 5863
GOLDEN Cockerel Press Ltd., 25 Sicilian Avenue, London
  WC1A 2QH Tel : 01.405 7979 Telex : 23565 -
  distributed by J.M.Dent & Sons Ltd.
GOLDEN Eagle Press Ltd., Montfort House, Frog Island,
  Leicester Tel : 0533 28851
GOLFERS Handbook, 246 West George Street, Glasgow G2 4OP
  Tel : 041.248 4667
GOLLANCZ Services, 14 Eldon Way, Lineside Estate, Littlehampton
  Sussex BN17 7EH Tel : 09064 21596
Victor GOLLANCZ Ltd., 14 Henrietta Street, Covent Garden
  London WC2E 8QJ Tel : 01.836 2006 - distributed
  by Gollancz Services Ltd.
GOMER Press, Llandysul, Dyfed, Wales Tel : 055932 2371
GOOD Elf Publications, 18 Clairview Road, Streatham, London
  SW16 Tel : 01.769 6911
GOOD News Crusade Publ., 15-17 High Cross Street, St.Austell
  Cornwall
GOOD Reading Ltd., 69 Fleet Street, London EC4Y 1HD
  Tel : 01.353 4781
Philip GOODALL Publishers, 92 Linden Way, Southgate, London
  N14 4NH Tel : 01.882 5877
GOODLIFFE Neale Ltd., Arden Forest Industrial Estate, Alcester
  Warwicks. B49 6ER Tel : 0789 763261
GOODWIN Dorman Publ.Ltd., 113 Westbourne Grove, London
  W2 4UP Tel : 01.229 9116
GOODYEAR Publ.Co., USA - distributed by Prentice Hall Intl.
GORDON & Breach Science Publ., 41-42 William IV Street,
  London WC2 4DE Tel : 01.836 5125 Telex : 23258
GORDON & Cremonesi Publ., New River House, 34 Seymour Road,
  London N8 0BE Tel : 01.348 7042 - distributed by
  Biblios Publishers Distribution Services Ltd.
GORDON & Gotch Books Ltd., Export Distribution Centre, 134
  Upper Road, Plaistow, London E13 0EY
  Tel : 01.476 5731 Telex : 897506 / Gotch House,
  30 St.Bride Street, London EC4A 4DJ
  Tel : 01.353 5211 Telex : 267382
GORDON Fraser Gallery Ltd., Fitzroy Road, London NW1 8TP
  Tel : 01.722 0077 Telex : 25848 / Eastcotts Road,
  Bedford MK42 0JX Tel : 0234 56531
GORHAM Intl.Inc., PO Box 8, Gorham, Maine 04038, USA
  Tel : 207 892 2216
GOTHARD House Publ.Ltd., Gothard House, Henley-on-Thames,
  Oxon.RG9 1AJ Tel : 0491 3602/4
Henry GOULDEN Ltd., 22 High Street, East Grinstead, Sussex
  RH19 3AW Tel : 0342 22669
O.A.GOULDEN & Partners, Quarry House, Stoke Hill, Stoke,
  Andover, Hants. Tel : 0264 73200
GOVERNMENT Publications - see HMSO and Irish Government
  Publications
GOVERNMENT Publications(EIRE), GPO Arcade, Dublin 1
GOWER Publ.Co.Ltd., Gower House, Croft Road, Aldershot,
  Hants.GU11 3HR Tel : 0252 331551 Telex : 858001
GRADUATE Press, Wroxton House, Chorleywood, Rickmansworth,
  Herts.

GRAHAM & Trotman Ltd., Sterling House, 66 Wilton Road,
  London SW1V 1DE Tel : 01.821 1123 Telex : 298878
Frank GRAHAM, 6 Queens Terrace, Newcastle upon Tyne
  NE2 2PL Tel : 0632 813067
The GRAMOPHONE, General Gramophone Publ.Ltd., 177-179
  Keston Road, Harrow, Middx.
GRANADA Publ.Ltd., PO Box 9, 29 Frogmore, St.Albans
  Herts.AL2 2NF Tel : 0727 72727 Telex : 262802
GRANARY Press, 10 Granary Lane, Budleigh Salterton,
  Devon EX9 6JD Tel : 03954 5488
GRANDREAMS Ltd., Jadwin House, 205-211 Kentish Town Road
  London NW5 2JU Tel : 01.485 0648/9
GRANGER Book Co.Inc., PO Box 406, Great Neck, NY11021,
  USA - distributed by Eurospan Ltd.
E.P.GRANT, Bradford Road, East Ardsey, Wakefield WF3 2JN
GRANT & Cutler Ltd., 11 Buckingham Street, Strand, London
  WC2W 6DQ Tel : 01.839 3136
GRANT McIntyre Ltd., 90-91 Great Russell Street, London
  WC1B 3PH Tel : 01.631 4141
GRANTA Editions Ltd., 7 Brooklands Avenue, Cambridge CB2
  2BB Tel : 0223 61762
GRAPHIC Communications Centre Ltd., Bernard House,
  Granville Road, Maidstone, Kent ME14 2BJ
  Tel : 0622 675324
GRAPHICS World, Miller House, Lower Stone Street, Maidstone
  Kent Tel : 0622 678551
GRAPHIS Press Corp., Dufourstrasse 107, CH-8008 Zürich
  Switzerland Tel : 01 251 92 11
GRASSHOPPER Press, 12 Church Street, Fenstanton,
  Huntingdon, Cambs.PE18 9JL Tel : 0480 69445
GRASSROOTS Publishers - distributed by IBD
Vivian GRAY, 108 Cuckfield Road, Hurstpierpoint, Hassocks,
  W.Sussex BNR 9RY Tel : 0273 832583
GRAY-Mills Publ.Ltd. - ceased trading 1976 - stocks and rights
  acquired by Basil Blackwell Publ.
GREAT Ouse Press, 82 Castle Street, Cambridge CB3 0AJ
  Tel : 0223 521030
GREATER London Council, GLC Research Library, Room 514
  County Hall, London SE1 7PB Tel : 01.633 6068
GREATER London Secondary Housing Association Ltd., 140-142
  Stockwell Road, London SW9 9TQ Tel : 01.737 3364
GREATER World Association Trust, 3 Lansdowne Road,
  Holland Park, London W11 3AL Tel : 01.727 7264/
  9795
GREEK Publishing Co.Ltd., 48a Artillery Lane, London E1
  Tel : 01.247 8574
GREEK Shipping Publications, 14 Skouze & Kolokotrani Street
  Piraeus, Greece
GREEN David Publications, Springfield House, The Parade,
  Oadby, Leicester Tel : 0533 27300
Philip GREEN Educational Ltd., 280 Evesham Road, Headless
  Cross, Redditch, Worcs.B97 5EP Tel : 0527 46145
Victor GREEN Publ.Ltd., Cavendish House, 128-134 Cleveland
  Street, London W1P 5DN Tel : 01.387 5050
  Telex : 8811108
W.GREEN & Son Ltd., Law Publishers, St.Giles Street,
  Edinburgh EH1 1PU Tel : 031.225 4879
GREEN,Belfield-Smith & Co., 20 Kingsway, London WC2B 6LH
  Tel : 01.405 3861 Telex : 893905
GREEN Tiger Press, 1061 India Street, San Diego, CA 92101,
  USA Tel : 619 238 1001
GREENACRES Publ.Co.Ltd., 34 Church Road, Hove, Sussex
  Tel : 0273 778168
GREENALL Whitley plc, Wilderspool Brewery, Warrington
  WA4 6RH Tel : 0925 51234
GREENCROFT Books, Trefelin, Cilgwyn, Newport, Dyfed
  SA42 0QN Tel : 023 976 470
Stephen GREENE Press, c/o European Book Service
GREENHAVEN Press, 577 Shoreview Park Road, St.Paul,
  MN55112, USA Tel : 612 482 1582
Henry GREENWOOD & Co.Ltd., 28 Great James Street, London
  WC1N 3HL Tel : 01.404 4202
GREENWOOD Press, c/o Westport Publ.Co., 3 Henrietta Street
  London WC2E 8LT Tel : 01.240 1009 - distributed
  by Eurospan Ltd.
GREGG International, The Distribution Centre, Blackhorse Road
  Letchworth, Herts.SG6 1HN Tel : 04626 72555
  Telex : 825372
The GREGG Press Inc., USA - distributed by Holt Saunders Ltd.
GRESHAM Books, The Gresham Press, PO Box 61, Henley-on-
  Thames, Oxon.RG9 3LQ Tel : 073 522 3789
GREYSTONE Corp., 6 Knole Road, Rottingdean, Sussex
Charles GRIFFIN & Co.Ltd., Charles Griffin House, Crendon
  Street, High Wycombe, Bucks HP13 6LE
  Tel : 0494 36341

GRIFFITH Institute, Ashmolean Museum, Oxford OX1 2PH - distributed by Aris & Philips Ltd.
GRIFFITH University, Nathan, Queensland 4111, Australia
GRISEWOOD & Dempsey Ltd., Elsley Court, 20-22 Great Titchfield Street, London W1P 7AD Tel : 01.631 0878 Telex : 27725
GROLIER Inc., USA - distributed by Franklin Watt Ltd.
GROSVENOR Books, 54 Lyford Road, London SW18 3JJ Tel : 01.870 2124 Telex : 917820
GROSVENOR Press, 50 Grosvenor Street, London W1X 9FH Tel : 01.491 1904 Telex : 23931
GROSVENOR Tax Publications, The Old House, 24 London Road, Horsham, W.Sussex RH12 1LQ Tel : 0403 62047
GROUPE des Editions, 13 Ave.Wladinieur Kamara, 78190 Trappes, France
GROUPE Expension, 67 Ave.de Wagram, 75017 Paris, France
GROVE Books, Bramcote, Notts.NG9 3DS Tel : 0602 251114
GROVE Press(Fleetbooks) - c/o TABS
GROWER Books, 50 Doughty Street, London WC1N 2LP Tel : 01.405 7135 Telex : 8811527
GRUB Street, 4 Kingly Street, London W1R 5LF Tel : 01.734 6428 Telex : 261426
GRUNE & Stratton Inc. - distributed by Academic Press Inc. (London)Ltd.
GRUNER & Jahr GmbH, PO Box 30-20-40, 2000 Hamburg 36, W.Germany Tel : 040 41181 Telex : 212376
Walter de GRUYTER & Co., Postfach 110240, 1000 Berlin, West Germany - distributed by IBD; represented by Global Book Resources Ltd.
CRYPHONE Press, 220 Montgomery Street, Highland Park, New York 08104, USA
The GUARDIAN, 119 Farringdon Road, London EC1R 3ER Tel : 01.278 2332 Telex : 8811746/8 / 164 Deansgate Manchester M60 2RR Tel : 061.832 7200
GUARDIAN Communications, Albany House, 3rd Floor, Hurst Street, Birmingham B5 4BD Tel : 021.622 4011
GUIDE Intl.Corp., 111 East Wacker Drive, Room 600, Chicago Ill.60601, USA
GUIDE to European Foundations, Edizioni della Fondazione, Via Ormea 37, 10125 Torino, Italy
GUIDES Ltd., Unit PP, Maidstone Industrial Centre, St.Peters Road, Maidstone, Kent Tel : 0622 681034
GUIDES to Multinational Business Inc., PO Box 92, Hanover Square, Cambridge, Mass.02138, USA
GUIDO Monaci, Via Francesco Crispi,10, 00187 Rome, Italy Tel : 06 48 34 01 Telex : 613462
GUILD of Master Craftsman Publications, Parklands House, Keymer Road, Burgess Hill, Sussex Tel : 04446 45267
GUILD of Pastoral Psychology, 37 Hogarth Hill, London NW11 6AY Tel : 01.458 3125
GUILD Press, Park Place House, PO Box 318, Tunnel Street, St.Helier, Jersey, Channel Islands Tel : 0534 20022
GUILD Sound & Vision, Woodston House, Oundle Road, Peterborough PE2 9PZ Tel : 0733 63122 Telex : 32659
GUILDFORD Educational Press, Philip Thorn Assocs.Ltd., Belvedere House, 53 Ridgemount, Guildford, Surrey GU2 5TH Tel : 0483 71986
GUILDHALL Library, Aldermanbury, Guildhall, London EC2P 2EJ Tel : 01.606 3030 X2858
GUILDHALL School of Music & Drama, Barbican, London EC2Y 8DT Tel : 01.628 2571
GUINNESS Superlatives Ltd., 2 Cecil Court, London Road, Enfield Middx.EN2 6DJ Tel : 01.367 4567 Telex : 23573
GULF Coast Oil Directory Publ., 111E Shoreline Drive, Sandustry Ohio 44870, USA - orders to Parrish Rodgers
GULF Publ.Co., PO Box 2608, Houston, Texas 77001, USA - distributed by Kogan Page Ltd.
GULLIVER Publ.Co.Ltd., White Lion Walk, Banbury, Oxon.OX16 8UD Tel : 0295 52002
A.E.GUNTHER, 35 Rudall Crescent, Hampstead, London NW3 1RR
GWASG Gee, Chapel Street, Denbigh, Clwyd Tel : 074 571 2020
GWASG Gwynedd, Nant Peris, Caernarfon, Gwynedd
GWASG Prifysgol Cymru - see University of Wales Press
GWASG y Dref Wen, 28 Church Road, Whitchurch, Cardiff Tel : 0222 617860
GWILYM Jenkins, 39 Broad Street, St.Helier, Jersey, Channel Islands
GWYNEDD Archives Service, Swyddfa'r Sir, Caernarfon, Gwynedd
GWYNN Publ.Co., Penygroes, Caernarfon, Gwynedd
GYL Dendaliske Boghandel, Nordisk Forlag AS, Klarebolerne 3, DK-1001 Copenhagen, Denmark

H

H&M Technical Publ.Ltd., 33 Oldfield Road, Bath, Avon Tel : 0225 314801
HATRA (formerly Hosiery & Allied Trades Research Ass'n.) 7 Gregory Boulevard, Nottingham NG7 6LD Tel : 0602 63311
HATRICS(Hampshire Technical Research Industrial Commercial Service), Hampshire County Library Headquarters, 81 North Walls, Winchester, Hants.SO23 8BY Tel : 0962 60644/9 Telex ; 47121
H.B.C.A., 10 King Street, Penrith, Cumbria CA11 7AI
HERTIS(Hertfordshire County Council Library & Information Service), PO Box 110, Hatfield, Herts AL10 9AD Tel : 07072 68100
HETP, 4 Victoria Road, Wilmslow, Cheshire SK9 5HN
HFL Publications, 9 Bow Street, London WC1E 7AL Tel : 01.379 6637 Telex : 299080 - distributed by Chatto, Bodley Head & Cape Services Ltd.
HLL Publications Ltd., 1 Westbourne Place, Hove, Sussex BN3 4GN Tel : 0273 70040
HM&M Publ.Ltd., Spectrum House, Hillview Gardens, London NW4 2JQ Tel : 01.203 5171
HMSO, Government Bookshop, PO Box 569, London SE1 9NH Tel : 01.928 6977
HMSO Retail Bookshops : Brazenrose Street, Manchester M60 8AS Tel : 061.832 7583 / 41 The Hayes, Cardiff CF1 1JW Tel : 0222 24306 / 258 Broad Street, Birmingham B1 2HE Tel : 021.643 3740 / Southey House, Wine Street, Bristol BS1 2BQ Tel : 0272 24306
HMSO - Northern Ireland, Government Bookshop, 80 Chichester Street, Belfast BT1 4JY Tel : 0232 34488
HMSO - Scotland, Government Bookshop, 13a Castle Street Edinburgh EH2 3AR Tel : 031.225 6333
H.P.D.Shipping, 31 Brook Street, Mayfair, London, W1Y 2LL
HPTA, Dept.of Chemical Engineering, Imperial College, London SW7
HPTA, Dept.of Mechanical Engineering, University of Leeds, Leeds LS2 9JT Tel : 0532 431751
HRAF Press (Human Relations Area Files), PO Box 2015, Yale Station, New Haven, Connecticut 06520, USA
HS Publications, 7 Epping Close, Mackworth Estate, Derby DE3 4HR
H.S.A., 15 Adam Street, London WC2
HSE - see Health & Safety Executive
HTV Ltd., The Television Centre, Cardiff CF1 9XL Tel : 0222 21021
H.V.C.A., 34 Palace Court, London W2 4JB
Michael HAAG Ltd., PO Box 369, London NW3 4ER Tel : 01.794 2647
HACHETTE Continental Publishers & Distributors Ltd., 4 Regent Place, London WC1R 6BH Tel : 01.734 5259
HACKETT Publ.Co., 109 Great Russell Street, London WC1B 3ND Tel : 01.580 1862
Peter HADDOCK Ltd., Pinfold Lane Industrial Estate, Bridlington YO16 5BT Te; : 0262 78121
HAFNER Publ.Co.Inc. - c/o Collier Macmillan Ltd.
HAIG Guides, 1-3 Central Buildings, 24 Southwork Street, London SE1 Tel : 01. 403 3366
HAKLUYT Society, c/o Map Library, The British Library,Great Russell Street, London WC1B 3DG
Erik HALE, River House, Golant, Fowey, Cornwall Tel : 072 683 3526
Robert HALE Ltd., Clerkenwell House, 45-47 Clerkenwell Green London EC1R 0HT Tel : 01.251 2661
HALIL Lola of London, PO Box 159, London NW1 7HZ
F.HALL & Sons, North Road, Woking, Surrey
James HALL (Publ.)Ltd., 2a Upper Grove Street, Leamington Spa, Warwicks.CV32 5AN Tel : 0926 32180
HALLCREST Press, Fulfilment Dept., EPO Box 251, Mclean, Virginia 22101, USA
John HALLEWELL(Publ.)Ltd., Hallewell House, 38 High Street Chatham, Kent Tel : 0634 43884
HALLIDAY Associates, Stanway, Colchester, Essex CO3 5LJ Tel : 0206 330395
HALLWAG,Bern - maps only distributed by William Collins Sons & Co.Ltd.
HALSTED Press Inc. - distributed by John Wiley & Sons Ltd.
HAMBLESIDE Publ.Ltd., 12 Southgate Street, Winchester, Hants.SO23 9EF Tel : 0962 604444 Telex : 477357
HAMBRO Company Guides, 6 Broad Street Place, London EC2M 7JH Tel : 01.628 3744
Alexander HAMILTON Inst.Inc., 1633 Broadway, New York 10019, USA

Hamish HAMILTON Ltd., Garden House, 57-59 Long Acre,
    London WC2E 9JZ Tel : 01.836 7733 Telex : 298265
    - distributed by TBL Book Service Ltd.
HAMILTON House Publishing, Hamilton House, Grooms Lane
    Creaton, Northampton NN6 8NS Tel : 060 124 612
HAMILTON Publ.Co., USA - distributed by John Wiley & Sons Ltd.
HAMLYN Publ.Group Ltd., Astronaut House, Hounslow Road
    Feltham, Middx.TW14 9AR Tel : 01.890 1480
    Telex : 25650 - orders to Sanders Lodge Industrial
    Estate, Rushden, Northants.NN10 9RZ
    Tel : 093 34 58521
Dag HAMMASSKJOLD Foundation, c/o Upslandsleanken, Box 276
    S-75105 Uppsala, Sweden
HAMMICKS, 16 Newman Lane, Alton, Hants.GU34 2PJ
    Tel : 0420 85822
HAMPSHIRE County Magazine, 74 Bedford Place, Soton, Hants.
HAMPTON House Productions Ltd., 9 York Road, Maidenhead
    Berks Tel : 0628 70014 Telex : 847295
HAN Shan Tang, 717 Fulham Road, London SW6 5UL
    Tel : 01.731 2447 Telex : 8953385
Heinrich HANAU Publ.Ltd., PO Box 2JG, London W1A 2JG
    Tel : 01.734 4353 Telex : 28604
HANDSWORTH Law Centre, 27 Clerkenwell Close, London EC1R
    0AT Tel : 01.251 4976
The HANDY Shipping Guide, 12-16 Laystall Street, London
    EC1R 4PB Tel : 01.837 7185/6
HANNAH Research Institute, Ayr KA6 5HL, Scotland
    Tel : 0292 76013/7
J.HANNANAND Co.(Publ.), 36 Great Clarendon Street, Oxford
    OX2 6LX Tel : 0865 57824
HANOVER Press Ltd., 207 Miller House, Miller Arcade, Preston
    Lancs. Tel : 0772 23150
HANSIB Publ.Ltd., Tower House, 139-149 Fonthill Road, London
    N4 3HF Tel : 01.263 8419 Telex : 888648
HANSOM Books, Artillery Mansions, 75 Victoria Street, London
    SW1H 0HZ Tel : 01.799 4452
HARCOURT Brace Jovanovich Ltd., 24-28 Oval Road, London
    NW1 7DU Tel : 01.485 7074/5 Telex : 25775
Patrick HARDY Books, 28 Percy Street, London W1P 9FF
    Tel : 01.636 9166 Telex : 22552
Thomas HARDY Society Ltd., 22 High East Street, Dorchester,
    Dorset DT1 1HA
HARLEY Books, Martins, Great Horkesley, Colchester, Essex
    CO6 4AH Tel : 0206 271216
HARMSWORTH Publ.Ltd., Carmelite House, Carmelite Street,
    London EC4Y 0JA Tel : 01.353 6000
Thomas HARMSWORTH Publ., 13 Nicosia Road, London SW18 3RN
    Tel : 01.874 1357
HARNSER Press, Black Boys, Thornage, Holt, Norfolk NR25 7QG
    Tel : 0263 861218
HARPER & Row, 28 Tavistock Street, London WC2E 7PN
    Tel : 01.836 4635 Telex : 267331 - distributed by
    Macdonald & Evans Ltd.
HARPER Trade Journals, Harling House, 47-51 Great Suffolk
    Street, London SE1 0BS Tel : 01.261 1604
HARRAP Ltd., 19-23 Ludgate Hill, London EC4M 7PD
    Tel : 01.248 6444
Paul HARRIS Publishing, 25 London Street, Edinburgh EH3 6LY
    Tel : 031.556 9696
HARRIS Publ.Ltd., 42 Maiden Lane, Strand, London WC2E 7CW
HARROW Computer Services Ltd., 346 Harrow Road, London
    W9 2HP Tel : 01.289 1158
Rupert HART-Davis Ltd. - distributed by Granada Publ.Ltd.
HARVARD Business Review, Soldiers Field, Boston, MA 02163
    USA
HARVARD Business Review Library - distributed by William
    Heinemann Ltd.
HARVARD Business School - distributed by IBD
HARVARD University, Center for Intl.Affairs, 6 Divinity Avenue,
    Cambridge MA02138, USA
HARVARD University Press, 126 Buckingham Palace Road,
    London SW1W 9SD Tel : 01.730 9208 Telex : 23933
    - distributed by IBD
HARVESTER Press Ltd., 16 Ship Street, Brighton BN1 1AD
    Tel : 0273 723031 Telex : 24224
HARVEY Miller Publ., 20 Marryat Road, Wimbledon, London SW19
    5BD Tel : 01.946 4426 - distributed by Oxford
    University Press
Vance HARVEY Publ., 37-39 Chartwell Drive, Wigston, Leicester
    LE8 2FL Tel : 0533 881334
HARVILL Press, 8 Grafton Street, London W1X 3LA
    Tel : 01.493 7070
HARWELL Industrial Research, Bldg.150, AERE, Harwell,
    Didcot, Oxon. OX11 0RA
HARWOOD Academic Publ.GmbH, POBox 197, London WC2N 4DE
    Tel : 01.836 5125 Telex : 23258

Verlag Otto HASSASSOIVITY, Postfach 2929, Taunasstrasse 6
    Wiesbaden, West Germany
HASTINGS House Publ.Inc., 10 East 40th Street, New York
    10016, USA
HATFIELD Polytechnic, PO Box 110, Hatfield, Herts AL10 9AD
    Tel : 070 72 68100
HAWKINS Publ.Ltd., Laxfield House, 2 Church Street,
    Coggeshall, Essex CO6 1TU Tel : 0376 62262
HAYDEN Book Co.Inc., USA - distributed by John Wiley & Sons
    Ltd.
R.HAYELL & Co., 117 Hatfield Road, St.Albans, Herts AL1 4JS
HAYES-Hill Inc., 220 E 42nd Street, New York 10017, USA
    Tel : 212 573 8750 Telex : 233468
HAYES Kennedy Ltd., 103 High Street, Thame, Oxford
HAYMARKET Publ.Ltd., 12-14 Ansdell Street, London W8 5TR
    Tel : 01.937 7288
HAYNES Publ.Group Ltd., Sparkford, Yeovil, Somerset BA22
    7JJ Tel : 0963 40635
R.HAZELL & Co., PO Box 39, Henley-on-Thames, Oxon RG9
    5UA Tel : 0491 641018
HAZLETON Publishing, 3 Richmond Hill, Richmond, Surrey
    TW10 6RE Tel : 01.948 1532 Telex : 946153
HEADLAND Press, 1 Henry Smith's Terrace, Headland,
    Hartlepool, Cleveland TS24 0PD Tel : 0429 31902
HEADLAND Publications, 38 York Avenue, West Kirby, Wirral
    Merseyside L48 3JF
HEADLEY Brothers Ltd., The Invicta Press, Queens Road,
    Ashford, Kent TN24 8HN Tel : 0233 23131
HEADLINE Promotions, Osborne House, 21-25 Lower Stone
    Street, Maidstone,Kent ME15 6YT Tel : 0622 671081
HEADLINE Publ.Ltd., Holywell House, 72-90 Worship Street
    London EC2 Tel : 01.247 8492
Chadwyck-HEALEY Ltd., 20 Newmarket Road, Cambridge CB5
    8DT Tel : 0223 311479
HEALTH & Safety Commission, Regina House, 259-269 Old
    Marylebone Road, London NW1 5RR
    Tel : 01.723 1262
HEALTH & Safety Executive, Baynards House, 1 Chepstow Place
    London W2 4TF Tel : 01.229 3456 X541 / Meadowbank
    House, 153 London Road, Edinburgh EH8 7AU
HEALTH Science Press, Hengiscote, Bradford, Holsworth,
    North Devon EX22 7AP Tel : 040 928 469
R.&W.HEAP(Publ.)Co.Ltd., Bowden Hall, Marple, Stockport
    Cheshire SK6 6NE Tel : 061.427 3513/4
D.C.HEATH & Co.(U.S.)Distributions - distributed by IBD
HEATHER Society, 7 Rossley Close, Highcliffe, Christchurch
    Dorset BH23 4RR Tel : 042 52 72191
HEATHERBANK Press, 163 Mugdock Road, Milngavie, Glasgow
    G62 6BR Tel : 041.956 2687
HEATING & Ventilating Contractors Association, Accounts &
    Publications Unit, Old Mansion House, Eamont
    Bridge, Penrith, Cumbria CA10 2BX Tel:0768 64771
    Telex : 64326
HEATING & Ventilating Publ.Ltd., Faversham House, 111 St.
    James's Road, Croydon, Surrey CR9 2TH
    Tel : 01.684 3891/2660 Telex : 943763
HEAVY Metal Books - c/o TABS
Sven R.HED, Bray Studios, Windsor Road, Windsor, Berks
    SL4 5UG Tel : 0628 22121 Telex : 849995
HEDDERWICK Stirling Grumbar & Co., 1 Moorgate, London EC2
HEFFERS Printers Ltd., Kings Hedges Road, Cambridge CB4
    2PQ Tel : 0223 51571 Telex : 81298
Peter A.HEIMS, 293 Kingston Road, Leatherhead, Surrey KT22
    7NJ Tel : 0372 374505
HEINEMANN Educational Books Ltd., 22 Bedford Square,
    London WC1B 3HH Tel : 01.637 3311 Telex : 261888
    - orders to Windmill Press, Kingswood, Tadworth,
    Surrey KT20 6TG Tel : 0737 3511 Telex : 947458
HEINEMANN Octopus, 59 Grosvenor Street, London W1X 9DA
    Tel : 01.493 5841 Telex : 27278 - distributed by
    WHS Distributors
William HEINEMANN Ltd., 10 Upper Grosvenor Street, London
    W1X 9PA Tel : 01.493 4141 Telex : 8954961 - orders
    to Windmill Press, Kingswood, Tadworth, Surrey
    KT20 6TG Tel : 0737 3511 Telex : 947458
William HEINEMANN Medical Books Ltd., 23 Bedford Square,
    London WC1B 3HH Tel : 01.637 3311 - orders to
    Windmill Press, Kingswood, Tadworth, Surrey KT20
    6TG Tel : 0737 3511 Telex : 947458
A.HELDOSMAN & Co., 19 Brunswick Road, Mount Claire, New
    Jersey 07042, USA
HELENA Press, PO Box 2, Slaithwaite, Huddersfield HD7 5JF
    Tel : 0484 842893
HELICON Press, Knight Street, Sawbridgeworth, Herts.CM21
    9AX Tel : 0279 722318 - distributed by Wentworth
    Book Co.Ltd.

HELIOS Books, 2 High Street, Glastonbury, Somerset BA6 9DU
   Tel : 0458 34184
The HELMINTHOLOGICAL Society of Washington, Business Office
   PO Box 368, Laurence, Kansas 66044, USA
HELP the Aged, Education Department, 218 Upper Street,
   London N1 Tel : 01.359 6316
HEMISPHERE Publ.Corp., 79 Madison Avenue, New York 10016
   USA Tel : 212 725 1999
HENDON Publ.Co.Ltd., Hendon Mill, Hallam Road, Nelson, Lancs.
   BB9 8AD Tel : 0282 63129
HENLEY Centre for Forecasting, 2 Tudor Street, Blackfriars
   London EC4Y 0AA Tel : 01.353 9961 Telex : 298817
HENLEY-The Management College, Greenlands, Henley-on-Thames
   Oxon. RG9 3AU Tel : 049 166 454
Ian HENRY Publ.Ltd., 38 Parkstone Avenue, Emerson Park,
   Hornchurch, Essex RM11 3LW Tel : 040 24 42042 -
   distributed by J.M.Dent & Sons Ltd.
HER Majesty's Consuls List, National Mutual House, South Park
   Sevenoaks, Kent TN13 1ED Tel : 0732 58646
HER Majesty's Stationery Office - see HMSO
HERALD Advisory Services, 23a Brighton Road, South Croydon
   Surrey CR2 6UE Tel : 01.681 3595/6 - distributed
   by Surridge Dawson & Co.(Publ.)Ltd.
HERALD & Weekly Times, 1 Maltravers Street, London WC2
   Tel : 01.836 5161
HERALD Books, 109 Great Russell Street, London WC1B 3ND
   Tel : 01.580 1862
HERALD Press Arbroath, Burnside Drive, Arbroath, Angus
   Tel : 0241 72274/5
HERALDRY Today, 10 Beauchamp Place, London SW3 1NW
   Tel : 01.584 1656 / Parliament Piece, Back Lane
   Ramsbury, Marlborough, Wilts. Tel : 067 22 617
Ian HERBERT, 12-13 Henrietta Street, London WC2
   Tel : 01.379 3478
HERBERT Press, 65 Belsize Lane, London NW3 5AU
   Tel : 01.794 5965 - distributed by A&C Black
HERDCROFT Ltd., Darville, Southview Road, Southwick,
   Sussex BN4 4TW
HERDER GmbH & Co.KG, Hermann-Herder-Str.4, 7800 Freiburg
   im Breisgau, W.Germany
Walton HERDEG Graphics Press, Dufounstrasse 107, CH-8008,
   Zurich, Switzerland
HEREFORD Press, 25 Elystan Place, London SW3 3JY
   Tel : 01.581 3044
HERELD Organization, Trimester International, PO Box 6042
   Lawrenceville, NJ 08648, USA Tel : 609 896 9447
HEREWARD Books Ltd., Unit 3, 33 Woodthorpe Road, Ashford
   Middx.TW15 2RP Tel : 0784 42941
HEREWARD Press, Brays Lane, Ely, Cambs.CB7 4HA
   Tel : 0353 3544/6
HERIOT-Watt University, Chambers Street, Edinburgh EH1 1HX
   Tel : 031.225 8432
HERIOT-Watt University, Institute of Offshore Engineering,
   Riccarton, Currie, Edinburgh EH4 4AS
   Tel : 031.449 5111
HERITAGE Books, 36 Great Russell Street, London WC1A 3PX
   Tel : 01.580 4168
HERITAGE of Music Ltd., 30 Agate Road, London W6
   Tel ; 01.748 0649
HERITAGE Press(Scotland), Towie Barclay Castle, Auchterless
   Aberdeen Tel : 088 84 347
HERITAGE Publications, Merchants House, Barley Market Street,
   Tavistock, Devon Tel : 0822 3592
HERMES Publ.Co., 1 Hermes Street, London N1 Tel : 01.837 7851
HERNER & Co., c/o Information Resources Press, 2100 M Street
   NW, Suite 316, Washington DC 20037, USA
HERON Books, Lawrence House, St.Andrews Hill, Norwich
W.E.HERSANT Ltd., 228 Archway Road, Highgate, London N6
   Tel : 01.340 3869
G.W.& A.HESKETH, PO Box 8, Ormskirk, Lancs.L39 5HH
   Tel : 0695 422227
HETTENA Associates Publications, 30 Westbourne Park Villas,
   London W2 5EA Tel : 01.229 3281 - orders to Studios
   5-9, 10-11 Archer Street, London W1 Tel : 01.734 2860
HEVAC Association, Unit 3, Phoenix House, Phoenix Way, Heston
   Middx.TW5 9ND Tel : 01.897 2848
HEYDON & Son Ltd., Spectrum House, Hillview Gardens, London
   NW4 2JQ Tel : 01.203 5171 Telex : 28303
HEYWOOD Books - distributed by Butterworths & Co.(Publ.)Ltd.
HIGH Hill Press Ltd., 6a Hampstead High Street, London NW3
   Tel : 01.435 2218
HIGHER Education Authority, 21 Fitzwilliam Square, Dublin 2,
   Ireland Tel : 0001 761545
HIGHLANDS & Islands Development Board, Bridge House, Bank
   Street, Inverness IV1 1QR Tel : 0463 34171

Adam HILGER Ltd., Techno House, Redcliffe Way, Bristol BS1
   6NX Tel : 0272 297481 Telex : 449149
HILL Farming Research Organisation, Bush Estate, Penicuik,
   Midlothian, Scotland
Harold HILL & Son, Sandy Lane, North Gosforth, Newcastle upon
   Tyne NE3 5HH Tel : 089 426 5146/7 Telex : 53188
Lawrence HILL - distributed by IBD
Leonard HILL - an imprint of Blackie Publ.Group
HILLBEX Press, 23 Queens Gate, London SW7
HILLIER Parker May & Rowden, 77 Grosvenor Street, London W1A
   2BT Tel : 01.629 7666 Telex : 267683
HILMARTON Manor Press, Calne, Wilts.SN11 8SB
   Tel : 024 976 208
J.A.HILTON, 19 Lonewood Way, Hadlow, Tonbridge, Kent
   Tel : 073 279 472 - distributed by J.Hannon & Co.
HINSDALE, Dryden - distributed by Holt Saunders Ltd.
HINWOOD Library of Ideas, Appletree Cottage, Crossways Road
   Grayshott, Hindhead GU26 6HE Tel : 042 873 4573
HISPANIC & Luso-Brazilian Council, Canning House, 2 Belgrave
   Square, London SW1X 8PJ Tel : 01.235 2303 -
   Diamante Series distributed by Grant & Cutler Ltd.
HISTORICAL Association, 59a Kennington Park Road, London
   SE11 4JH Tel : 01.735 3901/2974
HISTORICAL Research Unit, Stone House, Kings Sutton,
   Banbury, Oxon
J.HITCHCOCK, 5 Church Road, Great Bookham, Leatherhead
   Surrey KT23 3PN Tel : 0372 52804
HOARE Govett Ltd., Heron House, 319 High Holborn, London
   WC1V 7PE Tel : 01.404 0344 Telex : 885474
Margaret & Jack HOBBS (Publ.), 25 Bridge Street, Walton-on-
   Thames, Surrey Tel : 093 22 21267
HOBBY & Leisure Publ., 30 Parkhill Road, Hemel Hempstead,
   Herts.
HOBSONS Press (Cambridge)Ltd., Bateman Street, Cambridge
   CB2 1LZ Tel : 0223 69811 Telex : 81546
E.G.HOCHBERG & Associates, Box 222, Chester Professional
   Building, Chester, NJ 07930, USA Tel : 201 879 7170
HODDER & Stoughton Ltd., 47 Bedford Square, London WC1B
   3DP Tel : 01.636 9851 Telex : 885887 - distributed
   by Hodder & Stoughton Services Ltd.
HODDER & Stoughton Services Ltd., Mill Road, PO Box 6,
   Dunton Green, Sevenoaks, Kent TN13 2XX
   Tel : 0732 50111 Telex : 95122
Alison HODGE(Publisher), Bosulval Farmhouse, Newmill,
   Penzance, Cornwall TR20 8XA Tel : 0736 68093
William HODGE & Co.Ltd., 34-36 North Frederick Street, Glasgow
   G1 2BT Tel : 041.552 2248
A.R.HODGES, 10 Linton Road, Hastings, E.Sussex TN34 1TN
   Tel : 0424 434455
HODGETTS Ltd., Unisaf House, 32-36 Dudley Road, Tunbridge
   Wells, Kent TN1 1LH Tel : 0892 23184/6
   Telex : 95412
Francis HODGSON, PO Box 74, Guernsey, Channel Islands
   Tel : 0481 24332 - distributed by Longman Group Ltd.
   Directories Division
HOGARTH Press, 40 William IV Street, London WC2N 4DF
   Tel : 01.579 6637 Telex : 299080 - distributed by
   Chatto, Bodley Head & Cape Services Ltd.
John HODGSTON Assocs.Ltd., 23 Golden Square, London W1
   Tel : 01.439 8639
H.S.HOLAPPA & Associates, 9 Hart Road, Lynnfield, Mass.01940
   USA Tel : 617 334 5716
HOLCOT Press, Ivy House, Holcot, Northants.
HOLDAN Books Ltd., 15 Parade Avenue, Oxford OX2 0LX
   Tel : 0865 57971
HOLDEN Day Inc. - distributed by McGraw Hill Book Co.Ltd.
HOLLAND Press Ltd., 37 Connaught Street, London W2 2AZ
   Tel : 01.262 6184/01.723 1623
HOLLIS & Carter, 9 Bow Street, London WC2E 7AL
   Tel : 01.379 6637 Telex : 299080
HOLLIS Directories, Contact House, Lower Hampton Road,
   Sunbury-on-Thames, Middx.TW16 5HG
   Tel : 09327 84781/82054
HOLLOBONE Hibbert & Assocs.Ltd., 28-30 Little Russell Street
   London WC1A 2HN Tel : 01.405 3388/3386
   Telex : 267568
W.& R.HOLMES(Books), 30 Clydeholm Road, Glasgow G14 0BJ
   Tel : 041.954 2271/3
HOLMES & Meier Publishers, 131 Trafalgar Road, Greenwich,
   London SE10 9TX
HOLMES-McDougall Ltd., Allander House, 137-141 Leith Walk
   Edinburgh EH6 0JL Tel : 031.554 9444 Telex : 727508
HOLSWORTHY Publ.Ltd., 11 Suffolk Street, London SW1Y 4HG
   Tel : 01.839 6141
HOLT Blond - now Holt Saunders Ltd.

HOLT Rinehart & Winston Ltd. - see Holt Saunders Ltd.
HOLT Saunders Ltd., 1 St.Anne's Road, Eastbourne, E.Sussex BN21 3UN Tel : 0323 638221 Telex : 877503
HOME Birth Handbook, 47 Valence Road, Lewes, Sussex BN7 1SJ
HOME Grown Cereals Authority, Hamlyn House, Highgate Hill, London N19 5PR Tel : 01.263 3391
HOME Health Education Service, 653 St.Albans Road, Garston Watford, Herts WD2 6JP Tel : 092 73 71635
HOME Office Publns. London SW1 - distributed by Home Office Library
HOME Office Library, Room 1007, 50 Queen Anne's Gate, London SW1 9AT Tel : 01.213 7367
HOME Publ.Co.Ltd., Falcon House, 20-22 Belmont Road, Wallington, Surrey SM6 8TA Tel : 01.669 8131/5
HOMEFINDERS(1915)Ltd., 10 East Road, London N1 6AU Tel : 01.253 4628 Telex : 28177
HONEYGLEN Publ.Ltd., 16 Duchess of Bedford House, Duchess of Bedford Walk, London W8 7QL Tel : 01.937 3780
HONEYWELL Information Systems Ltd., 10 Cullen Way, Willesden, London NW10 6JZ Tel : 01.965 4283
HOOVER Institution, Room 32, Stanford University, Stanford California 94305, USA
HOPE Press Publications, Hope House, 45 Great Peter Street, London SW1P 3LT Tel : 01.222 6809
HOPKIN & Williams, PO Box 1, Romford, Essex
John HOPKINS University Press - distributed by IBD
HOPPENDSTEDT & Co., Hauptsitz D-6100 Darmstadt, Havelstrasse 9, Postfach 4006, West Germany
HORIZON Press, Stratford upon Avon, Warwicks.
Karen HORNEY Association, 27 Clerkenwell Close, London EC1R 0AT Tel : 01.251 4976
Thomas HORTON & Daughters, 22 Appleton Place, Box 3 Glen Ridge, New Jersey 07028, USA
B.HORWITZ Publ.Co., 462 Cheetham Hill Road, Manchester M8 7JW Tel : 061.740 5897
Ellis HORWOOD Ltd.Publisher, Market Cross House, Cooper Street, Chichester, Sussex PO19 1EB Tel : 0243 789942 Telex : 86290 - distributed by John Wiley & Sons Ltd.
HOSIERY & Allied Trade Research Association - see HATRA
HOSPITAL Research & Education Trust, 840 North Lake, Shore Drive, Chicago 60651, USA
HOTEL, Catering & Institutional Management Association, 191 Trinity Road, London SW17 7HN Tel : 01.672 4251
HOTELS & Catering Association, 13 Cork Street, London W1
HOUGHTON Mifflin Publ.Ltd., 41-45 Beak Street, London W1R 3LE Tel : 01.439 3485 - distributed by European Book Service
HOUSE Information Services Ltd., 178-202 Great Portland Street London W1N 6NH
HOUSING & Construction Research Associates, 1 Mercer Street London WC2H 9OL Tel : 01.836 0161
HOUSING Corporation, 149 Tottenham Court Road, London W1P 0BN Tel : 01.387 9466
HOUSMANS, 5 Caledonian Road, Kings Cross, London N1
Colin A.HOUSTON & Assoc.Inc., PO Box 416, Mamaroneck NY 10543, USA Tel : 914 698 3675
HOVE Foto Books, 34 Church Road, Hove, Sussex BN3 2GJ Tel : 0273 778166
C.W.HUBBER, 139 Mount Wise, Newquay, Cornwall Tel : 063 73 4767
Hans HUBER, Langgasstrasse 76, CH-3000 Berne 9, Switzerland - distributed by Holden Books
HUCA Publishers, 10 King Street, Penrith, Cumbria
HUDSON Institute, Quaker Ridge Road, Croton-on-Hudson, New York 10520, USA
Kelvin HUGHES(Charts & Maritime Supplies), 31 Mansell Street London E1 8AA Tel : 01.481 8741
HUGHES & Coleman Ltd., Spar Road, Norwich, Norfolk Tel : 0603 46159
HUGHES & Son (Publ.)Ltd., 88-90 Gower Road, Sketty, Swansea SA2 9BZ
HUGO's Language Books Ltd., 104 Judd Street, London WC1 Tel : 01.278 6136
HUGUENOT Society of London, 67 Victoria Road, London W8 5RH
HULL & Company, 5 Oak Street, Greenwich, CT 06830, USA Tel : 203 622 9120
HULTON Educational Publ.Ltd., Raans Road, Amersham, Bucks HP6 5BR Tel : 02403 4196 Telex : 837916
HULTON Technical Press Ltd., Warwick House, Swanley, Kent BR8 8JF Tel : 0322 68431
HUMAN Resource Development Press Inc. - distributed by MTP Press Ltd.
HUMAN Sciences Press, USA - distributed by Eurospan Ltd.
HUMAN Synergistics, 39819 Plymouth Road, Plymouth, Michigan 48170, USA
HUMANA Press Inc., New Jersey, USA - distributed by John Wiley & Sons Ltd.
HUMBERSIDE County Council, Grimsby Division Central Library Town Hall Square, Grimsby, S.Humberside DN31 1HG Tel : 0472 53123
HUNGARIAN Institute for Market Research, H1373 Budapest PO Box 617, Hungary Tel : 00361 185 679 Telex : 225064
HUNNYHILL Publications, Corner Cottage, Hunnyhill, Brighstone, Isle of Wight PO30 4DU Tel : 0983 740363
HUNT Institute for Botanical Documentation - distributed by Wheldon & Wesley Ltd.
Nicholas HUNTER Ltd., PO Box 22, Oxford Tel : 0865 52678
HUNTINGDON Research Centre, Huntingdon PE18 6ES Tel : 0480 890431
HUNTINGTON Publ.Ltd., 25 Nightingale Avenue, Cambridge CB1 4SG Tel : 0223 47471
HUNTSMAN Press, 25 Euston Road, London NW1 2SD Tel : 01.837 6400
C.HURST & Co.(Publ.)Ltd., 38 King Street, London WC2E 8JT Tel : 01.240 2666
HURTWOOD Publ.Ltd., London Road, Westerham, Kent TN16 1BX Tel : 0959 63431
HUTCHINS' Priced Schedules Ltd., 33 Station Road, Bexhill-on-Sea, E.Sussex TN40 1RG Tel : 0424 211908
HUTCHINSON Educational Ltd., 24 Highbury Crescent, London N5 1RX Tel : 01.359 3711 - distributed by Tiptree Book Service
HUTCHINSON Publ.Group Ltd., Hutchinson House, 17-21 Conway Street, London W1P 6JD Tel : 01.387 2811
HUTTON Press Ltd., 130 Canada Drive, Cherry Burton, Beverley, N.Humberside
HYDATUM, PO Box 4, Ross-on-Wye, HR9 6EB Tel : 0603 890599
HYDRAULICS Research Station, Wallingford, Oxon.OX10 8BA Tel : 0491 35381 Telex : 848552 - most titles distributed by HMSO
HYDROGRAPHIC Society, North East London Polytechnic, Forest Road, London E17 4JB Tel : 01.527 5666
HYMNS Ancient & Modern Ltd., St.Mary's Works, St.Mary's Plain, Norwich, Norfolk NR3 3BH Tel : 0603 612914
HYTHE Books, 37 Queen Street, Henley-on-Thames, Oxon. RG9 1AJ Tel : 0491 3602

I

IAEA, Vienna Intl.Centre, PO Box 100, Waanerstrasse 5, A-14100 Vienna, Austria
IAL - Industrial Aids Ltd., 14 Buckingham Palace Road, London SW1W 0QP Tel : 01.828 5036
IATA, Traffic Publications Dept., 26 Chemin de Joinville, PO Box 160, 1216 Cointrin, Geneva, Switzerland
IBD - International Book Distributors Ltd., 66 Wood Lane End, Hemel Hempstead, Herts. HP2 4RG Tel : 0442 58531 Telex : 82445
IBF Publications, 8th Floor, Bridge House, 121 Smallbrook Queensway, Birmingham B5 4JP Tel : 021.643 4523
IBG Transport Geog.Study Group, University of Keele, Dept. of Geography, Keele, Staffs.ST5 5BG
IBIS Information Services, Waterside, Lowbell Lane, London Colney, St.Albans, Herts.AL2 1DX Tel : 0727 25209
ICA-Forlaget AB, Stora Gatan 41, 5-721 85 Vasteras, Sweden Tel : 021 1104 40
I.C.A.E.W.(Inst.of Chartered Accountants in England & Wales) Moorgate Place, London EC2R 6ED - many titles distributed by Macdonald & Evans Ltd.
I.C.C. - see Inter Company Comparisons Ltd.
I.C.C. - see International Chamber of Commerce
I.C.I. - see Imperial Chemical Industry
I.C.M.A.(Institute of Cost & Management Accountants), 63 Portland Place, London W1N 4AB Tel : 01.637 2311
I.C.R.A., Gillow House, University of Lancaster, Lancaster
ICS Publ.Co.(U.K.)Ltd., Pebblecoombe, Tadworth, Surrey KT20 7PA Tel : 0372 379211/20 Telex : 915133
ICSU AB, Secretariat, 51 Bd.de Montmorency, 75016 Paris France Tel : 525 65 92
IDC Europa Ltd., 2 Bath Road, London W4 1LN Tel : 01.995 9222 Telex : 9178777
IEA Coal Research, 14-15 Lower Grosvenor Place, London SW1W 0EX Tel : 01.828 4661 Telex : 917624
I.E.E.Publications(Inst.of Electrical Engineers), PO Box 8 Southgate House, Stevenage, Herts.SG1 1HO
I.E.E.E.Computer Society, 5655 Naples Ph2a, Suite 301, Long Beech, California 90803, USA

IEEE Press - distributed by John Wiley & Sons Ltd.
I.E.R.E.(Inst.of Electronic & Radio Engineers) 99 Gower St., London WC1E 6AZ Tel : 01.388 3071
IFI/Plenum Data Corp., 227 W 17th Street, New York 10011, USA
IFLA International Office for UBC, c/o Reference Division, The British Library, Great Russell Street, London WC1B 3DG Tel : 01.580 8996
I.F.S.(Publ.)Ltd., 35-39 High Street, Kempston, Bedford MK42 7BT Tel : 0234 853605
IIED - see International Institute for Environment & Development
IIRS, PO Box 688, 3800 AR Amersfoort, The Netherlands
IIT Research Institute, 10 West 35th Street, Chicago, Il.60616 USA Tel : 312 567 4000
ILEA - see Greater London Council
ILO Publications - see International Labour Office
I.L.R.Publications Division, Cornell University, Box 1000 Ithaca, N.Y.14850, USA
IMAC Research, Lancaster House, More Lane, Esher, Surrey Tel : 0372 63121
IMAL Ltd., 229 Dawes Road, London SW6 7RD Tel : 01.381 0468
IMEDE Management Development Institution, PO Box 105 CH-1001 Lausanne, Switzerland
IMO - see International Maritime Organization
IMS World Publications Ltd., York House, 37 Queen Square, London WC1N 3BE Tel : 01.831 6806 Telex : 263298
INBUCON/AIC Management Consultants Ltd., Knightsbridge House, 197 Knightsbridge, London SW7 1RN Tel : 01.584 6171
INCOMTEC(Business Education & Training Service) - in liquidation 1980
INSPEC - see Institution of Electrical Engineers
I.O.E.X.Ltd. - see Institute of Export
IPC Building & Contract Journals Ltd., Surrey House, 1 Throwley Way, Sutton, Surrey SM1 4QQ Tel : 01.643 8040 Telex : 944546
IPC Business Press Info.Services Ltd., Windsor Court, East Grinstead House, East Grinstead, W.Sussex RH19 1XA Tel : 0342 26972 Telex : 95127
IPC Business Press Ltd., 40 Bowling Green Lane, London EC1R 0NE Tel : 01.837 3636 Telex : 23839 / 1-6 Paris Gardens, Stamford Street, London SE1 9LU
IPC Electrical-Electronic Press - distributed by IPC Business Press Ltd.
IPC Industrial Press, Dorset House, Stamford Street, London SE1 9LU Tel : 01.261 8000
IPC Marketing - now Mirror Group Newspapers
IPC Magazines Ltd., Kings Reach Tower, Stamford Street, London SE1 9LS Tel : 01.261 5000
IPC Science & Technology Press Ltd., PO Box 63, Westbury House, Bury Street, Guildford, Surrey GU2 5BH Tel : 0483 31261 - distributed by IPC Business Press Ltd.
IPST of Jerusalem, John Wiley & Sons Ltd., Baffins Lane, Chichester, Sussex PO19 1UD
I.R.C.N., 27 Rue Monceau, 75008 Paris, France
IRL Press, PO Box 1, Eynsham, Oxford OX8 1JJ Tel : 0865 882283 Telex : 28398
I.S.B.A., 2 Basil Street, London SW3 1AG Tel : 01.584 5221
ISO - International Organisation for Standardisation - distributed by B.S.I.
I.T.R.R.U., 32 Trumpington Street, Cambridge
ITV Publications Ltd., 247 Tottenham Court Road, London W1P 0AY Tel : 01.636 1599
IWSOM Publications, 1 Cecil Court, London Road, Enfield, Middx.
IGUANA Publ.Ltd., 178 Royal College Street, London NW1 0SP Tel : 01.485 3236
IKENGA Publ.Ltd., PO Box 83, Oxford OX2 6XD Tel : 0865 53563 Telex : 837184
ILIFFE Books Ltd. - some titles distributed by Butterworth & Co.(Publ.)Ltd.
ILLUMINATED Way Press, PO Box 2449, Menlo Park, California CA94025, USA - distributed in UK by Blue Light Publ., 10 Lefroy Road, London W12
ILLUSTRATED Newspapers Ltd., 23-29 Emerald Street, London WC1N 3QJ Tel : 01.404 5531
ILLUSTRATED Publications, 12-18 Paul Street, London EC4 - distributed by Argus
IMAGE Books(Doubleday) - c/o TABS
IMAGENES Press - distributed by IBD
IMPACT Publishers, PO Box 1094, San Luis Obispo, California CA93406, USA
IMPERIAL Chemical Industries Pharmaceuticals Division, Alderley Park, Macclesfield, Cheshire

IMPERIAL Chemical Industries, Plant Protection Division, Jealott's Hill Research Station, Bracknell, Berks RG12 6EY Tel : 0344 24701
IMPERIAL College of Science & Technology, London SW7 2AZ Tel : 01.589 5111 Telex : 261503
IMPERIAL Society of Teachers of Dairying, Birkhead Street, London WC1H 8BF
IMPERIAL Society of Teachers of Dancing, Euston Hall, Birkenhead Street, London WC1H 8BE Tel : 01.837 9967
IMPREX, 1 Brett Manor, Brett Road, London E8
IMPRINT Publications, 20 Pylewell Road, Hythe, Hants. Tel : 0703 847676
IMPRINT Software Ltd., 340 High Road, Chadwell Heath, Romford, Essex RM6 6AJ Tel : 01.599 7309
IMRAY Laurie Norie & Wilson Ltd., Wych House, The Broadway St.Ives, Huntingdon, Cambs.PE17 4BT Tel : 0480 62114
INCOMES Data Service Ltd., 140 Great Portland Street, London W1N 5TA Tel : 01.580 0521/9
INCORPORATED Council of Law Reporting for England & Wales, 3 Stone Buildings, Lincoln's Inn, London WC2A 3XN Tel : 01.242 6471/2
INCORPORATED Society of British Advertisers Ltd., 2 Basil Street, Knightsbridge, London SW3 1AG Tel : 01.584 5221
INCORPORATED Society of Musicians, 10 Stratford Place, London W1N 9AE Tel : 01.629 4413
INDEPENDENT Book Distributors - now Aquila Publ.Co.Ltd.
INDEPENDENT Broadcasting Authority - see ITV Publications
INDEPENDENT Labour Party, 27 Clerkenwell Close, London EC1R 0AT Tel : 01.251 4976
INDEPENDENT Magazines Ltd. - in liquidation 1980
INDEPENDENT Press Ltd. - distributed by Tavistock Bookshop
INDEPENDENT Publishers Guild, c/o Rosemary Petit, 52 Chepstow Road, London W2 Tel : 01.727 0919
INDEPENDENT Publ.Co., 38 Kennington Lane, London SE11 4LS Tel : 01.735 2101
INDEPENDENT Schools Association Inc., 45 Regent Street, Cambridge CB2 1AB Tel : 0223 355405
INDEX of New Products, 1 Lambeth High Street, London SE1 7JW
INDEX of Censorship, Writers & Scholars Intl.Ltd., 21 Russell Street, Covent Garden, London WC2B 5HP Tel : 01.836 0024
INDEX Publications, Peswera House, Barn Wood, Plymouth, Devon Tel : 0752 43369
INDIAN Books - The Bookcentre Ltd., Ranade Road, Dadan, Bombay, 400 028, India
INDIAN Institute of Technology, Have Khas, New Delhi, India
INDIANA University Press Ltd., c/o American University Publishers Group - distributed by IBD
INDUSTRIAL Aids Ltd., 14 Buckingham Palace Road, London SW1W 0QP Tel : 01.828 5036 Telex : 918666
INDUSTRIAL Data Ltd., 1-2 Berners Street, London W1P 3AG Tel : 01.637 1444 Telex : 25206
INDUSTRIAL Health Foundation Inc., 34 Penn Circle West, Pittsburgh, PA 15206, USA
INDUSTRIAL Institute for Economic & Social Research - distributed by Almqvist & Wiksell Ltd.
INDUSTRIAL Liaison Bureau Inc., 44 Lange Voorhout, The Hague, 2514 EG, The Netherlands Tel : 070 461020
INDUSTRIAL Market Research Ltd., 17 Buckingham Gate, London SW1 Tel : 01.834 7814
INDUSTRIAL Marketing Research Association, IMRA Office, 11 Bird Street, Lichfield, Staffs. WS13 6PW Tel : 054 32 23448
INDUSTRIAL Newspapers Ltd., Queensway House, 2 Queensway Redhill RH1 1QS Tel : 0737 68611 Telex : 948669
INDUSTRIAL Participation Association, 78 Buckingham Gate, London SW1E 6PO Tel : 01.222 0351
INDUSTRIAL Planning & Economics Ltd., 52 High Holborn, London WC1V 6RL Tel : 01.267 1805/01.242 3131
INDUSTRIAL Press Inc., USA - distributed by Holt Saunders Ltd.
INDUSTRIAL Railway Society, c/o R.E.West, 14 Charles Street Market Harborough, Leics.LE16 9AB
The INDUSTRIAL Relations Briefing, 346 Harrow Road, London W9 2HP Tel : 01.289 1158 - also Harrow Computer Services at same address
INDUSTRIAL Relations Research Association, 7226 Social Science Building, University of Wisconsin, Madison, WI53706 USA
INDUSTRIAL Relations Services, 67 Maygrove Road, London NW6 2EJ Tel : 01.328 4751/6 Telex : 267778
INDUSTRIAL Relations Training Resource Centre - now Employment Relations Ltd.

INDUSTRIAL Research & Information Services Ltd., 53 Cavendish Road, London SW12 0BL Tel : 01.675 1791
INDUSTRIAL Safety(Protective Equipment) Manufacturers Association, 69 Cannon Street, London EC4N 5AB
The INDUSTRIAL Society, 3 Carlton House Terrace, London SW1Y 5DG Tel : 01.839 4300
INDUSTRIAL Systems Research, 26 Brown Street, Manchester M2 1DN Tel : 061.834 5575
INDUSTRIAL Television Publ., 247 Tottenham Court Road, London W1P 6AV
INDUSTRIAL Training Research Unit Ltd., Lloyds Bank Chambers, Hobson Street, Cambridge CB1 1NL Tel : 0223 351576
INDUSTRIAL Tribunal Handbook - c/o New Comm. Publ.Co.
INDUSTRIESCHAIN-Verlagsgesellschafts, Postfach 4034, Berline Allee 8, 6100-Darmstadt, W.Germany
INDUSTRON Consultants, 2267 Coventry Road, Sheldon, Birmingham B26 3PD Tel : 021.742 4141 Telex : 337492
INFO Press Inc., 736 Center Street, PO Box 550, Lewiston New York 14092, USA
INFORM, 381 Park Avenue South, New York 10016, USA Tel : 212 689 4040
INFORMATION on Ireland, 27 Clerkenwell Close, London EC1R 0AT Tel : 01.251 4976
INFORMATION Petroleum Inc., 911 Jefferson Davies Highway, Suite 907, Arlington, VA22202, USA
INFORMATION Research Ltd., 40 Oxford Street, London W1N 9FS Tel : 01.580 3914 Telex : 24224
INFORMATION Resources Press - distributed by Gothard House Publ.Ltd.
INFORMATION Retrieval Ltd., 1 Falconberg Court, London W1V 5FG Tel : 01.437 5362
INFORMEDIA Ltd., 5 High Street, Beckenham, Kent BR3 1AZ Tel : 01.658 0286
INFOTECH Ltd., Nicholson House, High Street, Maidenhead, Berks SL6 1LD Tel : 0628 39101 Telex : 847319
INFRATEST Forschung GmbH & Co.KG, Landsbergerstrasse 338, D8000 Munchen 21, W.Germany Tel : 089 56001 Telex : 5212689
INGHAM White Ltd., Windmill House, 43 Windmill Road, Luton, Beds.LU1 3XL
INK Links Ltd., 271 Kentish Town Road, London NW5 2JS Tel : 01.267 6661 - distributed by Noonan Hurst
INLAND Revenue, Enquiry Service Unit, Room 7, New Wing Somerset House, Strand, London WC2R 1LB Tel : 01.438 7772/01.438 6325
INPUT-Output Publ.Co., 3 Wyndham Place, London W1H 1AP Tel : 01.262 0061
INPUT Two-Nine - imprint of Gower Publ.Co.Ltd.
IN-SEARCH Data, Jalan Nusa Indah 9, Tomang, Jakarta Barat, Tromol POS 3020, Jakarta, Indonesia Tel : 591729 Telex ; 46331
INSIGHT Research, 36 James Street, London W1M 5HS Tel : 01.935 3725
INSTITUT Francais du Petrole, BP311, 92506 Rueil-Malmalsou, Cedex, France Tel : 749 0214 Telex : 203050
INSTITUTE for Business Planning Inc. - distributed by Prentice Hall Intl.Ltd.
INSTITUTE for Cancer Research, 7701 Burholme Avenue, Fox Chase, Philadelphia, Penn.1911, USA
INSTITUTE for Economic Research, 56 Patrick Street, PO Box 54 Cork, Rep.of Ireland - distributed by Distribution & Media Sales
INSTITUTE for Fiscal Studies, 1-2 Castle Lane, London SW1E 6DR - distributed by Harris Publ.Ltd.
INSTITUTE for International Research, 57-61 Mortimer Street London W1N 7TD Tel : 01.637 4383 Telex : 8956007
INSTITUTE for Marine Environmental Research, Prospect Place The Hoe, Plymouth PL1 3DH Tel : 0752 21371
INSTITUTE for Medical Research & Occupational Health, 158 Mose Pijade, PO Box 291, Yu-41001, Zagreb, Yugoslavia
INSTITUTE for Policy Studies, 27 Clerkenwell Close, London EC1R 0AT Tel : 01.251 4976
INSTITUTE for Research into Mental & Multiple Handicap Ltd. 16 Fitzroy Square, London W1P 5HQ Tel : 01.387 9571
INSTITUTE for Science Technology, University Laboratory of Physiology, Parks Road, Oxford
INSTITUTE for Strategic Studies - see International Instiute for Strategic Studies
INSTITUTE for the Study of Conflict, 12-12a Golden Square, London W1R 3AF Tel : 01.439 7381
INSTITUTE for the Study of Drug Dependence, 3 Blackburn Road, London NW6 1XA Tel : 01.328 5541/2

INSTITUTE of Acoustics, University of Technology, Loughborough, Leics.LE11 3TU
INSTITUTE of Actuaries, 1 Staple Inn, High Holborn, London WC1V 7QL Tel : 01.242 6486
INSTITUTE of Administrative Management, 205 High Street Beckenham, Kent BR3 1BA Tel : 01.658 0171
INSTITUTE of Advanced Architectural Studies, University of York, The King's Manor, York YO1 2EP Tel : 0904 59861 X864
INSTITUTE of Advanced Legal Studies - see University of London Institute of Advanced Legal Studies
INSTITUTE of Advanced Motorists, Empire House, Chiswick High Road, London W4 5TJ Tel : 01.994 4403
INSTITUTE of Astronautics & Aeronautics, 1290 Ave of the Americas, New York 10019, USA
INSTITUTE of Bankers - distributed by Woodhead Faulkner (Publ.)Ltd.
INSTITUTE of Bankers in Scotland, 20 Rutland Square, Edinburgh EH1 2DE Tel : 031.229 9869
INSTITUTE of Biology, 41 Queens Gate, London SW7 5HU Tel : 01.589 9076/8
INSTITUTE of British Geographers, 1 Kensington Gore, London SW7 2AR Tel : 01.584 6371
INSTITUTE of Building - now called Chartered Institute of Building
INSTITUTE of Business Planning - distributed by IBD
INSTITUTE of Careers Officers, 2nd Floor, Old Board Chambers 37a High Street, Stourbridge, W.Midlands DY8 1TA Tel : 038 43 76464
INSTITUTE of Chartered Accountants, PO Box 433, Chartered Accountants Hall, Moorgate Place, London EC2P 2BJ Tel : 01.628 7060 Telex : 884443 - distributed by Macdonald & Evans (Publ.)Ltd.
INSTITUTE of Chartered Accountants in Scotland, 27 Queen Street, Edinburgh EH2 1LA Tel : 031.225 5673
INSTITUTE of Chartered Secretaries & Administrators - c/o Woodhead Faulkner(Publ.)Ltd.
INSTITUTE of Chartered Surveyors, 12 Great George Street, London SW1P 3AD
INSTITUTE of Chemical Engineers, 165-171 Railway Terrace Rugby, Warwicks. CV21 3HQ Tel : 0788 78214
INSTITUTE of Cost & Management Accountants, 63 Portland Place, London W1N 4AB Tel : 01.637 2311/4716
INSTITUTE of Development Studies, c/o University of Sussex Falmer, Brighton BN1 9RE Tel : 0273 606261 Telex : 877159
INSTITUTE of Directors, 116 Pall Mall, London SW1Y 5ED Tel : 01.839 1233
INSTITUTE of Economic Affairs, 2 Lord North Street, London SW1P 3LB Tel : 01.799 3745
INSTITUTE of Education Technology, Tuition & Counselling Research Group, Open University, Walton Hall, Milton Keynes MK7 6AA
INSTITUTE of Electrical & Electronics Engineers Inc., 445 Hoes Lane, Piscataway, New Jersey 08854, USA Tel : 201 981 1393
INSTITUTE of Employment Consultants Ltd., 6 Welbeck Street London W1M 7PB Tel : 01.486 6905/01.935 2631
INSTITUTE of Energy, 18 Devonshire Street, London W1N 2AU Tel : 01.580 7124
INSTITUTE of Export, World Trade Centre, London E1 9AA Tel : 01.488 4766
INSTITUTE of Family & Environmental Research 7a Kiderpore Avenue, London NW3
INSTITUTE of Fire Engineers, 148 New Walk, Leicester LE1 7QB Tel : 0533 553654
INSTITUTE of Fuel - now Institute of Energy
INSTITUTE of Geological Sciences, Exhibition Road, South Kensington, London SW7 2DE / 5 Princes Gate, London SW7 1QN Tel : 01.589 3444
INSTITUTE of Health Service Administrators, 75 Portland Place London W1N 4AN Tel : 01.580 5041
INSTITUTE of Heraldic & Genealogical Studies - see Achievements Ltd.
INSTITUTE of Housing, 12 Upper Belgrave Street, London SW1X 8BA Tel : 01.245 9933/7
INSTITUTE of Hydrology, Maclean Building, Crowmarsh Gifford Wallingford, Oxon. OX10 8BB Tel : 0491 38800
INSTITUTE of Incorporated Photographers, Amwell End, Ware Herts SG12 9HN Tel : 0920 4011
INSTITUTE of Information Scientists, Harvest House, 62 London Road, Reading, Berks RG1 5AS Tel : 0734 861345
INSTITUTE of Internal Auditors, 82z Portland Place, London W1N 3DH Tel : 01.580 0101
INSTITUTE of Labor & Industrial Relations, 504 E.Armory, University of Illinois, Urbana, Ill.61801, USA

INSTITUTE of Landscape Architects, 12 Carlton House Terrace London SW1Y 5AH Tel : 01.839 4044
INSTITUTE of Local Government Administrators, 127 Lexden Road, Colchester, Essex CO3 3RJ Tel : 0206 45212
INSTITUTE of Management Consultants, 23 Cromwell Place London SW7 2LG
INSTITUTE of Management Services, 1 Cecil Court, London Road, Enfield, Middx.EN2 6DD Tel : 01.363 7452
INSTITUTE of Manpower Studies, University of Sussex Mantell Building, Falmer, Brighton BN1 9RF Tel : 0273 686751
INSTITUTE of Marine Biochemistry, St.Fitticks Road, Aberdeen AB1 3RA Tel : 0224 875695
INSTITUTE of Marine Engineers, Marine Management(Holdings) Ltd., 76 Mark Lane, London EC3R 7JN Tel : 01.481 8493
INSTITUTE of Marital Studies, The Tavistock Centre, Belsize Lane, London NW3 5BA Tel : 01.435 7111
INSTITUTE of Marketing, Moor Hall, Cookham, Maidenhead Berks SL6 9ZH Tel : 06285 24922
INSTITUTE of Marketing Management, 205 High Street, Beckenham, Kent BR3 1BA
INSTITUTE of Medicine - distributed by Castle House
INSTITUTE of Municipal Treasurers & Accountants - now Chartered Institute of Public Finance & Accountancy
INSTITUTE of Noise Control Engineering, PO Box 3206, Arlington Branch, Poughkeepsie, New York 12603 USA
INSTITUTE of Oceanographic Sciences, Brook Road, Wormley Godalming, Surrey GU8 5UB Tel : 042 879 4141
INSTITUTE of Offshore Engineering, Heriot-Watt University, Edinburgh EH14 4AS Tel : 031.449 5111
INSTITUTE of Opthalmology, University of London, Judd Street, London WC1H 9QS Tel : 01.387 9621
INSTITUTE of Packaging, Fountain House, 1a Elm Park, Stanmore, Middx.HA7 4BZ Tel : 01.954 6277
INSTITUTE of Paper Chemistry, PO Box 1039, Appleton, Wisc. 54912, USA Tel : 414 734 9251
INSTITUTE of Personnel Management, IMP House, Camp Road Wimbledon, London SW19 4UW Tel : 01.946 9100
INSTITUTE of Petroleum, 61 New Cavendish Street, London W1M 8AR Tel : 01.636 1004
INSTITUTE of Physics, c/o Techno House, Redcliffe Way, Bristol BS1 6AX Tel : 0272 297481 Telex : 449149 - Journals orders to Blackhorse Road, Letchworth, Herts.SG6 1HN Tel : 04626 72555 - back issues distributed by Wm.Dawson & Sons Ltd.
INSTITUTE of Practitioners in Advertising, 44 Belgrave Square, London SW1X 8QS Tel : 01.235 7020 Telex : 918352
INSTITUTE of Practitioners in Work Study Organisation & Methods, 1 Cecil Court, London Road, Enfield, Middx.EN2 6DD
INSTITUTE of Public Administration, Hamilton House, Mabledon Place, London WC1H 9BD Tel : 01.388 0211
INSTITUTE of Public Administration, 57-61 Lansdowne Road, Dublin 4, Ireland Tel : 0001 686233
INSTITUTE of Purchasing & Supply, IPS House, High Street Ascot, Berks SL5 7HG Tel : 0990 23711
INSTITUTE of Quality Assurance, 54 Princes Gate, Exhibition Road, London SW7 2PG Tel : 01.584 9026
INSTITUTE of Race Relations, 247-249 Pentonville Road, London N1 9NG Tel : 01.837 0041 - distributed by Oxford University Press
INSTITUTE of Refrigeration, 76 Mill Lane, Carshalton, Surrey SM5 2JR Tel : 01.647 7033
INSTITUTE of Reprographic Technology, PO Box 101, Witham Essex CM8 1QS Tel : 0376 516297
INSTITUTE of Sales Management, 24 Warwick New Road, Leamington Spa, Warwicks. CV32 5JH Tel : 0926 25106/7
INSTITUTE of Shipping Economics, Am Dom 5a, D-2800 Bremen 1, W.Germany Tel : 0421 32 10 40
INSTITUTE of Supervisory Management, 22 Bare Street, Lichfield, Staffs.WS13 6LP Tel : 054 32 51346
INSTITUTE of Terrestrial Ecology, 68 Hills Road, Cambridge CB2 1LA Tel : 0223 69745/9 Telex : 817201
INSTITUTE of the Motor Industry, Fanshaws, Brickendon, Hertford SG13 8PG Tel : 099 286 282
INSTITUTE of Trading Standards, Trading Standards Dept., County Hall, St.Anne's Crescent, Lewes, E.Sussex BN7 1SW
INSTITUTE of Trading Standards Administration, Metropolitan House, 37 Victoria Avenue, Southend-on-Sea, Essex SS2 6DA
INSTITUTE of Vitreous Enammellers, Ripley, Nr.Derby DE5 3EB Tel : 0773 3136

INSTITUTION of Chemical Engineers, 165-171 Railway Terrace Rugby, Warwicks.CV21 3HQ Tel : 0788 78214 Telex : 311780
INSTITUTION of Civil Engineers, Thomas Telford Ltd., Marketing & Sales Dept., 1-7 Great George Street, London SW1P 3AA Tel : 01.222 9388
INSTITUTION of Electrical & Electronics Technician Engineers 2 Savoy Hill, London WC2R 0BS Tel : 01.836 3357
INSTITUTION of Electrical Engineers, Station House, Nightingale Road, Hitchin, Herts.SG5 1RJ Tel : 0462 53331
INSTITUTION of Electronic & Radio Engineers, 99 Gower Street London WC1E 6AZ Tel : 01.388 3071
INSTITUTION of Environmental Health Officers, Chadwick House, Rushworth Street, London SE1 0RB
INSTITUTION of Gas Engineers, 17 Grosvenor Crescent, London SW1X 7ES Tel : 01.245 9811
INSTITUTION of Gas Technology, Chicago 60611, Illinois, USA
INSTITUTION of Geologists, 2nd Floor, Geological Society Apartments, Burlington House, Piccadilly, London W1V 9HG Tel : 01.734 0751
INSTITUTION of Highway Engineers, 3 Lygon Place, Ebury Street, London SW1W 0JS
INSTITUTION of Mechanical Engineers, 1 Birdcage Walk, Westminster, London SW1H 9JJ Tel : 01.222 7899 Telex : 917944
INSTITUTION of Metallurgists, PO Box 471, 1 Carlton House Terrace, London SW1Y 5BE Tel : 01.839 1963
INSTITUTION of Mining & Metallurgy, 44 Portland Place London W1N 4BR Tel : 01.580 3802 Telex : 261410
INSTITUTION of Municipal Engineers, 25 Eccleston Square London SW1V 1NX Tel : 01.834 5082
INSTITUTION of Occupational Safety & Health, 222 Uppingham Road, Leicester LE5 0QG Tel : 0533 768424
INSTITUTION of Production Engineers, Rochester House, 66 Little Ealing Lane, London W5 4XX Tel : 01.579 9411
INSTITUTION of Structural Engineers, 11 Upper Belgrave Street London SW1X 8BH Tel : 01.235 4535
INSTITUTION of Water Engineers & Scientists, 31-33 High Holborn, London WC1V 6AX Tel : 01.831 6578
INSTITUTO de Ingeneeros de Minas, Alameda, B.O.Higgins, 1170 Off 911, Santiago, Chile
INSTITUTO Palin Inogico, Apartado 2UL, Lein, Spain
INSTRUMENT Society of America, 400 Stanwix Street, Pittsburgh Pennsylvania 15222, USA - distributed by John Wiley & Sons Ltd.
INSURANCE Institute of London, 20 Aldermanbury, London EC2V 7HY Tel : 01.606 5393
INSURANCE Technical Bureau, Terminal House, 52 Grosvenor Gardens, London SW1W 0AU Tel : 01.730 8847
INTEC Press Ltd., 54 Station Road East, Oxted, Surrey RH8 0PG Tel : 08833 6155 Telex : 95444
INTEC Publications, PO Box 15, Tadworth, Surrey KT20 6HQ Tel : 0737 833872
INTECO Corporation, 17 Bedford Square, London WC1 Tel : 01.637 9986
INTELLIGENCE International Ltd., 17 Rodney Road, Cheltenham Glos.GL50 1HX Tel : 0242 517774
INTELLIGENCE Publications(UK), 26 Meadow Lane, Sudbury Suffolk Tel : 0787 76374
INTER-ACTION Inprint, 15 Wilkin Street, London NW5 3NG Tel : 01.267 9421
INTERACTIVE Data, 80 Coleman Street, London EC2 Tel : 01.588 4807
INTER-AMERICAN Development Bank, 808 17th Street NW, Washington DC 20577, USA
INTERAUTO Publ.Ltd., Bercourt House, 51 York Road, Brentford Middx.TW8 0QP Tel : 01.560 3404 Telex : 936183
INTERAVIA S.A., Avenue Louis-Casai 86, CH-1216 Cointrin, Geneva, Switzerland
INTER-BANK Research Organisation, 32 City Road, London EC1Y 1AA Tel : 01.628 3070 Telex : 887440
INTERBOND Services Ltd., 56 Camden Road, London NW1 9LG Tel : 01.267 3823 Telex : 28905
INTERBOOK Ltd., 52 Manchester Street, London W1M 6DR Tel : 01.935 3441/3481
INTER COMMODITIES Ltd., 3 Lloyds Avenue, London EC3N 3DS Tel : 01.481 9827
INTER COMPANY Comparisons Ltd., 28-42 Banner Street, London EC1Y 8QE Tel : 01.253 3906
INTERCONTEX Publ.Ltd., 25 Manchester Square, London W1M 5AP Tel : 01.935 6136 Telex : 261479
INTERCONTINENTAL Book Productions, Berkshire House, Queen Street, Maidenhead, Berks SL6 1NF Tel : 0628 34433 Telex : 848036

INTERCRESCENT Publ.Co.Inc., POB 31413, Dallas, Texas
    75231, USA
INTEREUROPE Ltd., St.Peters Road, Maidenhead, Berks
    SL6 7QU Tel : 0628 34321 Telex : 848314
INTERFACE, National ZX80 & ZX81 Users' Club, 44-46 Earls
    Court Road, London W8 6EJ
INTERGOVERNMENTAL Maritime Consultative Organisation
    (IMCO), 101 Piccadilly, London W1V 0AE
    Tel : 01.499 9040 Telex : 23588
INTERMEDIATE Technology Publ.Ltd., 9 King Street, London
    WC2E 8HN Tel : 01.836 9434
INTERNATIONAL Aeradio Ltd., Hayes Road, Southall, Middx.
    UB2 5NJ Tel : 01.834 2411 Telex : 24114
INTERNATIONAL African Institute, 210 High Holborn, London
    WC1V 7BW Tel : 01.405 0351
INTERNATIONAL Agriculture Aviation Centre, c/o Cranfield
    Institute of Technology, Cranfield, Bedford
    MK43 0AL Tel : 0234 750141
INTERNATIONAL Air Transport Association, 26 Chemin de
    Joinville, PO Box 160, 1216 Cointrin, Geneva,
    Switzerland
INTERNATIONAL Association of Labour History Institute, c/o
    The Labour Party, Transport House, Smith Square
    London SW1
INTERNATIONAL Association of Technology, The Library of
    Chalmers University of Technology, S-4129
    Gothenburg, Sweden Tel : 031 81 01 00
    Telex : 2369
INTERNATIONALAtomic Energy Agency, Wagramerstrasse 5,
    PO Box 100, A-1400 Vienna, Austria
INTERNATIONAL Bee Research Association, Hill House,
    Gerrards Cross, Bucks SL9 0NR Tel : 0753 85011
INTERNATIONAL Book Distributors, 66 Wood Lane End,
    Hemel Hempstead, Herts.HP2 4RG
    Tel : 0442 58531 Telex : 82445
INTERNATIONAL Business Information KK, Izumiya Building
    1-1 Kojimachi 3-chome, Chiyoda-ku, Tokyo 102,
    Japan Tel : 03 230 2151 Telex : 78128117
INTERNATIONAL Carbide Data, 33 Oakhurst Aenue, East
    Barnet, Herts. EN4 8DN Tel : 01.368 4997
INTERNATIONAL Cargo Handling Co-ordination Association,
    (ICHCA), Abford House, 15 Wilton Road, London
    SW1V 1LX Tel : 01.828 3611 Telex : 261106G
INTERNATIONAL Chamber of Commerce, British National
    Committee, 103 New Oxford Street, London WC1A
    1QB Tel : 01.240 5558
INTERNATIONAL Chamber of Shipping - distributed by
    Witherby & Co.Ltd.
INTERNATIONAL Coffee Organisation, 22 Berners Street,
    London W1P 4DD Tel : 01.580 8595 Telex : 267659
INTERNATIONAL Communications, PO Box 261, Carlton House
    69 Great Queen Street, London WC2B 5BZ
    Tel : 01.404 4333
INTERNATIONAL Computer Programmes, 9000 Keystone Crossing
    Indianapolis, Indiana 46240, USA
INTERNATIONAL Computers Ltd., ICL House, Broadway,
    Letchworth, Herts. SG6 3PG Tel : 04626 5461 /
    ICL House, London SW15 1SW Tel : 01.788 7272
    Telex : 22971
INTERNATIONAL Consulting Associates Ltd., 1611 N.Kent
    Street, Arlington, VA 22209, USA
INTERNATIONAL Co-operative Alliance, 11 Upper Grosvenor
    Street, London W1X 9PA Tel : 01.499 5991
INTERNATIONAL Correspondence Schools Ltd., Intertext House
    Stewarts Road, London SW8 4UJ Tel : 01.622 9911
    Telex : 918658
INTERNATIONAL Council for Educational Development, 680 5th
    Avenue, New York 10019, USA
INTERNATIONAL Council of Nurses, PO Box 42, CH-1211
    Geneva 20, Switzerland
INTERNATIONAL Council of Scientific Unions, 51 Blvd.de
    Montmorency, 75016 Paris, France
INTERNATIONAL Council of Tanners, Leather Trade House
    9 St.Thomas Street, London SE1
    Tel : 01.407 1522
INTERNATIONAL Craft & Hobby Fair Ltd., 3 Rothesay Drive
    Highcliffe, Christchurch, Dorset BH23 4LB
    Tel : 04252 72711
INTERNATIONAL Crude Oil & Product Prices, c/o MEPEP,
    PO Box 4940, Nicosia, Cyprus
INTERNATIONAL Dance Teachers' Association Ltd., 76
    Bennett Road, Brighton BN2 5JL Tel : 0273 685652/3
INTERNATIONAL Data Corporation Europa - see IDC Europa
    Ltd.

INTERNATIONAL Defence & Aid Fund for Southern Africa,
    104 Newgate Street, London EC1A 7AP
    Tel : 01.606 6123
INTERNATIONAL Development Associates Inc., PO Box 3774,
    Wilmington, Del.19807, USA Tel : 215 388 1325
    Telex : 835409
INTERNATIONAL Development Centre - c/o Bowker
INTERNATIONAL Directory of Market Research Organisations,
    c/o Bridgewater House, 5-13 Great Suffolk Street
    London SE1 0NS Tel : 01.928 1200
INTERNATIONAL Drip Irrigation Association, c/o 3600 Gay Way
    Riverside, California 92504, USA
INTERNATIONAL Economic Association - distributed by
    Macmillan Publ.Ltd.
INTERNATIONAL Economic Publ.Ltd., 58 Haddington Road,
    Dublin 4, Ireland Tel : 0001 60272
INTERNATIONAL Federation for Documentation, 7 Hofweg,
    The Hague, The Netherlands
INTERNATIONAL Fluidics Services Ltd., 35-39 High Street,
    Kempston, Bedford MK42 7BT
INTERNATIONAL Food Information Service, Lane End House,
    Shinfield, Reading, Berks RG2 9BB
    Tel : 0734 883895 Telex : 847204
INTERNATIONAL Forest Science Consultancy, 21 Biggar Road
    Silverburn, Penicuik EH26 9LQ Tel : 0968 75112/
    77790
INTERNATIONAL Graphic Press Ltd., Danes Inn House, 263-
    265 Strand, London WC2 Tel : 01.580 8672
INTERNATIONAL Hydrographic Bureau, 7 Ave.President J.F.
    Kennedy, BP 345 MC Monaco, Principality of Monaco
    Tel : (93) 50 65 87 Telex : 469870
INTERNATIONAL Ideas Inc., 1627 Sprace Street, Philadelphia
    PA 19102, USA
INTERNATIONAL Institute for Economic Research, 2 Bedford
    Row, London WC1R 4BU Tel : 01.242 9238
INTERNATIONAL Institute for Environment & Development,
    10 Percy Street, London W1P 0DR Tel : 01.580 7656
INTERNATIONAL Institute for Land Reclamation & Improvement
    POB 45, 6700 AA Wageningen, The Netherlands
    Telex : 75230
INTERNATIONAL Institute for Strategic Studies, 23 Tavistock
    Street, London WC2E 7NQ Tel : 01.379 7676
INTERNATIONAL Institute of Communications, Tavistock House
    East, Tavistock Square, London WC1H 9LG
INTERNATIONAL Institute of Welding, 5a Princes Gate,
    Exhibition Road, London SW7 2PG Tel : 01.584 8556
INTERNATIONAL Laboratory Publ., 1 Woodside Road, Amersham
    Oxford
INTERNATIONAL Labour Office, 96-98 Marsham Street, London
    SW1 Tel : 01.828 6401
INTERNATIONAL Law Association, 3 Paper Buildings, Temple,
    London EC4Y 7EU Tel : 01.353 2904
INTERNATIONAL Learning Systems Inc., 1715 Connecticut Ave.
    NW, Washington DC 20009, USA
INTERNATIONAL Loss Control Institute, Highway 78, PO Box
    345, Loganville, GA30249, USA Tel : 404 466 2208
    - distributed by ROSPA
INTERNATIONAL Maritime Organisation, 4 Albert Embankment,
    London SE1 7SR Tel : 01.735 7611 Telex : 23588
INTERNATIONAL Marketing & Economic Services, Hurst House,
    157 Walton Road, East Molesey, Surrey KT8 0DX
    Tel : 01.941 5024 Telex : 932689
INTERNATIONAL Meehanite Metal Co.Ltd., Meerion House, 38
    Albert Road North, Reigate, Surrey RH2 9EH
    Tel : 073 72 44786 Telex : 28700
INTERNATIONAL Organisation for Standardisation - distributed
    by BSI
INTERNATIONAL Organisation of Consumers Unions, 9
    Emmastraat, 2595 EG The Hague, The Netherlands
    Tel : 47 63 31 Telex : 33561
INTERNATIONAL Planned Parenthood Federation, 18-20 Lower
    Regent Street, London SW1Y 4PW Tel : 01.839 2911
    Telex : 919573
INTERNATIONAL Planning Information, 134 Holland Park Avenue
    London W11 4VE Tel : 01.221 0998 Telex : 22861
INTERNATIONAL Potash Institute, PO Box CH-3048, Worblaufeu
    Bern, Switzerland
INTERNATIONAL Press Ltd., 669 Yonge Street, Toronto M4Y 2A7
    Canada
INTERNATIONAL Publishing Corp.Ltd., Kings Reach Tower,
    Stamford Street, London SE1 9LS Tel : 01.261 5000
INTERNATIONAL Railway Journal, PO Box 8, Falmouth, Cornwall
    Tel : 0326 313945

INTERNATIONAL Reports Inc., 200 Park Avenue South, New York 10003, USA Tel : 212 477 0003
INTERNATIONAL Research & Development Co.Ltd., Fossway Newcastle on Tyne NE6 2YD Tel : 0632 650451
INTERNATIONAL Research Directing, 6th Floor, Northwest House, Marylebone Road, London NW1 Tel : 01.723 7276
INTERNATIONAL Resource Development Inc., 30 High Street Norwalk, CT 06851, USA Tel : 203 866 6914 Telex : 643452
INTERNATIONAL Scholarly Book Services, 8 William Way Letchworth, Herts. SG6 2HG Tel : 046 26 3742
INTERNATIONAL Scientific Communications, 3 Woodside Road Amersham, Oxford
INTERNATIONAL Society for Horticultural Science, De Dreyen 6, 6703 BC Wageningen, Ther Netherlands
INTERNATIONAL Solar Energy Society, 19 Albermarle Street London W1X 3HA Tel : 01.493 6601
INTERNATIONAL Surveys Ltd., 20 Eglinton Avenue East, Toronto 12, Ontario M4P 1B2, Canada
INTERNATIONAL Tanker Owners Pollution Federation Ltd., Staple Hall, Stonehouse Court, 87-90 Houndsditch London EC3A 7AX Tel : 01.621 1255 Telex : 887514
INTERNATIONAL Technical Information Institute, Toranomon-tachikawa Building, 1-6-5 Nishishimbashi, Minatoku Tokyo, Japan
INTERNATIONAL Telecommunication Union, Place des Nations CH-1211 Geneva 20, Switzerland
INTERNATIONAL Textbook Co.Ltd., Wester Cleddens Road, Bishopbriggs, Glasgow G64 2NZ Tel : 041.772 2311
INTERNATIONAL Thomson Publ.Ltd., 93 Goswell Road London EC1V 7QA Tel : 01.253 9355
INTERNATIONAL Tin Council, Haymarket House, 1 Oxendon Street, London SW1Y 4EQ Tel : 01.930 0321
INTERNATIONAL Tin Research Institute, Fraser Road, Perivale Greenford, Middx.UB8 7AQ Tel : 01.997 4254
INTERNATIONAL Trade Centre UNCTAD/GATT, 54-56 Rue de Montbrillant, CH-1202 Geneva, Switzerland Tel : 34 60 21 Telex : 289052
INTERNATIONAL Trade Publ.Ltd., Queensway House, 2 Queensway, Redhill, Surrey RH1 1QS Tel : 0737 68611
INTERNATIONAL Union for Conservation of Nature & Natural Resources, CH-1196 Gland, Switzerland Tel : 022 64 71 81
INTERNATIONAL Union for Pure & Applied Chemistry - distributed by Pergamon Press
INTERNATIONAL Union of Crystallography, 5 Abbey Square Chester CH1 2HU Tel : 0244 42878
INTERNATIONAL Union of Public Transport, Avenue de l'Uruguay 19, B-1050 Brussels, Belgium
INTERNATIONAL Universities Press, Simon & Schuster, 239 Park Avenue S, New York 10003, USA
INTERNATIONAL Wheat Council, Haymarket House, 28 Haymarket London SW1Y 4SS
INTERNATIONAL Who's Who of the Arab World Ltd., 2 South Audley Street, London W1Y 5DQ Tel : 01.409 1525 Telex : 268663
INTERNATIONAL Youth Hostel Federation, Midland Bank Chambers, Howardsgate, Welwyn Garden City, Herts. AL8 6BT
INTERPHARM Press Inc., PO Box 530, Prairie View, IL 60069, USA
INTERPRESS Ltd., 51a-53a Chipstead Valley Road, Coulsdon, Surrey CR3 2RB Tel : 01.668 1306
INTERSCIENCE Publ.(Division of John Wiley Ltd.), Baffins Lane Chichester, W.Sussex PO19 1UD Tel : 0243 784531 Telex : 86290
INTERTEXT Publ.Ltd. - see Blackie & Son Ltd.
INTER-VARSITY Press, Norton Street, Nottingham NG7 3HR Tel : 0602 781054
INTRA-MARKET Analysis Ltd., 73 New Bond Street, London W1Y 9DB Tel : 01.493 3321 Telex : 261376
INVERESK Research Intl., Musselburgh, Midlothian EH21 7UB
INVEST in Britain Bureau, Dept.of Industry, Kingsgate House 66-74 Victoria Street, London SW1E 6SJ Tel : 01.212 6251
INVESTMENT Evaluator Ltd., Malcolm House, 12 Orange Street London WC2
INVESTORS Chronicle, Bracken House, Cannon Street, London EC4P 4BY Tel : 01.248 8000
INVOTECH Intl.Ltd., Nicholson House, Maidenhead, Berks SL6 1LD
IOLAIRE Marketing Services, PO Box 1, Portree, Isle of Skye Scotland
IQRA Publications, 52a Colegate, Norwich NR3 1DD Tel : 0603 23337

IRELAND Stationery Office(Dublin), St.Martins House, Waterloo Road, Dublin 4, Rep.of Ireland
IRELAND's Department of Foreign Affairs - distributed by Colin Smythe Ltd.
IRISH Academic Press, Kill Lane, Kill-o-the-Grange, Blackrock, Dublin, Rep.of Ireland Tel : 0001 850922
IRISH Government Publications, GPO Arcade, Dublin 1, Rep.of Ireland
IRISH Humanities Centre - distributed by Colin Smythe Ltd.
IRISH Management Institute, Sandyford Road, Dublin 4 Tel : 0001 983911
IRISH Messenger Publications, 37 Lower Leeson Street, Dublin 2, Rep.of Ireland Tel : 0001 767491/2
IRISH Productivity Centre, IPC House, 35-39 Shelbourne Road Dublin 4, Rep.of Ireland
IRISH University Press - distributed by Irish Academic Press
IRON & Steel Institute - see Metals Society
IRON & Steel Institute of Japan - distributed by Applied Science Publishers
IRVINGTON Publ.Inc. - distributed by John Wiley & Sons Ltd.
Richard D.IRWIN - c/o TABS
IRWIN Inc., c/o Feffer & Simons, Rijinhade 170, Box 112, Weesp The Netherlands
ISLAMIC Cultural Centre, 146 Park Road, London NW8 7RG Tel : 01.724 3363
ISLAMIC Foundation, 223 London Road, Leicester LE2 1ZE Tel : 0533 700725
ISLAMIC Information Services Ltd., Trafalgar House, 11 Waterloo Place, London SW1Y 4AS Tel : 01.930 8081/2
ISLAMIC Research Institute, PO Box 1035, Islamabad, Pakistan
ISOPUBLIC S.A., Witikonerstrasse 297, 8053 Zurich, Switzerland Tel : 01 53 72 72 Telex : 56153
ISSUES Publications, (University of Bradford), c/o 27 Clerkenwell Close, London EC1R 0AT Tel : 01.251 4976
ISSUING Houses Association, Granite House, 101 Cannon Street London EC4N 5BA Tel : 01.283 7334
ITEM Ltd., Centre House, Windmill Road, Fulmer, Berks SL3 6HD Tel : 028 16 3252
ITHACA Press, 13 Southwark Street, London SE1 1RQ Tel : 01.407 0393

J

J&M Publications Ltd., 1st Floor, 3 Crescent Place, Cheltenham, Glos. Tel : 0242 584203
J.E.Society, 49 Cadogan Square, London SW1X 0JB
JICNARS - see Joint Industry Committee for National Readership Surveys
J.K.Publishers, 23 Denne Road, Horsham, W.Sussex RH12 1JF Tel : 0403 50726
J.M.Books, The Corderries, Chalford Mill, Glos.
JACKDAW Publ.Ltd., 30 Bedford Square, London WC1B 3EL Tel : 01.636 5764/9395 - distributed by Chatto, Bodley Head & Cape Services Ltd.
JACKSON Moreley Publ.Ltd., 13 New Burlington Street, London W1 Tel : 01.234 4611
JACKSON Publications, 36 Moat Road, Loughborough, Leics. LE11 3PN
John I.JACOBS plc, 19 Great Winchester Street, London EC2N 2DB Tel : 01.588 1255
JAEGER & Waldman, POB 1103 34, D-6100 Darmstadt, W.Germany
JAGUAR Books, 3 Carlisle Place, London SW1 Tel : 01.834 1174
JAI Press Inc., 36 Sherwood Place, PO Box 1678, Greenwich Connecticut 06836-1678, USA Tel : 203 661 7602 - distributed by Eurospan Ltd.
JAICON Press Ltd. - distributed by IBD
Arthur JAMES Ltd., The Drift, Greenhill Park Road, Evesham, Worcs.WR11 4NW Tel : 0386 6566
JAMES & James, Cockburnhill Hall, Balerno, Midlothian - distributed by Godfrey Cave Associates, 42 Bloomsbury Street, London WC1B 3QJ Tel : 01.636 9177
JAMIESON, Davies & Associates, Great Chesterford, Saffron Walden, Essex CB10 1NR
JANES Publishing Co.Ltd., 5th Floor, 238 City Road, London EC1V 2PU Tel : 01.251 9281 Telex : 23168
JAPAN Company Handbook - see Oriental Economist
JAPAN Economic Research Center, Wikkei Building No.9-5, Otemachi, Chiyoda-ku, 1-chome, Tokyo, Japan
JAPAN Information, Kinokuniya Publ.Service of Japan Co., Rador House, 93-97 Regent Street, London W1
JAPAN Publ.Trading Co.Ltd., PO Box 5030, Tokyo International Japan - distributed by IBD
JAPAN Society of Civil Engineers, Yotsuya 1-chome, Shinjukee-ku, Tokyo 160, Japan
JAPAN Textile, Osaka, Senleur, Osaka, Japan

JAPAN Yellow Pages Ltd., St.Bldg.6-9 Lidabashi 4-Chome, Chiyoda-Ku, Tokyo 102, Japan Tel : (03) 239 3501
JARROLD Colour Publications, Barrack Street, Norwich NR2 1JF Tel : 0603 60211 Telex : 97497
JEDERMANN Verlag, Dr Otto Pfeffer, Postfach 103140, 6900 Heidelburg 1, W.Germany
JENCONS (Scientific)Ltd., Cherrycourt Way Industrial Estate, Stanbridge Road, Leighton Buzzard, Beds.LU7 8UA Tel : 0525 372010 Telex : 82164
Gwilym JENKINS & Partners Ltd., St.Leonard's House, St. Leonardgate, Lancaster LA1 1NN Tel : 0524 61831
JENKINS Publ.Co., The Pemberton Press, Box 2085, Austin. Texas 76768, USA Tel : 512 444 6616
E.A.JENSON, 39 Withdean Crescent, Brighton BN1 6WD Tel : 0273 501079
JEWISH Chronicle Publ., 25 Furnival Street, London EC4A 1JT Tel : 01.405 9252 - distributed by Wentworth Book Co.
JOBSON's Publ., 13 Wentworth Avenue, GPO Box 5338, Sydney NSW 2001, Australia
JOELMEAD Ltd., 636 Lansdowne Place, Hove, E.Sussex BN3 1FL Tel : 0273 773174
John HOPKINS University Press - distributed by CCJ Ltd. / IBD
R.H.JOHNS Ltd., 22 Mill Parade, Newport, Gwent NPT 2TH Tel : 0633 66906/7
Walter J.JOHNSON Inc., 355 Chestnut Street, Norwood NJ 07648, USA
JOHNSON Publ.Ltd., 11-14 Stanhope Mews West, London SW7 Tel : 01.373 8543 - distributed by Trade Counter Ltd.
JOHNSON Reprint Co.Ltd., 24-28 Oval Road, London NW1 7DX Tel : 01.267 4466/01.300 0155 Telex : 25775
JOHNSTON & Bacon Books Ltd., PO Box 1, Stirling Tel : 0786 84867
JOHNSTON Green & Co.(Publ.) Ltd., 27 Hamilton Drive, Glasgow G12 8DN Tel : 041.339 2711 - orders to J.B.Thomson, 12 Canal Terrace, Paisley, Renfrewshire PA1 2HS
JOHNSTON International Publ.Group, 51-53 Gray's Inn Road London WC1X 8PP Tel : 01.242 2202
JOINT Industry Committee for National Readership Surveys, 44 Belgrave Square, London SW1X 8QS
JOINT Press & Publications Co., 69-71 Monmouth Street, London WC2
JOINT University Company for Soc.& Public Administration, Hamilton House, Mabledon Place, London WC1H 9BD Tel : 01.388 0211
John JONES(Cardiff)Ltd. - ceased trading 1980 - many titles stocked by Welsh Books Centre
Peter JONES, Audley House, 11 Margaret Street, London W1N 8AT Tel : 01.580 3866
JONES Yarrell & Co.Ltd., 227-239 Tooley Street, London SE1 2PA Tel : 01.225 6255
JONES-SANDS Publishing, c/o 26 Exhall Green, Exhall, Coventry CV7 9GL
JORDAN Dataquest - now Jordan & Sons (Surveys)Ltd.
JORDAN & Sons(Surveys)Ltd., Jordan House, 47 Brunswick Place, London N1 6EE Tel : 01.253 3030 Telex : 261010
Michael JOSEPH Ltd., 44 Bedford Square, London WC1B 3DU Tel : 01.323 3200 Telex : 21322 - distributed by TBL Book Service Ltd.
JOSSEY Bass, 28 Banner Street, London EC1Y 8QE Tel : 01.253 1516 - distributed by Sage
JOURNAL of Commerce & Shipping Telegraph Ltd., 213 Tower Building, 22 Water Street, Liverpool L3 1LN Tel : 051.236 4511 Telex : 627772
JOURNAL of Educational Administration & History, Room 14 Parkinson Court, The University, Leeds LS2 9JT Tel : 0532 31751 X6159
JOURNEYMEN Press, 97 Ferme Park Road, Crouch End, London N8 9SA Tel : 01.348 9261/01.253 2659 Telex : 25247 - distributed by Central Books Ltd.
E.E.JUDGE & Sons Inc., PO Box 866, Westminster, MD21157, USA
JUNCTION Books, 15 St.John's Hill, London SW11 Tel : 01.223 8200
D.W.JUNK, PO Box 13713, 2501 ES The Hague, The Netherlands - distributed by Kluwer Academic Publ.
JUNIPER Press, 22 Hyde Street, Winchester, Hants. Tel : 0962 64213
JUNIUS Publ.Ltd., 38 Electric Avenue, London SW9 8JR Tel : 01.274 3951
JUPITER Books(London)Ltd., 167 Hermitage Road, Harringay, London N4 1LZ Tel : 01.800 6601/4

JURISPUBLICATIONS Ltd., 44 London Wall, London EC2M 5TB
JURY Publ.Ltd. - in liquidation
JUSTICE, 95a Chancery Lane, London WC2A 1DT Tel : 01.405 6018
JUTA & Co.Ltd., PO Box 30, Cape Town, South Africa Tel : Cape Town 711181 - general distribution by Bailey Bros.& Swinfen Ltd., law & textbooks distributed by Hammick, Sweet & Maxwell Ltd.

K

K.Books, Waplington Hall, Allerthorpe, York Tel : 075 92 2142
K&R Books Ltd., Edlington Hall, Edlington, Horncastle, Lincs. Tel : 065 82 3383
K.B.Publications & Tourist Publications, 115 North Lane, East Preston, Sussex Tel : 090 62 73494
KC Publications, Box 14883, 2901 Industrial Road, Las Vegas Nevada 89114, USA Tel : 702 731 3123
K.R.P.Publ.Ltd., 26 Meadow Lane, Sudbury, Suffolk CO10 6TD Tel : 0787 76374
KSL Publications, Ballards, Knotting Green, Bedford MK44 1AA Tel : 0234 781224
Jeff KAHANE, 27 Clerkenwell Close, London EC1R 0AT Tel : 01.251 4976
KAHN & Averill, 21 Pennard Mansions, Goldhawk Road, London W12 8DL Tel : 01.743 3278
KAIMAN & Polon Inc., 456 Sylvan Avenue, Englewood Cliffs, NJ07632, USA
S.KARGER - distributed by John Wiley & Sons Ltd.
Michael KATAMKA Ltd., 103 Stanmore Hill, Stanmore, Middx. HA7 3BZ Tel : 01.954 0490
KAWABATA Press, Knill Cross House, Hr Anderton Road, Millbrook, Torpoint, Cornwall
K.&G.KAY Publishers, Horizon House, 5 Victoria Drive, Bognor Regis, W.Sussex PO21 2RH Tel : 02433 21772/29421
Richard KAY Publications, 80 Sleaford Road, Boston, Lincs. PE21 8EU Tel : 0205 64423
KAYE & Ward Ltd., The Windmill Press, Kingswood, Tadworth Surrey KT20 6TG Tel : 0737 833511 Telex : 947458
KEELER Instruments Ltd., 21-27 Marylebone Lane, London W1M 6DS Tel : 01.935 8512
KEESINGS Publications, Longman Group Journal Division, Longman House, Burnt Mill, Harlow, Essex CM20 2JE Tel : 0279 26721
KEGAN, Paul Trench Trubner Ltd. - see Routledge & Kegan Paul Ltd.
KELLY's Directories Ltd., Windsor Court, East Grinstead House, East Grinstead, W.Sussex RH19 1XB Tel : 0342 26972 Telex : 95127
KEMBLE Press Ltd., PO Box 44, Banbury, Oxon.OX15 4EQ Tel : 0295 61190
KEMPS Group(Printers & Publ.)Ltd., 1-5 Bath Street, London EC1V 9QA Tel : 01.253 4761 - orders to Bowker Publ.Co.Ltd.
KENBE Reproductions, 11 Bourne Road, Soton, Hants.
KENDALL Hunt, 2460 Kerper Bd, Dubuque, IA 52001, USA
KENEDY Hudson Ltd., 8 Dury Lane, Solihull, W.Midlands B91 3BD Tel : 021.704 3301/2
J.G.KENNEDY & Co.Ltd., 22 Methuen Park, London N10 2JS Tel : 01.883 5533 Telex : 8952838
KENNEDY Brothers Publ.Ltd., Healey Works, Goulbourne Street, Keighley, W.Yorks BD21 1PN Tel : 0535 600714
KENNIKAT Press Inc., 90 South Bayles Avenue, Port Washington NY 11050, USA - orders to Dunellen Press
KENNY's Bookshop & Art Galleries Ltd., High Street, Galway, Ireland Tel : 091 62739
KENT County Council, County Hall, Maidstone, Kent Tel : 0622 671411 Telex : 965212/95356
H.KENT Ltd., 135 South Street, Bishops Stortford, Herts. Tel : 0279 5406
KENT State University Press, Kent, Ohio 44242, USA - distributed by European Book Service
KENTUCKY University Press - distributed by IBD
KENYON-Deane Ltd., 129 St.John's Hill, London SW11 1TD Tel : 01.223 3472
KERRYMAN Ltd., Clash Industrial Estate, Tralee, Co.Kerry Eire Tel : Tralee 21666 Telex : 28100 / c/o Independent Newspapers Ltd., Aitken House, 118 Fleet Street, London EC4A 2BA Tel : 01.353 9009
KERSHAW Publ.Co., 109 Great Russell Street, London WC1B 3ND Tel : 01.580 1862

A.S.KERSWILL Ltd., Leeder House, Erskine Road, London NW3 3AJ Tel : 01.586 0135
KESTREL Books - see Penguin Books Ltd.
KETER Publ.Ltd., Israel - distributed by Jewish Chronicle Publications
KETTLEWELL Transport Information Trade Services, Mill House, Station Road, Eastville, Boston, Lincs. PE22 8LS Tel : 020 584 377
KEY Book Service Inc., 425 Asylum Street, Bridgeport, Conn.06610, USA
KEYDEX Publishers(Unitoken Ltd.), Eyot House, Walton Lane, Weybridge, Surrey KT13 8LX Tel : 0932 48586
KEYNOTE Publ.Ltd., 28-42 Banner Street, London EC1Y 8QE Tel : 01.253 3006
KEYSTONE Press Agency Ltd., 52-62 Holborn Viaduct, London EC1A 2FE Tel : 01.236 3331/4
KEYSER Ullmann Ltd., 25 Milk Street, London EC2V 8JE Tel : 01.606 7070
KIBBLE Books, 27 Clerkenwell Close, London EC1R 0AT Tel : 01.251 4976
W.KIMBER & Co.Ltd., Godolphin House, 22a Queen Anne's Gate, London SW1H 9AE Tel : 01.222 7684/6
KIME's International Law Directory Ltd., 170 Sloane Street, London SW1X 9QG
Henry KIMPTON Publishers, 205 Great Portland Street, London W1N 6LR Tel : 01.580 6381
KIMES Development Ltd., Woodcote Grove, Ashley Road, Epsom, Surrey KT18 5BW Tel : 03727 26140
James F.KING, 20 Haldane Terrace, Newcastle upon Tyne
KING Edward's Hospital Fund for London, c/o Pitman Medical Ltd., Kings Fund Centre, 126 Albert Street London NW1 7NF Tel : 01.267 6111
KING Features, 235 East 45th Street, New York, NY 10017, USA
KING Publications Ltd., 6-7 Great Chapel Street, London W1V 4BR Tel : 01.734 9452
KINGFISHER Books Ltd., Elsley Court, 20-22 Great Titchfield Street, London W1P 7AD Tel : 01.631 0878 Telex : 27725
KINGFISHER Publ.Ltd., Newtown Street, Woodford, Northants. Tel : 080 12 4301
KINGSCLERE Publications, 11 Swan Street, Kingsclere, Newbury, Berks Tel : 0635 298839
KINGSMEAD Press, Watermead, Nailsea Wall, Kenn Pier, Clevedon, Avon BS21 6UE
KINGSMOOR Publications Ltd., 9 Market Street, Harlow Tel : 0279 29731
KINGSTON Publications, The Old Manse, Mevagissey, St. Austell, Cornwall PL26 6TQ Tel : 072 684 2401
KINGSWAY Publications Ltd., Lottbridge Drive, Eastbourne E.Sussex BN23 6NT Tel : 0323 27454 Telex : 877415
KINGSWOOD Educational Services, 1 Headley Road, Grayshott, Surrey GU26 6LE Tel : 042873 4939
KINGSWOOD Publications Ltd., Granville House, St.Peters Street, Winchester, Hants. Tel : 0962 67603
KITE Books, 3 Newton Grove, Bedford Park, London W4 Tel : 01.994 3399 / 135 South Street, Bishops Stortford, Herts. Tel : 0279 54060
KIVER Communications, 149-155 Ewell Road, Surbiton, Surrey
B.KLEIN Publications, PO Box 8503, Coral Springs, Florida 33065, USA Tel : 305 752 1708
Ernst KLETT Verlag, Postfach 809, D-7000 Stuttgart 1, West Germany Tel : 0711 66720 Telex : 721715
Charles H.KLINE & Co.Inc., 330 Passaic Avenue, Fairfield New Jersey 07006, USA Tel : 201 227 6262 Telex : 139170
KLINKHARDT & Biermann, Rosenheimer Strasse 12, D-8000 München 80, West Germany Tel : 089 448 77 48
KLUWER Academic Publ.Group, Kamerlingh Onnesweg 7-11, PO Box 989, 3300 AZ Dordrecht, The Netherlands Tel : 078 178222 Telex : 20083
KLUWER Business Books, PO Box 23, Deventer, The Netherlands
KLUWER General Services, Lange Voorhout 9-11, The Hague, The Netherlands
KLUWER Harrap Handbooks - now Kluwer Publ.Ltd.
KLUWER Law & Taxation Publishers - distributed by Kluwer Academic Publ.Group
KLUWER Publ.Ltd., 1 Harlequin Avenue, Great West Road, Brentford, Middx.TW8 9EW Tel : 01.568 6441/7
Charles KNIGHT Ltd., c/o Benn Publ.Ltd., Sovereign Way, Tonbridge, Kent TN9 1RW Tel : 0732 364422
KNITTING International, Eastern Boulevard, Leicester LE2 7BW Tel : 0533 548271
Alfred A.KNOPF - distributed by European Book Service
KNOW Future, 27 Clerkenwell Close, London EC1R 0AT Tel : 01.251 4976

KNOWLEDGE Industry Publications Inc., 701 Westchester Avenue, White Plains, New York 10604, USA - distributed by Eurospan Ltd.
KODAK Ltd., PO Box 66, Hemel Hempstead, Herts. HP1 1JU - distributed by Patrick Stephens Ltd.
KODANSHA International, 12-21 Otowa 2-chome, Bunkyo-ku, Tokyo 112, Japan - distributed by IBD
KOGAN Page Ltd., 120 Pentonville Road, London N1 9JN Tel : 01.837 7851/4
KOHLER & Coombes Ltd., 12 Horsham Road, Dorking, Surrey RH4 2JL Tel : 0306 81532
Verlag W.KOHLHAMMER GmbH, Augsburger Strasse 722, 7000 Stuttgart 61, West Germany
KOLISKO Archive Publications, 8 Albemarle Road, Bournemouth Dorset BH3 7LZ Tel : 0202 519282
KOMPASS Publ.Ltd., Windsor Court, East Grinstead House, East Grinstead, W.Sussex RH19 1XD Tel : 0342 26972 Telex : 95127
KONA Publications Ltd., 335 City Road, London EC1V 1LJ Tel : 01.278 6914
KONINKLYKE Fabrieken, Posthumus BV, Winkel, St.Lucienstweg 25, Amsterdam, The Netherlands
KOREA Directory Co., CPO Box 3955, Seoul 100, Korea
KOREAN Traders Association, World Trade Centre, Chung-kic, Seoul, Korea
KORN/Kerry Intl.Ltd., 2-4 King Street, St.James, London SW1Y 6QL Tel : 01.930 5524
KOSEI Publ.Co. - distributed by IBD
R.M.KOSSOFF & Assocs.Inc., 10 Rockefeller Plaza, New York 10020, USA Tel : 212 246 4035 Telex : 426832
KOZMIK Press Centre, 48a Astonville Street, London SW18 5AL Tel : 01.874 8218
Karl KRAMER Verlag, Schulze-Delitzsch-Strasse 15, D-7000 Stuttgart 80, West Germany Tel : 0711 610700
Verlag Waldeman KRAMER, Bornheimen, Landwihe 579, Postfach 600445, D-6000 Frankfurt-am-Main 60, W.Germany
KRAUSHAR & Eassie, 20 Buckingham Street, London WC2N 6EE Tel : 01.839 3276
KRAUS-Thomson Organization, 27 Red Lion Street, London WC1R 4PS Tel : 01.404 3055
R.E.KRIEGER, 645 New York Avenue, Huntington, New York 11743, USA - distributed by Global Book Resources
KRISHNAMURTI Foundation Trust Ltd., 24 Southend Road, Beckenham, Kent BR3 1SD Tel : 01.650 7023
KUGLER Medical Publ., PO Box 516, Amsteleevn 1134, The Netherlands
The KYLIN Press, Darbonne House, High Street, Waddesdon, Nr.Aylesbury, Bucks Tel : 0296 651 411

L

LAAS International, 39 Great Fox Meadow, Doddinghurst, Brentwood, Essex CM15 0AU - distributed by The Aviation Hobby Shop, 4 Horton Parade, Horton Road, West Drayton, Middx.
LAMSAC - see Local Authorities Management Services & Computer Committee
LINSAC, 68 Barker Road, Linthorpe, Middlesbrough, Cleveland TS5 5ES
L.P.Enterprises, 8-11 Cambridge House, Cambridge Road, Barking, Essex IG11 8NT
L.S.P.Books Ltd., 8 Farncombe Street, Farncombe, Godalming, Surrey GU7 3AY Tel : 048 68 28622 Telex : 919101
LA Haule Books Ltd., West Lodge, La Haule, Jersey, Channel Islands Tel : 0534 44957
LABELS & Labelling, 10 Torrington Drive, Potters Bar, Herts EN6 5HR Tel : 0707 56828
LABORATORY Animals Ltd., 1 Thrifts Mead, Theydon Bois, Essex CM16 7NF
LABORATORY of the Government Chemist, Cornwall House, Stamford Street, London SE1 9NQ
LABOUR Party, 150 Walworth Road, London SE17
LABOUR Research Department, 78 Blackfriars Road, London SE1 8HF Tel : 01.928 3649
LACY (Hylton)Publ.Ltd., Dial House, 6 Park Street, Windsor Berks SL4 1UU Tel : 07535 69777
LADYBIRD Books Ltd., PO Box 12, Beeches Road, Loughborough Leics.LE11 2NQ Tel : 0509 268021 Telex : 341347
G.H.LAKE & Co.Ltd., 33 Station Road, Bexhill-on-Sea, E.Sussex TN40 1RG Tel : 0424 211908
H.K.LAKE & Associates, 4500 Campus Drive, Suite 348, Newport Beach, CA 92660, USA Tel : 714 846 9402 Telex : 678401

LAKE District Special Planning Board, National Park Office,
    Busher Walk, Kendal, Cumbria CA9 4RQ
    Tel : 0539 24555
LAKELAND Paperbacks, 1 Bath Street, London EC1V 9LB
    Tel : 01.251 2925 Telex : 262364 - orders to Unit 14,
    Trident Industrial Estate, Pindar Road, Hoddesdon,
    Herts Tel : 0992 42033
LAMBEG Industrial Research Association, Research Institute,
    Lambeg, Lisburn, Co.Antrim, N.Ireland BT27 4RJ
    Tel : 023 82 2255
LAMBERT Publ.Inc., 1030 Fifteenth Street NW, Washington DC
    20005, USA Tel : 202 682 1111 Telex : 248597
The LAMP Press, 26 Bothwell Street, Glasgow G2 6PA
LANCASHIRE & Cheshire Antiquarian Society, c/o Portico Library
    57 Mosley Street, Manchester 2 Tel : 061.236 6785
Stephen & Jean LANCE Publications, Brook House, Mint Street,
    Godalming, Surrey GU7 1HE Tel : 04868 22184
The LANCET, 7 Adam Street, Adelphi, London WC2N 6AD
    Tel : 01.836 7228
Jay LANDESMAN Ltd., 159 Wardour Street, London W1
    Tel : 01.439 1643 - distributed by Kogan Page Ltd.
Allen LANE, Bath Road, Harmondsworth, Middx.UB7 0D7
    Tel : 01.759 5722 Telex : 933349
LANE Publ.Co. - c/o TABS
P.LANG Verlag - distributed by Bowker
LANGE Medical Publ., Drawer Los Altos, California 94022,
    USA Tel : 415 948 4526 - distributed by Proost &
    Brandt Distribution
LANGESCHEIDT Universal - distributed by Hodder & Stoughton
LANGEWIESCHE, Postfach 1327, D-6240 Konigstein im Taunus,
    West Germany
LANGFORD Press, 115 The Furlongs, Ingatestone, Essex CM4
    0AL Tel : 02775 3700
LANGLEY Technical Services, 27 Clerkenwell Close, London
    EC1R 0AT Tel : 01.251 4976
C.M.LANGSTON, 29 Green Way, Bromley, Kent BR2 8QX
    Tel : 01.462 3561
LANSDOWNE Press - see Rigby International Pty.
LANSDOWNE Publications Ltd., Design House, The Mall, London
    W5 5LS Tel : 01.579 2282
LANTERN Books Ltd., PO Box 1, Aberdeen AB9 8PE
    Tel : 0224 55878
LANTHORN Press, Peredur, East Grinstead, Sussex
LARMAN Associates, Tavistock House North, Tavistock Square,
    London WC1H 9HX Tel : 01.388 7207
LARSEN Sweeney Assocs.Ltd., PO Box 36, Maidstone, Kent
    ME14 5QE Tel : 0622 670962 Telex : 96433
Roger LASCELLES, 47 York Road, Brentford, Middx.TW8 0QP
    Tel : 01.847 0935
LATIMER House Ltd., Maxwell House, 74 Worship Street, London
    EC2A 2EN Tel : 01.377 4600
LATIMER New Dimensions Ltd., 14 West Central Street, London
    WC1A 1JH Tel : 01.246 1594
LATIMER Press, 18 Foxes Dale, Blackheath, London SE3
    Tel : 01.852 6936
LATIN America Bureau, 1 Amwell Street, London EC1R 1UL
    Tel : 01.278 2829
LAUREATE Press London, 10 Wandon Road, London SW6 2JF
    Tel : 01.736 0005
T.Werner LAURIE Ltd., 9 Bow Street, London WC2E 7AZ
    Tel : 01.836 9081 - distributed by Bodley Head Ltd.
LAURIE Milbank & Co., Portland House, 72-73 Basinghall Street,
    London EC2V 5DP Tel : 01.606 6622
Wilfrid LAURIER University Press - distributed by Colin
    Smythe Ltd.
LAVES-Chemie, Hamburger Allee 12, D-6000 Frankfurt-am-Main
    West Germany Tel : 0611 774026
LAW & Business Inc., USA - distributed by Harcourt Brace
    Jovanovich Ltd.
LAW Society, Law Society House, 113 Chancery Lane, London
    WC2A 1PL Tel : 01.242 1222 Telex : 261203 -
    distributed by Oyez
LAWRENCE & Wishart Ltd., 39 Museum Street, London WC1A 1LQ
    Tel : 01.405 0103/4
LAZY Summer Books, 88 Southmoor Road, Oxford OX2 6RB
    Tel : 0865 59161
LE Play House Press - stock transferred to University of Keele
LEA & Febiger, c/o Henry Kimpton, 7 Leighton Place, Leighton
    Road, London NW5 2QL Tel : 01.267 5483
LEAD Development Association, 34 Berkeley Square, London
    W1X 6AJ Tel : 01.499 8422
LEAGUE of Arab States, 52 Green Street, London
LEARNED Information, Besselsleigh Road, Abingdon, Oxford
    OX13 6LG Tel : 0865 730275
LEARNING Development Aids, Aware House, Duke Street, Wisbech
    Cambs.PE13 2AE Tel : 0945 63441

LEARNING Systems Company(Irwin) - c/o TABS
David LEE Publ.Ltd., 38 High Street, Thornbury, Avon
    Tel : 0454 418497
LEE Donaldson Associates, 21-24 Bury Street, London SW1Y
    6AL Tel : 01.839 3881
LEEDS University Press, The University, Leeds LS2 9JT
    Tel : 0532 31751 X304
LEGAL Action Group, 28a Highgate Road, London NW5 1NS
    Tel : 01.485 1189
LEICESTER University Press, Fielding Johnson Building,
    University of Leicester, Leicester LE1 7RH
    Tel : 0533 551860
LEIDEN University Press - distributed by Kluwer Academic Publ.
LEISURE Arts Ltd., 154-156 Upper Richmond Road, London
    SW15 2SW Tel : 01.789 6699
LEISURE Consultants, Lint Growis, Foxearth, Sudbury, Suffolk
    Tel : 0787 75777
LEISURE Life Ltd., Atlas House, Atlas Mills, Chorley Old Road,
    Bolton, Lancs. Tel : 0204 494281
LEMON Tree Press Ltd., 27 Bedfordbury, London WC2N 4BJ
    Tel : 01.240 3782
LEPUS Books, 7 Leighton Place, Leighton Road, London NW5
    2QL Tel : 01.267 5483/7
LESTER Star, 375 Upper Richmond Road, Westet, London SW1
Charles LETTS & Co.Ltd., Diary House, Borough Road, London
    SE1 1DW Tel : 01.407 8891 Telex : 884498
LEVEL Ltd., PO Box 438, Hampstead, London NW3 1BH
Lionel LEVENTHAL Ltd., 2-6 Hampstead High Street, London
    NW3 1QQ Tel : 01.794 0246 Telex : 896691
LEVIATHAN House - in liquidation
A.LEWIS (Masonic Publ.)Ltd., Terminal House, Shepperton,
    Middx.TW17 8AS Tel : 09322 28950
A.F.LEWIS & Co.Inc., 79 Madison Avenue, New York 10016,
    USA Tel : 212 679 0770
F.LEWIS Publ.Ltd., 35 Bedford Row, London WC1R 4JH
    Tel : 01.242 0946 - distributed by A.&C.Black
H.K.LEWIS & Co.Ltd., 136 Gower Street, London WC1E 6BS
    Tel : 01.387 4282/6
J.D.LEWIS & Son Ltd., GWASG Gomer Press, Llandysul, Dyfed
    SA44 4BQ Tel : 055932 2371/2
LEWIS Brooks Ltd., 52 Manchester Street, London W1M 6DR
    Tel : 01.935 3441
LEWIS Publications Ltd., 31 Castle Street, Kingston upon Thames
    Surrey KT1 1ST Tel : 01.549 7688
LEXINGTON Books, USA - distributed by Gower Publ.Co.Ltd.
LEYFORD Publ.Ltd., 47 Julian Street, Plymouth, Devon
    Tel : 0752 28883
John LIBBEY & Co.Ltd., 80-84 Bondway, Vauxhall, London SW8
    1SF Tel : 01.582 5266
LIBER, Sloltsgatan 24, S-205 10 Malmö, Sweden
    Tel : 040 706 50 Telex : 12801 S
LIBERAL Party, Publication Department, 1 Whitehall Place,
    London SW1A 2HE Tel : 01.839 3839
LIBERTARIAN Books - distributed by Cranfield Book Service
LIBRAIRIE Marcel Didier, c/o Librairie A-Matier, 8 Rue d'Assas
    75278 Paris Cedex 06, France
LIBRAIRIE Payot SG, Case Postale 3212, 1002 Lausanne,
    Switzerland
LIBRARIES Unlimited Inc., PO Box 263, Littleton, CO 80160-0263
    USA - distributed by Eurospan Ltd.
LIBRARY & Information Services Council, c/o Dept.of Education
    & Science, Elizabeth House, York Road, London SE1
    7PH Tel : 01.928 9222 Telex : 23171
LIBRARY Association - now Library Association Publishing Ltd.
LIBRARY Association Publishing Ltd., 7 Ridgmont Street,
    London WC1E 7AE Tel : 01.636 7543 Telex : 21897
LIBRARY of Congress, Building 159, Navy Yard Anney,
    Washington DC 20541, USA
LIBRARY of the Institute of Chartered Accountants, PO Box 433
    Chartered Accountants Hall, Moorgate Place, London
    EC2P 2BJ Tel : 01.628 7060 - see also entry for
    ICAEW Publications
LIBRARY Management, Research Unit, University of Technology,
    Loughborough, Leics. LE11 3TU
LIBRESSO BV, Postbus 23, 7400 GA Deventer, The Netherlands
LIBRUSA Ltd., 3 Henrietta Street, London WC2E 8LU
    Tel : 01.240 0856
LIFE Insurance Marketing Research Association, 170 Sigowney
    Street, Hartford, Connecticut 06105, USA
LIFE Officers Association, Aldermary House, Queen Street,
    London EC4N 1TP Tel : 01.236 5117
LIFE Publications Ltd., 88 Newland, Lincoln LN1 1YA
    Tel : 0522 37491
LIFEBOAT Associates Ltd., PO Box 125, London WC2H 9LU
    Tel : 01.836 9028

LIFESKILLS Associates, Ashling, Back Church Lane, Leeds
    LS16 8DN Tel : 0532 610060
LIFESPAN, 27 Clerkenwell Close, London EC1R 0AT
    Tel : 01.251 4976
LIGHT Rail Transit Association, 65 Harlington Street, Chatham
    Kent ME4 5PJ / 37 Highfields, Towcester, Northants
    NN12 7EY
LIGHT Trades House Ltd., Melbourne Avenue, Sheffield S10 2QJ
Anthony D.LILLY, 1 North Place, Western Road, Littlehampton,
    W.Sussex Tel : 0303 39881
LIME Tree Bower Press, 46 Brookfield, Highgate West Hill,
    London N6 6AT Tel : 01.340 7217
LINCOLN Electric Co., 22801 St.Clair Avenue, Cleveland, Ohio
    44117, USA
Frances LINCOLN Ltd., Apollo Works, Charlton Kings Road,
    London NW5 2SB Tel : 01.622 9933 Telex : 918066
James F.LINCOLN Associated Welding Foundation, PO Box 17035
    Cleveland, Ohio 44117, USA
LINDEN Press, Fontwell, Arundel, W.Sussex BN18 0TA
    Tel : 024 368 3302
The LINDSEY Press, 1-6 Essex Street, London WC2R 3HY
    Tel : 01.836 0525
LINGUAPHONE Institute Ltd., Linguaphone House, Beavor
    Lane, Hammersmith, London W6 9AR Tel : 01.741 1655
LINK House Magazines (Croydon)Ltd., Link House, 9 Dingwall
    Avenue, Croydon CR9 2TA Tel : 01.686 2599
LINK House Publications Ltd. - now Link House Magazines
    (Croydon)Ltd.
LINKLINE Publications, 50 Providence Place, Brighton, Sussex
    BN1 4GE Tel : 0273 698181/4
LINNET Books - c/o European Book Service
W.& J.LINNEY Ltd., 121 Newgate Lane, Mansfield, Notts.NG18
    2PA Tel : 0623 26262/6 Telex : 377149
LION Publishing, Icknield Way, Tring, Herts HP23 4LE
    Tel : 0442 82 5151 Telex : 826715
LIPMAN Management Resources Ltd., 54-70 Moorbridge Road,
    Maidenhead, Berks SL6 8BN Tel : 0628 3123
J.B.LIPPINCOTT Co., USA - distributed by Macdonald & Evans
Alan R.LISS, 150 5th Avenue, New York 10011, USA
LIST Surveys Ltd., Bridge House, Great Missenden, Bucks
    Tel : 02406 4271/2
LITHARNE Ltd., Litharne House, The Rosary, Long Marston,
    Stratford-upon-Avon, Warwicks. CV37 8RG
    Tel : 0789 720604
LITHOGRAPHIC Training Services Ltd., 333-350 Royal Exchange
    Manchester M2 7FJ Tel : 061.832 6806
    Telex : 669160
LITOR Publ.Ltd., 45 Grand Parade, Brighton BN2 2QA
    Tel : 0273 603254 Telex : 87369
Arthur D.LITTLE Inc., Berkeley Square House, Berkeley Square
    London W1 Tel : 01.493 6801
LITTLE Brown & Co.Publ. - c/o TABS
LITTLE Dean Book Service Ltd., 23 Wroslyn Road, Freeland,
    Oxon. Tel : 0993 881354
LIVE Leads Corporation, 200 Madison Avenue, New York 10016
    USA Tel : 212 689 7202
LIVERPOOL Area Health Authority, Dept.of Pharmacy, Alder
    Hen Children's Hospital, Eaton Road, Liverpool
    L12 2AP
LIVERPOOL Free Press, 27 Clerkenwell Close, London EC1R 0AT
    Tel : 01.251 4976
LIVERPOOL University Press, Press Building, 123 Grove Street
    Liverpool L7 7AF Tel : 051.709 3630 - distributed
    by The Stonebridge Press
LIVING Stream, 44 Queen Street, Blackpool, Lancs.
    Tel : 0253 55067
LIVRARIA Bertrand, Sarl, Rua Joao de Deus-Venda Nova, 2700
    Amadora Codex, Portugal Tel : 97 45 71
    Telex : 12709
LIVREXPORT, 21 Rue Froidevaux, 75014 Paris, France
LLOYD Institute of Management, 72-74 Brewer Street, London
    W1R 4DA Tel : 01.437 2427
LLOYD Luke (Medical Books)Ltd., 49 Newman Street, London
    W1P 4BW Tel : 01.580 4255
LLOYDS Management, 125 High Holborn, London WC1 6BR
    Tel : 01.405 3499
LLOYDS of London Press, Lime Street, London EC3M 7HA
    Tel : 01.623 7100 - orders to Sheepan Place,
    Colchester CO3 3LP Tel : 0206 69222
LLOYDS Register of Shipping, 71 Fenchurch Street, London
    EC3M 4BS Tel : 01.709 9166 Telex : 888379
    - orders to Printing House, Manor Royal, Crawley,
    W.Sussex RH10 2QN
LOCAL Authorities Management Services & Computer Committee,
    Vincent House, Vincent Square, London SW1P 2NB
    Tel : 01.828 2333

LOCAL Government Operational Research Unit, 201 Kings Road
    Reading, Berks RG1 4LH Tel : 0734 661234
LOCAL Government Training Board, 8 The Arndale Centre,
    Luton LU1 2TS
LOCAL Population Studies, Tawney House, Matlock, Derbyshire
    DE4 3BT
LOCATION of Offices Bureau, 27 Chancery Lane, London WC2A
    1NS Tel : 01.405 2921
A.M.LOCK & Co.Ltd., Neville Street, Oldham, Lancs.
    Tel : 061.624 0333
LOCK Distribution, Neville Street, Middleton Road, Oldbury
    Warley, West Midlands
LOCKSLEY Press, 101 Locksley Park, Belfast BT10 0AT
LOCKWOOD, Crosby, Staples, PO Box 9, 29 Frogmore, St.
    Albans, Herts. AL2 2NF
LODENEK Press, 17 Duke Street, Padstow, Cornwall
    Tel : 0841 532283
LODESTONE Books, 73 Robertson Street, Glasgow G2
LODGEMARK Press, Bank House, Summerhill, Chislehurst,Kent
    BR7 5RD Tel : 01.467 6533
LOFTHOUSE Publications, 1 West Close, Carleton, Pontefract
    W.Yorks WF8 3NR Tel : 0977 701315
LOGICA Ltd., 64 Newman Street, London W1A 4SE
    Tel : 01.637 1511 Telex : 27200
Y.LOLFA, Talybont, Dyfed
LOMOND Systems Inc., PO Box 56, Mt.Airy, Maryland 21771
    USA
LONDINIUM Press, 24 Week Street, Maidstone, Kent ME14 1RN
    Tel : 0622 861861
Keith LONDON Associates, 40 Stonehills, Welwyn Garden City,
    Herts. AL8 6PD Tel : 07073 30114/5
LONDON & Continental Publ.Co., 33-35 Bowling Green Lane,
    London EC1R 0DA Tel : 01.837 1212 Telex : 299049
LONDON & Home Counties Regional Advisory Council for
    Technological Education, Tavistock House South,
    Tavistock Square, London WC1H 9LR
    Tel : 01.388 0027
LONDON & Sheffield Publ.Co.Ltd., 5 Pond Street, Hampstead
    London NW3 2PW Tel : 01.794 0800
LONDON Borough Management Services Unit - now part of
    L.A.M.S.A.C.
LONDON Business School, Sussex Place, Regent's Park, London
    NW1 4SA Tel : 01.262 5050
LONDON Chamber of Commerce, 69 Cannon Street, London
    EC4N 5AB Tel : 01.248 4444
LONDON Chartered Accountants, 38 Finsbury Square, London
    EC2A 1PX Tel : 01.628 2467
LONDON County Bus Service, Lesbourne Road, Reigate, Surrey
    RH2 7LE Tel : 07372 42411
LONDON Cycling Campaign, 27 Clerkenwell Close, London EC1R
    0AT Tel : 01.251 4976
LONDON Editions, 70 Old Compton Street, London W1V 5PA
    Tel : 01.734 5186
LONDON Graduate School of Business Studies - now London
    Business School
LONDON Information(Rowse Muir)Ltd., Index House, Ascot,
    Berks SL5 7EU Tel : 0990 23377
LONDON Labour Library, 27 Clerkenwell Close, London EC1R
    0AT Tel : 01.251 4976
LONDON, Magazine Edition, 30 Thurloe Place, London SW7
    Tel : 01.589 0618
LONDON Researchers, Alan Armstrong & Assocs.Ltd., 72 Park
    Road, London NW1 4SH Tel : 01.723 3902
    Telex : 297635
The LONDON Review of Books, 6a Bedford Square, London
    WC1B 3RA Tel : 01.631 0884
LONDON School of Economics & Political Science, Houghton Street
    Aldwych, London WC2A 2AE Tel : 01.405 7686
LONDON School of Hygiene, Kepper Street, London WC1
LONDON Syndication, The Old Forge, Redhill, Nr.Buntingford
    Herts. Tel : 0763 88348
LONDON Transport Executive, 55 Broadway, London SW1H 0BD
    Tel : 01.222 5600 - hardbacks distributed by Ian
    Allan Ltd., other orders to The Publicity Officer,
    Poster Shop, Griffith House, 280 Marylebone Road
    London NW1 5RJ Tel : 01.262 3444
LONGCROSS Press Ltd., c/o Astron, 5 Fitzhardinge Street,
    London W1
LONGLEAT Press, Longleat, Warminster, Wilts. BA12 7NW
    Tel : 098 53 324
LONGMAN Cheshire Pty.Ltd., 346 St.Kilda Road, Melbourne
    Victoria 3004, Australia Tel : 03 699 1522
    Telex : 33501
LONGMAN Group Ltd., Longman House, Burnt Mill, Harlow,
    Essex CM20 2JE Tel : 0279 26721

LONGMAN Group Ltd.(Journals), Fourth Avenue, Harlow, Essex CM19 5AA Tel : 0279 29655 Telex : 817484
LONSDALE Technical Ltd., 21 The Promenade, Cheltenham, Glos. Tel : 0242 35244
William T.LORENZ & Co., 311 Commonwealth Avenue, Boston, Mass.02115, USA Tel : 617 266 1784
LORNE Caldeugh Ltd., 1 Whitehall Place, London SW1 Tel : 01.839 7465
LORRIMER Publ.Ltd., 47 Dean Street, London W1V 5HL Tel : 01.734 7792 - distributed by LSP Books Ltd.
LOTUS Press Ltd., Moelfre, Gwynedd LL72 8HU Tel : 024 888 423
LOW Pay Research Unit, 9 Poland Street, London W1V 3DG
Peter LOWE, 49 Uxbridge Road, London W5 5SA Tel : 01.840 4411 Telex : 934610
Robson LOWE Ltd., 50 Pall Mall, London SW1Y 5JZ Tel : 01.839 4030 Telex : 915410
LOWNDES, Lambert Group, PO Box 144, Norfolk House, Wellesley Road, Croydon CR9 3EB Tel : 01.686 2466
Herman LUCHTECHAND Verlag, Postfach 1780, 5450 Henwied 1, W.Germany
LUCIS Press Ltd., Suite 54, 3 Whitehall Court, London SW1A 2EF Tel : 01.839 4512/3
LUND Humphries Publ.Ltd., 26 Litchfield Street, London WC2H 9NJ Tel : 01.836 4243
LUNING Prak Assocs.Inc., 200 Summit Avenue, Montvale, NJ07645, USA Tel : 201 573 1400
William LUSCOMBE Publ.Ltd., Artists House, 14-15 Manette Street, London W1V 5LB Tel : 01.434 1694 Telex : 24892 - distributed by Mitchell Beazley Marketing Ltd.
LUTTERWORTH Press, Luke House, Farnham Road, Guildford Surrey GU1 4XD Tel : 0483 77536 Telex : 858623 - orders to TBL Book Service Ltd.
Dr Helmut LUTZ, Haussmannstrasse 46, 6 Stuttgart 0, West Germany
LUXON Press Ltd., 2-4 Abbeymount, Edinburgh EH8 8JH Tel : 031.661 9339
LUZAC Co.Ltd., PO Box 157, 46 Great Russell Street, London WC1B 3PE Tel : 01.636 1462
LYLE Publications Ltd., Glenmayne, Galashiels, Selkirkshire TD1 3NR, Scotland Tel : 0896 2005 Telex : 727195
LYNXPLAN Ltd., Prudential House, 28-40 Blossom Street, York YO2 2AJ Tel : 0904 24885/6
LYREBIRD Press, 14 Cornwall Gardens, London SW7 4AN Tel : 01.589 1626
LYTHWAY Press Ltd., 93-100 Locksbrook Road, Bath BA1 3HB Tel : 0225 331945 Telex : 449897

Mc

McAlpine, Thorpe & Warrier Ltd., 1 Montague Street, London WC1B 5BP Tel : 01.580 9792 Telex : 888941
McANALLY Montgomery & Co., Barber-Surgeons' Hall, Monkwell Square, Wood Street, London EC2Y 5BL Tel : 01.726 6060
McBRIDE Bros.& Broadley Ltd., 52 Statford Road, Wolverton, Bucks MK12 5LS Tel : 0908 312278
McCARTA Ltd., 122 Kings Cross Road, London WC1X 9DS Tel : 01.278 8278
McCARTHY Information Ltd., Manor House, Ash Walk, Warminster Wilts. BA12 8PY Tel : 0985 215151
Harold McCARTHY Publ., 601-4 Fleetway House, 200 Bree Street, PO Box 4258, Johannesburg, South Africa
McCRONE Research Assocs.Ltd., 2 McCrone Mews, Belsize Lane, London NW3 5BG Tel : 01.435 2282/3
McCUTCHAN Publ.Group, 25-26 Grove Street, Berkeley, CA94704 USA
McCUTCHEON Publ., 175 Rock Road, Glen Rock, New Jersey 07452, USA
MacDONALD & Evans Ltd., Estover Road, Plymouth PL6 7PZ Tel : 0752 705251 Telex : 45635
MacDONALD Educational Ltd., Holywell House, Worship Street, London EC2A 2EN Tel : 01.247 5499 Telex : 885233 - orders to Macdonald Publishing Services(Paulton)Ltd.
MacDONALD (Futura) Publishing Group, Paulton House, 8 Shepherdess Walk, London N1 7LW Tel : 01.251 1666 Telex : 23168 - orders to Macdonald Publishing Services(Paulton)Ltd.
MacDONALD General Books, Paulton House, 8 Shepherdess Walk Lonon N1 7LW Tel : 01.251 1666 Telex : 23168 - orders to Macdonald Publishing Services(Paulton)Ltd.
McDONALD Publications of London Ltd., 268 High Street, Uxbridge, Middx.UB8 1UA Tel: 0895 30726

MacDONALD Publishers, Edgefield Road, Loanhead, Midlothian EH20 9SY Tel : 031.440 0246
MacDONALD Publishing Services(Paulton)Ltd., Paulton, Bristol BS18 5IQ Tel : 0761 413301/7 Telex ; 44713
MacGIBBON & Kee Ltd. - see Granada Publishing Ltd.
McGILL Queen's University Press - c/o Canada Books Intl. - distributed by IBD
McGRAW-Hill Book Co.(U.K.)Ltd., Shoppenhangers Road, Maidenhead, Berks SL6 2QL Tel : 0628 23431 Telex : 848484
McGRAW-Hill Publications, 1221 Avenue of the Americas, New York 10020, USA Tel : 212 997 1221
Jean MacGREGOR & Associates, The Corderries, Chalford Hill, Stroud, Glos. Tel : 0453 88 3176
MacGREGOR Centrex Ltd., 50 Salisbury Road, Hounslow, Middx. TW4 6JP Tel : 01.572 0912 Telex : 935727
The McILVAINE Company, 2970 Maria Avenue, Northbrook, Illinois 60062, USA Tel : 312 272 0010
Grant McINTYRE Ltd., 39 Great Russell Street, London WC1B 3PH Tel : 01.631 4141 - distributed by J.M.Dent & Sons
James A.MACKAY, 11 Newall Terrace, Dumfries DG1 1LN
MACKINTOSH Publications Ltd., Mackintosh House, Napier Road Luton, Beds Tel : 0582 412716 Telex : 826818
McKNIGHT Publishing Company - distributed by Taplinger
MACLAREN & Sons, Applied Science Publishers, 22 Rippleside Commercial Estate, Ripple End, Barking, Essex Tel : 01.595 2121
MACLAREN Publ.Ltd., PO Box 109, Davis House, 69-77 High Street, Croydon CR9 1QH Tel : 01.688 7788
William MacLELLAN Ltd., 268 Bath Street, Glasgow G2 4JR Tel : 041.332 8507
James McNAUGHTON Paper Group, 10-11 Atlantic Road, Avon- bridge Trading Estate, Avonmouth, Bristol BS11 9LQ Tel : 0272 828431 Telex : 449446
Julia MacRAE Books, 12a Golden Square, London W1R 4BA Tel : 01.437 0713 Telex : 262655 - distributed by J.M.Dent & Sons Ltd.

M

M.A.R.K.Book Distribution Ltd., 18 Ursula Street, London SW11 3DW Tel : 01.223 5398
MC Publishing Co., 175 Roak Road, Glen Rock, New Jersey 07452, USA
M.C.B.Publ.Ltd., 198-200 Keighley Road, Bradford, W.Yorks BD9 4JQ Tel : 0274 43823/492583
M.D.Research & Services Ltd., 98 Roebuck House, Stag Place, London SW1E 5AA Tel : 01.828 0795 Telex : 886227
MEFIS - see Middle East Financial Information Service
MENAS Press Ltd. - see Middle East & North African Studies Press Ltd.
MENCAP, 123 Golden Lane, London EC1Y 0RT Tel : 01.253 9433
MEP Ltd., PO Box 24, Northgate Avenue, Bury St.Edmunds, Suffolk IP32 6BW Tel : 0284 63277
MERAG, 27 Clerkenwell Close, London EC1R 0AT Tel : 01.251 4976
M.E.W.Research, 7 Layer Gardens, London W3 9PR Tel : 01.992 6294
MIRA - see Motor Industry Research Association
MIT Energy Laboratory, Rm.E40-454, Cambridge, Mass.02139, USA
M.I.T.Press, 126 Buckingham Palace Road, London SW1W 9SD Tel : 01.730 9208 Telex : 23933 - distributed by IBD
ML Petroleum Services Ltd., 32 St.James Street, London SW1
MTP Press, Falcon House, Queen Square, Lancaster LA1 1Rn Tel : 0524 68765 Telex : 65212
MW Publishers, 290a Hale Lane, Edgware, Middx.HA8 8NP Tel : 01.958 3155
MWH London Publishers, 233 Seven Sisters Road, London N4 2DA Tel : 01.263 3071 Telex : 8812176
M.W.S. Scientific Ltd., Parham Drive, Boyatt Wood Industrial Estate, Eastleigh, Hants. SO5 4NU Tel : 0703 619171
MACHINE & Allied Production Engineers Institute, 1200 18th Street, Washington DC 20036, USA
MACHINE Tool Industry Research Association, Hulley Road, Hurdsfield, Macclesfield, Cheshire SK10 2NE Tel : 0625 25421
MACHINE Tools Trade Association, 62 Bayswater Road, London W2 3PH
MACHINERY Buyer's Guide, 1 Copers Cope Road, Beckenham, Kent BR3 1NB Tel : 01.650 4877

MACHINERY Press Ltd., 1 Copers Cope Road, Beckenham, Kent BR3 1NB Tel : 01.650 4877
MACK Publ.Company, 20th & Northampton Streets, Easton, PA 18042, USA
MACKINTOSH Publ.Ltd., Mackintosh House, Napier Road, Luton, Beds. LU1 1RG Tel : 0582 412716 Telex : 826818
MACLEAN-Hunter Ltd., 76 Oxford Street, London W1N 0HH Tel : 01.434 2233
MACMILLAN Co., New York - see Collier Macmillan Ltd.
MACMILLAN Journals Ltd., Brunel Road, Basingstoke, Hants. RG21 2XS Tel : 0256 29242
MACMILLAN London Ltd., 4 Little Essex Street, London WC2R 3LF Tel : 01.836 6633
MACMILLAN Martin Ltd., Charles Roe House, Chestergate, Macclesfield, Cheshire SK11 6DZ Tel : 0625 613000
MACRO Marketing Ltd., Burnham Lane, Slough, Berks SL1 6LN Tel : 06286 4422 Telex : 847945
Charles S.MADAN & Co.Ltd., Vortex Works, Atlantic Street, Broadheath, Altrincham, Cheshire WA14 5DA
H.T.MADDOCK & Son, Upperboat Trading Estate, Pontypridd, Glamorgan CF37 5BP Tel : 044 385 2371
MADE in Europe Ltd., 12 Woodlodge, Woodfield Lane, Ashtead, Surrey KT21 2DS
MADE Simple - imprint of William Heinemann
MAGILL Books Intl. - distributed by Bowker
MAGNA Flux Ltd., South Dorcan Industrial Estate, Swindon, Wilts. SN3 5HE Tel : 0793 24566
MAGNA Print Books, Magna House, Long Preston, Nr.Skipton, N.Yorks BD23 4ND Tel : 07294 225
MAGNUM Books, 11 New Fetter Lane, London EC4P 4EE Tel : 01.583 9855 - distributed by Associated Book Publishers
MAGNUM Publ.Ltd., 110-112 Station Road East, Oxted, Surrey RH8 0QA Tel : 08833 7755 Telex : 95359
MAIL Order Music, Dettingen Way, Bury St.Edmunds, Suffolk IP33 3BR
Bruce MAIN-Smith Ltd., PO Box 20, Leatherhead, Surrey Tel : 0306 2255
MAINSTREAM Publishing, 25a South West Thistle Street Lane, Edinburgh EH2 1EW Tel : 031.225 2804/9618
MAISONNEUVE S.A., B.P.39-57160 Moulins-les-Metz, France Tel : (8) 760 11 80
Paul MAITLAND, 13 Sutherland Road, Tunbridge Wells, Kent TN1 1SE Tel : 0892 26092 Telex : 95275
MAKROTEST Ltd., Sinclair House, The Avenue, London W13 8NT Tel : 01.998 7733 Telex : 934821
MALCOLM Stewart Books Ltd., PO Box 265, London N3 2QF
MANAGEMENT Centre Europe, European HQ of the International Management Association, Avenue des Arts 4, B1040 Brussels, Belgium
MANAGEMENT Editions(Europe), 4 Cours de Bastions, 1205 Geneva, Switzerland
MANAGEMENT Games Ltd., George Street, Maulden, Bedford MK45 2DD Tel : 0525 404248
MANAGEMENT Personnel, York House, Chertsey Street, Guildford Surrey
MANAGEMENT Publications - distributed by British Institute of Management
MANAGEMENT Research, 35 Connaught Street, London W2 Tel : 01.262 8941
MANAGEMENT Services Ltd., Finsbury Circus House, 4-10 Blomfield Street, London EC2M 7BU Tel : 01.588 4111
MANAGEMENT Update Ltd., 43 Brodrick Road, London SW17 7DX Tel : 01.767 7542
MANAGING Your Own Business Ltd., Vine House, Portsmouth Road, Cobham, Surrey
MANCHESTER Business School, Booth Street West, Manchester M15 6PB Tel : 061.273 8228 Telex : 668354
MANCHESTER, City of, Public Relations Office, Town Hall, Manchester M60 2LA Tel : 061.236 3377 X501
MANCHESTER Statistical Society, c/o Aldersyde, Maynestone Road, Chinley, Stockport, Cheshire SK12 6AH Tel : 0663 50234
MANCHESTER University Press, Oxford Road, Manchester M13 9PL Tel : 061.273 5539
MANDERLEY Press Ltd., Selkirk House, 73 Prestbury Road, Cheltenham, Glos. Tel : 0242 25702
MANHATTEN Publ.Ltd., Sandhurst House, 72 St.Peters Avenue, Kettering, Northants. NN16 0HB Tel : 0536 3829 - distributed by Tiptree Book Services Ltd.
George MANN Books, PO Box 22, Maidstone, Kent ME14 1AH Tel : 0622 59591
MANNING Eapley Publ.Ltd., 42 High Street, Croydon, Surrey

MANPOWER Services Commission, Selkirk House, High Holborn, London WC1 Tel : 01.836 1213
MANSELL Publishing, 6 All Saints Street, London N1 9RL Tel : 01.837 6676/7
MANSK-Svenska Publ.Co.Ltd., 17 North View, Peel, Isle of Man Tel : 0044 624842855
W.S.MANSY & Son Ltd., Hudson Road, Leeds LS9 7DL
MANTEC Publ.Ltd., 150 Railway Terrace, Rugby, Warwicks. CV21 3HN Tel : 0788 890419
MANUFACTURING Chemists Association, 1825 Connecticut Ave. NW, Washington DC 20009, USA
MAP Productions Ltd., Olwen House, Quarry Hill Road, Tonbridge, Kent TN9 2RH Tel : 0732 351946
MARBNAIN Ltd., St.Margaret's Road, Twickenham, Middx. TW1 1RJ Tel : 01.892 4411
Peter MARCAN, 31 Rowliff Road, High Wycombe, Bucks
MARCEL Dekker AG, Elisabethenstrasse 19, Postfach 34, 4010 Basel, Switzerland Tel : (061) 23 10 30 Telex : 63475
MARCHAM Manor Press, Appleford, Abingdon, Oxon.OX14 4PB Tel : 023 582 319
MARCHES Tropicaux et Mediterranéens, 190 Boulevard Hausmann 75008 Paris, France Tel : 563 1155 Telex : 290131
MARCHMONT Publ., Longdene, Haslemere, Surrey GU27 2PH Tel : 0428 53841 Telex : 858543
MARCOM Publishing, Western Lodge, Station Road, Andoversford Cheltenham, Glos. GL54 4LA Tel : 0242 82749
MARCONI Instruments Ltd., Long Acres, St.Albans, Herts AL4 0JN Tel : 0727 59292
MARGOLIS Marketing & Research Co., 232 Madison Avenue, Suite 905, New York 10016, USA Tel : 212 685 1278
MARINE Biological Association of U.K., The Laboratory, Citadel Hill, Plymouth PL1 2PB Tel : 0752 21761
MARINE Ecological Surveys Ltd., PO Box 6, Faversham, Kent Tel : 022775 523
MARINE Management(Holdings)Ltd., 76 Mark Lane, London EC3R 7JN Tel : 01.481 8493 Telex : 886841
MARINE Media Manpower, 76 Mark Lane, London EC3R 7JN
MARK One Publications Intl.Ltd., Mark House, Locksbrook Road Bath, Avon Tel : 0225 26277
A/S MARKEDS-Data, 16 Ahlefeldtsgade, DK-1359, Copenhagen K Denmark Tel : 01 15 90 90
MARKET Assessment Publications, 2 Duncan Terrace, London N1 8BZ
MARKET Facts of Canada Ltd., 1240 Bay Street, Toronto, Ontario M5R 3L9, Canada Tel : 416 964 6262
MARKET Location Ltd., 17 Waterloo Place, Warwick Street, Royal Leamington Spa, Warwicks.CV32 5LA Tel : 0926 34235
MARKET Research Society, 15 Belgrave Square, London SW1X 8PF Tel : 01.235 4709
MARKET Studies International, 28-42 Banner Street, London EC1Y 8QE Tel : 01.250 3922 Telex : 23678
MARKET Data Enterprises, PO Box 1218, New York 10010, USA
MARKETING & Research Consultancy Ltd., Churchill House, 87 Jesmond Road, Newcastle-upon-Tyne NE2 1NH Tel : 0632 812257/8 Telex : 537020
MARKETING Development, 402 Border Road, Concord, Mass. 01742, USA Tel : 617 369 5382
MARKETING House Publ.Ltd., Moor Hall, Cookham, Berks SL6 9QH Tel : 06285 24922
MARKETING Improvements Ltd., Ulster House, 17 Ulster Terrace, Outer Circle, Regent's Park, London NW1 4PJ Tel : 01.487 5811
MARKETING Intelligence Service Ltd., 33 Academy Street, Naples NY 14512, USA Tel : 510 254 5590
MARKETING Office/INFORCO, 19 Rue Greneta, 75002 Paris France Tel : 236 29 64 Telex : 212576
MARKETING Research Bureau, 4001 Westerley Place, Suite 103 Newport Beach, CA 92660, USA Tel : 714 752 0575 Telex : 678401
MARKETING Science Institute, 14 Story Street, Cambridge, MA02138, USA Tel : 617 491 2060
MARKETING Strategies for Industry, 22 Wates Way, Mitcham, Surrey CR4 4HR Tel : 01.640 6621 Telex : 27950
MARKETING Systems GmbH, Hunsrveckstrasse 9A, D-4300 Essen 1 (Bredeney), W.Germany Tel : 0201 42901
MARKETING Thrust Ltd., GordonHouse, 276 Banbury Road, Oxford OX2 7HA Tel : 0865 512673
MARKETING Yearbook, Diplomatic House, 12-18 High Road, London W2 9PJ
MARKHAM House Press, 17 Montpelier Place, Brighton, BN1 3BF Tel : 0273 25544
MARLBOROUGH Publ.Ltd., 75 Lower Camden, Chislehurst, Kent BR7 5JD Tel : 01.467 1937 Telex : 943763

MARLIN Publ.Intl., 485 Fifth Avenue, New York 10017, USA - some titles distributed by Alan Armstrong & Assocs. Ltd.
MARQUIS Publications, 200 East Ohio Street, Dept.5667, Chicago, Illinois 60611, USA Tel : 312 787 2008
Alan MARSH(Management & Development)Ltd., 110-111 Strand, London WC2R 0AA Tel : 01.836 8918 Telex : 24973
MARSHALL Cavendish Publ.Ltd., 58 Old Compton Street, London W1V 5PA Tel : 01.734 6710 Telex : 23880 - distributed by Sidgwick & Jackson
MARSHALL Editions Ltd., 71 Eccleston Square, London SW1V 1PJ Tel : 01.834 0785/7
MARSHALL Morgan & Scott Publ.Ltd., 1 Bath Street, London EC1V 9LB Tel : 01.251 2925 - orders to Unit 14, Trident Industrial Estate, Pindar Road, Hoddesdon Herts.EN11 0LD Tel : 0992 42033
MARSHALL Pickering, 3 Beggarwood Lane, Basingstoke, Hants.RG23 7LP Tel : 0256 59211
MARSTON Book Service Ltd., PO Box 87, 54 Marston Street, Oxford OX4 1LB Tel : 0865 724041
MARTIN Books, 8 Market Passage, Cambridge CB2 3PF - part of Woodhead Faulkner Ltd.
Barry MARTIN Travel Ltd., Suite 309-310 Albany House, 324 Regent Street, London W1R 5AA Tel : 01.637 0373/7
MARTIN Brian & O'Keeffe Ltd., 37 Museum Street, London WC1 Tel : 01.405 8302 - distributed by Bookpoint Ltd.
Chris MARTIN & Associates, 6 Innage Road, Northfield, Birmingham B31 2DX Tel : 021.475 2088
John MARTIN Publ.Ltd., 24 Old Bond Street, London W1X 3DA Tel : 01.629 6461 Telex : 23442
MARTIN Robertson & Co.Ltd., 108 Cowley Road, Oxford OX4 1JF Tel : 0865 19109
MARTIN Marietta Corp., PO Box 5837, Orlando, Florida 32805, USA
MARTINDALE Hubbell Inc., 1 Prospect Street, Summit, New Jersey 07901, USA
MARTIN-HAMBLIN Research, 14-20 Headfort Place, London SW1X 7HN Tel : 01.235 5444 Telex : 896691
MARTINS Publ.Group, 18 Bedford Square, London WC1B 3JN Tel : 01.580 8236
MARTINUS Nijhoff BV, Box 269, 9-11 Lange Voorhout, The Hague, The Netherlands Tel : 70 469460
MARUZEN Publ.Co. - c/o TABS
MARVELL Press, 40 Lowfield Road, London NW6 2PR Tel : 01.328 1563
MARWAIN Publ.Ltd., 245 Queensway, Bletchley, Milton Keynes Tel : 0908 643022
MASHTOTS Press, BCM-Mashtots, London WC1V 6XX Tel : 01.242 2320
MASON & Lipscombe, 44 Wallington Square, Wallington, Surrey SM6 8RN
MASON Charter, USA - distributed by Van Nostrand Reinhold
Kenneth MASON Publ.Ltd., 13-14 Homewell, Havant, Hants. PO9 1EE Tel : 0705 486262/3 - distributed by J.M.Dent & Sons Ltd.
MASSON-Editeur, 120 Boulevard Saint-Germain, 75280 Paris Cedex 06, France
MASSON & Lic S.A., 120 Boulevard Saint-Germain, 75280 Paris Cedex 06, France
F.C.MATHIESON & Sons Ltd. - gone away, 1983
J.M.J.MAUS Ltd., 6-10 Tudor Road, Hampton, Middx.TW12 2NQ Tel : 01.979 0201 Telex : 929805
G.W.MAY Ltd., 94 Wigmore Street, London W1H 0BR Tel : 01.935 0665
MAYFLOWER Books Ltd., c/o Granada Publ.Ltd., Park Street, St.Albans, Herts.
Kevin MAYHEW Publ., 55 Leigh Road, Leigh-on-Sea, Essex SS9 1SP Tel : 0702 76425/715236
MAYHEW McCrimmon Ltd., 10-12 High Street, Great Wakering, Essex SS3 0EQ Tel : 0702 218956
Eric MAYLIN Ltd., 87-89 Curtain Road, London EC2A 3BR Tel : 01.739 6333 Telex : 24817
MAYPOLE Press, 2a Market Hill, Maldon, Essex CM9 7PZ Tel : 0621 56608/58111
MEADOWFIELD Press Ltd., ISA Building, Dale Road Industrial Estate, Shildon, Co.Durham MD24 2QZ Tel : 0388 773065
Thomas MEADOWS Co.Ltd., 36 Grosvenor Gardens, London SW1W 0ED
MECHANICAL Engineering Publ.Ltd., PO Box 24, Northgate Avenue, Bury St.Edmunds, Suffolk IP32 6BW Tel : 0284 63277
MECHANICAL Engineers Association, 16 Dartmouth Street, London SW1H 9BL Tel : 01.222 2367

MECHANICAL Properties Data Center, Battelle Memorial Institute, Columbus, Ohio, USA
Herbert E.MECKE Assoc.Inc., 274 Madison Avenue, New York 10016, USA Tel : 212 689 9536
MECKLER Publishing, 3 Henrietta Street, London WC2E 8LU Tel : 01.240 0856
MEDIA Publ., Hale House, 290-296 Green Lanes, London N13 5TP Tel : 01.882 0155
MEDICAL & Technical Publ.Co.Ltd. - see MTP Press Ltd.
MEDICAL Education(International)Ltd., Pembroke House, 36-37 Pembroke Street, Oxford OX1 1BL Tel : 0865 724631 Telex : 83147
MEDICAL Marketing Information Ltd., 38 Hockerhill Street, Bishops Stortford, Herts.
MEDICAL Missionary Association, 6 Canonbury Place, London N1 2NJ Tel : 01.359 1313
MEDICAL Products Marketing Services, 778 Frontage Road, Northfield, IL 60093, USA Tel : 312 446 0194
MEDICAL Research Council, 20 Park Crescent, London W1N 4AL Tel : 01.636 5422
MEDICI Society Ltd., 34-42 Pentonville Road, London N1 9HG Tel : 01.837 7099
MEDICO-Pharmaceutical Forum, 1 Wimpole Street, London W1M 8AE Tel : 01.580 2070
MEDUSA Press, 21 Lynford Gardens, Seven Kings, Ilford, Essex Tel : 01.590 1701/7027
William A.MEEUWS Publisher, Wightwich, Boars Hill, Oxford OX1 5DR Tel : 0865 735380/57971
MELBOURNE House(Publ.)Ltd., Glebe Cottage, Glebe House, Station Road, Cheddington, Leighton Buzzard LU7 0SQ Tel : 01.405 6347 - orders to 131 Trafalgar Road Greenwich, London SE10
MELBOURNE University Press - distributed by Prentice-Hall Intl.Inc.
MELROSE Press Ltd., 7 Regal Lane, Soham, Ely, Cambs.CB7 5BA Tel : 0353 721091 Telex : 81584
MENARD Press, 8 The Oaks, Woodside Avenue, London N12 8AR Tel : 01.446 5571
MENAS Press Ltd., Gallipoli House, Outwell, Wisbech, Cambs. PE14 8TN
MENDIP Press - now Mendip Publishing
MENDIP Publishing, Cleeve House, Theale, Wedmore, Somerset BS28 4SL Tel : 0934 712995
MENOSHIRE Ltd., 49 Churchfield Road, Acton, London W3 6AY Tel : 01.992 2623
MENTOR Books - distributed by New English Library Ltd.
John MENZIES(London)Ltd., Highbury House, Drayton Park, London N5 Tel : 01.226 8741
MERCAT Press, c/o James Thin Ltd., 53-59 South Bridge, Edinburgh Tel : 031.556 6743
MERCIER Press, PO Box 5, 4 Bridge Street, Cork, Ireland Tel : Cork 504022 Telex : 75463 - distributed by Fowler Wright Books
MERCK Sharp & Dohme Ltd., Hoddesdon, Herts. EN11 9BU Tel : 09924 67272
MERCURIONS Books, Nant-Gwilw, Llanfynydd, Carmarthen SA32 7TT Tel : 055 84 531
MERCURY House Reference Books, Mercury House, Business Publications Ltd., Waterloo Road, London SE1 8UL Tel : 01.928 3388 Telex : 21977
MERCURY House Publishers Ltd., Portland Street, Staple Hill, Bristol BS16 4PG Tel : 0272 658908
MERIDIEN Medical Publ.Ltd., 145a Croydon Road, Beckenham, Kent BR3 3RB Tel : 01.650 4929
MERLIN Books Ltd., Stonycroft, East Hill, Braunton, Devon EX33 2LD Tel : 0271 812117
The MERLIN Press Ltd., 3 Manchester Road, London E14 Tel : 01.987 7959
MERRIAM Co., USA - distributed by Longman Group Ltd.
Charles E.MERRILL Publ.Co., Alperton House, Bridgewater Road Wembley, Middx. HA0 1EG Tel : 01.902 8812 Telex : 261378 - distributed by IBD
MERRION Press, 16 Groveway, London SW9 0AR Tel : 01.735 7791 - orders to 91a Landor Road, London SW9 9RT Tel : 01.733 5173
MERROW Publ.Co.Ltd., ISA Building, Dale Road Industrial Estate, Shildon, Co.Durham Tel : 0670 55860 - distributed by Meadowfield Press Ltd.
MERSEYSIDE Aviation Society Ltd., Room 14, Hangar 2, Liverpool Airport, Merseyside L24 8QE
MESSAGERIES du Livre Commission, 45 Rue Benard, 75014 Paris France Tel : 543 23 48
METAL Box plc, General Line Division, Queens House, Forbury Road, Reading, Berks RG1 3JH Tel : 0734 581177 Telex : 847437

METAL Bulletin plc, Park House, Park Terrace, Worcester Park, Surrey KT4 7HY   Tel : 01.330 4311   Telex : 21383
METAL Finishing Book Centre, 28 High Street, Teddington, Middx.TW11 8EW   Tel : 01.943 2610
METALS & Minerals Research Services, 222-225 The Strand, London WC2R 1BA   Tel : 01.353 1914   Telex : 896691
METALS Society, 1 Carlton House Terrace, London SW1Y 5DB   Tel : 01.839 4071   Telex : 8814813
METAS Ltd., Chobham, Woking, Surrey   Tel : 048 62 7121
METCALFE Publ.Ltd., 10 East Road, London W1 6AM   Tel : 01.251 1533
METEOROLOGICAL Office, London Road, Bracknell, Berks RG12 2SZ   Tel : 0344 20242
METHOD Publishing Co.Ltd., Duke Street, Golspie, Sutherland KW10 6RR   Tel : 040 83 3430
METHODIST Publ.House, Wellington Road, Wimbledon, London SW19 8EU   Tel : 01.947 5256/9
METHUEN & Co.Ltd. - see Associated Book Publ.(UK)Ltd.
METHUEN Children's Books Ltd. - see Associated Book Publ. (UK)Ltd.
METHUEN Educational Ltd. - see Associated Book Publ.(UK)Ltd.
METHUEN London Ltd. - see Associated Book Publ.(UK)Ltd.
METRA Consulting Group Ltd., St.Mary's House, 42 Vicarage Crescent, London SW11 3LD   Tel : 01.223 7634   Telex : 919173
METRO Publ.Ltd., Bull Green House, Halifax, W.Yorks HX1 2EB   Tel : 0422 42008
MICAWBER Publications, The Old Ship, High Street, Wingham, Kent CT3 1BJ   Tel : 0227 72655
S.MICHAEL's Abbey Press, Farnborough, Hants.GU14 7NQ   Tel : 0252 47573
MICHELIN Tyre Co., Maps & Guides Dept., 81 Fulham Road, London SW3 6RD   Tel : 01.589 1460   Telex : 919071
MICHIE Company, PO Box 7587, Charlottesville, Virginia 22906, USA
MICHIGAN State University Press - distributed by TABS
MICROBIOLOGICAL Research Establishment, Porton Down, Salisbury, Wilts. SP4 0JG   Tel : 0980 610391
MICROFICHE Publ., PO Box 3513, Grand Central Station, New York 10017, USA
MICROFORM Association of G.B.Ltd., Dellfield, Pednor, Chesham, Bucks HP5 2SX   Tel : 02406 5991
MICROFORM Ltd., East Ardsley, Wakefield WF3 2AT   Tel : 0924 825700
MICRO Information Ltd.(Microinfo), PO Box 3, Newman Lane, Alton, Hants.   Tel : 0420 84300
MICROSCOPE Publications, 2508 South Michigan Avenue, Chicago, IL 60616, USA
MICROWAVE Exhibitions & Publishers Ltd., Convex House, 43 Dudley Road, Tunbridge Wells, Kent TN1 1LE   Tel : 0892 44027   Telex : 95604
MIDAS Books(Planned Action Ltd.), 12 Dene Way, Speldhurst, Tunbridge Wells, Kent TN3 0NX   Tel : 089 286 2860 - orders to Noonan Hurst Ltd.
The MIDDLE East, 63 Long Acre, London WC2E 9JH   Tel : 01.836 4221/2
MIDDLE East & North African Studies Press Ltd., Gallipoli House, Outwell, Wisbech, Cambs.PE14 8TN   Tel : 094 571 2733
MIDDLE East Economic Digest, MEED House, 21 St.John Street, London WC1N 2BP   Tel : 01.404 5513   Telex : 27165
MIDDLE East Economic Survey, PO Box 4940, Nicosia, Cyprus   Tel : (021) 74691 45431   Telex : 2198
MIDDLE East Executive Reports, 1115 Massachusetts Avenue NW No.16, Washington DC 20005, USA   Tel : 202 289 3900   Telex : 440462
MIDDLE East Financial & Industrial Services S.A., PO Box 174, Birmingham B5 7PJ   Tel : 021.440 1703
MIDDLE East Financial Information Service, PO Box 174, Birmingham B5 7PJ   Tel : 021.446 1703
MIDDLE East International Publications, 21 Collingham Road, London SW5 0NU   Tel : 01.373 5228
MIDDLE East Marketing Research Bureau Ltd., Mitsis Building 3, Makarios 111 Avenue, PO Box 2098, Nicosia, Cyprus   Tel : 45413   Telex : 2488
MIDDLE East Review Co.Ltd., 21 Gold Street, Saffron Walden, Essex CB10 1EJ   Tel : 0799 21150
MIDLAND Consultants, 97 Little Sutton Road, Four Oaks, Sutton Coldfield
MIDLAND Counties Publ.(Aerophile)Ltd., 24 The Hollow, Earl Shilton, Leicester LE9 7NA   Tel : 0455 47256
MILESTONE Publications, 62 Murray Road, Horndean, Hants. PO8 9JL   Tel : 0705 597440
MILITARY Vehicles & Engineering Establishment, Chobham Lane, Chertsey, Surrey KT16 0EE   Tel : 0990 23366

MILK Marketing Board, Thames Ditton, Surrey KT7 0EL   Tel : 01.398 4101   Telex : 928239
Harvey MILLER Publishers, 20 Marryatt Road, London SW19 5BD   Tel : 01.946 4426
J.Garnet MILLER, 129 St.John's Hill, London SW11 1TD   Tel : 01.228 8091
MILLER Freeman Publications, 500 Howard Street, San Francisco CA 94105, USA   Tel : 415 397 1881   Telex : 278273
MILLINGTON Books, 54 Elgin Avenue, London W9 2HA - orders & distribution Noonan Hurst Ltd.
MILLINGTON Ltd., 109 Southampton Row, London WC1 4HH   Tel : 01.637 2541 - orders & distribution Noonan Hurst Ltd.
MILLS & Boon Ltd., 15-16 Brook Mews, London W1A 1DR   Tel : 01.493 8131   Telex : 24420 - distributed by Distribution & Management Services Ltd.
MIMRAM Press, 11 Harmer Green Lane, Digswell, Welwyn, Herts. AL6 0AY   Tel : 043 871 6367
MIND (National Association for Mental Health), 22 Harley Street London W1N 2ED   Tel : 01.637 0741 - distributed by MIND Bookshop, 157 Woodhouse Lane, Leeds LS2 3EF
MINE of Information Ltd., 1 Francis Avenue, St.Albans, Herts. AL3 6BL   Tel : 0727 52801   Telex : 925859
MINERALOGICAL Association of Canada, Dept.of Minerology, Royal Ontario Museum, 100 Queens Park, Toronto, Ontario M5S 2L6, Canada
MINERVA Press Ltd., 44 Great Russell Street, London WC1B 3PA   Tel : 01.580 7200   Telex : 22158
Paul P.B.MINET, c/o Piccadilly Rare Books, 30 Sackville Street London W1   Tel : 01.437 2135
MINICONSULT Ltd., 35 Richmond Avenue, Islington, London N1 0NB   Tel : 01.607 6839
MINIMAX Books Ltd., Broadgate Lane, Deeping St.James, Peterborough   Tel : 0778 344388
MINING Group Newspapers, Holborn Circus, London EC1P 1DQ   Tel : 01.353 0246
MINING Journal Books Ltd., PO Box 10, Edenbridge, Kent TN8 5NE   Tel : 073 271 4333/4
MINISTRY of Agriculture, Fisheries & Food - see Agriculture, Fisheries & Food, Ministry of
MINISTRY of Overseas Development, Tropical Products Institute 127 Clerkenwell Road, London EC1R 5DB   Tel : 01.405 7943
MINNESOTA University Press, Oxford University Press, Ely House, 37 Dover Street, London W1X 4AH
MINORITY Press Group, 27 Clerkenwell Close, London EC1R 0AT   Tel : 01.251 4976
MINORITY Rights Group, Benjamin Franklin House, 36 Craven Street, London WC2N 5NG   Tel : 01.930 6659
MINTEL Publications Ltd., 20 Buckingham Street, London WC2N 6EE   Tel : 01.839 1542
MIRO, Switzerland - UK Agents : European Data & Research Ltd. 77 George Street, London W1H 5PL   Tel : 01.486 7621
MIRROR Books Ltd., Athene House, 66-73 Shoe Lane, London EC4P 4AB   Tel : 01.353 0246   Telex : 27286
MIRROR Group Newspapers, Holborn Circus, London EC1P 1DQ   Tel : 01.353 0246 X4780
MISS Carter Publications, 25 Silverwell Street, Bolton, Lancs.   Tel : 0204 386608
MITCHELL Beazley London Ltd., 14-15 Manette Street, London W1V 5LB   Tel : 01.434 3272 - distributed by Bookpoint
MITRE Press, 115 Old Street, London EC1V 9JR   Tel : 01.251 4995
MITRE Publications, 59-61 High Street, Newport Pagnell   Tel : 0908 610780
Andrew MOBBS Publ.Ltd., 16 The Square, Kenilworth, Warwicks.CV8 1EB   Tel : 0926 511524
MODEL & Allied Publishers, PO Box 35, Bridge Street, Hemel Hempstead, Herts.HP1 1EE
MODERN English Publications Ltd., PO Box 129, Oxford OX2 8JU   Tel : 0865 53539
MODERN Humanities Research Association, Kings College, Strand, London WC2R 2LS   Tel : 01.836 5454
MODERN Library, USA - c/o Wildwood House
MODERN Management Techniques, 121a-125a Sefton Street, Southport, Lancs.   Tel : 0704 59581
MODERN Metal Publications, 14 Knoll Road, Dorking, Surrey   Tel : 0306 884079
MODERN Plastics International, 50 Avenue de la Gare, 1003 Lausanne, Switzerland
MOLENDINAR Press, 16 Laurel Street, Glasgow G11 7QR   Tel : 041.334 8540
MOMENTA Publ.Ltd., 7 Dunkenshaw Crescent, Lancaster LA1 4LQ - distributed by Biblios Publ.Distribution Services Ltd.

Arnoldo MONDADORI Co.Ltd., 1-4 Argyll Street, London
    W1V 1AD   Tel : 01.734 6301 Telex : 24610
MONEY Management, 2 Greystoke Place, Fetter Lane,
    London EC4   Tel : 01.405 6969
MONITOR Press, Rectory Road, Great Waldingfield, Sudbury,
    Suffolk CO10 0TL   Tel : 0783 78607 Telex : 21120
MONKMAN-Rumsey, PO Box 3760, Wilmington, Del.19807,
    USA   Tel : 302 658 7587 Telex : 835409
MONKS Publications, Debden Green, Saffron Walden, Essex
    CB11 3LX   Tel : 0371 830598
MONTEC Publications Ltd., 150 Railway Terrace, Rugby,
    Warwicks. CV21 3HN   Tel : 0788 890 419
MONTHLY Review Press, 47 The Cut, London SE1 8LL
    Tel : 01.261 1354
MOODY's Investors Service, 6-8 Bonhill Street, London EC2A
    4BU   Tel : 01.628 3691 Telex : 886697
MOONRAKER Press, 26 St.Margarets Street, Bradford-on-Avon,
    Wilts.   Tel : 022 16 3469
MOOR Platt Press Ltd., c/o E.& W.Bleasdale, 13 Starling Road,
    Radcliffe, Manchester   Tel : 061.764 1654
MOOR Press, Bank House, Baildon Green, Shipley, Yorks.
    BD17 5JA   Tel : 0274 583450
MOORE Publishing, Abacus House, Hendon Street, Grimsby
    DN3 3QD   Tel : 0472 52537
MOORE Special, PO Box 4088, Bridgeport, Conn.06607, USA
MOORLAND Publ.Co.Ltd., PO Box 2, 11 Station Street,
    Ashbourne, Derbyshire DE6 1DZ   Tel : 033 55 5086
MORAL Re-Armament Books, 54 Lyford Road, London SW18 3JJ
    Tel : 01.870 2124 Telex : 917820
A.MORCA,C.E., Rue Jules Lejeune 55, B-1060 Brussels, Belgium
MORGAN Grampian(Publ.)Ltd., 30 Calderwood Street, London
    SE18 6QH   Tel : 01.855 7777
R.MORGAN Publishing, Morgans, Southill Road, Chislehurst,
    Kent BR7 5EE   Tel : 01.467 2703 - distributed by
    Argus Books Ltd.
A.E.MORGAN Publications Ltd., Stanley House, 9 West Street,
    Epsom, Surrey KT18 7RL
MORGANITE Electrical Carbon Ltd., Clase Road, Morriston,
    Swansea SA6 8PP   Tel : 0792 721817 Telex : 48280
MORRELL Publ. - now Economic Forecasters Publ.Ltd.
Robert MORRIS Associates, PO Box 8500, S-1140 Philadelphia,
    PA 19178, USA
MORRIS International Ltd., 133 Regency Street, London SW1E
    6AJ   Tel : 01.828 2557
E.J.MORTEN(Booksellers)Ltd., 6 Warburton Street, Didsbury,
    Manchester M20 0RA   Tel : 061.445 7629
MOSBY-Yearbook Ltd., Barnard's Inn, Holborn, London EC1N
    2JA   Tel : 01.242 9613 Telex : 268633
MOTOR Industry Research Association, Watling Street,
    Nuneaton, Warwicks. CV10 0TU   Tel : 0682 68541
MOTOR Racing Directory, The Mill House, Station Road,
    Eastville, Boston, Lincs. PE22 8LS
    Tel : 020 584 377
MOTOR Racing Publications Ltd., 28&32 Devonshire Road,
    Chiswick, London W4 2HD   Tel : 01.994 6783
MOTORBOOKS International Publishers & Wholesalers Inc.,
    729 Prospect Avenue, Osceola, WI 54020, USA
    Tel : 715 294 3345
Anthony MOTT Ltd., 50 Stile Hall Gardens, London W4 3BU
    Tel : 01.994 3875
MOUETTE Press, Wightwick, Boars Hill, Oxford OX1 5DR
    Tel : 0865 735380
MOUTON Publ., PO Box 482, Frankenslag 173, The Hague,
    The Netherlands - distributed by IBD - represented
    by Global Book Resources
MOVEMENT Publications, c/o PO Box 226, Pennant Hills 2120,
    Australia
A.R.MOWBRAY & Co.Ltd., St.Thomas House, Becket Street,
    Oxford OX1 1SJ   Tel : 0865 242507 - distributed by
    J.M.Dent & Sons(Distribution)Ltd.
Abigail MOZLEY Ltd., 8 Wood Lane, Falmouth, Cornwall
    Tel : 0326 314758
MULLARD Ltd., T.P.D., New Road, Mitcham, Surrey CR4 4XY
    Tel : 01.648 3471 Telex : 22194
Frederick MULLER Ltd., Dataday House, 8 Alexandra Road,
    London SW19 7JZ   Tel : 01.946 9188
MULTICARE Soldtes Ltd., Maylands Avenue, Hemel Hempstead,
    HP2 9EP
MULTILINGUAL Matters, Bank House, 8a Hill Road, Clevedon,
    Avon BS21 7HH   Tel : 0272 876519
MULTIMEDIA Publ.Ltd., PO Box 76, Chislehurst, Kent BR7 5HL
    Tel : 01.467 7416
MULTINATIONAL Business Guides Inc., Harvard Square, Boston,
    Mass., USA
MULTINATIONAL Executive Inc., Harvard Square, Box 92,
    Cambridge, MA 02138, USA

MUNICIPAL Publ.Ltd., 178-202 Great Portland Street, London
    W1N 6NH   Tel : 01.631 2400 Telex : 262568
MUNKSGAARD International Publ.Ltd., 35 Nørre Søgade,
    DK-1370 Copenhagen K, Denmark
James MUNRO & Co.Ltd., c/o Youngi Raith Road, Fenwick,
    Kilmarnock, Ayrshire KA3 6DQ   Tel : 05606 454
MUNRO-Barr Publications Ltd., 256 West George Street, Glasgow
    G2 42P   Tel : 041.248 4667
Thomas MURBY & Co., Park Lane, Hemel Hempstead, Herts HP2
    4TE   Tel : 0442 3244 Telex : 826261
A.J.MURPHY, 152 Yarmouth Road, Norwich, Norfolk
    Tel : 0603 38246
John MURRAY (Publ.)Ltd., 50 Albemarle Street, London W1X
    4BD   Tel : 01.493 4361/3 Telex : 21312
MURRAYS Remainder Books Ltd. - gone away 1982
MUSEUM Association, 34 Bloomsbury Way, London WC1A 2SF
    Tel : 01.404 4767
MUSEUM of Cider Ltd., The Cider Mills, Ryelands Street,
    Hereford HR4 0LW   Tel : 0432 54207
MUSEUM of Modern Art, New York - c/o TABS
MUSEUM Prints, 25 Brunswick Road, Gloucester
    Tel : 0452 421827
MUSHROOM Books & Crafts, 10 Heathcote Street, Nottingham
MUSHROOM Publishing, 102 Gloucester Place, London W1
MUSIC Research, 36 Packington Street, London N1 8OB
MUSIC Sales Ltd., Distribution Centre, Newmarket Road, Bury
    St.Edmunds, Suffolk IP33 3YB   Tel : 0284 68011
MUSLIM Educational Trust, 130 Stroud Green Road, London N4
    3RZ   Tel : 01.272 8502

N

NACAB (National Association of Citizens' Advice Bureaux), 27
    Clerkenwell Close, London EC1R 0AT
    Tel : 01.251 4976
NACE, PO Box 1891, Houston, Texas 14001, USA
N.A.G.Press Ltd., Elm House, 10-16 Elm Street, London WC1X
    0BP   Tel : 01.278 2345 - orders to 93-99 Goswell Road,
    London EC1V 7QA   Tel : 01.253 9355
NATCO U.K.Ltd., 19th Floor, Station House, Harrow Road,
    Wembley, Middx.HA9 6EN   Tel : 01.903 1424
NATO - see North Atlantic Treaty Organisation
NBA, 7 Arundel Street, London WC2R 3AZ
NBCC Ltd., NBA House, 7 Arundel Street, London WC2R 3AZ
    Tel : 01.836 4488 - orders to PO Box 87, 1-3
    Pemberton Row, London EC4P 4HL   Tel : 01.353 3300
NCC Publications, The National Computer Centre Ltd., Oxford
    Road, Manchester M1 7ED   Tel : 061.228 6333
    Telex : 668962 - orders to J.M.Dent & Sons(Distrib.)
    Ltd.
N.C.H., Sales Division, Ambrose Lane, Harpenden, Herts AL5
    4BY   Tel : 05827 62150
NCLC Publishing Society Ltd., 11 Dartmouth Street, London
    SW1H 9BN   Tel : 01.222 8877
NCRP Publications, 7910 Woodmont Avenue, Suite 1016, Bethesda
    Maryland 20814, USA
NEDO Books - see National Economic Development Office
NFBTE Publications, Federation House, 2309 Coventry Road,
    Sheldon, Birmingham B26 3PL   Tel : 021.742 5121
NFER-Nelson Publ.Co.Ltd., 2 Oxford Road East, Windsor, Berks
    SL4 1DF   Tel : 07535 58961
NFPA - see National Fire Protection Association
N.G.Middle East Communication Services Ltd., 18 Curzon Street
    London W1   Tel : 01.409 2622/3
NIFES (National Industrial Fuel Efficiency Service Ltd.),
    Orchard House, Great Smith Street, London SW1P
    3BU   Tel : 01.222 0961
NIGP Borba, TRG Marksa 1, Engelsa 7, 1101 Beograd,
    Jugoslavia
NIOSH, 4676 Columbia Parkway, Cincinnati, Ohio 45226, USA
NMI Ltd. - see National Maritime Institute
N.O.P.Market Research Ltd., Tower House, Southampton Street
    London WC2E 7HN   Tel : 01.836 1511
NOWA Polish Independent Publ.House, c/o Miroslow Chojecki,
    Vl.Sarbiewskiego 2m47, Warsaw, Poland - distributed
    by Aleksander Smolar, 9 Rue Dr.A.Schweitzer,
    92220 Bagneux, France   Tel : 664 3846
N.R.C.d. - see National Reprographic Centre for documentation
NRDC - see National Research Development Corporation
NTIS - see National Technical Information Service of U.S.
NTL Institute for Applied Behavioural Science, N.Dorr Avenue,
    Fairfax, VA 22030, USA
NTL Learning Resources Corp.7594 Eads Avenue, La Jolla,
    California 92037, USA

NUS Publications, 3 Endsleigh Street, London WC1 0DU
    Tel : 01.387 1277 Telex : 25951
NAFFERTON Books(Studies in Education Ltd.), Railway Cottages, Wansford Road, Driffield, E.Yorks. Tel : 0377 46861
NAGEL Publ., 42 Bloomsbury Street, London WC1
NANOGENS International, PO Box 487, CA 95019, USA
NÄRINGSLIVETS Förlagsdistribution, 103 20 Stockholm, Sweden
NASE Delo (Our Works), 53 Hawthorne Drive, Harrow, Middx. HA2 7NU Tel : 01.868 8080
NATIONAL Abortion Campaign, 374 Grays Inn Road, London WC1X 8BB Tel : 01.278 0153
NATIONAL Academy of Engineering - orders to Castle House Publ.
NATIONAL Academy of Sciences, 2101 Constitution Ave., Washington DC, USA - orders to Castle House Publ.
NATIONAL Advisory Centre on Careers for Women, 251 Brompton Road, London SW3
NATIONAL Aeronautics & Space Administration, 400 Maryland Ave.SW, Washington DC 20546, USA - orders to American Information Retrieval Service
NATIONAL Anti-Vivisection Society Ltd., 51 Harley Street, London W1N 1DD Tel : 01.580 4034
NATIONAL Army Museum, Royal Hospital Road, London SW3 4HT
NATIONAL Association for the Care & Resettlement of Offenders, 169 Clapham Road, London SW9 0PU Tel : 01.582 6500 - distributed by Barry Rose (Publ.)Ltd.
NATIONAL Association of Accountants, 919 3rd Avenue, New York 10022, USA
NATIONAL Association of Boys' Clubs, 24 Highbury Grove, London N5 2EA Tel : 01.359 9281
NATIONAL Association of Corrosion Engineers, PO Box 986, Katy, Texas 77450, USA
NATIONAL Association of Drop Forgers & Stampers, Grove Hill House, 245 Grae Lane, Handsworth, Birmingham B20 2HB Tel : 021.554 3311
NATIONAL Association of Head Teachers, Holly House, 6 Paddockhall Road, Haywards Heath, W.Sussex RH16 1RG Tel : 0444 453291/2
NATIONAL Association of Pension Funds, Sunley House, Bedford Park, Croydon CR0 0XF
NATIONAL Association of Plumbing, Heating & Mechanical Services Contractors, 6 Gate Street, London WC2A 3HX
NATIONAL Association of Port Employers, Commonwealth House, 1-19 New Oxford Street, London WC1A 1DZ Tel : 01.242 1200 Telex : 295741
NATIONAL Association of Teachers in Further & Higher Education, Hamilton House, Mabledon Place, London WC1H 9BH Tel : 01.387 6806
NATIONAL Association of Youth Clubs, Keswick House, 30 Peacock Lane, Leicester Tel : 0533 29514
NATIONAL Bible Society of Scotland, 7 Hampton Terrace, Edinburgh EH12 5XU Tel : 031.337 9701/2
NATIONAL Board of Boiler & Pressure Vessel Inspectors, 1055 Crupper Avenue, Columbus, Ohio 43229, USA Tel : 614 888 8320 Telex : 246 625
NATIONAL Book League, Book House, 45 East Hill, London SW18 2QZ Tel : 01.870 9055 / 15a Lynedoch Street, Glasgow G3 6EF Tel : 041.332 0391
NATIONAL Building Agency, NBA House, 7 Arundel Street, London WC2R 3DZ Tel : 01.836 4488 Telex : 268312
NATIONAL Bureau for Handicapped Students, 40 Brunswick Square, London WC1N 1AZ Tel : 01.278 3459
NATIONAL Bureau of Economic Research, 1050 Massachusetts Avenue, Cambridge, Mass.02138, USA Tel : 617 868 3900
NATIONAL Bureau of Standards, Office of Technical Information & Publications, Washington DC 20234, USA
NATIONAL Bus Company Publications, 25 New Street Square, London EC4 Tel : 01.583 9177
NATIONAL Cancer Institute, Building 31, Room 10A18, Bethesda, Maryland 20205, USA
NATIONAL Caravan Council Ltd., 43-45 High Street, Weybridge Surrey KT13 8BT Tel : 0932 51376/9 Telex : 928800
NATIONAL Cattle Breeders Association, Cholesbury, Tring, Herts. Tel : 024 029 544
NATIONAL Centre for Alternative Technology, Llwyngwern Quarry, Machynlleth, Powys, Wales Tel : 0654 2400
NATIONAL Centre for School Technology, Trent Polytechnic, Burton Street, Nottingham NG1 4BU Tel : 0602 48248
NATIONAL Children's Bureau, 8 Wakley Street, London EC1V 7QE Tel : 01.278 9441
NATIONAL Children's Homes, 85 Highbury Park, London N5 1UD Tel : 01.226 2033
NATIONAL Christian Education Council, Robert Denholm House, Nutfield, Redhill RH1 4HW Tel : 073 782 2411
NATIONAL Clearinghouse for Drug Abuse Information, PO Box 416, Kensington, Maryland 20795, USA
NATIONAL Coal Board, Hobart House, Grosvenor Place, London SW1X 7AE Tel : 01.235 2020
NATIONAL Coal Board, Library, Coal House, Doncaster DN1 3HD Tel : 0302 66611
NATIONAL Company of Paper Industry, 260 Madison Avenue, New York, USA
NATIONAL Computing Centre, Oxford Road, Manchester M1 7ED Tel : 061.228 6333 - distributed by J.M.Dent & Sons (Distribution)Ltd.
NATIONAL Consumer Council, 18 Queen Anne's Gate, London SW1H 9AA Tel : 01.930 5752
NATIONAL Council for Civil Liberties, 21 Tabard Street, London SE1 4LA Tel : 01.403 3888 - distributed by Southern Distribution
NATIONAL Council for One Parent Families, 255 Kentish Town Road, London NW5 2LX Tel : 01.267 1361
NATIONAL Council for Voluntary Organisations, 26 Bedford Square, London WC1B 3HU Tel : 01.636 4066 - orders to Macdonald & Evans Distribution Services Ltd.
NATIONAL Council of Social Services, 26 Bedford Square, London WC1B 3HU - orders to Bedford Square Press
NATIONAL Council of Teachers of Mathematics, 1906 Association Drive, Reston, VA 22091, USA Tel : 703 620 9840
NATIONAL Council on Alcoholism, 3 Grosvenor Crescent, London SW1X 7EE Tel : 01.235 4182
NATIONAL Dairymen's Association, 19 Cornwall Terrace, London NW1 4QP Tel : 01.486 7244 Telex : 262027
NATIONAL Development Programme in Computer Assisted Learning, 37-41 Mortimer Street, London W1N 7RJ Tel : 01.637 0552/01.580 2226
NATIONAL Economic Development Office, NEDO Books, Millbank Tower, Millbank, London SW1P 4QX Tel : 01.211 5989 or 5985
NATIONAL Eczema Society, Tavistock House North, Tavistock Square, London WC1H 9SR Tel : 01.388 4097
NATIONAL Electronics Manufacturers Association, 2101 N.W. L Street, Washington DC 20037, USA
NATIONAL Engineering Laboratory, East Kilbride, Glasgow G75 0QU Tel : 035 52 20222 Telex : 777888
NATIONAL Enterprise Board - now British Technology Group
NATIONAL Extension College, 18 Brooklands Avenue, Cambridge CB2 2HN Tel : 0223 316644
NATIONAL Federation of Building Trade Employees, Crompton Way, Crawley, Sussex RH10 2QP
NATIONAL Federation of Building Trade Employers - see NFBTE Publications
NATIONAL Federation of Demolition Contractors, Cowdray House 6 Portugal Street, London WC2A 2HH Tel : 01.404 4020 Telex : 8955101
NATIONAL Federation of Housing Associations, 30-32 Southampton Street, London WC2E 7HE Tel : 01.240 2771
NATIONAL Federation of Roofing Contractors, 15 Soho Square London W1V 5FB
NATIONAL Federation of Women's Institutes, 39 Eccleston Street London SW1W 9NT Tel : 01.730 7212
NATIONAL Fire Protection Association, Batterymarch Park Quincy, MA 02269, USA
NATIONAL Froebel Foundation, Froebel Institute, Grove House, Roehampton Lane, London SW15 5PJ Tel : 01.876 2242
NATIONAL Gallery, Publications Dept., Trafalgar Square, London WC2N 5DN Tel : 01.839 3321
NATIONAL Gallery of Ireland - distributed by Colin Smythe Ltd.
The NATIONAL Gardens Scheme, 57 Lower Belgrave Street, London SW1W 0LR Tel : 01.730 0359
NATIONAL Gas Turbine Establishment, Pyestock, Farnborough Hants. Tel : 0252 44411
NATIONAL Geographic Society, Washington DC, USA
NATIONAL Housebuilding Council, 58 Portland Place, London W1N 4BU
NATIONAL Illumination Committee of G.B., c/o Jules Thorn Lighting Laboratory, Thorn EMI Lighting Ltd., Great Cambridge Road, Enfield, Middx.EN1 1UL
NATIONAL Industrial Conference Board, 845 Bad Avenue, New York 10022, USA
NATIONAL Industrial Fuel Efficiency Service Ltd. - see NIFES
NATIONAL Institute for Research in Dairying, Shinfield, Reading, Berks RG2 9AT Tel : 0734 883103
NATIONAL Institute for Social Work, Mary Ward House, 5-7 Tavistock Place, London WC1H 9SS Tel : 01.387 9681
NATIONAL Institute of Adult Education, De Montfort House, 19b De Montfort Street, Leicester LE1 7GE Tel : 0533 551451
NATIONAL Institute of Agricultural Botany, Huntindon Road, Cambridge CB3 0LE Tel : 0223 76381

NATIONAL Institute of Economic & Social Research, 2 Dean Trench Street, Smith Square, London SW1P 3HE Tel : 01.222 7665
NATIONAL Institute of Industrial Psychology - see NFER
NATIONAL Institute on Drug Abuse, 5600 Fishers Lane, Rockville, Maryland 20852, USA
NATIONAL Institution of Agricultural Engineering, Wrest Park, Silsoe, Bedford MK45 4HS Tel : 0525 60000
NATIONAL Lampoon Books - c/o TABS
NATIONAL League of Cities, 1020 Eye Street NW, Washington DC 20006, USA
NATIONAL Library of Scotland, George IV Bridge, Edinburgh EH1 1EW Tel : 031.226 4531
NATIONAL Library of Wales, Aberystwyth, Dyfed SY23 8BU Tel : 0970 3816
NATIONAL Magazine Co.Ltd., National Magazine House, 72 Broadwick Street, London W1V 2BP Tel : 01.437 7833 Telex : 263879 - magazine distribution : COMAG, Tavistock Road, West Drayton, Middx.
NATIONAL Maritime Institute, Feltham, Middx.TW14 0LQ Tel : 01.977 0933 Telex : 263118
NATIONAL Maritime Museum, Greenwich, London SE10 9NF Tel : 01.858 4422
NATIONAL Marriage Guidance Council, Little Church Street, Rugby, Warwicks. CV21 3AP Tel : 0788 73241
NATIONAL Materials Handling Centre, Cranfield Institute of Technology, Cranfield, Bedford MK43 0AL Tel : 0234 750323
NATIONAL Microfilm Association, 8719 Colesville Road, Silver Spring, MD.20910, USA
NATIONAL Micrographics Association, 8719 Colesville Road, Silver Spring, MD 20910, USA
NATIONAL Museum of Wales, Cathays Park, Cardiff CF1 3NP Tel : 0222 397951
NATIONAL Physical Laboratory, Teddington, Middx.TW11 0LW Tel : 01.977 3222
NATIONAL Playing Fields Association, 25 Ovington Square, London SW3 1LQ Tel : 01.584 6445
NATIONAL Portrait Gallery, 2 St.Martins Place, London WC2H 0HE Tel : 01.930 1552 X54 & 29
NATIONAL Ports Council - ceased publishing, 1981
NATIONAL Pure Water Association, Southern Ash, Gilberts Lane, Whixall, Whitchurch, Shropshire SY13 2PR Tel : 094872 642
NATIONAL Radiological Protection Board, Chilton, Didcot, Oxon. OX11 0RQ Tel : 0235 831600 Telex : 837124 - publications via HMSO
NATIONAL Register Publ.Co., 5201 Old Orchard Road, Skokie, Ill.60076, USA
NATIONAL Reprographic Centre for documentation, The Hatfield Polytechnic, Bayfordbury, Lower Hatfield Road, Hertford, Herts. SG13 8LD Tel : 0992 552341/2
NATIONAL Research Council - orders to Castle House Publ.
NATIONAL Research Council of Canada, Montreal Road, Ottawa, Ontario, K1A 0R6, Canada
NATIONAL Research Development Corporation - now British Technology Group
NATIONAL Semiconductor (UK)Ltd., 301 Harpur Centre, Horne Lane, Bedford MK40 1TR Tel : 0234 47147
NATIONAL Sheep Association, Cholesbury, Tring, Herts. Tel : 024 029 544
NATIONAL Society for Clean Air, 136 North Street, Brighton BN1 1RG Tel : 0273 26313
NATIONAL Society of Duck Keepers, Pheasants' Coombe, Hambleden, Henley-on-Thames, Oxon. RG9 6SD
NATIONAL Terotechnology Centre, Cleeve Road, Leatherhead, Surrey KT22 7SA Tel : 037 23 7842
NATIONAL Textbook Co., USA - distributed by Sweet & Maxwell
NATIONAL Trust, 42 Queen Anne's Gate, London SW1H 9AS Tel : 01.222 9251 / Western Way, Melksham, Wilts.
NATIONAL Union of Students, 3 Endsleigh Street, London WC1 0DU
NATIONAL Union of Teachers, Hamilton House, Mabledon Place, London WC1H 9BD Tel : 01.387 2442/7
NATIONAL Vegetable Research Station, Wellesbourne, Warwick CV35 9EF Tel : 0789 840382
NATIONAL Water Council, 1 Queen Anne's Gate, London SW1H 9BT Tel : 01.222 8111
NATIONAL Westminster Bank Ltd., Business Development Div., 41 Lothbury, London EC2P 2BP Tel : 01.726 1000
NATIONAL Women's Aid Federation, 26 Clerkenwell Close, London EC1R 0AT Tel : 01.251 4976
NATIONAL Wool Textile Export Corp., Lloyds Bank Chambers, 43 Hustlergate, Bradford, Yorks. BD1 1PE
NATIONAL Youth Bureau, 17-23 Albion Street, Leicester

NATIONWIDE Book Service, 5 Buckingham Gate, London SW1 Tel : 01.828 3942
NATTALI & Maurice, 9 Bow Street, London WC2E 7AL Tel : 01.836 9081 - distributed by Bodley Head Ltd.
NATURAL Energy Centre, 161 Clarence Street, Kingston-upon-Thames, Surrey KT1 1QT
NATURAL Environment Research Council, Alhambra House, 27-33 Charing Cross Road, London WC2H 0RX Tel : 01.930 9232
NATURAL History Museum, Cromwell Road, London SW7 5BD Tel : 01.589 6323
NATURAL History Press - c/o TABS
NATURE Conservancy Council, Attingham Park, Shrewsbury, Shropshire SY4 4TW Tel : 074377 611
NAUTICAL Books, 4 Little Essex Street, London WC2R 3LF Tel : 01.836 6633 Telex : 262024
NAUTICAL Publ.Co.Ltd., Nautical House, Lymington, Hants. SO4 9BA Tel : 0590 72578 Telex : 47674
NAVAL Institute Press, 2-6 Hampstead High Street, London NW3 Tel : 01.794 7868
NAYLOR Press, Skerry Lore, Undercliff, Sandygate, Folkestone Kent CT20 3AT Tel : 0303 38178
NEALE Watson Academic Publ., Room 110, 156 5th Avenue, New York 10010, USA
NELPRESS, Danbury Park, Danbury, Chelmsford, Essex CM3 4AT Tel : 024541 2141
Anthony NELSON Ltd., 7 St.Johns Hill, Shrewsbury, Shropshire SY1 1JE Tel : 0743 3651
Don NELSON Publications Ltd., PO Box 193, Barnet, Herts. EN4 8LP Tel : 01.368 5534
Thomas NELSON & Sons Ltd., Nelson House, Walton-on-Thames Surrey KT12 5PL Tel : 093 22 46133 Telex : 929365
W.R.NELSON & Co., 11 Elm Place, Rye, New York 10580, USA
NEM Chand & Bros., Civil Lines, Roorkee 247667, Uttar, Pradesh, India
NETHER Halse Books, Winsford, Minehead, Somerset TA24 7JE Tel : 064 385 314
NETHERLANDS State Printers, Christoffel Plan Tijustraat, The Hague, The Netherlands
NETHERLANDS Chamber of Commerce in the U.K., 307-308 High Holborn, London WC1V 7LS Tel : 01.405 1358
NETWORK, Printers Mews, Market Hill, Buckingham MK18 1JX Tel : 028 02 5226/7
NETWORK Communications, Index House, 29 Junction Road, Lightwater, Surrey GU18 5TQ Tel : 0276 75160
NEW African Yearbook - distributed by International Communications
NEW American Library Inc., 1301 Ave.of the Americas, New York 10019, USA - distributed by New English Library
NEW Cavendish Books, 23 Craven Hill, London W2 Tel : 01.262 7905
NEW Caxton Library Services Ltd., Holywell House, 72-90 Worship Street, London EC2A 2EN Tel : 01.247 5400
NEW Commercial Publ.Co.Ltd., 4 St.John's Terrace, London W10 Tel : 01.289 6504
NEW Encyclopaedia of Employment Law & Practice, 3 New Burlington Street, London W1X 2AA Tel : 01.439 2431
NEW English Library - distributed by Hodder & Stoughton Services
NEW Era Press, Lambourn Woodlands, Newbury, Berks RG16 7TW Tel : 0488 72666
NEW Fiction Society, 7 Albemarle Street, London W1 Tel : 01.493 9001
NEW Forest Leaves, Bisterne Close, Burley, Ringwood, Hants. BH24 4BA Tel : 04253 3315
NEW Foundations, 83 Heath Lane, Bladon, Oxford OX7 1SA
NEW Horizon General Publishers, 25 Station Road, Bognor Regis PO21 2RH Tel : 0243 821772/829421
NEW Knowledge Books, 18 Elizabeth Crescent, East Grinstead, W.Sussex - distributed by Rudolf Steiner Press
NEW Leaf Books Ltd., 38 Camden Lock, Commercial Place, Chalk Farm Road, London NW1 8AF Tel : 01.267 6183
NEW Left Books, 15 Greek Street, London W1V 5LF Tel : 01.437 3546 - distributed by IBD
NEW Library World, Clive Bingley (Journals) Ltd., 16 Pembridge Road, London W11 Tel : 01.229 1825
NEW Opportunity Press Ltd., 76 St.James Lane, London N10 Tel : 01.444 7281 Telex : 28604-137-607
NEW Park Publications Ltd., 216 Old Town, London SW4 0JT Tel : 01.622 7029
NEW Perspectives Publ.Ltd., 46 Bloomsbury Street, London WC1B 3QQ Tel : 01.637 0908
NEW Playwrights' Network, 35 Sandringham Road, Macclesfield Cheshire SK10 1QB Tel : 0625 25312

NEW Science Publications, New Scientist Readers Services, 2614 Kings Reach Tower, Stamford Street, London SE1 Tel : 01.261 5000 Telex : 915748
NEW University of Ulster, Coleraine, Co.Derry BT52 1SA Tel : 0265 4141
NEW York Academy of Sciences, 2 East 63rd Street, New York 10021, USA
NEW York Botanical Garden Press - distributed by Bowker
NEW York State School of Industrial Labour Relations, Cornell University, PO Box 1000, Ithaca, NY 14853, USA
NEW York Times Co., Book Division, 330 Madison Avenue, New York 10017, USA - distributed by Harper & Row
NEW York University Press - distributed by Eurospan
NEWBURY House Publ.Ltd., 35 Woodland Gardens, London N10 Tel : 01.883 6110 - distributed by IBD
R. & R.NEWKIRK, PO Box 1727, Indianapolis, Indiana 46206, USA Tel : 317 297 4360
NEWMAN Books Ltd., 48 Poland Street, London W1V 4PP Tel : 01.439 0335
NEWMAN Communications Ltd., Suite 68, 13 Henrietta Street, London WC2E 8LH Tel : 01.836 4688
NEWMAN-Howells Assocs.Ltd., Wolvesey Palace, Winchester, Hants. SO23 9NB Tel : 0962 63173
NEWNES Books, Astronaut House, Hounslow Road, Feltham, Middx.TW14 9AR Tel : 01.890 1480
NEWNES Technical Books - distributed by Butterworth & Co.
NEWS & Media Ltd., 33 Stroud Green Road, London N4 3EF Tel : 01.263 1417
NEWSPAPER Archive Developments Ltd. - now called Research Publications Ltd.
NEWSWEEK International, Newsweek House, Wellington Street, Slough, Berks SL1 1UG
NEXUS, 26-27 West India House, Baldwin Street, Bristol, Avon. Tel : 0272 279528
NICHOLAS Publ.Co., PO Box 96, New York 10024, USA
Robert NICHOLSON Publ.Ltd., 17-21 Conway Street, London W1P 5HL Tel : 01.387 2811
NICHOLSON & Bass Ltd., 3 Clarence Street West, Belfast BT2 7GP Tel : 0232 27491
NIELSEN Clearing House, 1900 North 3rd Street, Clinton, Iowa 52732, USA Tel : 319 242 4505
NIHON Brain Publ.Co., c/o Maruzen Co.Ltd., PO Box 5050 Tokyo International, 100-31 Japan
Martinus NIJHOFF Ltd., Lange Voorhout 9-11, PO Box 269, The Hague, The Netherlands Tel : 010 31 70 469460 Telex : 34164 - distributed by Kluwer Academic Publ. Group, The Netherlands
NILE & Mackenzie Ltd., 43 Dover Street, London W1X 3RE Tel : 01.493 0351 Telex : 268312
James NISBET & Co.Ltd., Digswell Place, Welwyn Garden City, Herts. AL8 7SX Tel : 070 73 25491
George NOBBS Publishing, 90 Hall Road, Norwich, Norfolk Tel : 0603 611406
NOBELS Explosives Co.Ltd. - distributed by Callerton Explosives Sales Dept., Street Houses, Ponteland, Newcastle upon Tyne NE20 9BT
NOMAD Publ.Ltd., 2 Great Marlborough Street, London W1V 1DE Tel : 01.434 2853 Telex : 27269
NOMURA Research Institute, Japan - orders to Financial Times Business Publ.Ltd.
NONESUCH Library, 9 Bow Street, London WC2E 7AL Tel : 01.379 6637 Telex : 299080 - distributed by Bodley Head Ltd.
NOONAN Hurst Ltd., 131 Trafalgar Road, Greenwich, London SE10 9TX Tel : 01.692 1475/6 - orders to Unit 6, Seager Building, Brookmill Road, Deptford, London SE8 Tel : 01.692 1475
NOORDHOFF Intl.Publ. - now Sijthoff & Noordhoff Intl.Publ.
Paul NORBURY Publ.Ltd., Caxton House, High Street, Tenterden Kent TN30 6BD Tel : 05806 4141
NORDISK Handelskalender, Sydvestrej 49, DK-2600 Glostrup Copenhagen, Denmark
NORFOLK Press Ltd., 82 Hurlingham Court, Ranelagh Gardens, London SW6 3UR Tel : 01.736 0189
NORMAL Press, 25 Vicarage Lane, Upper Hale, Farnham, Surrey
Jill NORMAN Ltd., 90-91 Great Russell Street, London WC1B 3PY Tel : 01.631 4141 - distributed by J.M.Dent & Sons (Distribution)Ltd.
NOROIL Publ.House Ltd., 50 Gresham Street, London EC2V 7AY Tel : 01.606 3266
NORRIS Modern Press Ltd., 6 Victoria Street, Douglas, Isle of Man Tel : 0624 5054
NORRIS, Oakley Richardson & Glover, Kent House, Telegraph Street, London EC2 Tel : 01.588 4080
NORSK Opinionsinstitutt AS, Huitfeldtsgade 51, Postboks 2306-Solli, Oslo 2, Norway Tel : 11 10 54

NORSK Petroleumsforening,.(Norwegian Petroleum Society), PO Box 1897, Vika, Oslo 1, Norway
NORTH Atlantic Treaty Organisation - distributed by Ministry of Defence, Station Square House, St.Mary Cray, Orpington, Kent BR5 3RE
NORTH of England Development Council, Bank House, Carliol Square, Newcastle upon Tyne NE1 6XE
NORTH of England Law Book Publ.Co., PO Box 11, Heaton, Newcastle upon Tyne NE7 7DW
NORTH of Scotland College of Agriculture, 581 King Street, Aberdeen AB9 1UD Tel : 0224 40291
NORTH East London Polytechnic, Romford Road, London E15 4LB Tel : 01.590 8236
NORTH Sea Oil Directory - see Spearhead Publications Ltd.
NORTH Semiconductor (UK) Ltd., Larkfield Industrial Estate, Greenoak PA16 0EP, Scotland Tel : 0475 33251
NORTHAMPTONSHIRE Record Society, Delapre Abbey, Northampton NN4 9AW Tel : 0604 62297
J.W.NORTHEND Ltd., 49 West Street, Sheffield S1 3SH Tel : 0742 730341
NORTHERN Business Information, 287 MacPherson Avenue, Toronto M4V 1A4, Canada Tel : 416 961 1201
NORTHERN House Poets, 19 Haldane Terrace, Jesmond, Newcastle upon Tyne NE2 3AN Tel : 0632 812614
NORTHERN Publishing Workshop, 5 Charlotte Square, Newcastle upon Tyne NE1 4XF Tel : 0632 22634
NORTHERN Technology Books, Box 62, Evanston, IL 60204, USA
NORTHERN Times Ltd., Main Street, Golspie, Sutherland KW10 6RD Tel : 040 83 3784
NORTHGATE Publ.Co.Ltd., PO Box 24, Northgate Avenue, Bury St.Edmunds, Suffolk IP32 6BW Tel : 0284 63277
NORTH-Holland Publ.Co., PO Box 211, 1000AE Amsterdam, The Netherlands Tel : 20 5803 911 Telex : 18582
NORTHUMBRIAN Pipers Society, 33 Dunsgreen, Ponteland, Newcastle upon Tyne NE20 9EH Tel : 0661 24466 / 15 Parkside Crescent, Seaham, Co.Durham Tel : 0670 813248 X56
NORTHWESTERN University Press, 1735 Benson Avenue, Evanston Ill. 60201, USA
NORTHWICK Publishers, 14 Bevere Close, Worcester WR3 7QH Tel : 0905 56876
NORTHWOOD Publications Ltd. - now International Thomson Publishing Ltd.
W.W.NORTON & Co.Ltd., 25 New Street Square, London EC4A 3NT Tel : 01.353 7076 - orders to Ernest Benn Ltd.
NORTON Bailey & Co., 103 Lonsdale Road, London SW13 Tel : 01.748 8519
NORWEGIAN Chamber of Commerce, London, Inc., Norway House 21-24 Cockspur Street, London SW1Y 5BN
NORWICH & Norfolk Chamber of Commerce & Industry, 112 Barrack Street, Norwich NR3 1UB Tel : 0603 25977 Telex : 975247
NOSTALGIA Press, PO Box 293, Franklin Square, New York 11010, USA
NOTTINGHAM Alternative Publications, 27 Clerkenwell Close, London EC1R 0AT Tel : 01.251 4976
NOTTINGHAM Court Press, 44 Great Russell Street, London WC1B 3PA Tel : 01.637 2156
NOVA Hrvatska, 30 Fleet Street, London EC4Y 1AJ Tel : 01.946 9649 Telex : 8811204
NOVELLO & Co.Ltd., Borough Green, Sevenoaks, Kent TN15 8DT Tel : 0732 883261
NOVOSTI Press Agency, 3 Rosary Gardens, London SW7 4NW Tel : 01.373 7350
John L.NOYCE, Publisher, 27 Clerkenwell Close, London EC1R 0AT Tel : 01.251 4976
NOYES Intl.Corp. - distributed by Gothard House Publ.Ltd.
NUCLEAR Energy Intelligence, Teal House, Moat Lane, Prestwood, Great Missenden, Bucks HP16 9DA
The NUFFIELD Foundation, Nuffield Lodge, Regent's Park, London NW1
NUFFIELD Provincial Hospitals Trust, 3 Prince Albert Road, London NW1 7SP Tel : 01.485 8207 - distributed by Oxford University Press
NUMERICAL Algorithms Group Ltd., NAG Central Office, Mayfield House, 256 Banbury Road, Oxford OX2 7DE Tel : 0865 511245 Telex : 83354
NUMISMATIC Publ.Co., Sovereign House, Brentwood, Essex CM14 4SE Tel : 0277 219876
NURSERY World, Cliffords Inn, Fetter Lane, London EC4A 1PJ Tel : 01.242 0935/9
NUTRITION & Food Sciences, Forbes Publications, Hartree House Queensway, London W2 4SH
NYT Nordisk Forlag, Njalsgade 21, Bygning 5, 3 Sal, 2300 Copenhagen, Denmark

O

O & B Books, 1215 NW Kline Place, Carvallis, OR 97330, USA
OAPEC - see Organization of Arab Petroleum Exporting Countries
OCIMF, c/o Witherby & Co., 5 Plantain Place, Crosby Row, London SE1 1YN
O.D.I., 10-11 Percy Street, London W1P 0JB Tel : 01.637 3622
O.E.C.D.(Organisation for Economic Co-operation & Development) - distributed by HMSO
OMF Books, Belmont, The Vine, Sevenoaks, Kent TN13 3TZ
O.P.E.C., Public Relations, Obere Donaustrasse 93, 1-1020 Vienna, Austria
OPS, 190 Camden Hill Road, London W8
ORYX Press, 3930E Camel Back Road, Phoenix, AZ 85018, USA
O.U.E.E. - see Open University Press
OVP, 11 Rue Quentin Bauchart, 75384 Paris, Cedex 08, France
OAK Tree Press Co.Ltd., Unit 14, Trident Industrial Estate, Pindar Road, Hoddesdon, Herts EN11 0LD Tel : 0992 42033 / 47 Marylebone Lane, London W1 Tel : 01.486 3271
OAKWOOD Press, Old School House, Church Hill, Tarrant Hinton, Blandford Forum, Dorset DT11 8JB Tel : 025 889 274
O'BRIAN Press, 20 Victoria Road, Rathgar, Dublin 6
OCEAN Books Ltd., 74 Long Lane, London EC1 Tel : 01.606 9371
OCEANA Group of Publishers, 58 Carey Street, London WC2A 2JB Tel : 01.405 5464
A.S.O'CONNOR & Co.Ltd., 26 Sheen Park, Richmond, Surrey TW9 1UW Tel : 01.940 8371/2
OCTAGON Press Ltd., 14 Baker Street, London W1M 1DA Tel : 01.935 0084 Telex : 261034
OCTOBER Press Ltd., 112-116 Miller Drive, Fareham, Hants. PO16 7LN Tel : 0329 237622
OCTOPUS Books, 59 Grosvenor Street, London W1X 9DA Tel : 01.493 5841 Telex : 27278
OELGESCHLAGER Gun & Hain Inc. - distributed by Eurospan
OFFERPACE Ltd., 47 Balstonia Drive, Stanford-le-Hope, Essex SS17 8HX Tel : 03756 42166
OFFICE du Livre SA, Route de Villars 101, Fribourg, Switzerland
OFFICE for the Official Publications of the European Communities, Rue de Commerce 5, PO Box 1003, Luxembourg
OFFICE of Health Economics, 12 Whitehall, London SW1A 2DY Tel : 01.930 9203
OFFICE of Population Census & Surveys, St.Catherine's House, London WC2B 6JP Tel : 01.242 0262
OFFICE Publ.Inc., 1200 Summer Street, Stamford, Connecticut 06904, USA
John OFFORD Publ.Ltd., PO Box 64, Eastbourne, E.Sussex BN21 3LW
OFFSHORE Engineering, 1-7 Great George Street, London SW1P 3AA Tel : 01.222 9389
OFFSHORE Promotional Services Ltd., 190 Campden Hill Road, Lodon W8 7TH Tel : 01.727 8415
OFICYNA Poetow I Malarzy - see Poets' & Painters' Press
OFREX Ltd., Ofrex House, Stephen Street, London W1A 1EA Tel : 01.636 3686
OGILVY & Mather Ltd., Brettenham House, Lancaster Place, London WC2E 7EZ Tel : 01.836 2466
OGUZ Press Ltd., 193a Shirland Road, London W9 2EU Tel : 01.286 1889/4527
OHIO University, Centre for International Studies - distributed by IBD
OHIO University Press - distributed by IBD
OIL & Colour Chemical Association, 967 Harrow Road, Wembley Middx.HA0 2SF
OIL & Energy Trends, Energy Economics Research Ltd., Guildgate House, The Terrace, Wokingham, Berks RG11 1BP Tel : 0734 789470
OIL & Gas Consult Intl., Suite 1210, 320 South Boston Buildings, Tulsa, Oklahoma 74103, USA
OIL Companies International Marine Forum - distributed by Witherby & Co.Ltd.
OILFIELD Publications Ltd., PO Box 11, Ledbury, Herefordshire HR8 1SN Tel : 0531 4563 Telex : 35566
A.S.ØKONOMISK Litteratur, Postboks 9123 Vaterland, Ebbelsgt.3 Oslo 1, Norway Tel : (02) 20 90 73 Telex : 18536
OLAF Norlis Bokhandel, Universitetsyt 24, Oslo 1, Norway
OLD Safety Valve, Fornceff St.Peter, Norwich NR16 1JA Tel : 0508 30530
R.OLDENBOURG Verlag, Rosenheimer Str.145, D-8000 München 80 Germany Tel : (089) 4112 248
The OLEANDER Press, 17 Stansgate Avenue, Cambridge CB2 2QZ Tel : 0223 44688
OLIPHANTS, 1 Bath Street, London EC1V 9LB Tel : 01.251 2925 Telex : 262364 / Unit 14, Trident Industrial Estate, Pindar Road, Hoddesdon, Herts. EN11 0LD

OLIVER & Boyd, Robert Stevenson House, 1-3 Baxter's Place Leith Walk, Edinburgh EH1 3BB Tel : 031.556 2424 Telex : 727511
OLIVER's Guides, 9 Courtleigh Gardens, London NW11 9JX Tel : 01.458 1607
OMEGA - see BPC Publishing
OMICRON Publ.Ltd., Sunderland House, Sunderland Street, Macclesfield, Cheshire SK11 6JN Tel : 0625 25527 Telex : 667854
OMNIBUS Book Service, 25 East Street, Farnham, Surrey GU9 7SD Tel : 0252 725607
OMNIBUS Press, 78 Newman Street, London W1P 3LA Tel : 01.636 9033 Telex : 21892
OMNIBUS Society, Publications Dept., 216 Hastings Road, Bromley, Kent BR2 8QH Tel : 01.674 5280
ONE Parent Families, National Council for One-Parent Families, 255 Kentish Town Road, London NW5 2LX Tel : 01.267 1361
ONLINE Computer Systems - now Online Conferences Ltd.
ONLINE Conferences Ltd., Argyle House, Joel Street, Northwood Hills, Middx.HA6 1TS Tel : 09274 28211
ONLINE Publications Ltd., Argyle House, Joel Street, Northwood Hills, Middx. HA6 1TS Tel : 09274 28211 Telex : 923498
ONLINE Publishing Ltd. - distributed by Online Conferences Ltd.
ONLYWOMEN Press, 27 Clerkenwell Close, London EC1R 0AT Tel : 01.251 4976
ONYX Press Ltd., 86 Lauriston Road, London E9 7HA Tel : 01.985 9921
Anthony OORLOFF Publications Ltd., 18 Priors Road, Windsor Berks SL4 4PD Tel : 07535 52013
OPEN Books Publ.Ltd., West Compton House, Shepton Mallet Somerset Tel : 074 989 264 - distributed by J.M. Dent & Sons (Distribution)Ltd.
OPEN Court Publ.Co., USA - distributed by Eurospan Ltd.
The OPEN University, Publishing Division, Walton Hall, Milton Keynes MK7 6AA Tel : 0908 74066
OPEN University Educational Enterprises Ltd., 12 Cofferidge Close, Stony Stratford, Milton Keynes MK11 1BY Tel : 0908 566744 Telex : 826147
OPINION Research Centre, 251-259 Regent Street, Oxford Circus, London W1A 4YZ
OPTICAL Publ.Co.Inc., Berkshire Common, PO Box 1146, Pittsfield, Mass.01202, USA
ORAL History Society, Dept.of Sociology, University of Essex Colchester, Essex
ORBACH & Chambers, 74 Long Acre, London EC1A 9ET Tel : 01.606 9371
ORBIS Books (London)Ltd., 66 Kenway Road, London SW5 0RD Tel : 01.370 2210
ORBIS Publ.Ltd., 20 Bedfordbury, London WC2N 4BT Tel : 01.379 6711 Telex : 22725 - distributed by George Philip & Son Ltd.
ORBIT - see BPC Publishing
ORDNANCE Survey, Romsey Road, Maybush, Southampton SO9 4DH Tel : 0703 775555
ORESKO Books Ltd., 30 Notting Hill Gate, London W11 3HX Tel : 01.727 3188 - distributed by Jupiter Books (London)Ltd.
ORGANISATION for Economic Co-operation & Development (O.E.C.D.) - distributed by HMSO
ORGANISATION Of Arab Petroleum Exporting Countries, PO Box 20501, Safat, Kuwait Telex : 2166 - some titles distributed by Graham & Trotman Ltd.
ORGANIZATION of Petroleum Exporting Countries (OPEC), Obere Donaustrasse 93, 1020 Vienna 2, Austria
ORIEL Press Ltd., Stocksfield Studio, Branch End, Stocksfield NE43 7NA Tel : 066 15 3065 - orders to Broadway House, Newtown Road, Henley-on-Thames, Oxon. RG9 1EN
ORIENTAL Economist, 1-4 Hongokucho, Nihonbashi, Chuo-ku Tokyo 103, Japan
A.D.ORIENTEM Ltd., 2 Cumberland Gardens, St.Leonards, Sussex TN38 12OQ
ORION Books, 13 Salisbury Road, Eastbourne, E.Sussex BN20 7UB Tel : 0323 23776
ORLANDO Language Texts Ltd., 4 Church Street, Abbey Green Bath BA1 1NL Tel : 0225 61929 Telex : 444337
ORMONDE Publications Ltd., 76 Clancarty Road, London SW6 3AA Tel : 01.736 4886
ORYX Press, 2214 North Central at Encanto, Phoenix, AZ85004 USA Tel : 602 254 6156 Telex : 910 951 1333 - distributed by Library Association Publ.Ltd.
Adam OSBORNE Associates, USA - distributed by McGraw Hill Book Co.Ltd.

Alan OSBORNE & Assocs.Ltd., 22 Nelson Road, Greenwich,
　　London SE10 8BP　Tel : 01.858 7176/7
OSCAR Publications Inc., 64 Clissold Crescent, London N16 9AT
　　Tel : 01.254 6136
OSPREY Publ.Ltd., 12-14 Long Acre, London WC2E 9LP
　　Tel : 01.836 7863　Telex : 21667 - distributed by
　　George Philip & Son Ltd.
The OTHER Press, 27 Clerkenwell Close, London EC1R 0AT
　　Tel : 01.251 4976
OTO Research Corporation, Sumi Building, 4-1-6 Takatanobaba,
　　Shinjuku ku, Tokyo 160, Japan
OTTO Vieth Verlag, Alfredstrasse, D-2000 Hamburg 76,
　　W.Germany
OUTER Circle Policy Unit - ceased trading, 1980
OUTLET Book Company - c/o TABS
OUTPOSTS Publications, 72 Burwood Road, Walton-on-Thames,
　　Surrey KT12 4AL
OVAL Projects, 335 Kennington Road, London SE11 4QE
　　Tel : 01.582 4887
OVERSEAS Development Council, 1717 Massachusetts Ave.NW
　　Washington DC 32036, USA
OVERSEAS Development Institute, 10 Percy Street, London W1P
　　0JB　Tel : 01.580 7683 / ODI Sales, Montagu House,
　　High Street, Huntingdon, Cambs. PE18 6EP
OVERSEAS Press Media Association, 122 Shaftesbury Avenue,
　　London W1V 3HA
OVERSEAS Publications Interchange Ltd., 8 Queen Anne's
　　Gardens, London W4 1TU　Tel : 01.997 7025
Peter OWEN Ltd., 73 Kenway Road, London SW5 0RE
　　Tel : 01.373 5628
OWEN Wells, 30 St.James Road, Ilkley, W.Yorks
　　Tel : 0934 608394
OWEN's Commerce & Travel Ltd. - now Owen's Publications Ltd.
OWEN's Publications Ltd., 32 Mount Pleasant, Alperton, Wembley
　　Middx.HA0 1TU　Tel : 01.930 7799　Telex : 261577
OWENS S.A., Box 248, 1630 Bulle, Switzerland
OXENHAM Technology Associates, PO Box 42888, Dept.278,
　　Houston, Texas 77042, USA
OXFAM Educational Dept., 274 Banbury Road, Oxford OX2 7DZ
　　Tel : 0865 56777　Telex : 83610
OXFAM Public Affairs Unit, Parnell House, 25 Milan Road,
　　London SW1　Tel : 01.828 0346
OXFORD Bibliographical Society, c/o Bodleian Library, Oxford
　　OX1 3BG　Tel : 0865 44675　Telex : 83656
OXFORD Centre for Management Studies, Kennington, Oxford
　　OX1 5NY　Tel : 0865 735422
OXFORD Education Systems, 23 Divinity Road, Oxford OX4 1LH
OXFORD Group, 12 Palace Street, London SW1E 5JT
　　Tel : 01.828 6591　Telex : 917820 - distributed by
　　Grosvenor Books (The Good Road Ltd.)
OXFORD Illustrated Press Ltd., Little Holcombe, Stag Lane,
　　Newington, Oxford OX9 8AJ　Tel : 0865 890026
OXFORD Microform Publ.Ltd., 19a Paradise Street, Oxford OX1
　　1LD　Tel : 0865 46252
OXFORD Polytechnic Press, Headington, Oxford OX3 0BP
　　Tel : 0865 64777
OXFORD Publishing Co. - see Blandford Press
OXFORD Railway Publ.Co.Ltd., 8 The Roundway, Headington
　　Oxford OX3 8DH　Tel : 0865 66215
OXFORD School Publications, 126 High Street, Oxford
　　Tel : 0993 72124　- orders to Bridge House, Witney,
　　Oxon.
OXFORD University, Dept.of Forestry - see Commonwealth
　　Forestry Institute
OXFORD University Press, Ely House, 37 Dover Street, London
　　W1X 4AH　Tel : 01.629 8494 / Walton Street, Oxford
　　OX2 6DP　Tel : 0865 56767　Telex : 837330 /
　　213 Stafford Street, Glasgow G4
OXFORD University Press (Distribution), Saxon Way West,
　　Corby, Northants. NN18 9ES　Tel : 0536 741519
　　Telex : 34313
OXFORD University Press Music Department, Ely House, 37
　　Dover Street, London W1　Tel : 01.629 8494
OYEZ Longman Publ.Co., 21-27 Lamb's Conduit Street,
　　London WC1N 3NJ　Tel : 01.242 2548
OYEZ Publ.Ltd., Norwich House, 11-13 Norwich Street,
　　London EC4A 1AB　Tel : 01.404 5721　Telex : 888870
OZIMEK Data Corp., 92 Mendota Avenue, Rye, New York 10580,
　　USA　Tel : 914 967 8420

P

P.A.Computers & Telecoms Ltd., 33 Greycoat Street, London
　　SW1　Tel : 01.828 7744　Telex : 8813082
P.A.Management Consultants Ltd., Hyde Park House, 60a
　　Knightsbridge, London SW1X 7LE　Tel : 01.235 6060
PBI Publications Ltd., Britannica House, High Street, Waltham
　　Cross, Herts. EN8 7DY　Tel : 0992 23691
　　Telex : 23957 - distributed by Biblios Publishers
PBS (International) Ltd. - see Philograph Publications Ltd.
P.D.A.S.(Cowley)Ltd., Unit 6, 2 Derby Road, Greenford, Middx.
　　UB6 8UJ　Tel : 01.575 5756
P.E.Consulting Group, Park House, Egham, Surrey TW20 0HW
　　Tel : 0784 34411
PEP - now Political Studies Institute
P.E.R.A., Melton Mowbray, Leics. LE14 0PB　Tel : 0664 4133
PEVA, Iman Sokak 1, Beyoglu, Istanbul, Turkey
PG Publishing Pte.Ltd., Suite 609, Mt.Elizabeth Medical Centre,
　　Mount Elizabeth, Singapore 0922　Tel : 2350006
　　Telex : RS 39967
P.H.Publishing Ltd., Waterloo Road, Stockport, Cheshire SK1
　　3BN　Tel : 061.480 2128
PIRA(Research Association for the Paper & Board Printing &
　　Packaging Industries), Randalls Road, Leatherhead
　　Surrey KT22 7RU
PM International, Treganna, Marsh Lane, Leonard Stanley, Glos.
　　GL10 3NJ　Tel : 045382 3535
PPC Books, PO Box 1260, Tulsa, Oklahoma 74101, USA
P.S.G.Publ.Co. - c/o TABS
PSI - see Policy Studies Institute
PUDOC, Centre for Agricultural Publ.& Documentation, PO Box
　　4, 6700 AA Wageningen, The Netherlands
　　Tel : 08370 19146
PACEMAKER Publ.Ltd., 20 Oxford Road, Newbury, Berks RG13
　　1PA　Tel : 0635 30690
PACIFIC Economics Pty.Ltd., PO Box A771, Sydney South 2000
　　NSW, Australia
PACIFIC Publications, c/o Global Books, 109 Great Russell Street
　　London WC1B 3NA　Tel : 01.580 2633
PACKAGED Facts, 274 Madison Avenue, New York 10016, USA
　　Tel : 212 532 5533
PACKARD Publ.Ltd., 16 Lynch Down, Funtington, Chichester
　　Sussex PO18 9LR　Tel : 024 358 621
PADDINGTON Press Ltd., 21 Bentinck Street, London W1M 5RL
　　Tel : 01.935 3738　Telex : 27604 - distributed by
　　Biblios Publishers' Distribution Services Ltd.
PAGODA Books, 30 Museum Street, London WC1A 1LH
　　Tel : 01.637 0890
PAINE Webber Mitchell Hutchins, 140 Broadway, New York 10005
　　USA　Tel : 212 437 7480
PAINT Research Association, Waldegrave Road, Teddington,
　　Middx.TW11 8LD　Tel : 01.977 4427/9
　　Telex : 928720
PAINTMAKERS Association, Alembic House, 93 Albert Embankment
　　London SE1 7TY　Tel : 01.582 1185
PAKISTAN Publications, 1st Floor, V.C.Chambers, 2 Abdullali
　　Haroon Road, Karachi, Pakistan
PALACE Publ.Ltd., 44 Conduit Street, London W1R 9FB
　　Tel : 01.437 7131
PALADIN Books Ltd. - see Granada Publ.Ltd.
PALANTYPE Organization Ltd., 4 North Mews, London WC1
　　Tel : 01.242 3460
PALESTINE Exploration Fund, 2 Hinde Mews, Marylebone Lane
　　London W1M 5RH　Tel : 01.935 5379
PALGRAVE Publ.Co.Ltd., 25 Windsor Street, Chertsey, Surrey
　　KT16 8AX　Tel : 09328 64477
PALL Mall Press - see Phaidon Press Ltd.
PALLADIO Press, 99 High Street, Aberdeen AB2 3ER
　　Tel : 0224 46102
PALLENT Press, 13 The Pallent, Havant, Hants.
PALLET Enterprises Ltd., PO Box 33W, Wembley, Middx. HA9
　　9NU　Tel : 01.908 2122
PALM Publishers Ltd., Canada - distributed by Colin Smythe Ltd.
Robert PALMER, 35 Isabel House, 46-47 Victoria Road, Surbiton
　　Surrey KT6 4JL　Tel : 01.390 5348　Telex : 291561
Rosemary PALMER Ltd., 33 Killigrew Gardens, Trevispian Parc
　　St.Erme, Cornwall　Tel : 0872 79123
PALMERSTAN Publ.Co., 6285 Barnell Road, H.Hanta 30328,
　　Georgia, USA
PALSHAW Measurement Inc., PO Box 1439, Pebble Beach, CA
　　93953, USA　Tel : 408 625 2500
PAN Am World Airways, 193 Piccadilly, London W1
PAN Books, 18 Cavaye Place, London SW10 9PG　Tel : 01.373 6070
　　Telex : 917466 / Prunel Road, Basingstoke, Hants.
PANAF Books Ltd., 243 Regent Street, London W1R 8PN
　　Tel : 01.408 1611

PANDA Publishing, 64 Cross Street, Manchester M2 4JS
    Tel : 061.834 7271
PANDEMIC, 24 Red Lion Street, London WC1R 4PX
    Tel : 01.242 0373   Telex : 28257
PANDON Publications, Millburn House, Dean Street, Newcastle
    upon Tyne   Tel : 0632 20330
PANGBOURNE English Centre, Shooters Hill, Pangbourne,
    Reading RG8 7DU   Tel : 07357 2462
PANMURE Gordon & Co., 9 Moorfields Highwalk, London
    EC2Y 9DS   Tel : 01.638 4010
PANTHEON Books, c/o Pendemic Ltd.
PANTHER Books Ltd. - see Granada Publ.Ltd.
PAPER Industries Research Association, Randalls Road,
    Leatherhead, Surrey KT22 7RU   Tel : 0372 76161
    Telex : 929810
PAPER Sack Development Association, 12-14 Market Square
    Leighton Buzzard, Beds. LU17 7EY   Tel : 0525 381893
PAPER Tiger Books - see Dragon's World Ltd.
David PARADINE Developments Ltd., Broadbent House, 64-65
    Grosvenor Street, London W1X 9DB   Tel : 01.629 3793
PARADISE Press Ltd., Townside Cottage, Wispington, Lincs.
    LN9 5RN   Tel : 065887 259
PARENT's Magazine Press, USA - distributed by McGraw Hill
    Book Co.Ltd.
Paul PAREY, Spitalerstrasse 12, Postfach 10 63 04, D-2000
    Hamburg 1, W.Germany   Tel : 040 32 15 11/14
    Telex : 2161 391
PARIS Match, 99 Rue d'Amsterdam, 75009 Paris, France
    Tel : 280 6855
PARKE Sutton Publishing, 59 London Street, Norwich NR2 1HL
    Tel : 0603 615661/667021
PARKES Library Ltd. - titles taken over by Univ.of Southampton
PARKINSONS Disease Society, 81 Queens Road, London SW19
PARLIAMENTARY Profiles Services Ltd., 3-4 Palace Chambers,
    Bridge Street, Westminster, London SW1A 2JT
    Tel : 01.930 2677
PARLIAMENTARY Research Services, 18 Lincoln Green,
    Chichester, W.Sussex PO19 4DN   Tel : 0243 787272
PARRISH Rogers International - now Beacon Publishing
PARTIALLY Sighted Society, 40 Wordsworth Street, Hove,
    E.Sussex BN3 5BH   Tel : 0273 736053
The PASOLD Research Fund Ltd., Becketts House, Edington,
    Nr.Westbury, Wilts.   Tel : 0380 342
PASTON Publ.Inc., 6366 Gross Point Road, PO Box 312 Niles,
    Ill.60648, USA
PATENT Office, 25 Southampton Buildings, London WC2A 1AY
PATERNOSTER Press Ltd., Paternoster House, 3 Mount Radford
    Crescent, Exeter EX2 4JW   Tel : 0392 50631
PATERSON-Brown, Norwood, Hawick, Roxburghshire TD9 7HP
    Tel : 0450 2352
PATEST Service, PO Box 81, Hemel Hempstead, Herts.HP1 1UR
    Tel : 0442 52113
PATHFINDER Press Ltd., 47 The Cut, London SE1 8LL
    Tel : 01.735 5566
PATIENTS Association, 11 Dartmouth Street, London SW1H 9BN
    Tel : 01.222 4992
PATRIA Translations Ltd., West Bexington, Dorchester, Dorset
    DT2 9DL   Tel : 030 587 349
Stanley PAUL & Co.Ltd., 3 Fitzroy Square, London W1P 6JD
    - distributed by Hutchinson Publ.Group Ltd.
Peter PAUPER Publishing, PO Box 303, Two Rivers, WI 54241,
    USA
PAVILION Books, 44 Bedford Square, London WC1B 3DU
    Tel : 01.323 3200
F.E.PEACOCK Publ.Inc. - c/o Pandemic Ltd.
A.& F.PEARS Ltd. - Cyclopaedia published by Pelham Books Ltd.
C.Arthur PEARSON Ltd. - distributed by Hamlyn Publ.Group
David PEARSON Associates, Spring House, Mill Lane, Broxbourne
    Herts.   Tel : 09924 65783   Telex : 298951
PEAT Marwick Mitchell & Co., 7 Ludgate Broadway, London EC4V
    6DX   Tel : 01.248 1685   Telex : 8812908
PEBBLE Press, 27 Clerkenwell Close, London EC1R 0AT
    Tel : 01.251 4976
PEBBLE Prints, 16 Robertson Drive, Sheffield S6 5DY
PECKHAM Publishing Project, 13 Peckham High Street, London
    SE15   Tel : 01.701 1757
PECO Publications & Publicity Ltd., Underleys, Beer, Seaton,
    Devon EX12 3NA   Tel : 0297 20580
PEDDER Associates Ltd., Lark House, 199 Westminster Bridge
    Road, London SE1 7UT   Tel : 01.633 0866
PEDERSEN's Highland Maps, 25 Glenburn Drive, Inverness
    Tel : 0463 41107
PELHAM Books Ltd., 44 Bedford Square, London WC1B 3DU
    Tel : 01.323 3200   Telex : 21322 - distributed by
    TBL Book Service Ltd.
PEMBERTON Books (Pemberton Publ.Co.Ltd.), 88 Islington
    High Street, London N1 8EN   Tel : 01.226 7251/2

PEMBRIDGE Press Ltd., 16 Pembridge Road, London W11
    Tel : 01.229 1825
PENDOMER Press, The Raswell, Loxhill, Godalming, Surrey
    GU8 4BQ   Tel : 048 632 473
PENDRAGON House(UK)Ltd., Lizard Town, Helston, Cornwall
    TR12 7PG   Tel : 032 629 741
PENDYKE Publications, 37 Pendyke Street, Southam, Leamington
    Spa, Warwicks. CV33 9PB
PENGUIN Books Ltd., Bath Road, Harmondsworth, Middx.UB7
    0DA   Tel : 01.759 1984/5722 / 536 Kings Road,
    London SW10 0UH   Tel : 01.351 2393   Telex : 263130
PENINSULA Publ., USA - distributed by Prentice Hall
PENNINE Publ.Ltd., 745 Abbeydale Road, Sheffield S7 2BG
    Tel : 0742 550602
PENNSYLVANIA State University Press, 215 Wagner Building
    University Park, PA16802, USA - distributed by
    IBD
PENNWELL Books, PO Box 21288, Tulsa, Oklahoma 74121, USA
PENTECH Press, 4 Graham Lodge, Graham Road, London NW4
    3DG   Tel : 01.202 5373
PEOPLE at Work Ltd., PO Box 3, 158 Chesterfield Road North,
    Mansfield, Notts. NG19 7JH   Tel : 0623 640203
PEOPLE's Publications, 27 Clerkenwell Close, London EC1R 0AT
    Tel : 01.251 4976
PEOPLE's Publ.House(Private)Ltd., Rani Jhansi Road, New
    Delhi 110055, India
PEPAR Publications, 50 Knightlow Road, Harborne, Birmingham
    B17 8QB
PEPPER Press, Montague House, Russell Square, London WC1B
    5BX   Tel : 01.637 1466   Telex : 8811713
PER Selvig AS, PO Box 152 Centrum, Oslo 1, Norway
    Tel : 02 42 57 53
Peter PEREGRINUS Ltd., PO Box 8, Southgate House, Stevenage
    Herts.SG1 1HQ   Tel : 0438 3311
PERFORMING Rights Society, 29-33 Berners Street, London
    W1P 4AA
PERGAMON-Infoline, 12 Vandy Street, London EC2A 2DE
    Tel : 01.377 1225   Telex : 8814614
PERGAMON Press Ltd., Headington Hill Hall, Oxford OX3 0BW
    Tel : 0865 64881   Telex : 83177
N.M.PERYER Ltd., PO Box 883, 93 Cambridge Terrace,
    Christchurch 1, New Zealand   Tel : 64 771 3 -
    distributed by Whitcoulls Ltd.
PERMANENT Press, RD No.2, Noyac Road, Sag Harbor, New
    York, USA   Tel : 516 725 1101
PERMANENT Way Institution, 27 Lea Wood, Fleet, Hants.GU13
    8AN
Colin PERRY Ltd., Rowanhurst Drive, Farnham Common, Bucks
    SL2 3HG   Tel : 02814 5585
PERSEPHONE Press, 27 Clerkenwell Close, London EC1R 0AT
    Tel : 01.251 4976
PET Library(London)Ltd., 30 Borough High Street, London SE1
    1XU   Tel : 01.407 3668   Telex : 883288
PETERHOUSE Press, High Street, Wendover HP22 6DU
    Tel : 0296 34183
Malcolm PETERS, 28 Thorpe Street, Birmingham B5 4AX
    Tel : 021.622 4380
PETERSBURG Press Ltd., 59a Portobello Road, London W11 3DB
    Tel : 01.229 0165 - orders to Tiptree Book Services
PETROBROS (UK), International Press Centre, 13th Floor,
    76 Shoe Lane, London EC4A 3JB
PETROCELLI Books Inc. - distributed by Van Nostrand Reinhold
PETROCONSULTANTS Ltd., Hill Samuel House, Adelaide Road,
    Dublin 2, Ireland   Tel : Dublin 688830
PETROLEUM Economist, 107 Charterhouse Street, London EC1M
    6AA   Tel : 01.251 3501   Telex : 27161
PETROLEUM Extension Service, University of Texas at Austin,
    Box 5 University Station, Austin, Texas 78712, USA
PETROLEUM Information Corp., 4100 E.Dry Creek Road,
    Littleton, CO 80122, USA   Tel : 303 740 7100
PETROLEUM Information Ltd., Green Dragon House, 64-70 High
    Street, Croydon, Surrey CR0 9XN   Tel : 01.680 7031
Institute of PETROLEUM, 61 New Cavendish Street, London W1M
    8AR   Tel : 01.636 1004 - distributed by Heyden &
    Son Ltd.
PETROLEUM Publ.Co., PO Box 1260, Tula, Oklahoma 74101, USA
PHAIDON Press Ltd., Littlegate House, St.Ebbe's Street,
    Oxford OX1 1SQ   Tel : 0865 46681   Telex : 83308
    - orders to 2b Ridgeway Trading Estate, Iver, Bucks
    SL0 9HW   Tel : 0753 654747
PHARMACEUTICAL Data Services, PO Box 20831, Phoenix,
    AZ 85036, USA   Tel : 602 257 1500
PHARMACEUTICAL Press, 1 Lambeth High Street, London SE1
    7JN   Tel : 01.735 9141
PHARMAPROJECTS, 18 Hill Rise, Richmond, Surrey TW10 6UA
PHARMIND Publications Ltd., 162 Regent Street, London W1R 6DD

PHAROS Rare Books Ltd., 5-11 Lavington Street, London SE1 0NZ   Tel : 01.261 9790/9734
PHASE Separations Ltd., Deeside Industrial Estate, Queensferry, Clwyd CH5 2LR   Tel : 0244 816444   Telex : 61459
PHILATELIC Publ.Ltd., Robell Way, Storrington, Pulborough, W.Sussex   Tel : 090 66 3269
George PHILIP Alexander Ltd., Norfolk House, Smallbrook Queensway, Birmingham B5 4LJ   Tel : 021.643 8641/4
George PHILIP Services Ltd., Arndale Road, Wick, Littlehampton W.Sussex BN17 7EN   Tel : 090 64 5599, 7453/5
PHILIP & Tacey Ltd., North Way, Andover, Hants. SP10 5BA   Tel : 0264 61171   Telex : 47496
PHILIP, Son & Nephew Ltd., 7 Whitechapel, Liverpool L1 6HF   Tel : 051.236 0246/8
Alan PHILIPP, 9 Courtleigh Gardens, London NW11 9JX   Tel : 01.458 1607
PHILLIMORE & Co.Ltd., Shopwyke Hall, Chichester, W.Sussex PO20 6BQ   Tel : 0243 787636
Phoebe PHILLIPS Editions, 44 Earlham Street, London WC2H 9LA   Tel : 01.379 6837
PHILLIPS & Drew Research, Lee House, London Wall, London EC2Y 5AP   Tel : 01.628 4444   Telex : 291163
PHILLODGE Ltd., 1st Floor, 198 Kettering Road, Northampton   Tel : 0604 30391
PHILOGRAPH Publ.Ltd., North Way, Andover, Hants.SP10 5BA   Tel : 0264 61171   Telex : 47496
PHIN Publ.Ltd., Phin House, 12-14 Bath Road, Cheltenham, Glos.GL53 7HA   Tel : 0242 510129   Telex : 95631
PHOEBUS Publ.Co., 52 Poland Street, London W1A 2JX   Tel : 01.734 9131   Telex : 23451
PHONIC Blend Systems Ltd., Gordon House, Forest Avenue, Mansfield, Notts.NG18 4BX   Tel : 0623 26251   Telex : 377866
PHOTO Precision Ltd., Caxton Road, St.Ives, Huntingdon, Cambs.PE17 4LS   Tel : 0480 64364
PHYSICAL Education Association of G.B.& N.Ireland, Ling House, 10 Nottingham Place, London W1M 4AY   Tel : 01.486 1301/2
PHYSICS Trust Publications, Blackhouse Road, Letchworth, Herts. SG9 6HN   Tel : 04626 72555
Judy PIATKUS Publ.Ltd., 17 Brook Road, Loughton, Essex IG10 1BW   Tel : 01.508 7362 - distributed by George Philip & Son Ltd.
PICKERING & Inglis Ltd., 3 Beggarwood Lane, Basingstoke Hants. RG23 7LP   Tel : 0256 59211
PICTON Publ.Ltd., Citadel Works, Bath Road, Chippenham Wilts. SN15 2AB   Tel : 0249 50391
PICTORIAL Charts Educational Trust, 27 Kirchen Road, London W13 0UD   Tel : 01.567 9206
PICTURE Researchers Handbook, 11 Granville Park, London SE13 7DY
PIERCE & Warriner (UK)Ltd., 44 Upper Northgate Street, Chester, Cheshire CH1 4EF   Tel : 0244 382525   Telex : 617057
PIERROT Publ.Ltd., 60 Greek Street, Soho Square, London W1V 5LR   Tel : 01.439 2596
James PIKE Ltd. - gone away, 1981
PILGRIM Press Ltd., Lodge Lane, Derby DE1 3HE   Tel : 0332 47087
PILKINGTON Brothers Ltd., St.Helens, Merseyside WA10 3TT   Tel : 0744 28882
PILLAY Publications, 48 Welbeck Avenue, Southampton, Hants.   Tel : 0703 551500
PINERIDGE Press Ltd., 91 West Cross Lane, West Cross, Swansea, W.Glamorgan SA3 5LU
PINNACLE Electronic Components, Electron House, Cray Avenue, St.Mary Cray, Orpington, Kent BR5 3PJ
Francis PINTER (Publ.)Ltd., 5 Dryden Street, London WC2E 9NW   Tel : 01.240 2430
PION Ltd., 207 Brondesbury Park, London NW2 5JN   Tel : 01.459 0066/7
PIPELINE Research Inc., 122 East 42nd Street, New York 10168, USA   Tel : 212 661 1777
PIPES & Pipelines International, PO Box 21, Beaconsfield, Bucks HP9 1NS   Tel : 04946 5139
PIRATE Press, 107 Valley Drive, Kingsbury, London NW9 9NT   Tel : 01.204 7464
PITKIN Pictorials Ltd., 11 Wyfold Road, London SW6 6SG   Tel : 01.385 4351/3
PITMAN Books Ltd., 128 Long Acre, London WC2E 9AN   Tel ; 01.379 7383   Telex : 261367
PITMAN Correspondence College, Worcester Road, London SW19 7QQ   Tel : 01.947 6993
PLAID Books - c/o TABS
PLAIN English Campaign, 78 Wiltshire Street, Salford M7 0BD   Tel : 061.795 5042/061.792 8531

PLAN Magazines Ltd., 45 Station Road, Redhill, Surrey RH1 1QH   Tel : 0737 68261
PLANNING & Development Publications, 8 Norfolk Road, Brighton Sussex BN1 3AA
The PLANNING Exchange, 186 Bath Street, Glasgow G2 4HG
PLANT Assessment(London)Ltd., 60a North Street, Chichester Sussex PO19 1NB   Tel : 0243 788696
PLANTECON(Overseas)Research Ltd., 148-150 Lordship Lane, London SE22 8HB   Tel : 01.299 0534   Telex : 896691
PLASTICS & Rubber Institute, 11 Hobart Place, London SW1W 0HL
PLENUM Publ.Co.Ltd., 88-90 Middlesex Street, London E1 7EZ   Tel : 01.377 0686
PLEXUS Publ.Ltd., 30 Craven Street, London WC2N 5NT   Tel : 01.839 1315/6   Telex : 261234
PLOUGH Publ.House, Society of Brothers Ltd., Darvell Community, Robertsbridge, Sussex TN32 5DR   Tel : 0580 880626
PLUNKETT Foundation, 31 St.Giles, Oxford OX1 3LF   Tel : 0865 53960
PLUTO Press Ltd., Unit 10, Spencer Court, 7 Chalcot Road, London NW1 8LH   Tel : 01.722 0141   Telex : 21879
  - distributed by J.M.Dent & Sons (Distribution)Ltd.
PLYMOUTH Gazette, 12 Byland Road, Lower Compton, Plymouth Devon   Tel : 0752 667785
POCKET Books, Simon & Schuster, 1230 Ave.of the Americas, New York 10020, USA
POCKET Guides - see BPC Publ.Ltd.
POCKETFAX, 46 The Avenue, Loughton, Essex IG10 4PX   Tel : 01.508 1279
POETS' & Painters' Press, 146 Bridge Arch, Sutton Walk, London SE1 8XU   Tel : 01.928 7533
POINTON York (Publ.)Ltd., 25 Bedford Row, London WC1R 4HE   Tel : 01.405 6813
POLAND Street Publ.Ltd., 9 Poland Street, London W1V 3DG   Tel : 01.734 0875
POLICE Foundation, 1909 K Street NW, Suite 400, Washington DC 20006, USA
POLICE Review Publ.Co.Ltd., 14 St.Cross Street, Hatton Garden London EC1N 8FE   Tel : 01.242 1432/3
POLICY Studies Institute, 1-2 Castle Lane, London SW1E 6DR   Tel : 01.828 7055
POLISH Cultural Foundation Ltd., 9 Charleville Road, London W14 9JL   Tel : 01.385 9008
G.POLITI, 36 via Annatello, 20131 Milan, Italy
POLITICAL & Economic Planning - now Political Studies Institute
POLITICAL Ecology Research Group Ltd., 34 Cowley Road, Oxford   Tel : 0865 725354
POLITICAL Reference Publications - see Macmillan Publ.Ltd.
The POLITICS of Health Group, 27 Clerkenwell Close, London EC1R 0AT   Tel : 01.251 4976
R.C.POLK & Co., 2001 Elm Hill Pike, PO Box 1340, Nashville, Tennessee 37202, USA
POLONIA Book Fund Ltd., 8 Queen Anne's Gardens, London W4 1TU   Tel : 01.747 0844
POLYBOOKS Ltd., 2-4 Abbeymount, Edinburgh EH8 8JH   Tel : 031.661 9339
POLYGON Books, 1 Buccleuch Place, Edinburgh EH8 9LW   Tel : 031.667 5718
POLYGRAPH Verlag GmbH, 6000 Frankfurt am Main 70, Scharmainkai 85, W.Germany
POLYSTYLE Publ.Ltd., 382-386 Edgware Road, London W2   Tel : 01.723 3022 - distributed by Argus Dist.Ltd.
POLYTECH Publ.Ltd., 36 Hayburn Road, Offerton, Stockport Cheshire SK2 5DB   Tel : 061.427 6606
The POLYTECHNIC of Central London, 309 Regent Street, London W1R 8AL   Tel : 01.580 2020
POLYTECHNIC of North London, School of Librarianship, 207-225 Essex Road, Islington, London N1 3PN   Tel : 01.607 2789   Telex : 25228
POLYTECHNIC of the South Bank, Centre for Energy Studies, Borough Road, London SE1 0AA
Samuel A.POND, 425 Family Farm Road, Woodside, CA94062, USA
POND Press, 7 Beasleys Ait, Sunbury, Middx.TW16 6AS   Tel : 093 27 80091
PONTIFICIA Commissio Iustitia et Pax - distributed by Colin Smythe Ltd.
PONY Club, The British Equestrian Centre, Stoneleigh, Kenilworth, Warwicks. CV8 2LR   Tel : 0203 27192/5
Robert POOLEY Ltd. - distributed by Airlife Publ.Ltd.
POPLAR Press Ltd., 13 Burlington Lodge Studios, Rigault Road, London SW6 4JJ   Tel : 01.731 5938
PORCUPINES, 11 Boutport Street, Barnstaple, Devon   Tel : 0271 3641
Henry PORDES Ltd., 529b Finchley Road, London NW3 7BH   Tel : 01.435 9878/9

PORT City Press, Baltimore, Maryland, USA
PORT of London Authority, London Dock House, 1 Thomas Moore Street, London E1 9HZ Tel : 01.476 6900 Telex : 887719
PORTCULLIS Press Ltd., Queensway House, 2 Queensway, Redhill, Surrey RH1 1QS Tel : 0737 68611 - distributed by Argus Books Ltd.
PORTFOLIO Graphics Ltd., Granville House, Cranville Road, Maidstone, Kent Tel : 0622 671289/56455
PORTICO Publications, 84 Fetter Lane, London EC4A 1EQ Tel : 01.831 6861
PORTSMOUTH City Council, Civic Offices, Guildhall Square, Portsmouth PO1 2AL Tel : 0705 822251
PORTWAY Press Ltd., Timeform House, Halifax, W.Yorks. HX1 1XE Tel : 0422 63322 Telex : 51353
POSEIDON Press, 6 Turnpin Lane, London SE10 9JA Tel : 01.858 5789
POSITIONING To Win, PO Box 1928, La Mesa, CA 92041, USA Tel : 714 462 5536
POST News, Stoke-sub-Hamdon, Somerset TA14 6BR Tel : 093 588 245
POST Office National Users Council, Waterloo Bridge House, Waterloo Road, London SE1 8UA
POSTAL History Society, Sea Meadow, Higher Sea Lane, Charmouth, Bridport, Dorset DT6 6BB Tel : 029 76 60447
J.D.POTTER Ltd., 145 Minories, London EC3N 1NH Tel : 01.709 9076
The POUND House, Market Square, Newent, Glos. GL18 1PS Tel : 0531 820650
J.D.POWER & Associates, 3325 Wilshire Blvd., Los Angeles, CA 90010, USA Tel : 213 480 1717
T.& A.D.POYSER Ltd., Town Head House, Calton, Waterhouses, Staffordshire ST10 3JQ Tel : 053 86 366
PRACTISING Law Institute, 810 Seventh Avenue, New York 10019, USA Tel : 212 765 5700
PRACTITIONER, 36 Calderwood Street, London SE18 6QH
PRAEGER International - c/o Holt Saunders Ltd.
PRECISION Press, 15 High Street, Marlow, Bucks SL7 1AV
PREDICASTS Ltd., 199-201 High Street, Orpington, Kent BR6 0PF Tel : 0689 38488 Telex : 898239
PRENTICE-Hall International, 66 Wood Lane End, Hemel Hempstead, Herts. HP2 4RG Tel : 0442 58531 Telex : 82445
PRESCHOOL Playgroups Association, Alford House, Aveline Street, London SE11 5DH Tel : 01.582 8871
PRESERVATION Press, National Trust for Institute Press, 740-748 Jalon Place NW, Washington DC 20006, USA
PRESS Association Ltd., PO Box 67, 85 Fleet Street, London EC4P 4BE Tel : 01.353 7440
PRESS Council, 1 Salisbury Square, London EC4Y 8AE Tel : 01.353 1248
PRESSED Felt Manufacturers' Association, Hudcar Mills, Hudcar Lane, Bury BO9 6HD Tel : 0274 24235
PRESSES Universitaires de Bruxelles, Avenue Paul Heger 42, 1050 Brussels, Belgium Tel : 02 649 97 80
PRESSURE Vessel Handbook Publ.Inc., USA - distributed by Coronday Ltd., Marston Court, 102 Manor Road, Wallington, Surrey
PRESTON Publ.Inc., PO Box 48312, Niles, Illinois 60648, USA Tel : 312 647 0566
John PRICE Business Courses Ltd., Prudential House, 28-40 Blossom Street, York YO2 2AJ Tel : 0904 24885/6
Norman PRICE Ltd., 17 Tottenham Court Road, London W1P 9DP Tel : 01.636 4900
PRICE Waterhouse & Co., Southwark Towers, 32 London Bridge Street, London SE1 9SY Tel : 01.407 8989
PRIDEAUX Press, PO Box 1, Letchworth, Herts. Tel : 046 26 4499
PRIMARY Communications Research Centre, University of Leicester, Leicester LE1 7RH Tel : 0533 556223
PRIMROSE Publishing, Primrose Farm, Wicklewood, Wymondham, Norfolk NR18 9PX Tel : 0953 605256 Telex : 975194
PRINCETON University Press, 3175 Princeton Pike, Lawrenceville NJ 08648, USA
PRINT & Press Services Ltd., 69 Beech Hill, Barnet, Herts. EN4 0JW Tel : 01.440 3690
The PRINTED Shop, 7 Langley Street, Covent Garden, London WC2H 9JX Tel : 01.379 3555
PRINTING & Graphic Services Ltd., Golf Course Lane, Filton, Bristol BS12 7QS Tel : 0272 695471/2
PRINTING Industries of America Inc., 1730 N.Lynn Street, Arlington, VA 22209, USA Tel : 703 841 8168
George PRIOR Associated Publ.Ltd., 37-41 Bedford Row, London WC1R 4JH Tel : 01.405 6603/6626 -distributed by Biblios Publishers' Distribution Services Ltd.

PRIORY Press Ltd., 49 Lansdowne Place, Hove, E.Sussex BN3 1HS Tel : 0273 722562
PRISM Press, Stable Court, Chalmington, Dorchester, Dorset DT2 0HB Tel : 0300 20524 - distributed by George Philip & Sons Ltd.
PROBE Research Inc., PO Box 590, Morristown, NJ 07960, USA Tel : 201 285 1503
Arthur PROBSTHAIN, 41 Great Russell Street, London WC1B 3PH Tel : 01.636 1096
PRODUCTION Engineering Research Association of Great Britain, Melton Mowbray, Leicestershire LE13 0PB Tel : 0664 4133
PROFESSIONAL & Scientific Publications, BMA House, Tavistock Square, London WC1H 9JR Tel : 01.387 4499
PROFESSIONAL Books Ltd., Milton Trading Estate, Abingdon Oxon. OX14 4SY Tel : 0235 834821
PROFESSIONAL Book Distributors Inc., 555 East Hudson Street Columbus, Ohio 43211, USA
PROFESSIONAL Publ.Ltd., Alhambra House, 27-31 Charing Cross Road, Trafalgar Square, London WC2H 0AU Tel : 01.930 3951
PROFILE Books, 65 Victoria Street, Windsor, Berks SL4 1EH Tel : 07535 69777
PROGNOS AG, Steingraben 42, CH-4011 Basel, Switzerland Tel : 061 223200 Telex : 63323
PROGRESS House(Publ.)Ltd., 36 Home Farm Road, Dublin 9 Eire Tel : 0001 370588
PROGRESSIVE Publ., 37 College Street, Calcutta 12, West Bengal, India
PROJECTA U.K.Ltd., PO Box 15, Royston, Herts. SG8 5NQ Tel : 0763 47003
PROMETHEUS Books, 700 East Amherst Street, Buffalo, New York 14215, USA
PROOST En Brandt NV, Strijkviertel 63, 3454 PK de Meern, The Netherlands Tel : 010 31 3406 2344
PROPERTY Services Agency, SGS Library, Whitgift Centre, Wellesley Road, Croydon CR9 3LY Tel : 01.686 8710
PROPHETIC Witness Movement, Upperton House, The Avenue, Eastbourne, Sussex BN21 3YB
PROSPERITY Publications, PO Box 159, London NW1 7HZ
PROTECTION of the Rights of Prisoners (PROP), 27 Clerkenwell Close, London EC1R 0AT Tel : 01.251 4976
PROTEUS (Publ.)Ltd., Suite 3, Bremar House, Sale Place, London W2 1PT Tel : 01.262 2271 Telex : 21969
J.R.PROUS SA, Apartado de Correos 540, Barcelona, Spain
PROVEPLAN Ltd., 1a College Green, Gloucester Tel : 0452 422984
PSYCHIC Press Ltd., 23 Great Queen Street, London WC2B 5BB Tel : 01.405 2914/5
PUBLIC Health Advisory Service, 27 Clerkenwell Close, London EC1R 0AT Tel : 01.251 4976
PUBLIC Libraries Group of the Library Association, Penzance Library, Morrab Road, Penzance, Cornwall TR18 4EY
PUBLIC Library Research Group, c/o C.Bath, Central Library, Church Street, Brighton, E.Sussex
PUBLIC Opinion Research of Israel Ltd., PO Box 20114, 12 Carlebach Street, Tel-Aviv 61200, Israel Tel : 261598 Telex : 341118
PUBLICATION Services, 33-35 Foxley Lane, High Salvington, Worthing, Sussex BN13 3AD Tel : 0903 65405.204283
PUBLICATIONS Citizen Health Research Group, 2000 P Street NW, Washington DC 20036, USA
PUBLICATIONS Distribution Co-operative, 27 Clerkenwell Close London EC1R 0AT Tel : 01.251 4976 / Birchcliffe Centre, Hebden Bridge, W.Yorks HX7 8DG Tel : 042 284 3315 / 45 Niddry Street, Edinburgh EH1 1LG Tel : 031.557 0133
PUBLICATIONS for Companies, Cutting Hill House, Benington Stevenage, Herts. SG2 7DJ Tel : 043.885 656 - distributed by Ward Lock Ltd.
PUBLICATIONS India, 112 Whitfield Street, London W1 Tel : 01.848 0670
PUBLICITY Press Ltd., 29-31 Meaghen Street, Chippendale NSW 2008, Australia
PUBLISH or Perish Inc., 901 Washington Street, Wilmington DE 19801, USA
PUBLISHERS Association, 19 Bedford Square, London WC1B 3HJ Tel : 01.580 6321/5 Telex : 21792
PUMP Manufacturers Association, 37 Castle Street, Guildford Surrey GU1 3UQ Tel : 0483 37997
PUMPKIN Press, 113 Westbourne Grove, London W2 4UP Tel : 01.229 9116
PURNELL Books, Paulton, Bristol BS18 5LQ Tel : 0761 413301
PUTNAM & Co.Ltd., 9 Bow Street, Covent Garden, London WC2E 7AL Tel : 01.379 6637 Telex : 299080

Q

QED Information Sciences Publications, c/o Online Publications, Argyle House, Joel Street, Northwood Hills, Middx. Tel : 09274 28211

QUAKER Home Service, Friends Book Centre, Friends House, Euston Road, London NW1 2BJ Tel : 01.387 3601

QUANTUM Science Corporation, 16 Charles II Street, London SW1Y 4QU Tel : 01.839 5347 Telex : 917720

Bernard QUARITCH Ltd., 5-8 Lower John Street, Golden Square London W1R 4AU Tel : 01.734 2983 Telex : 8955509

QUARTERMAINE House Ltd., 110 Windmill Road, Sunbury on Thames, Middx. Tel : 093 27 86262/5 Telex : 928185

QUARTET Books Ltd., 27 Goodge Street, London W1P 2FD Tel : 01.636 3992/5 Telex : 919034

QUARTILLES Ltd., 9 Colne Road, Couneshall, Colchester, Essex CO6 1TH

QUARTO Publ.Ltd., 32 Kingly Court, London W1 Tel : 01.734 4611

QUEEN Anne Press, Holywell House, Worship Street, London EC2A 2EN Tel : 01.377 4600

QUEEN's University of Belfast, University Road, Belfast BT7 1NN Tel : 0232 45133

QUEST Medical Publishers, 145a Croydon Road, Beckenham, Kent BR3 3RB Tel : 01.650 4929/5093 - distributed by European Book Service

QUEST Research Publications Ltd., PO Box 168, London SE26 6PR Tel : 01.659 0790

QUIGLEY Publ.Co.Inc., 159 West 53rd Street, New York 10019, USA

QUILL Publishing Ltd., 32 Kingly Court, London W1 Tel : 01.734 4611

QUINTA Publ.Ltd., 68a Wigmore Street, London W1 Tel : 01.935 3478

QUINTESSENCE Publ.Co.Ltd., 52 Manchester Street, London W1M 6DR

QUORUM Books Inc. - distributed by Greenwood Press

R

R&D Publications Ltd., 30-34 Langham Street, London W1N 5LB Tel : 01.580 6972

R&E Research Publishers, PO Box 2008, Saratoga, CA 95070, USA

RAC, RAC House, Lansdowne Road, Croydon, Surrey CR9 6HN Tel : 01.686 2525 Telex : 21418 - distributed by Biblios Publishers Distribution Services

R.A.P.R.A. - see Rubber & Plastics Research Association

RCA Ltd., Sunbury on Thames, Middx.TW6 7HW Tel : 093 27 85511

R.H.S.Enterprises Ltd. - distributed by Cassell Ltd.

RIBA Publications Ltd., The Finsbury Mission, 35-37 Morland Street, London Ec1V 8VB Tel : 01.251 0791

RICS, Norden House, Basing View, Basingstoke, Hants.RG21 2HN

R.I.P.A. - see Royal Institute of Public Administration

RM Associates, 151 East Forrest Avenue, PO Box 816, Neenah, Wisc.54956, USA

RoSPA, Cannon House, The Priory, Queensway, Birmingham B4 6BS Tel : 021.233 2461

R.P.Bookservice, Alphonsus House, Chawton, Alton, Hants. GU34 3HQ Tel : 0420 88222

RPS, Victoria Hall, East Greenwich, London SE10 0RF Tel : 01.858 1717/7768

R.S.Productions, Hamilton House, Nelson Close, Totnes, Devon

RSM Publications, 27 Clerkenwell Close, London EC1R 0AT Tel : 01.251 4976

RSPCA, Causeway, Horsham, W.Sussex RH12 1HG Tel : 0403 64181

R.T.P.I., 26 Portland Place, London W1

RVR Consultants, PO Box 553, Shawnee Mission, Kansas 66201 USA Tel : 913 722 5795

RWA Report on World Affairs, 3 Alma Square, London NW8 9QD Tel : 01.286 0712

A.B.RABEN & Sjögren Bokförlag, Box 45022, S-104 30 Stockholm 45, Sweden Tel : 08 34 99 60 Telex : 19490

RACE Today Ltd., 74 Shakespeare Road, London SE24 Tel : 01.737 2268

RACEFORM, 2 York Road, London SW11 3PZ Tel : 01.223 1183 Telex : 263792

RADICAL Statistics Group, 27 Clerkenwell Close, London EC1R 0AT Tel : 01.251 4976

RADIO Society of Great Britain, Alma House, Cranborne Road, Potters Bar, Herts. EN6 3JW Tel : 0707 59015

RADIOPRESS Inc., Fuji Television Annex, No.7 Kawada-Cho Ichigaya, Shinjuku-ku, Tokyo 162, Japan

RAFTWAIN Ltd. - see Guild Press

RAINBIRD Publ.Group Ltd., 40 Park Street, London W1Y 4DE Tel : 01.491 4777 Telex : 261472 - orders to Remlap Book Services, 6 Ruskin Drive, Offmore Farm, Kidderminster, Worcs.

RAINBOW/Celtion Books, 171 Victoria Road, Aberdeen AB1 3ND

RAINTREE Publishers Intl., 31 Southampton Row, London WC1B 5HJ Tel : 01.404 4321

RAM Publ.Co.Ltd. - ceased publishing, 1980

RAMAKRISHNA Vedanta Centre, Blind Lane, Bourne End, Bucks SL8 5LG Tel : 062 85 26464

RAMBORO Books, 64 Pentonville Road, London N1 Tel : 01.837 6301 Telex : 24224

RAMCROFT Ltd., PO Box 9, Twyford, Berks Tel : 0734 345535

RAMSEY Head Press, 36 North Castle Street, Edinburgh EH2 3BN Tel : 031.226 6692

RAND McNally & Co., Box 7600, Chicago, Ill.60680, USA

RAND McNally College Publ.Co., USA - distributed by Eurospan

RANDOM House Inc., 400 Hahn Road, Westminster, MD 21157, USA - distributed by TABS

RANELAGH Editions Ltd., 82 Hurlingham Court, Ranelagh Gardens, London SW6 3UR Tel : 01.736 0189

RANK & File, 27 Clerkenwell Close, London EC1R 0AT Tel : 01.251 4976

RAPP & Whiting Ltd., 105 Great Russell Street, London WC1B 3LJ Tel : 01.580 2746

RAVEN Press, 1140 Ave.of the Americas, New York 10036, USA Tel : 212 575 0335 Telex : 640073

RAVEN Publishing - ceased trading 1980

RAVENSWOOD Publ.Ltd., PO Box 24, 205 Croydon Road, Beckenham, Kent BR3 3QH Tel : 01.777 6291

RAVETTE Ltd., 12 Star Road, Partridge Green, Horsham, Sussex RH13 8RA Tel : 0403 710392

David RAYNER Publisher, 6 Woodbury Lane, Clifton, Bristol BS8 2SD Tel : 0272 730535

READER's Digest Association Ltd., 25 Berkeley Square, London W1X 6AB Tel : 01.629 8144 Telex : 264631

READERS Union Ltd., Brunel House, Forde Road, Newton Abbot Devon TQ12 2DW Tel : 0626 61121 Telex : 42904

RED Notes, 27 Clerkenwell Close, London EC1R 0AT Tel : 01.251 4976

REDCLIFFE Press Ltd., 14 Dowry Square, Bristol BS8 4SH Tel : 0272 290158

REDEMPTORIST Publishers, Alphonsus House, Chawton, Alton, Hants. GU34 3HQ Tel : 0420 88222

David REDFERN Photography, 83-84 Long Acre, London WC2E 9NG Tel : 01.240 1883 Telex : 28221

REDWING, 27 Clerkenwell Close, London EC1R 0AT Tel : 01.251 4976

A.H.& A.W.REED Ltd., 68-74 Kingsford-Smith Street, Wellington New Zealand - distributed by Prentice Hall/IBD

Thomas REED Industrial Press Ltd., Saracen's Head Buildings 36-37 Cock Lane, London EC1A 9BY Tel : 01.248 7881

Thomas REED Publications Ltd., PO Box 36, High Street West, Sunderland SR1 1UP Tel : 0783 75211/4 Telex : 53376

William REED Ltd., 5-7 Southwark Street, London SE1 1RQ Tel : 01.407 6981

REED International Ltd., Reed House, 82 Piccadilly, London W1A 1EJ

REEDBOOKS Ltd., Fox Lane North, Chertsey, Surrey KT16 9HW Tel : 09328 64234

REEDMINSTER Publ.Ltd., c/o The Bishopsgate Press, 21 New Street, London EC2 Tel : 01.283 1711

REEDMOOR Magazine Co., 1028 Chestnut Street, Philadelphia PA 19187, USA

Geo.R.REEVE Ltd., Damgate, Wymondham, Norfolk NR18 0BD Tel : 0953 602297

William REEVES Bookseller Ltd., 1a Norbury Crescent, London SW18 4JR Tel : 01.764 2108

REFERENCE Intl.Publ.Ltd., c/o Mitchell Beazley, Artists House 14-15 Manette Street, London W1V 5LB Tel : 01.437 7624

REGAL Print Co., 218 New Kings Road, London SW6 4XE Tel : 01.731 4755

REGENBOGEN-Verlag, 27 Clerkenwell Close, London EC1R 0AT Tel : 01.251 4976

REGENCY Intl.Publications Ltd., Newstone House, 127 Sandgate Road, Folkestone, Kent CT20 2BL Tel : 0303 54691

REGENCY Press, 125 High Holborn, London WC1V 6QA Tel : 01.242 8481

REGENT School of English, 19-23 Oxford Street, London W1R 1RF Tel : 01.734 7455

REGENTS Publ.Co.Inc., USA - distributed by European Book Service

REGIONAL Advisory Council for Technological Education, Tavistock House, South Tavistock Square, London WC1H 9LR
REGIONAL Publications(Bristol)Ltd., 5 Springfield Road, Abergavenny, Gwent NPT 5TD Tel : 0873 2207
REGIONAL Reference Press, 72 Sackville Street, Manchester
REGISTER of Companies, Companies House, Crown Way, Maindy, Cardiff CF4 3UZ Tel : 0222 388588
Alex P.REID & Son, 28 Market Street, Aberdeen AB9 2EQ Tel : 0224 56386
D.REIDEL Publ.Co., PO Box 17, 3300 AA Dordrecht, The Netherlands - distributed by Kluwer Academic Publ.Group
Max REINHARDT Ltd., 9 Bow Street, London WC2E 7AL Tel : 01.379 6637 Telex : 299080
REINHOLD Publ.Corp., USA - see Van Nostrand Reinhold & Co.
RELEASE Publ.Ltd., 27 Clerkenwell Close, London EC1R 0AT Tel : 01.251 4976
RELIABILITY Analysis Centre, Griffins Air Force Base, New York 13441, USA
RELIABILITY Data Books, London Information (Rowse Muir) Ltd., Index House, Ascot, Berks SL5 7EU Tel : 0990 23377
RELIANCE School of Investment Ltd., c/o Unwin Brothers Ltd., The Gresham Press, Old Woking, Surrey GU22 9LH
RELIGIOUS & Moral Education Press, Hennock Road, Exeter Devon EX2 8RP Tel : 0392 74121/4 Telex : 42749 - orders to E.J.Arnold & Son Ltd.
RELIGIOUS Education Council, St.Martin's College, Lancaster LA1 3JD Tel : 0524 63446
REMPLOY Ltd., 1 Boston Road, Gorse Hill Industrial Estate, Beaumont Leys, Leicester LE4 1BB Tel : 0533 355971
RENTOKIL Group plc, Rentokil House, Garland Road, East Grinstead, W.Sussex RH19 1DY Tel : 0342 27171
RESEARCH & Development Society, 47 Belgrave Square, London SW1X 8QX Tel : 01.235 6111
RESEARCH & Finance Management Ltd., 8 Bryanston Square, London W1
RESEARCH Associates, The Radfords, Longton Road, Stone, Staffs.ST15 8DJ Tel : 0785 813164 Telex : 36459
RESEARCH Bureau Ltd., PO Box 203, Green Bank, London E1 9PA Tel : 01.488 1366 Telex : 884823
RESEARCH Defence Society, Grosvenor Gardens House, Grosvenor Gardens, London SW1W 0BS Tel : 01.828 8745
RESEARCH International, PO Box 31, Salisbury Square House, London EC4P 4HA Tel : 01.353 3494 Telex : 28395
RESEARCH Publications Ltd., PO Box 45, Reading RG1 8HF Tel : 0734 583247/8
RESEARCH Publications Services Ltd., Victoria Hall, Fingal Street, East Greenwich, London SE10 0RF Tel : 01.858 1717/2574
RESEARCH Publ.Co. - now Skilton & Shaw
RESEARCH Services Ltd., Station House, Harrow Road, Wembley, Middx. Tel : 01.903 8511
RESEARCH Studies Press, 8 William Way, Letchworth, Herts. SG6 2HG Tel : 04626 3742
RESEARCH Studies Press Inc. - distributed by John Wiley & Sons
RESEARCH Surveys of G.B.Ltd., Research Centre, West Gate, London W5 1EL Tel : 01.997 5555 Telex : 261978
RESEARCH Unit, Barnoak, Crieff, Perthshire Tel : 0764 2696 - distributed by St.Ninian's Training Centre, Book Dept.
RESIDENTIAL Care Association, 3rd Floor, 357 Strand, London WC2R 0HB
RESTON Publ.Co. (division of Prentice Hall, USA) - distributed by IBD
RETAIL Audits Ltd., Imperial Life House, 390 High Road, Wembley, Middx.HA9 6TB Tel : 01.902 8887
RETAIL Banker International, 392 Goldhawk Road, London W6 0SB Tel : 01.741 4771 Telex : 8812128
RETAIL Journals Ltd., Queensway House, 2 Queensway, Redhill Surrey RH1 1QS Tel : 0737 68611
RETAIL Management Development Programme, 5-6 East Street, Brighton, Sussex BN1 1HP Tel : 0273 722687 Telex : 877159
RETAIL Outlets Research Trust, PO Box 88, Amersham, Bucks HP8 4TB Tel : 02404 4883
RETAIL Research Unit - c/o Manchester Business School
RETAILING & Planning Associates, PO Box 5, Corbridge, Northumberland NE45 5AA
RETIREMENT Choice Magazine Co.Ltd., Bedford Chambers, Covent Garden, London WC2E 8HA Tel : 01.836 8772
REVELATION Press, The Red House, Kelham, Newark, Notts. NG23 5QP Tel : 0636 2807
REVISTA Espanola de Micropaleontologia, Serrano, 116 Madrid 6 Spain

REWARD Regional Surveys Ltd., 1 Mill Street, Stone, Staffs. ST15 8BA Tel : 078 583 4554
RIBAND Books, Sedgwick Park, Horsham, W.Sussex RH13 6QH Tel : 040 376 369
RICARDO Consulting Engineers, Bridge Works, Shoreham by Sea, Sussex BN4 5FG Tel : 079 17 5611
The RICHMOND Publ.Co.Ltd., Orchard Road, Richmond, Surrey TW9 4PD Tel : 01.876 1091
R.G.RIDDELL Pty.Ltd., 1st Floor, 100 Alexander Street, Crows Rest 2065, PO Box 282, Australia
Eric RIDDER, 110 Wall Street, New York 10005, USA
RIDER Press, 27 Clerkenwell Close, London EC1R 0AT Tel : 01.251 4976
RIDGWAY Press, Sunrise House, 23 Midford Lane, Limpley Stoke Bath BA3 6JR Tel : 022 122 3502
RIDINGS Publ.Co., 33 Beverley Road, Driffield, N.Humberside YO25 7SD Tel : 0377 43232
RIGBY Intl.Pty.Ltd., 5 Great James Street, London WC1 Tel : 01.242 5969/6706 Telex : 296616
RIGHT Way Books - see Elliot Right Way Books
RING Publications, 1-3 Wine Office Court, Fleet Street, London EC4A 3AL Tel : 01.353 4060
RISK Research Group Ltd., Bridge House, 181 Queen Victoria Street, London EC4V 4DD Tel : 01.236 2175 Tel : 8811636
RIVERSDOWN Publ.Ltd., Riversdown House, Warnford, Southampton SO3 1LH Tel : 096 279 244 Telex : 8954623
RIVINGTON's (Publ.)Ltd., Montague House, Russell Square, London WC1B 5BX Tel : 01.637 1466 Telex : 8811713
RIZZOLI Intl.Publications Inc., 712 Fifth Avenue, New York 10019, USA - distributed by A.Zwemmer Ltd.
ROAD Haulage Association Ltd., Roadway House, 104 New Kings Road, London SW6 4LN Tel : 01.736 1183 Telex : 298404
ROAD Transport Industry Training Board, MOTEC, High Ercall, Telford, Shropshire TF6 6RB Tel : 0952 770441
Glyn ROBERTS, 1 Little Anglesey Road, Gosport, Hants.
James ROBERTSON, 7 St.Anne's Villas, London W11 4RH
Martin ROBERTSON & Co.Ltd., 108 Cowley Road, Oxford OX4 1JF Tel : 0865 724041 Telex : 837022
ROBERTSON & Associates Inc., 34 Maple Street, Summit, NJ 07901, USA Tel : 201 622 3135
ROBERTSON Research Canada Ltd., 3rd Floor Lougheed Building, 604 First Street SW, Calgary, Alberta, T2P 2M8, Canada Tel : 403 233 7750
ROBERTSON Research Intl.Ltd., Tyn-y-Coed, Llanrhos, Llandudno, Gwynedd, N.Wales LL30 1SA Tel : 0492 81811
ROBINSON & Associates, The Chapel, 5 Salisbury Street, Cranborne, Hants. Tel : 072 54 327
ROBINSON & Watkins Books Ltd., Bridge Street, Dulverton Somerset Tel : 0389 23395
ROBOTICS Press Ltd. - distributed by Computer Research Press
ROBSON Books, Bolsover House, 5-6 Clipstone Street, London W1P 7EB Tel : 01.637 5937/8
ROBSON Lowe Ltd., 39 Poole Hill, Bournemouth, Dorset BH2 5PX Tel : 01.839 4034/5
ROCHDALE's Alternative Press Ltd., 27 Clerkenwell Close, London EC1R 0AT Tel : 01.251 4976
ROCKET Propulsion Co., Box 15346, Del City, OK 73115, USA
RODALE & Co.Ltd., Chestnut Close, Potter End, Berkhamsted Herts. HP4 2QL
RODALE Press, Griffin Lane, Aylesbury, Bucks HP19 3AS Tel : 0296 25952
RODALE Press Inc. - distributed by Rodale Press
ROHR Publ.Co., 28 Carteret Street, Upper Montclair, NJ 07043, USA
C.H.W.ROLES & Associates Ltd., Centronic House, King Henry's Drive, New Addington, Croydon CR9 0BG Tel : 0689 48221
J.Y.ROLLIN Electronics Data Source, 19 Rue Huche, 92150 Suresnes, France Tel : 609 95 95 Telex : 641055
George RONALD, 46 High Street, Kidlington, Oxford OX5 2DN Tel : 086 75 5273 Telex : 837646
RONALD Press Co., 79 Madison Avenue, New York 10016, USA - distributed by John Wiley & Sons Ltd.
Egon RONAY Org.Ltd., Greencoat House, Francis Street, London SW1P 1DH Tel : 01.828 6032 Telex : 8954759 - some guides published by Penguin Books
John S.ROPER, 4 Mount Pleasant, Bilston, W.Midlands Tel : 0902 43631
Barry ROSE (Publ.)Ltd., Little London, Chichester, Sussex PO19 1PG Tel : 0243 783637

ROSHFIELD Publ.Ltd., Kenwolde Lodge, Callow Hill, Virginia Water, Surrey
O.W.ROSKILL & Co.Ltd. - see Dun & Bradstreet Ltd.
ROSKILL Information Services Ltd., 2 Clapham Road, London SW9 0JA Tel : 01.582 5155 Telex : 917867
ROSTOMIES, 118 Wandsworth High Street, London SW18
Bertram ROTA (Publ.)Ltd., 30-31 Long Acre, London WC2E 9LT Tel : 01.836 0723
ROTHAMSTED Experimental Station, Harpenden, Herts. AL5 2JQ
ROTOGRAPHIC Publications, 37 St.Efrides Road, Torquay, Devon TQ2 5SG Tel : 0803 211316
ROTO-Vision SA, 10 Rue de l'Arquebuse, 1204 Geneva, Switzerland
ROTTERDAM University Press, Badhuisweg 232, The Hague, The Netherlands - distributed by Gower Publ.Co.Ltd.
ROUNDWOOD Press, Warwick Road, Kineton, Warwick Tel : 0926 640400
Les ROUTIERS - see British Relais Routiers
ROUTLEDGE & Kegan Paul Ltd., 39 Store Street, London WC1E 7DD Tel : 01.637 7651
ROWETT Research Institute, Greenburn Road, Bucksburn, Aberdeen AB2 9SB Tel : 0224 712751
ROXBY & Lindsey Press Ltd., 98 Clapham Common North Side, London SW4 9SG Tel : 01.228 2558 Telex : 261234
ROYAL Academy of Arts, Piccadilly, London W1V 0DS Tel : 01.734 9052
ROYAL Aeronautical Society, 4 Hamilton Place, London W1V 0BQ Tel : 01.499 3515
ROYAL Agricultural Society of England, National Agricultural Centre, Stoneleigh, Kenilworth, Warwicks. CV8 2LZ Tel : 0203 555100
ROYAL Aircraft Establishment, Farnborough, Hants.GU14 6TD Tel : 0252 24461
ROYAL Albert Memorial Museum, Queen Street, Exeter, Devon EX4 3RX Tel : 0392 56724
ROYAL Anthropological Institute, 56 Queen Anne Street, London W1M 9LA Tel : 01.486 6832
ROYAL Asiatic Society, 56 Queen Anne Street, London W1M 9LA Tel : 01.935 8944
ROYAL Association for Disability & Rehabilitation, 25 Mortimer Street, London W1N 8AB Tel : 01.637 5400
ROYAL Automobile Club - see RAC
ROYAL Central Asian Society, 42 Devonshire Street, London W1N 1LN Tel : 01.580 5728
ROYAL College of Art, Kensington Gore, London SW7 2EU Tel : 01.584 5020
ROYAL College of General Practitioners, 14 Princes Gate, London SW7 1PU Tel : 01.581 3232
ROYAL College of Nursing of the U.K., Henrietta Place, Cavendish Square, London W1M 0AB Tel : 01.580 2646
ROYAL College of Obstetricians & Gynaecologists, 27 Sussex Poace, Regent's Park, London NW1 4RG
ROYAL College of Physicians, 9 Queen Street, Edinburgh EH2 1JQ Tel : 031.225 7175
ROYAL College of Veterinary Surgeons, 32 Belgrave Square, London SW1X 8QP Tel : 01.235 4971/2
ROYAL Commonwealth Society, Information Bureau, Northumberland Avenue, London WC2N 5BJ Tel : 01.930 6733
ROYAL Economic Society, Nuffield College, Oxford OX1 1NF
ROYAL Entomological Society of London, 41 Queensgate, London SW7 5HU Tel : 01.584 8361
ROYAL Genealogies, 128 Kensington Church Street, London W8 4BH
ROYAL Geographical Society, 1 Kensington Gore, London SW7 2AR Tel : 01.589 5466
ROYAL Historical Society, University College London, Gower Street, London WC1E 6BT Tel : 01.387 7532 - guides & handbooks distributed by Boydell Press Ltd. studies in history distributed by Swift Printers Ltd.
ROYAL Horticultural Society - see R.H.S.Enterprises Ltd.
ROYAL Institute of British Architects - see RIBA Publ.Ltd.
ROYAL Institute of Chemistry - see Royal Society of Chemistry
ROYAL Institute of International Affairs, Chatham House, 10 St.James's Square, London SW1Y 4LE Tel : 01.930 2233 X27 Telex : 896691
ROYAL Institute of Public Administration, 3 Birdcage Walk, London Sw1H 9JJ Tel : 01.222 2248
Royal Institution of Chartered Surveyors, 12 Great George Street, London SW1P 3AD Tel : 01.222 7000 Telex : 915443 / Nordon House, Basing View, Basingstoke, Hants. RG21 2HN Tel : 0256 55234/9
ROYAL Institution of Chartered Surveyors, Scottish Branch, 7 Manor Place, Edinburgh EH3 7DN Tel : 031.225 7078

ROYAL Institution of Naval Architects, 10 Upper Belgrave Street, London SW1X 8BQ Tel : 01.235 4622
ROYAL Meteorological Society, James Glaister House, Grenville Place, Bracknell, Berks RG12 1BX Tel : 0344 22957/8
ROYAL National Institute for the Deaf, 105 Gower Street, London WC1E 6AH Tel : 01.387 8033
ROYAL Observatory, Edinburgh EH9 3JH Tel : 031.667 3321
ROYAL Philatelic Society, 41 Devonshire Place, London W1N 1PE Tel : 01.486 1044/5
ROYAL Photographic Society, 14 South Audley Street, London W1Y 5DP Tel : 01.493 3967
ROYAL School of Church Music, Addington Palace, Croydon Surrey CR9 5AD Tel : 01.654 7676/1671
The ROYAL Society, 6 Carlton House Terrace, London SW1Y 5AG Tel : 01.839 5561 Telex : 917876
ROYAL Society for Mentally Handicapped Children & Adults - see MENCAP
ROYAL Society for the Prevention of Accidents - see RoSPA
ROYAL Society of Arts, John Adam Street, London WC2N 6EZ Tel : 01.839 2366
ROYAL Society of Chemistry, Burlington House, Piccadilly, London W1V 0BN Tel : 01.734 9864 - orders to The Distribution Centre, Blackhorse Road, Letchworth, Herts. SG6 1HW
ROYAL Society of Health, 13 Grosvenor Place, London SW1X 7EN Tel : 01.235 9961
ROYAL Society of Medicine, Chandos House, 2 Queen Anne Street, London W1M 0BR
ROYAL Society of Tropical Medicine & Hygiene, Manson House 26 Portland Place, London W1N 4EY Tel : 01.580 2127
ROYAL Sovereign Group, Britannia House, 100 Drayton Park London N5 1NA Tel : 01.226 4455 Telex : 267668
ROYAL Town Planning Institute, 26 Portland Place, London W1N 4BE Tel : 01.636 9107
ROYAL Tropical Institute, Dept.of Tropical Hygiene, Mauritskade 63, Amsterdam, The Netherlands
ROYAL United Services Institute (Defence Studies), Whitehall London SW1A 2ET Tel : 01.930 5854
ROYDON Publ.Ltd., 4 St.Stephens Close, London NW8
RUBBER & Plastics Research Association of G.B., Shawbury, Shrewsbury, Shropshire SY4 4NR Tel : 0939 250383
RUBBER Red Book, Palmerton Publ.Co.Inc., 6285 Barfield Road Atlanta, Georgia 30328, USA
RUDDICK & Associates, 6149 South Sheridan, Suite 107, Tulsa Oklahoma 74133, USA Tel : 918 492 7300
A.RUDKIN Assocs., PO Box 15, 15 Cornmarket Street, Oxford OX1 3EB
I.L.RUFFINO, Italy - distributed by Davis-Poynter Ltd.
RUNNING Angel, 55 Telegraph Lane East, Norwich NR1 4AR Tel : 0603 611795
RUNNING Press, 385 19th Street, Philadelphia, PA 19103, USA
The RUNNYMEDE Trust, 37a Gray's Inn Road, London WC1X 8PP Tel : 01.404 5266
Peter RUSEK Publ.Ltd., Little Store House, High Street, Marlow, Bucks. Tel : 0494 40829
Bertrand RUSSELL House, Gamble Street, Nottingham NG7 4ET Tel : 0602 708318
Compton RUSSELL Ltd., The Old Brewery, Tisbury, Salisbury Wilts. SP3 6NH Tel : 074 787 747
Michael RUSSELL Publ.Ltd., The Chantry, Wilton, Salisbury Wilts. SP2 0JU Tel : 072 274 3150
RYER Associates Inc., 5 Sharon Drive, Whippany, NJ 07981 USA Tel : 201 887 2178
RYLAND's Directory,Queensway House, 2 Queensway, Redhill Surrey RH1 4QS Tel : 0737 68611
RYSTON Publ.Ltd., 11 London Road, Downham Market, Norfolk PE38 9BX

S

S.A.E. - see Society of Automotive Engineers
SATRA - see Shoe & Allied Trades Research Association
S.B.S.Publ., 4320 Stevens Great Blvd., Suite 230 Can Jose, California 95129, USA
S.C.A.T.Publications (Services to Community Action & Tenants) 27 Clerkenwell Close, London EC1R 0AT Tel : 01.253 3627
SCM Press Ltd., 26-30 Tottenham Road, London N1 4BZ Tel : 01.249 7262
SCRAM, 27 Clerkenwell Close, London EC1R 0AT Tel : 01.251 4976
SDP, 4 Cowley Street, London SW1P 3NB Tel : 01.222 4141/1200

S.E.P., Apartado 8111, Madrid, Spain
S.E.P.M. - see Society of Economic Paleontologists & Mineralogists
SERA (Socialist Environmental Resources Assoc.), 27 Clerkenwell Close, London EC1R 0AT Tel : 01.251 4976
SGM Publishing House, Radstock House, 3 Eccleston Street, London SW1W 9LZ Tel : 01.730 2155/7
SGS-Ates (UK)Ltd., Planar House, Walton Street, Aylesbury, Bucks. Tel : 0296 5977
SHAC (The London Housing Aid Centre), 189a Old Brompton Road, London SW5 0AR Tel : 01.373 7841/7276
SIAR Planning Ltd., 86 Prince Albert Road, London NW8
SINTEF, N7034 Trondheim - NTH, Norway Tel : 075 93 000
SIPRI - see Stockholm International Peace Research Institute
SIRA Institute Ltd., South Hill, Chislehurst, Kent BR7 5EH Tel : 01.467 2636 Telex : 896649
SITPRO, Almack House, 26-28 King Street, London SW1Y 6QW Tel : 01.214 3399 Telex : 919130
SLA - see Scottish Library Association
 - or Special Libraries Association, USA
SLA Rose Inc., 224 Commerce Place, Greensbord, NC 27420, USA
S.N.A.M.E., 1 World Trade Centre, Suite 1369, New York 10048, USA
SPCK, Holy Trinity Church, Marylebone Road, London NW1 4DU Tel : 01.387 5282
SPIE, PO Box 10, Bellingham, Washington DC 98225, USA
SRAMA - see Spring Research & Manufacturers' Association
S.R.H.E. - see Society for Research into Higher Education
SRI Europe, Middle East & Africa, 12-16 Addiscombe Road, Croydon CR0 0XT Tel : 01.686 5555 Telex : 946125
SSRC - see Social Science Research Council
S.T.Publ., 407 Gilbert Avenue, Cincinnati, Ohio 45202, USA Tel : 513 421 2050
STBS, PO Box 197, London WC2N 4DE
STE Generale de Presse, 13 Avenue de l'Opera, 75001 Paris France
STL Distributors, PO Box 48, 1 Sherman Road, Bromley, Kent BR1 3JH Tel : 01.460 4470 Telex ; 896706
SABBERTON Publications, PO Box 35, Southampton SO9 7BU Tel : 0703 769361
SACKETT & Marshall Ltd., 2 Great Marlborough Street, London W1 Tel : 01.437 6006 Telex : 298344 - distributed by WHS Distributors
Richard SADLER Ltd., Halfpenny Furze, Mill Lane, Chalfont St. Giles, Bucks HP8 4NR Tel : 024 07 2509
SAFARI Books (Export)Ltd., 32 Hue Street, St.Helier, Jersey Channel Islands Tel : 0534 74717 Telex : 4192012
SAFETY Engineering Laboratory Health & Safety Executive, Red Hill, Sheffield S3 7HQ Tel : 0742 78141
SAFETY Officers, SEC House, 33 Elm Road, New Malden, Surrey
SAFETY Technology Ltd., Twickenham Road, Feltham, Middx. TW13 6HA Tel : 01.894 5511 Telex : 27419
SAGE Publications, 28 Banner Street, London EC1Y 8PE Tel : 01.253 1516
SAGITTARIUS Bloodstock Associates Ltd., Suite 53, 26 Charing Cross Road, London WC2H 0DJ Tel : 01.836 4628
SAIGA Publ.Co.Ltd., 1 Royal Parade, Hindhead, Surrey GU26 6TD Tel : 0428 73 6141/6854
ST.Albert's Press, Whitefriars, Faversham, Kent ME13 7JN Tel : 079 582 2607
ST.Andrew Press, 121 George Street, Edinburgh EH2 4YN Tel : 031.225 5722
ST.Anthony's Press, St.Anthony's Hall, Peasholme Green, York YO1 2PW Tel : 0904 59861 X274
ST.Clair Press College Publ., 4 East Huron Street, Chicago, Ill. 60611, USA
ST.James's Group - see Economist Intelligence Unit
ST.James's Press Ltd., 5-11 Worship Street, London EC2A 2AY Tel : 01.588 6631
ST.John's Ambulance Association & Brigade, Priory House, St. John's Gate, Clerkenwell, London EC1M 4DA Tel : 01.253 6644
ST.Martin's Press, 175 Fifth Avenue, New York 10010, USA
ST.Mary's Press, The Convent, Wantage, Oxon. OX12 9DJ Tel : 023 57 3141
ST.Michael's Organisation, 80 Highgate West Hill, London N6 Tel : 01.340 1810
ST.Ninian's Training Centre, Book Dept., Crieff, Perthshire Tel : 0764 3766
ST.Paul's Bibliographies, Foxbury Meadow, Godalming, Surrey GU8 4AE Tel : 048632 228
ST.Paul's Publications, St.Paul's House, Middlegreen, Slough Berks SL3 6BT Tel : 0753 20621
ST.Trillo Publications, St.Trillo, 92 Hillside Road, Portishead, Bristol BS20 8LJ

SALAMANDER Books, Salamander House, 27 Old Gloucester Street, London WC1N 3AF Tel : 01.242 6693 Telex : 261113 - distributed by New English Library
SALES & Marketing Management, 633 Third Avenue, New York 10017, USA Tel : 212 986 4800
The SALES Machine Ltd., 22 St.James Street, Covent Garden, London WC2E 8NS
SALESIAN Publications, Blaisdon Hall, Longhope, Glos. GL17 0AQ Tel : 0452 830247
SALOP County Council, Shire Hall, Abbey Foregate, Shrewsbury SY2 6ND Tel : 0743 222100
SALTIRE Society, Saltire House, 13 Atholl Crescent, Edinburgh EH3 8HA Tel : 031.228 6621
SALVATIONIST Publ.& Supplies Ltd., 117-121 Judd Street, London WC1H 9NN Tel : 01.387 1656/5621
SAMPSON Low, Berkshire House, Queen Street, Maidenhead, Berks SL6 1NF Tel : 0628 37171
SAMSON Books Ltd., Down House, Redlynch, Salisbury, Wilts. SP5 2JP Tel : 0725 20347
SAMSON Publ.Ltd., 12-14 Hill Rise, Richmond, Surrey TW10 6UA Tel : 01.948 4251
SAMSON Uitgeverij BV, Box 4 Alphen, Aan den Rijn, The Netherlands
SANDLE Brothers Ltd., c/o World Intl.Publ.Ltd., PO Box 111 61 Great Ducie Street, Manchester M60 3BL
SANGAM Books Ltd., 51 Manchester Street, London W1M 6JD Tel : 01.935 8453
SANTA Monica Publ.Co., 1210 Galisteo Parkway, Santa Fe, NM 87501, USA
SATELLITE Books, Kendell House, 9 Kendall Road, Isleworth, Middx.
SATURDAY Ventures, 11 Granville Park, London SE13 7DY Tel : 01.318 0034
W.B.SAUNDERS Co.Ltd. - c/o Holt Saunders Ltd.
K.G.SAUR - distributed by Library Association Publishing
SAVANT Institute, 2 New Street, Carnforth, Lancs. LA5 9BX
SAVE Britain's Heritage, 3 Park Square West, London NW1 4LJ Tel : 01.486 4953
E.B.SAVORY Milln & Co., 3 London Wall Buildings, London EC2M 5PU Tel : 01.638 1212
SAVOY Books Ltd., 279 Deansgate, Manchester M3 4EW Tel : 061.832 2168
SAWELL Publ.Ltd., 127 Stanstead Road, London SE23 1JE Tel : 01.699 6792
R.G.SAWERS Publ.Ltd., 13-14 New Bond Street, London W1Y 9PF Tel : 01.499 7291/7209
SAXON House, 27 Clerkenwell Close, London EC1R 0AT Tel : 01.251 4976
SCAN Publ.Co.Ltd., Scan House, Southwick Street, Southwick Brighton BN4 4TE Tel : 0273 595969
SCANDINAVIAN Inst.of African Studies, PO Box 2126, 5750 02 Uppsala, Sweden
SCANDINAVIAN Journal of Work Environment & Health, Haastmaninkatu 1, Fin 00290, Helsinki 29, Finland
SCARECROW Press, USA - distributed by Bailey Bros. & Swinfen Ltd.
SCHIFFER Publ.Ltd., Box E, Exton, Pennsylvania 19341, USA Tel : 215 696 1001
G.SCHIRMER Ltd., Stockley Close, Stockley Road, West Drayton, Middx.UB7 9BE Tel : 08954 43945
Mustor SCHMIDT, Rossmastt 23, 6000 Frankfurt am Main, West Germany
SCHOCKEN Books, 67 Park Avenue, New York 10016, USA / 9 Sidney Square, London E1 Tel : 01.790 8437/1381 - orders to Noonan Hurst Ltd.
SCHOFIELD & Sims Ltd., Dogley Mills, Fenay Bridge, Huddersfield HD8 0NQ Tel : 048 483 5643
SCHOLAR Press Ltd., 59-61 East Parade, Ilkley, Yorks.LS29 8JP Tel : 0943 600321
SCHOLARS Book Co., 4431 Mount Vernon, Houston, Texas 77006, USA Tel : 713 528 4395
SCHOLASTIC Publ.Ltd., 141-143 Drury Lane, London WC1B 5TG Tel : 01.379 7333
SCHOOL Government Publ.Co., Darby House, Bletchingly Road Merstham, Redhill, Surrey RH1 3DN Tel : 073 74 2223
SCHOOL Library Association, Victoria House, 29-31 George Street, Oxford OX1 2AY Tel : 0865 722746 / 35 Bloomfield Place, Arbroath, Angus DD11 3LP Tel : 0241 74060
SCHOOL Natural Science Society - see Association for Science Education
SCHOOL of Oriental & African Studies, London University, Malet Street, London WC1E 7HA
SCHOOL of Rural Economics & Related Studies, Wye College, Ashford, Kent TN25 5AH Tel : 0233 812401 X283

SCHOOLS Council, 160 Great Portland Street, London W1N 6LL Tel : 01.580 0352
SCHOONMAKER Associates, Mainly Marketing, PO Drawer M, Coram, NY 11727, USA Tel : 516 473 8741
SCHOTLAND Business Research, PO Box 511, Princeton, NJ 08540, USA Tel : 609 466 1400
SCHWAB Marketing GmbH, Zieblandstrasse 16, D-8000 Munich 40, W.Germany
SCHWEIGER Buchyentrum, Postfach 522, CH-4600 Olten 1, Switzerland
E.SCHWEIZERBART'SCHE Verlagsbuchhandlung, Johannesstrasse 3A, D-7000 Stuttgart 1, Germany Tel : 0711 623541/3
SCHWEIZERISCHER Verein für Schweisstechnik, Postcheck 40-1454, St.Alban - Varstadt 95, 4006 Basle, Switzerland
SCHWEIZERISCHER Apothekerverein, Societe Suisse de Pharmacie, 3000 Bern 6, Postfach 3006, Marktgasse 52, Switzerland
SCICON, Sanderson House, 49-57 Berners Street, London W1P 4AQ Tel : 01.580 5599
SCIENCE & Behaviour Books - c/o TABS
SCIENCE & Engineering Research Council, Polaris House, North Star Avenue, Swindon, Wilts. SN2 1ET Tel : 0793 26222 X2256
SCIENCE Press, PO Box 496, Princeton, NJ 08540, USA - distributed by TABS
SCIENCE Reference Library, Store Street, London WC1E 7DG el : 01.405 8721
SCIENCE Research Associates Ltd., Newtown Road, Henley-on-Thames, Oxon RG9 1EN Tel : 0491 575959 - orders to IBD
SCIENCE Research Council - now Science & Engineering Research Council
SCIENCE Reviews Ltd., 3-4 St.Andrews Hall, London EC4V 4BY
SCIENTECHNICA (Publ.)Ltd. - see John Wright & Sons Ltd.
SCIENTIFIC American, 415 Madison Avenue, New York 10017, USA
SCIENTIFIC Computing Service Ltd., 17 Balfe Street, Kings Cross, London N1 9EB
SCIENTIFIC Era Publications, 4 St.Mary's Place, Stamford, Lincs. Tel : 0780 2550
SCIENTIFIC Information Consultants Ltd., 661 Finchley Road, London NW2 2HN Tel : 01.794 2217
SCIENTIFIC Methods Inc., Box 195, Austin, Texas 78767, USA Tel : 512 477 5781 Telex : 776443
SCIENTIFIC Press, The Stanford Barn, Palo Alto, California 94304, USA
SCIENTIFIC Press Ltd., 4 Burkes Parade, Beaconsfield, Bucks. HP9 1NS Tel : 049 46 5139
SCIENTIFIC Publ.(GB)Ltd., More Hall, Brockton, Much Wenlock Shropshire TF13 6JU Tel : 074 636 294
SCIENTIFIC Publ.Company, 40 Dalton Street, Rochdale Road, Manchester M4 4JP Tel : 061.205 1514
SCIENTIFIC Subscription Service, 329 Addiscombe Road, Croydon Surrey CR0 7LF Tel : 01.654 1853
SCIENTIFIC Technical Book Service Ltd., 41-42 William IV Street London WC2N 4DF
SCOLAR Press, 13 Brunswick Centre, London WC1N 1AF Tel : 01.278 6381/2
SCOPE Books, 3 Sandford House, Kingsclere, Newbury, Berks RG15 8PA Tel : 0635 298439
SCORPION Publ.Ltd., 377 High Street, Stratford, London E15 5EX Tel : 01.555 3339
SCOTT Foresman & Co. - orders to IBD
SCOTTISH Academic Press Ltd., 33 Montgomery Street, Edinburgh EH7 5JX Tel : 031.556 2796
SCOTTISH Adult Literacy Agency, 4 Queensway Street, Edinburgh EH2 4PA
SCOTTISH Arts Council, 19 Charlotte Square, Edinburgh EH2 4DF Tel : 031.226 6051
SCOTTISH Association for Spastics, 22 Corstorphine Road, Edinburgh EH12 6HP
SCOTTISH Civic Trust, 24 George Square, Glasgow G2 1EF Tel : 041.221 1466/7
SCOTTISH Community Education Council, 4 Queensferry Street Edinburgh EH2 4PA Tel : 031.225 9451
SCOTTISH Consumer Council, 4 Somerset Place, Glasgow G3
SCOTTISH Council (Development & Industry), 23 Chester Street Edinburgh EH3 7ET
SCOTTISH Council for Civil Liberties, 27 Clerkenwell Close London EC1R 0AT Tel : 01.251 4976
SCOTTISH Council for Educational Technology Ltd., Dowanhill 74 Victoria Crescent Road, Glasgow G12 9JN Tel : 041.334 9314

SCOTTISH Council for Research in Education, 15 St.John Street, Edinburgh EH8 8JR Tel : 031.557 2944
SCOTTISH Council of Social Service, 18-19 Claremont Crescent Edinburgh EH7 4QD Tel : 031.556 3882
SCOTTISH Council on Alcoholism, 147 Blythswood Street, Glasgow G2 4EN Tel : 041.333 9677
SCOTTISH Council Research Institute - gone away, 1982
SCOTTISH Health & Home Dept., New St.Andrew's House, St.James Centre, Edinburgh
SCOTTISH Health Service Centre, Crewe Road South, Edinburgh EH4 2LF Tel : 031.332 2335
SCOTTISH Institute of Adult Education, 4 Queensferry Street, Edinburgh EH2 4PA Tel : 031.226 7200
SCOTTISH Institute of Agricultural Engineering, Bush Estate Penicuik, Midlothian EH26 0PH Tel : 031.445 2147
SCOTTISH Library Association, The Mitchell Library, North Street, Glasgow G3 7DN
SCOTTISH Marine Biological Association, Dunstaffnage Marine Research Labs., PO Box 3, Oban, Argyll, PA34 4AD Tel : 0631 2244
SCOTTISH Mountaineering, 4 Morven Road, Bearsden, Glasgow G61 2BU
SCOTTISH Office, Scottish Office Library, New St.Andrew's House, St.James Centre, Edinburgh EH1 3TG Tel : 031.556 8400
SCOTTISH Special Housing Association, 15-21 Palmerston Places, Edinburgh EH12 5AT
SCOTTISH Tourist Board, 23 Ravelston Terrace, Edinburgh EH4 3EU Tel : 031.332 2433 Telex : 72272
SCOTTISH Volleyball Association, Castlecliff, 25 Johnston Terrace, Edinburgh EH1 2NH Tel : 031.225 7311
SCOTTISH Youth Hostels Association, National Office, 7 Glebe Crescent, Stirling FK8 2JA Tel : 0786 2821 Telex : 779689
SCOUT Association, Scout Shop Ltd., Churchill Industrial Estate, Lancing, Sussex BN15 8UG / Baden-Powell House, Queen's Gate, London SW7 5JS Tel : 01.584 7030
Charles SCRIBNER & Sons, 597 Fifth Avenue, New York 10017, USA - distributed by European Book Service
SCRIPWORLD Pharmaceutical News, 18-20 Hill Rise, Richmond Surrey TW10 6UA Tel : 01.948 3262
SCRIPTORIA, Belgielei 147a, B-2000 Antwerp, Belgium
SCRIPTURE Union, 130 City Road, London EC1X 2NJ Tel : 01.250 1966
SEA Fish Industry Authority, Sea Fisheries House, 10 Young Street, Edinburgh EH2 4JQ Tel : 031.225 2515 Telex : 727225
D&P SEABROOK Ltd., 10 Oxford Road, Kidlington, Oxford OX5 1AA Tel : 08675 2719
SEABY's Numismatic Publ.Ltd., Audley House, 11 Margaret Street, London W1N 8AT Tel : 01.580 3677
SEAGULL SA, PO Box 44, The Grange, St.Peter Port, Guernsey Channel Islands Tel : 0481 27111 Telex : 4191316
SEARCH Press Ltd., Wellwood, North Farm Road, Tunbridge Wells, Kent TN2 3DR Tel : 0892 44037/8 Telex : 957258
SEATRADE Publications, Fairfax House, Colchester, Essex CO1 1RJ Tel : 0206 45121 Telex : 98517
Martin SECKER & Warburg Ltd., 54 Poland Street, London W1V 3DF Tel : 01.437 2075 Telex : 26188
SECOND Aeon Publications, 19 Southminster Road, Penylan Cardiff CF2 5AT Tel : 0222 68697
SECRETARIES Journal Ltd., 98 Park Street, London W1Y 4BR
SECTOR Publ.Ltd., 10 Perryfield Way, Ham, Richmond, Surrey TW10 7SP
The SECURI Book Co., 8 Topside, Grenoside, Sheffield S30 3RD, Yorks
SECURITY World Books, 2639, 80 La Cienega Blvd., Los Angeles, California 90034, USA
SEER Books, 6 Borneo Street, London SW15 1QQ
SEELEY Service Co.Ltd. - stock acquired by F.Warne Ltd.
SEIBT-Verlag GmbH, Bavariaring 24, D-8000 Munchen 2, West Germany Tel : 089 530 9005
SELDON Society, c/o Faculty of Law, Queen Mary College, Mile End Road, London E1 4NS Tel : 01.980 4811
SELECTION & Industrial Training Administration Ltd., 15a The Broadway, Wimbledon, London SW19 1PD
SELL's Publications Ltd., Sell's House, 39 East Street, Epsom Surrey KT17 1BQ Tel ; 037 27 26376 Telex : 21792
SELPRESS Books Ltd., 35 High Street, Wendover, Aylesbury Bucks HP22 6DU Tel : 0296 624113 Telex : 83273
SEMICON Indexes Ltd., 7 Kings Road, Fleet, Hants. GU13 9AB Tel : 025 14 28526

SEMINAR for Arabian Studies, c/o Institute of Archeology, 31 Gordon Square, London WC1H 0PY
SEMINAR Indexes Ltd., 7 King's Parade, Kings Road, Fleet Hants.GU13 9AB Tel : 025 14 28526
SEMINAR Press, 111 5th Avenue, New York 10003, USA
SEND The Light Trust - see STL Distributors
SENECIO Publ.Co.Ltd., 7 Little Clarendon, Oxford OX1 2HP Tel : 0865 54466
SENTRY Books, 10718 White Oak Avenue, Granad Hills, CA 91344 USA
SERINDIA Publications, 10 Parkfields, London SW15 6NH Tel : 01.788 1966 Telex : 923421
SERVICE Station Publ.Ltd., 178-202 Great Portland Street London W1N 6NH Tel : 01.637 2400 Telex : 262568
William SESSIONS Ltd., Ebor Press, York YO3 9HS Tel : 0904 21711 Telex : 57712 / 19 Bedford Row London WC1R 4EB Tel : 01.405 8086
SETSQUARE Design Ltd., 52 London Street, Reading RG1 4SQ
SETTLE & Bendall(Wigmore), 32 Savile Row, London W1X 1AG Tel : 01.734 0171
SEVERN House, 4 Brook Street, London W1Y 1AA - distributed by Tiptree
Ronald SEWELL & Assocs.Ltd., 1 Queen Square, Bath BA1 2HG Tel : 0225 318500 Telex : 449728
SEYMOUR Press Ltd., 334 Brixton Road, London SW9 7AG Tel : 01.733 4444 Telex : 8812945
SHAKESPEARE Head Press Ltd., 108 Cowley Road, Oxford OX4 1JF Tel : 0865 724041 - distributed by Marston Book Services
SHALWATER Ltd., Meadway Garden Reach, Chalfont St.Giles Bucks HP8 4BE
SHANTI Sadan, 29 Chepstow Villas, London W11 3DR Tel : 01.727 7846
SHAP Crest Ltd., 2 Catherine Street, London WC2B 5JS
SHARE Community Ltd., 177 Battersea High Street, London SW11 3JS Tel : 01.223 0924
I.P.SHARP Assoc.Ltd., 132 Buckingham Palace Road, London SW1W 9SA Tel : 01.730 4567
M.E.SHARPE Inc., 80 Business Park Drive, Armonk, NY 10504 USA - UK representative : Eurospan Ltd.
SHAW & Sons Ltd., Shaway House, Bell Green Lane, Lower Sydenham, London SE26 5AE Tel : 01.778 5131
SHAWS Linton Publ., 35 Market Place, Wantage, Oxon.OX12 8AE Tel : 02357 4672
SHEAF Publishing, 35 Moorooaks Road, Sheffield S10 1BX Tel : 0742 662934
SHEARSON/American Express, St.Alphage House, 2 Fore Street London EC2Y 5DA Tel : 01.588 7505
SHEARWATER Press Ltd., Eastfield, Sulby, Ramsey, Isle of Man Tel : 0624 813733
SHEBA Books, 31 Dashwood Rise, Duns Tew, Oxford OX5 4JQ
SHEBA Feminist Publishers, 488 Kingsland Road, London E8 4AE Tel : 01.254 1590
SHEED & Ward Ltd., 6 Blenheim Street, London W1Y 0SA Tel : 01.629 0306
SHEEO Andrews & McMeel, 6700 Squibb Road, Mission, Kansas 66202, USA
SHEET Metal Layout Books, 14189 Madison Avenue, Detroit Michigan 48239, USA
SHEFFIELD City Libraries, Central Library, Surrey Street, Sheffield S1 1XZ Tel : 0742 734711/3 Telex : 54243
SHELDON Press, Holy Trinity Church, Marylebone Road, London NW1 4DU - orders to The Trade Dept., 7 Castle Street Reading RG1 7SB Tel : 0734 599011
SHELL (UK)Ltd., Shell Mex House, Strand, London WC2R 0DX Tel : 01.438 3530 - maps distributed by Robert Nicholson Publ.Ltd.
SHELTER (National Campaign for the Homeless), 157 Waterloo Road, London SE1 8UU Tel : 01.633 9377
SHEPHEARD-Walwyn Publ.Ltd., Suite 34, 26 Charing Cross Road London WC2H 0HY Tel : 01.240 5992
SHEPPARD Press Ltd., PO Box 42, Russell Chambers, Covent Garden, London WC2E 8AX Tel : 01.240 0406 Telex : 25247
SHEPPARDS & Chase, Clements House, Gresham Street, London EC2V 7AU Tel : 01.606 8099 Telex : 886268
SHEPPEY Publ.Ltd., Brenchley House, High Street, Sittingbourne Kent Tel : 0795 79139
SHERIDON Publishing, 220 Melfort Road, Thornton Heath, Surrey
John SHERRATT & Son Ltd., St.Ann's Press, 78 Park Road, Timperley, Altrincham, Cheshire WA14 5QQ Tel : 061.973 5711
Peter SHERWOOD Associates Inc., 20 Haarlem Avenue, White Plains, New York 10603, USA Tel : 914 761 3033
SHETLAND Island Council, Lower Hillhead, Lerwick

SHIPPING Guides Ltd., Shipping Guides House, 75 Bell Street Reigate, Surrey RH2 7AN Tel : 073 72 42255/7
SHIPPING World & Shipbuilder, 25 New Street Square, London EC4A 3JA Tel : 01.353 3212 Telex : 27844
Keith SHIPTON Dev.Ltd., Adelaide House, London Bridge, London EC4R 9DS Tel : 01.623 5210
SHIRE Publications Ltd., Cromwell House, Church Street, Princes Risborough, Aylesbury, Bucks HP17 9AJ Tel : 084 44 4301
SHIRLEY Institute, Didsbury, Manchester M20 8RX Tel : 061.445 8141 Telex : 668417
SHIVA Publ.Ltd., 4 Church Lane, Nantwich, Cheshire CW5 5RQ Tel : 0270 628272 Telex : 367258
SHOE & Allied Trades Research Association, SATRA House, Rockingham Road, Kettering, Northants. NN16 9JH Tel : 0536 516318
SHOE & Leather News, 84-88 Great Eastern Street, London EC2A 3ED Tel : 01.739 2071
The SHOE String Press - see Archon Books
SHOEMAKER Press, c/o Nigel Gray, 18 East Priors Court, Northampton
SHRINE of Wisdom, Fintry Brook, Godalming, Surrey GU8 5UQ Tel : 042 879 2621
Barry SHURLOCK & Co.(Publ.)Ltd., 3 Mill Lane, Abbots Worthy, Winchester, Hants. SO21 1SD Tel : 0962 884058
SHUTTLEWORTH Collection, Old Warden Aerodrome, Biggleswade Beds. SG18 9EP Tel : 076 727 288
SIDGWICK & Jackson Ltd., 1 Tavistock Chambers, Bloomsbury Way, London WC1A 2SG Tel : 01.242 6081/3 - distributed by Gollancz Services Ltd.
La SIESTA Press, PO Box 406, Glendale, California 91209, USA
SIGMA Technical Press, 5 Alton Road, Wilmslow, Cheshire SK9 5DW
SIGN of the Times Publ.Co., 407 Gilbert Avenue, Cincinnati OH 45202, USA
SIGNET Books - distributed by New English Library Ltd.
SIJTHOFF & Noordhoff Intl.Publ.BV - c/o Kluwer Academic Publishers Group
SILCO Book Ltd., 7 Russell Gardens, London NW11 9NJ Tel : 01.455 0716 Telex : 24224
SILVER Burdett Co., 250 James Street, Morristown, New Jersey 07960, USA
SIMMONS Market Research Bureau, 219 East 42nd Street, New York 10017, USA Tel : 212 867 1414
Gordon SIMMONS Research Ltd., 80 St.Martin's Lane, London WC2 Tel : 01.836 1822
SIMON & Schuster Inc. - distributed by Silco Books Ltd.
SIMON Books, The Old Hop Exchange, 1-3 Central Buildings 24 Southwark Street, London SE1 - orders to Bailey Bros.& Swinfen Ltd.
SIMON Books Directories, Barton House, 69 Sandgate Road, Folkestone, Kent CT20 2AF
SIMPLIFICATION of International Trade Procedures Board - see SITPRO
SINAUER Assoc.Inc., Sunderland, Mass.01375, USA - orders to Addison Wesley
SINGER (School Books) - division of Random House - orders to European Book Service
SIRON Publishing, 20 Queen Anne Street, London W1N 9FB Tel : 01.580 4900
SIXART Studios & The Golden Head Press, Sixart Studios, Hampton Poyle, Oxford OX5 2PZ Tel : 08675 3134
SIZE Report, 145-147 High Street, Kelvedon, Essex
SKEIST Laboratories Inc., 112 Naylon Avenue, Livingston, New Jersey 07039, USA Tel : 201 994 1050
SKI Specialists Ltd., 4 Douro Place, London W8 5PH
Charles SKILTON Ltd., 2-4 Abbeymount, Edinburgh EH8 8JH Tel : 031.661 9339
Anthony SKINNER Management Ltd., 565 Fulham Road, London SW6 1ES Tel : 01.385 1992
Thomas SKINNER Directories, Windsor Court, East Grinstead House, East Grinstead, W.Sussex RH19 1XE Tel : 0342 26972
SKY Publishing Corp., 49 Bay State Road, Cambridge, Mass. 02238-1290, USA
Lee SLURZBERG Research Inc., 120 East 56th Street, New York 10022, USA Tel : 212 980 3335
SMALL Firms Information Centre, 65 Buckingham Palace Road, London SW1W 0QX Tel : 01.828 2384
SMALLER Businesses Advisory Services Ltd., 34-36 Streetley Lane, Sutton Coldfield, West Midlands B74 4TU
A.SMITH Institute, 50 Westminster Mansions, Little Smith Street London SW1P 3DQ Tel : 01.222 4995

John SMITH & Sons (Glasgow)Ltd., 57-61 St.Vincent Street, Glasgow G2 5TB Tel : 041.221 7472
Maurice Temple SMITH Ltd., Gloucester Mansions, Cambridge Circus, London WC2H 8HD Tel : 01.836 5188
SMITH Stanley & Co.Inc., 72 Old Kings Highway North, PO Box 1651, Darien, Conn. 06820, USA Tel : 203 655 7664
W.H.SMITH & Son Ltd., Strand House, New Fetter Lane, London EC4A 1AD Tel : 01.353 0277 Telex : 887777
W.H.SMITH Distributors, Euston Street, Freemen's Common, Aylestone Road, Leicester LE2 7SS Tel : 0533 547671
SMITHSONIAN Institution Press - distributed by Eurospan Ltd.
Colin SMYTHE Ltd., PO Box 6, Gerrards Cross, Bucks SL9 8XA Tel : 0753 86000
H.SNELL Ltd., 354 High Road, Wembley, Middx. HA9 6AP
SOCIAL Affairs Unit, 2 Lord North Street, Westminster, London SW1 Tel : 01.799 3745
SOCIAL Audit Ltd., Munro House, 9 Poland Street, London W1V 3BG
SOCIAL Development Corp., 266 Pearl Hartford, CT 06103, USA
SOCIAL Organisation Ltd., 32 Copley Road, Stanmore, Middx. HA7 4PF Tel : 01.954 1201
SOCIAL Science Research Council, 1 Temple Avenue, London EC4Y 0BD Tel : 01.353 5252 Telex : 28902 - distributed by School Govt.Publ.Co.Ltd.
SOCIALIST Medical Association, 9 Poland Street, London W1V 3DG Tel : 01.439 3395
SOCIALIST Worker Publications, 27 Clerkenwell Close, London EC1R 0AT Tel : 01.251 4976
SOCIALISTS Unlimited, 27 Clerkenwell Close, London EC1R 0AT Tel : 01.251 4976
SOCIEDAD Mexicana de Mecanica de Suelos AC, Londris Wo 44, Coyoacoen, Mexico 21, D.F.Mexico
SOCIETÄTS Verlag, Postfach 2929, 6000 Frankfurt am Main 1, W.Germany
SOCIETE des Publications du Moniteur, 17 Rue d'Uzes, 75002 Paris, France
SOCIETE Didcot-Bottin, 28 Rue du Docteur Finlay, 75338 Paris Cedex 15, France
SOCIETE Generale de Presse, 13 Ave de l'Opera, 75001 Paris France
SOCIETY for Analytical Chemistry - see Royal Society of Chemistry
SOCIETY for Applied Mathematics, 33 South 17th Street, Philadelphia, PA 19103, USA - distributed by Heyden & Sons Ltd.
SOCIETY for Occupational Environmental Health, 2914 M Street NW, Washington DC 20007, USA
SOCIETY for Promoting Christian Knowledge, Holy Trinity Church Road, Marylebone Road, London NW1 4DU Tel : 01.387 5282 - orders to 7 Castle Street, Reading Berks RG1 7SB Tel ; 0734 599011
SOCIETY for Research into Higher Education, University of Surrey, Guildford, Surrey GU2 5XH Tel : 0483 39003
SOCIETY for the Protection of Ancient Buildings, 55 Great Ormond Street, London WC1N 3JA Tel : 01.405 2646
SOCIETY for Underwater Technology, 1 Birdcage Walk, London SW1H 9JJ Tel : 01.222 8658
SOCIETY of Antiquaries of London, Burlington House, Piccadilly London W1V 0HS Tel : 01.437 9954
SOCIETY of Archivists, Guildhall Library, Aldermanbury, London EC2P 2EJ
SOCIETY of Authors, 84 Drayton Gardens, London SW10 9SD Tel : 01.373 6642
SOCIETY of Automotive Engineers, 400 Commonwealth Drive, Warrendale, Penn. 15096, USA - distributed by American Technical Publ.Ltd.
SOCIETY of Chemical Industry, 14 Belgrave Square, London SW1X 8PS Tel : 01.235 3681
SOCIETY of Civil Engineering Technicians, 1-7 Great George Street, Westminster, London SW1P 3AA Tel : 01.222 7722
SOCIETY of County Treasurers, County Treasurers Department, County Hall, Northallerton, N.Yorks. DL7 8AL Tel : 0609 3123
SOCIETY of Dairy Technology, 72 Ermine Street, Huntingdon Cambs. PE18 6EZ Tel : 0480 50741
SOCIETY of Dyers & Colourists, PO Box 244, Perkin House, 82 Gratton Road, Bradford, Yorks. BD1 2JB
SOCIETY of Economic Paleontologists & Mineralogists, Box 4756 Tulsa, Oklahoma 74104, USA Tel : 918 743 9765
SOCIETY of Electronic & Radio Technicians Ltd., 57-61 Newington Causeway, London SE1 6BL Tel : 01.403 2351
SOCIETY of Genealogists, 37 Harrington Gardens, London SW7 4JX

SOCIETY of Glass Technology, Thornton, 20 Hallam Gate Road, Sheffield S10 5BT Tel : 0742 663168
SOCIETY of Investment Analysis, 211-213 High Street, Bromley Kent BR1 1NY Tel : 01.464 0811
SOCIETY of Leather Technologists & Chemists, 1 Edges Court Moulton, Northampton NN3 1UJ Tel : 0604 47318
SOCIETY of Manufacturing Engineers - distributed by American Technical Publ.Ltd.
SOCIETY of Metaphysicians Ltd., Archers Court, Stonestile Lane, The Ridge, Hastings, E.Sussex TN35 4PG Tel : 0424 751577
SOCIETY of Mining Engineers of AIMF, 540 Arapeen Drive, Salt Lake City, Utah 54108, USA
SOCIETY of Motor Manufacturers & Traders, Forbes House, Halkin Street, London SW1X 7DS Tel : 01.235 7000 Telex 21628
SOCIETY of Naval Architects & Marine Engineers, One World Trade Centre, Suite 1369, New York 10048, USA
SOCIETY of Occupational Medicine, 11 St.Andrew's Place, Regent's Park, London NW1 4LE Tel : 01.486 2641
SOCIETY of Petroleum Engineers, 6200 North Central Expressway Drawer 64750, Dallas, Texas 75206, USA Tel : 214 361 6601 Telex : 730989
SOCIETY of Photo-Optical Instrumental Engineers, PO Box 10, Bellingham, WA 98225, USA Tel : 206 676 3290
SOCIETY of Radiographers, 14 Upper Wimpole Street, London W1M 8BN Tel : 01.935 5726/7
SOCIETY of the Faith & Church Union Trustees Inc., Faith House, 7 Tufton Street, Westminster, London SW1
SOCIETY of the Plastics Industry Inc., 355 Lexington Avenue New York 10017, USA
SOCIOLOGICAL Review Monographs, University of Keele, Keele Staffs. ST5 5BG
SODEMAE, 11b Ave. de la Porte Neuve, Luxembourg
SOFTCOVER Library Ltd., 44 Hill Street, London W1X 8LB
SOIL & Water Management Assoc.Ltd., National Agricultural Centre, Stoneleigh, Kenilworth, Warwicks. CV8 2LZ Tel : 0203 555100
SOLAR Energy Information Services, PO Box 19475, Sacramento, CA 95819, USA Tel : 916 739 1376
SOLIDARITY(London), 123 Lathom Road, London E6 Tel : 01.552 3985
SOLSTICE Productions Ltd., 85 Carnwath Road, London SW6 3HZ Tel : 01.736 3008
SOMERSET House Inc., USA - distributed by Chadwyck-Healey Ltd.
SONCINO Press Ltd., Audley House, North Audley Street, London W1 Tel : 01.629 6506
SONICAID Ltd., Hook Lane, Nyetimber, Bognor Regis, Sussex PO21 3PA
SOTHEBY, King & Chasemore, Station Road, Pulborough, W.Sussex RH20 1AJ Tel : 079 82 2081
SOTHEBY Parke Bernet Publ.Ltd., 36 Dover Street, London W1X 3RB Tel : 01.499 4551/2 Telex : 24454
SOTHEBY Publications, Russell Chambers, Covent Garden, London WC2E 8AA Tel : 01.240 1091 Telex : 22158
SOUTH African Institute of Race Relations, PO Box 97, 2000 Johannesburg, South Africa Tel : 011 724 4441
SOUTH EAST & Asia Iron & Steel Institute, Tower 1003, DBS Building, 6 Shenton Way, Singapore 1
SOUTH Group Publ.Ltd., 11 North Street, Ashburton, Devon Tel : 0364 53389
SOUTH West Scotland Tourist Association, Douglas House, Newton Stewart, Wigtownshire DG8 6DG Tel : 0671 2549
SOUTHAMPTON Civic Record Office, c/o City Archivist, Civic Centre, Southampton SO9 4XL Tel : 0703 23855
SOUTHEND-on-Sea Museum Service, Central Museum, Victoria Avenue, Southend-on-Sea, SS2 6EX Tel : 0702 330214
SOUTHERN Collectors Publications, 80 Northam Road, Southampton, Hants. Tel : 0703 23255
SOUTHERN Distribution, Building K, Ablion Yard, 17a Balfe Street, London N1 Tel : 01.837 1460
SOUTHERN Forest Experimental Station, Federal Buildings, 701 Loyola Avenue, New Orleans, LA 70013, USA
SOUTHERN Regional Council for Further Education, 26 Bath Road Reading, Berks RG1 6NT
SOUTHSIDE Publ.Ltd., 17 Jeffrey Street, Edinburgh EH1 1DR Tel : 031.556 0023
SOUVENIR Press Ltd., 43 Great Russell Street, London WC1B 3PA Tel : 01.580 9307/8 / 01.637 5711/3 - orders to Tiptree Book Services Ltd.
SOVEREIGN Grace Advent Testimony, 1 Donald Way, Chelmsford Essex CM2 9JB Tel : 0245 68815

SOVEREIGN International, Sovereign House, Brentwood, Essex CM14 4SE
SPACE Educational Aids Society, 12 Boosborough Gardens, London SW1K 2IT
SPARTAN Books, Hayden Book Co., 50 Essex Street, Rochelle Park, New Jersey 07662, USA - distributed by Butterworth & Co.Ltd.
SPEARHEAD Publications Ltd., Rowe House, 55-59 Fife Road, Kingston-upon-Thames, Surrey KT1 1TA Tel : 01.549 5831
Neville SPEARMAN Ltd., Priory Gate, 57 Friars Street, Sudbury Suffolk Tel : 078 73 71818
SPECIAL Libraries Association, 235 Park Avenue South, New York 10003, USA
SPECIALISED Book Marketing, 22 Newhaven Road, Evington Leicester LE5 6JG Tel : 0533 415238
SPECIALISED Publications Ltd., 5 Grove Road, Surbiton, Surrey KT6 4BT Tel : 01.390 0222 Telex : 8954665
SPECIALISTS in Business Information Inc., 3375 Park Avenue Wantagh, NY 11793, USA Tel : 516 781 7277
SPECTRUM Books Ltd., 6 Miletas Place, Fairhaven, Lytham St. Annes, Lancs. FY8 1BQ Tel : 0253 735381
SPECTRUM Publishing, Spectrum House, 183-185 Askew Road London W12 9AX Tel : 01.749 6746
SPEED Sport Motobooks, Bercourt House, 51 York Road, Brentford, Middx.TW8 0QP Tel : 01.560 3404 Telex : 936183
SPENCER Agency Ltd., 1 Warwick Avenue, Wickham, Newcastle upon Tyne
John SPENCER & Co.(Publ.)Ltd., 131 Brackenbury Road, London W6 Tel : 01.748 8560
SPHERE Books, 30-32 Grays Inn Road, London WC1X 8JL Tel : 01.405 2087 Telex : 858846 - orders to TBL Bookservice Ltd.
Der SPIEGEL Verlag AG, Brandsweite 19, 2000 Hamburg 11 West Germany
The SPINAL Injuries Association, 126 Albert Street, London NW1 7NF
SPINDLEWOOD, 70 Lynhurst Avenue, Barnstaple EX31 2HY Tel : 0271 71612
SPINK & Son Ltd., 5-7 King Street, St.James, London SW1Y 6QS Tel : 01.930 7888 Telex : 916711
SPIRITUALIST Association of G.B., 33 Belgrave Square, London SW1X 8QL Tel : 01.235 3351/4
SPIRITUALIST Press, 23 Great Queen Street, London WC2B 5BB Tel : 01.405 2914/5
SPOKESMAN Books, Bertrand Russell House, Gamble Street, Nottingham NG7 4ET Tel : 0602 708318 - distributed by Publications Distribution Co-operative
E.& F.N.SPON Ltd., 11 New Fetter Lane, London EC4P 4EE Tel : 01.583 9855 Telex : 263398 - distributed by Associated Book Publishers
SPORTING Chronicle Publ.Ltd., Thomson House, Withy Grove Manchester M60 4BJ Tel : 061 834 1234
SPORTING Handbooks Ltd., 12 Dyott Street, London WC1A 1DF Tel : 01.836 8911
SPORTING Life, 9 New Fetter Lane, London EC4A 1AR Tel : 01.353 0246
The SPORTS Council, 16 Upper Woburn Place, London WC1H 0QP Tel : 01.388 1277
SPORTVERLAG - distributed by Central Books
The SPOTLIGHT Casting Directory & Contacts, 42 Cranbourn Street, London WC2 Tel : 01.437 7631
SPRING Research & Manufacturers Association, Henry Street, Sheffield S3 7EQ Tel : 0742 70771
SPRINGBORN Laboratories Inc., 21 Ludlow Avenue, Luton Beds. LU1 3RW
SPRINGER Publ.Co.Inc., 200 Park Avenue South, New York 10003, USA
SPRINGER Verlag, Heidelberger Platz 3, D-1000 Berlin 33, Germany Tel : 030 8207-1 Telex : 01 83 319
SPRINGWOOD Books Ltd., 22 Chewter Lane, Windlesham Surrey GU20 6JP Tel : 0276 74741 - distributed by George Philip & Son Ltd.
SPURBOOKS, Allander House, 137-141 Leith Walk, Edinburgh EH6 8NS Tel : 031.554 9444
SQUIRTS Guide Ltd., PO Box 6, Kettering, Northants
Maxwell SROGE Publications, 731 N.Cascade, Colorado Springs CO 80903, USA
STACEY International Publishers, 128 Kensington Church Street London W8 4BH Tel : 01.221 6109 Telex : 298768 - orders to Glenside Industrial Estate, Star Road Partridge Green, Horsham, W.Sussex Tel : 0403 710971
STACEY Publications, 1 Hawthorndene Road, Hayes, Bromley BR2 7DZ Tel : 01.462 6461

STACKPOLE Books, Cameron & Kelker Streets, Box 1831, arrisburg, PA 17105, USA Tel : 717 234 5091
STAFFORDSHIRE County Library, Friars Terrace, Stafford ST17 4AY Tel : 0785 3121 X8350
STAGE 1, 47 Red Lion Street, London WC1R 4PF Tel : 01.405 7780
STAHLSCHLÜSSEL - distributed by J.M.J.Maus Ltd.
STAINER & Bell Ltd., 82 High Street, East Finchley, London N2 9PW Tel : 01.444 9135
STAM Press Ltd., Raans Road, Amersham, Bucks HP6 6JJ Tel : 02403 4196 Telex : 837916
STAMEX BV, 36a GraafFlorislaan, PO Box 505, Hilversum, The Netherlands
STAMFORD Research Institute, Crolyn House, Dingwall Road Croydon, Surrey Tel : 01.681 1751
STANBOROUGH Press Ltd., Alma Park, Grantham, Lincs. NG31 9SL Tel : 0476 4284/6
STANBROOK Abbey Press, Callow End, Worcester WR2 4TD Tel : 0905 830209
STANDARD & Poor's Corporation, 25 Broadway, New York 10004 USA Tel : 212 248 2525
STANDARD & Poor's International SA, Boulevard Bischoffsheim 45, Box 2, 1000 Brussels, Belgium Tel : 218 52 08
STANDARD Catalogue Information Services Ltd., Medway Wharf Road, Tonbridge, Kent TN9 1QR Tel : 0732 365251/2
STANDARD Press (Montrose)Ltd., 66 High Street, Montrose, Angus Tel : 0674 2251
STANDARD Rate & Data Service, 5201 Old Orchard Road, Skokie Ill. 60076, USA - orders to British Rate & Data Ltd., 76 Oxford Street, London W1N 0HH
STANDARDS for Material Products Systems & Services, 1916 Race Street, Philadelphia, Penn. 19103, USA
STANDING Conference of Principals & Directors of Colleges & Institutes in Higher Education, Worcester College of Higher Education, Henwick Grove, Worcester WR2 6AJ Tel : 0905 428080
STANFORD Maritime Ltd., 12-14 Long Acre, Covent Garden London WC2E 9LP Tel : 01.836 1321 Telex : 21667 - orders to George Philip & Son Ltd.
STANFORD Research Institute, SRI International, 333 Ravenswood Avenue, Menlo Park, California 94025, USA Tel : 415 326 6200 Telex : 334463
STANFORD University Press, Stanford, CA 94305, USA
STANILAND Hall Associates Ltd., 42 Colebrooke Row, London N1 8AF Tel : 01.359 6054 - distributed by Graham & Trotman Ltd.
STANWELL Distributors, 96 Stanwell Road, Penarth, South Glamorgan CF6 2LP Tel : 0222 700256
STAPLES Printers Ltd., 94 Wigmore Street, London W1H 0BR Tel : 01.935 0665
STAR Books, 44 Hill Street, London W1X 8LB Tel : 01.493 6777 Telex : 28117 - distributed by Tiptree Book Services Ltd.
STARFISH Books Ltd., 1 Royal Parade, Hindhead, Surrey GU26 6TD Tel : 042873 6141 & 6854/5
Harold STARKE Ltd., Pegasus House, 116-120 Golden Lane, London EC1Y 0TL Tel : 01.253 2145 - orders to The Barn, Northgate, Beccles, Suffolk Tel : 0502 713239
STARLING Press Ltd., Tredegar Street, Risca, Newport, Gwent NP1 6YB Tel : 0633 612251
STARTRACK Publications, 15 Park Road, Wellingborough, Northants. NN8 4PW
STATE Research Publications, 27 Clerkenwell Close, London EC1R 0AT Tel : 01.251 4976
STATE University of New York Press - distributed by Hodder & Stoughton Ltd.
STATISTICAL Yearbook Netherlands - orders to Joop van Halm, PO Box 688, 3800 Amersfoort, The Netherlands
STEAM Press, 43 Floral Street, Covent Garden, London WC2E 9DW Tel : 01.836 7557
STECHERT Macmillan Inc., 866 3rd Avenue, New York 10022, USA
STEEL Castings Research & Trade Association, 5 East Bank Road Sheffield S2 3PT Tel : 0742 28647 Telex : 54281
STEEL Structures Painting Council, Publications Dept., 4400 5th Avenue, Pittsburgh, PA 15213, USA
STEIN &Day, USA - distributed by Wildwood House Ltd.
Franz STEINER Verlag, D-6200 Wiesbaden, Postfach 5529, Friedrichstrasse 24, W.Germany Tel : 0 61 21 / 37 20 11
Rudolf STEINER Press, 35 Park Road, London NW1 6XT Tel : 01.723 9514 / 38 Museum Street, London WC1 Tel : 01.242 4249

STEMMER House Publ.Inc., 2627 Caves Road, Owings Mills Maryland 21117, USA
H.F.STENFERT Kroese BV, Pieterskirkhof 38, Postbus 33, Leiden, The Netherlands
Patrick STEPHENS Ltd., Bar Hill, Cambridge CB3 8EL Tel : 0954 80010 Telex : 817677
T.STEPHENSON & Sons Ltd., Market Place, Prescot, Merseyside L34 5SD Tel : 051.426 5161
STEREOSCOPIC Society, 40 Elgan Avenue, Surbiton, Surrey
STERLING Publ.Ltd., PO Box 839, 86-88 Edgware Road, London W2 2YW Tel : 01.258 0066 Telex : 8953130
STERLING Publishing Company - distributed by Blandford Press
STEVENS & Sons Ltd. - see Associated Book Publ.(UK)Ltd.
STEWARD & Sons Publisher, Long Beach, California, USA
Angus STEWART Publ.Ltd., The Old Rectory, Roughton, Norwich, Norfolk NR11 8SU Tel : 026 376 626
Malcolm STEWART Books Ltd., PO Box 265, London N3 2QF Tel : 01.349 2045
William STEWART Intl.Ltd., Carlton Chambers, Station Road, Shortlands, Bromley, Kent BR2 0EY
STILLIT Books Ltd., 72 New Bond Street, London W1Y 0QY Tel : 01.493 1177 Telex : 23475
Leslie STINTON & Partners, 39a London Road, Kingston-upon-Thames, Surrey KT2 6ND Tel : 01.546 7276
STOATE & Bishop, St.James Square, Cheltenham, Glos. Tel : 0242 36741
STOBART & Son Ltd., 67-73 Worship Street, London EC2A 2EL Tel : 01.247 0501/5
The STOCK Exchange, London EC2N 1HP Tel : 01.588 2355 X8708
STOCKHOLM Intl.Peace Research Institute, c/o Taylor & Francis Ltd., 4 John Street, London WC1N 2ET Tel : 01.405 2237/9 Telex : 858540
STOCKHOLM School of Economics, Economic Research Institute Box 6501, 11383 Stockholm, Sweden
Arthur H.STOCKWELL Ltd., Elms Court, Torrs Park, Ilfracombe, Devon EX34 8BA Tel : 0271 62557
STONE & Cox Publ.Ltd., Mitre House, 44 Fleet Street, London EC4Y 1BS Tel : 01.353 1622
The STONEBRIDGE Press, 823-5 Bath Road, Brislington, Bristol BS4 5NU Tel : 0272 775375
STONEHAM Publ.Ltd., Stoneham Park, Eastleigh, Hants. SO5 3HT Tel : 0703 766715
STONESHIRE Co.Ltd., Lloyds Bank Chambers, 841 High Road, North Finchley, London N12 8PT
STONEHART Publ.Ltd., 13 Golden Square, London W1R 4AG
STORES & Clothing Research & Development Establishment, Flagstaff Road, Colchester, Essex CO2 7SS Tel : 0206 5121
STRAKER Bros. Ltd., 21 New Street, London EC2M 4NT Tel : 01.283 1711
STRAMULLION, 43 Candlemaker Row, Edinburgh EH1 2QB Tel : 031.225 2612
STRATEGIC Analysis Inc., 2525 Prospect Street, Reading, PA 19606, USA Tel : 215 779 2800
STRATEGIC Incorporated, 4320 Stevens Creek Blvd., Suite 215 San Jose, CA 95129, USA
STRATEGIC Management Learning, 27 Great Ormond Street, London WC1N 3JB Tel : 01.242 9172
STRATHCLYDE Convergencies, 15 Spence Street, Glasgow G20 0AW Tel : 041.946 2423
STRATMAN Conseil, 17 Rue Marsollier, F-75002 Paris, France Tel : 296 8915
STRATTON Intercontinental, 381 Park Avenue South, New York 10013, USA
STRUCTURE Publishing, 21 Caterham Road, London SE13 5AP Tel : 01.318 4607
STUBBS Directory Ltd., Dun & Bradstreet Ltd., 6-8 Bonhill Street, London EC2A 4BU Tel : 01.628 3691
STUDENT Christian, Monument Press, 56-58 Bloomsbury Street, London WC1B 3QX
STUDIO B, 1 Beaufort Street, London SW3 5AQ Tel : 01.352 9277
STUDIO Publ.(Ipswich) Ltd., 32 Princes Street, Ipswich, Suffolk IP1 1RJ Tel : 0473 217127
STUDIO Vista Ltd., 35 Red Lion Square, London WC1R 4SG Tel : 01.831 6100 - distributed by Cassell Ltd.
STUDY Commission on the Family, 3 Park Road, London NW1 6XN Tel : 01.486 8211/2
STYLUS Publications, 62 Bergholt Road, Colchester, Essex CO4 5AU Tel : 0206 853985
SUBMEX Ltd., 19 Roland Way, London SW7 3RF Tel : 01.373 3069 Telex : 8814824
SUFFOLK Records Society, County Hall, Ipswich, Suffolk IP4 2JS Tel : 0473 55801 - distributed by Boydell & Brewer
SUFI Publ.Co.Ltd., 23 East Street, Farnham, Surrey GU9 7SD Tel : 0252 721879 Telex : 858193 - distributed by Momenta Publ.Ltd.

SUMMERFIELD Press Ltd. - see Philip Wilson Publ.Ltd.
SUMMIT Publications, 38 High Street, Thornbury, Avon Tel : 0454 417472
SUNFLOWER Books - c/o TABS
SUNNY Publications, Unit 3, Taveners, Southfield Road, Nailsea Avon Tel : 0272 854175
SUNSET Books - c/o TABS
SURELINK Publishers' Services Ltd., Church House, Church Street, Godalming, Surrey Tel : 048 68 22071
SURREY University Press, Bishopbriggs, Glasgow G64 2NZ Tel : 041.772 2311 - orders to J.M.Dent & Sons Ltd.
SURRIDGE Dawson & Co.(Publ.)Ltd., 136 New Kent Road London SE1 Tel : 01.703 5480
SURVEY Force Ltd., 140 Bordon Lane, Sittingbourne, Kent Tel : 0795 23778
SURVEY Research Group Ltd. (Asia Pacific Centre), 6 Camden High Street, London NW1 0JH Tel : 01.388 5021 Telex : 887560
SUSSEX Genealogical Centre, 33 Sussex Square, Brighton, Sussex BN2 5AB Tel : 0273 602813
SUSSEX University Press, Refectory Terrapin, Falmer, Brighton, Sussex BN1 9QZ Tel : 0273 66755 - distributed by Scottish Academic Press Ltd.
Alan SUTTON Publ.Ltd., 17a Brunswick Road, Gloucester GL1 1HG Tel : 0452 419575
SUTTON Courtenay Press, Appleford, Abingdon, Oxon.OX14 4PB Tel : 023 582 319
SUTTON Publ.Co.Inc., 707 Westchester Avenue, White Plains NY 10604, USA Tel : 914 949 8500
SWALLOW Publ.Ltd., 32 Hermes Street, London N1 Tel : 01.278 1677/0733
SWEATMAN & Fordham, Alain Charles House, 27 Wilfred Street London SW1 Tel : 01.828 6107
SWEDENBORG Society, 20-21 Bloomsbury Way, London WC1A 2TH Tel : 01.405 7986
SWEDISH Research Council, Wennergren Centre, Box 6710 S-11385 Stockholm, Sweden Tel : 08 15 15 80 Telex : 13599
SWEDISH Trade Council, Storgatan 19, Box 5513, S-114 85 Stockholm, Sweden
SWEET & Maxwell Ltd. - see Associated Book Publ.(UK)Ltd.
SWETS Publ.Service, Heereweg 3476, 2161 CA Lisse, The Netherlands Tel : 02521 19113
SWINDON Book Co., 13-15 Lock Road, Kowloon, Hong Kong
SWIFT Printers(Publ.)Ltd., 1-7 Albion Place, Britton Street, London EC1M 5RE Tel : 01.405 0015
SWISS Financial Yearbook SA, PO Box 694, CH 6830 Chiasso Switzerland Tel : 091 435056 Telex : 842116
SYBEX, USA - distributed by The Computer Bookshop, Temple House, 43-45 New Street, Birmingham B2 4LH Tel : 021.643 4577
SYCAMORE Press Ltd., Wymondham, Melton Mowbray, Leics. LE14 2AZ
SYDNEY University Press, c/o Scholarly Book Services, 8 William Way, Letchworth, Herts.
SYENTEK Inc., PO Box 26588, San Francisco, CA 94126, USA Tel : 415 928 0471
SYSTEM Three (Scotland)Ltd., 16 York Place, Edinburgh EH1 3EP Tel : 031.556 9462
SYSTEMS Publications Ltd. - now Caxton Publications Ltd.

T

TABS - see Transatlantic Book Service
TBL Book Services Ltd., 17-23 Nelson Way, Tuscam Trading Estate, Camberley, Surrey GU15 3EU Tel : 0276 62667/62144 Telex : 858846
T.E.A.M. (The European Atlantic Movement) 7 Cathedral Close Exeter, Devon EX1 1EZ Tel : 0392 74908
T.F.H. (G.B.)Ltd., 11 Ormside Way, Holmethorpe Industrial Estate, Redhill RH1 2PX Tel : 0737 68311
THR Book Centre, Capacity House, 2-6 Rothsay Street, London SE1 4UD Tel : 01.407 6444
TIM, PO Box 7627, 11182 J.Schiphol Airport, The Netherlands
TRADA, Hughenden Valley, High Wycombe, Bucks HP14 4ND Tel : 0240 24 3091
T.U.C. - see Trades Union Congress
TA Ha Publishers Ltd., 68a Delancey Street, London NW1 7RY Tel : 01.485 7804
TAB Books Inc., Blue Ridge Summit, PA 17214, USA - distributed by W.Foulsham & Co.Ltd.
TABB House, 11 Church Street, Padstow, Cornwall PL28 8BG Tel : 0841 532 316
TACK Research Ltd., Tack House, PO Box 251, Longmoore St., London SW1V 1JJ Tel : 01.834 5001

TACTICAL Marketing Ltd., 73 New Bond Street, London W1Y
    9BD Tel : 01.493 3321 Telex : 261376
TALBOT Press Ltd., PO Box 43a, Ballymount Road, Dublin 12
    Republic of Ireland Tel : 0001 500611 Telex : 5864
TALISCOURT Ltd., Tavistock House, Tavistock Square, London
    WC1H 9HD Tel : 01.388 6743
TALISMAN Books, 27 Sumatra Road, London NW6 1PS
TALLIS Press Ltd., 3-4 Abbeymount, Edinburgh EH8 8JH
    Tel : 031.661 9339
TALMY, Franklin Ltd., 29 Rupert House, Nevern Square,
    London SW5 Tel : 01.584 7545 - orders to Bookpoint
    Ltd.
TAMARISK Books, West Hill Cottage, Exmouth Place, Hastings
    E.Sussex TN34 3JA Tel : 0424 420591
TANDEM Publishing, 44 Hill Street, London W1X 8LB
    Tel : 01.493 6777 - distributed by Tiptree Book
    Services Ltd.
TANKER & Bulker International, Intec Press Ltd., 3 Station
    Parade, Whyteleafe, Surrey Tel : 01.668 1306.3718
TANTIVY Press, Magdalen House, 136-148 Tooley Street, London
    SE1 2TT Tel : 01.407 7566
TAPLINGER Publ.Co., 132 West 22nd Street, New York 10011
    USA Tel : 212 741 0801
TARA Books, Southend House, Church Lane, Lymington, Hants.
    SO4 9RA Tel : 0590 76848
TARGET Books, 44 Hill Street, London W1X 8LB
    Tel : 01.493 6777 Telex : 937943 - distributed by
    Tiptree Book Services Ltd.
TARQUIN Publications, Stradbroke, Diss, Norfolk IP22 2BR
    Tel : 037 984 218
TATE Gallery Publications, Millbank, London SW1P 4RG
    Tel : 01.834 5651/2
TAURUS Press, 2 Willow Dene, Bushey Heath, Watford WD2 1PS
    Tel : 01.950 4625
TAURUS Press, VAP House, Station Fields, Kidlington, Oxford
    OX5 1LL Tel : 086 75 5461/3
TAVISTOCK Bookshop, c/o United Reform Church, 86 Tavistock
    Place, London WC1H 9RT Tel : 01.837 9116/9028
TAVISTOCK Publ.Ltd. - see Associated Book Publ.(UK)Ltd.
TAX Haven Review Book Centre - see THR Book Centre
TAX Lawyer Publ.Co., PO Box 1, Watlington, Oxon.OX9 5SF
    Tel : 0844 54092
TAX Management International, 17 Dartmouth Street, London
    SW1H 9BL Tel : 01.222 8831
TAXATION Publ.Co.Ltd., 98 Park Street, London W1Y 4BR
    Tel : 01.629 7888
TAXWISE Ltd., 272 London Road, Wallington, Surrey SM6 7DJ
    Tel : 01.773 0921
TAY Press Ltd., 3 Carlisle Place, London SW1 Tel : 01.834 1174
J.A.TAYLOR, c/o Dept.of Geography, Univ.College of Wales,
    Llandinam Building, Penglais, Aberystwyth, Dyfed
    Tel : 0970 3111 X3264
TAYLOR & Francis Ltd. (Intl.Scientific Publ.), 4 John Street,
    London WC1N 2ET Tel : 01.405 2237/9
    Telex : 858540 - orders to Rankine Road, Basingstoke
    Hants. RG24 0PR Tel : 0256 68011
TAYLOR Hall Publishing, PO Box 156, Chearsley, Aylesbury,
    Bucks HP18 0DQ Tel : 0844 208474
TAYLOR Nelson & Assocs.Ltd., 457 Kingston Road, Ewell, Epsom
    Surrey Tel : 01.394 0191
TEACH Yourself Books - see Hodder & Stoughton Ltd.
TEACHER Publ.Co.Ltd., Derbyshire House, Lower Street,
    Kettering, Northants. NN16 8BB Tel : 0536 518407
TEACHERS College Press - c/o Kershaw Publ.Co.Ltd.
TEAKFIELD Ltd. - now Gower Publ.Co.Ltd.
TECHALERT, T.R.C.Orpington, Kent BR5 3RF
TECHNICAL & Medical Studies Ltd., 29 Dorset Square, London
    NW1 6QJ Tel : 01.724 0811 Telex : 25247
TECHNICAL Association of the Pulp & Paper Industry (TAPPI),
    Technology Park, PO Box 105113, Atlanta, GA 30348
    USA
TECHNICAL Authors Group (Scotland), 100 Findhorn Place,
    Edinburgh
TECHNICAL Book Services, PO Box 79, Maidenhead, Berks SL6
    2FC - distributed by Macmillan
TECHNICAL Indexes Ltd., Willoughby Road, Bracknell, Berks
    RG12 4DW Tel : 0344 26311 Telex : 849207
TECHNICAL Industrial Services, 1 London Place, Newmills,
    Stockport, SK12 4ER
TECHNICAL Formulae, 10 Worton Drive, Fareham, Hants.
    PO16 7PY
TECHNICAL Insights Inc., PO Box 1304, Fort Lee, NJ 07024,
    USA Tel : 201 944 6204
TECHNICAL Press, Freeland, Oxford OX7 2AP Tel : 0993 881788
    Telex : 847777

TECHNICOPY Ltd., 66 High Street, Stonehouse, Glos. GL10
    2NA Tel : 045 382 2444
TECHNIP, 27 Rue Ginoux, 75737 Paris, Cedex 15, France
TECHNISCHE Hogeschule Eindoven, Postbus 513, Eindover
    The Netherlands
TECHNOLOGY Forecasts & Technical Surveys, Suite 208,
    South Beverly Drive, Beverly Hills, CA 90212, USA
TECHNOLOGY Marketing Group Ltd., 950 Lee Street, Des
    Plaines, IL 60016, USA Tel : 312 297 1404
TECHNOLOGY Reports Centre, Dept.of Industry, Orpington
    Kent BB5 3RF Tel : 0689 32111
TECHNOMIC Publ.Co.Inc., 265 Port Road West, Westport,
    Connecticut 06880, USA
TECHNOMIC Research Assoc.Inc., 1 North Wacker Drive,
    Chicago, ILL 60606, USA Tel : 312 346 5091
TECHNOMICA Ltd., Manor House, Moreton, Dorchester, Dorset
    DT2 8RG Tel : 0929 462470
TEE & Whiten (Distributors) Ltd., Standard House, Bonhill
    Street, London EC2A 4DA Tel : 01.628 4741
    Telex : 888602
TEKNISK Hogskolelitteratur, 10044 Stockholm 70, Sweden
The TELECOM Library, 205 W 19th Street, New York 10011,
    USA Tel : 212 691 8215
TELECOMMUNICATIONS Press, 2 Queen Anne's Gate, London
    SW1H 9BY Tel : 01.222 4333
TELECOMMUNICATIONS Users' Association, Tress House, 3-7
    Stamford Street, London SE1 9NT Tel : 01.928 5989
TELEGRAPH Publications, 135 Fleet Street, London EC4P 4BL
    Tel : 01.353 4242 Telex : 22874
TELEGRAPHIC Cable & Radio Registrations Inc., PO Box 14
    Larchmont, NY 10538, USA
TELEPHONY Publ.Corp., 136 Broomfield Road, Chelmsford
    Essex CM1 1RN Tel : 0245 58257 Telex : 995801
TELEPHONY Research, 55 E.Jackson Boulevard, Chicago, ILL
    60604, USA Tel : 312 922 2435
TELEPRESS Ltd., 6 The Broadway, White Hart Lane, Barnes
    London SW13 0NY Tel : 01.878 2076
Thomas TELFORD Ltd., Telford House, 1-7 Great George Street
    London SW1P 3AN Tel : 01.253 9999 Telex : 298105
TELLES Langdon Publ.Ltd., 29 Park Street, Croydon, Surrey
    CR0 1YD Tel : 01.686 2740
TELLEX Monitors Ltd., 47 Gray's Inn Road, London WC1X 8PN
    Tel : 01.405 7151
TEMPLAR North Publications, 12 Marchbank, New Springs,
    Wigan Tel : 0942 34767
TEMPLE University Press, Broad & Oxford Streets, Philadelphia
    PA 19122, USA Tel : 215 787 8787
TEMPLEGATE Press Ltd., PO Box 3, Woking, Surrey
    Tel : 09323 51991
TEN Speed Press, PO Box 7123, Berkeley, CA 94707, USA -
    distributed by Umbrella Publ.Services Ltd.
TENNYSON Society, c/o Central Library, Free School Lane,
    Lincoln LN2 1EZ Tel : 0522 33541
TEREDO Books Ltd., PO Box 430, 19 Waldegrave Road, Brighton
    BN1 6GR Tel : 0273 505432 - distributed by George
    Philip & Sons Ltd.
TERGO Data, 34 Edinburgh Drive, Darlington, Co.Durham DL3
    8AT Tel : 0325 68998
TERMINAL Operators Ltd., Rodwell House, Middlesex Street,
    London E1 7HJ Tel : 01.377 9366
TERRA Nova Editions Ltd., 12 Lambs Conduit Passage, London
    WC1V 6XX Tel : 01.404 5364 - orders to PO Box 5
    Leominster, Herefordshire
TERRACE Project, 27 Clerkenwell Close, London EC1R 0AT
    Tel : 01.251 4976
TERRESTRIAL Environmental Studies, 103-107 Waterloo Road
    London SE1 8UL Tel : 01.633 0033 Telex : 27706
TERTIARY Publications, 41 The Drive, Esher, Surrey
TETRADON Publications Ltd., 40 Hadzor Road, Oldbury, Warley
    W.Midlands B68 9LA Tel : 021.429 4397
TEXAS Instruments Ltd., PO Box 50, Market Harborough, Leics.
    Tel : 0858 64613
TEXTEL Publishing, 4-6 Victoria Terrace, Leamington Spa,
    Warwicks. CV31 3AB
TEXTILE Business Press Ltd., 91 Kirkgate, Bradford, W.Yorks
    Tel : 0274 26357
TEXTILE Institute, 10 Blackfriars Street, Manchester M3 5DR
    Tel : 061.834 8457 Telex : 668297
TEXTILE Trade Press - distributed by Textile Institute
THAMES & Hudson Ltd., 30 Bloomsbury Street, London WC1B
    3QP Tel : 01.636 5488 Telex : 25992
THAMES Enterprise Agency Ltd., 29-37 Wellington Street,
    Woolwich, London SE18 6PW Tel : 01.854 8888
THAMES Valley Regional Management Centre, Wellington Street
    Slough, Berks SL1 1YG Tel : 0753 33680

THAT's Entertainment, Cabin V, 25 Horsell Road, London
    N5 1XL Tel : 01.607 4492
THEATRICAL Management Association Council of Regional Theatre
    Ltd., Bedford Chambers, The Piazza, Covent
    Garden, London WC2E 8HQ Tel : 01.836 09712/3
THEOREX, 8327 La Jolla Scenic Div., La Jolla, CA 92037, USA
THEOSOPHICAL Publ.House Ltd., 68 Great Russell Street,
    London WC1B 3BU Tel : 01.405 2309
THEOSOPHICAL University Press, 124 Church Lane, Marple,
    Stockport, Cheshire SK6 7AY Tel : 061.427 2606
THERAPEUTIC Research Press Inc., PO Box 514, Tenafly
    New Jersey 07670, USA
THERMAL Insulation, St.Atwood Road, Didsbury, Manchester
    M20 0TB Tel : 061.445 1173
THETA Technology Corp., 462 Ridge Road, Wethersfield, CA
    06109, USA Tel : 203 563 9400
Georg THIEME Verlag, Postbox 732, D-7000 Stuttgart 1, West
    Germany
THIMBLE Press, Lockwood, Station Road, South Woodchester,
    Stroud, Glos. GL5 5EQ Tel : 045 387 2208
James THIN, 53-59 South Bridge, Edinburgh EH1 1YS
    Tel : 031.556 6743
THIRD World Foundation, 13th Floor, New Zealand House,
    Haymarket, London SW1Y 4TS Tel : 01.839 6167/
    01.439 6447
THIRD World Publ.Ltd., 151 Stratford Road, Birmingham B11
    1RD Tel : 021.773 6572
THIS England Ltd., Alma House, Rodney Road, Cheltenham,
    Glos. Tel : 0242 35185
THOMAND Books, PO Box 85, Limerick, Ireland Tel : 061 61944
THOMAS Intl.Publ.Co., 1 Penn Plaza, New York 10001, USA
Charles C.THOMAS Publisher, 2600 South 1st Street, Springfield
    Illinois 62717, USA Tel : 217 789 8980
THOMPSON Henry Ltd., London Road, Sunningdale, Berks SL5
    0EP Tel : 0990 24615
Richard H.THOMPSON Ltd., 97 Elgin Crescent, London W11 2JF
    Tel : 01.229 4500 Telex : 261234
THOM's Directories Ltd., 38 Merrion Square, Dublin 2, Republic
    of Ireland Tel : 0001 767481
D.C.THOMSON & Co.Ltd., Courier Buildings, 2 Albert Square
    Dundee DD1 9QJ Tel : 0382 23131 Telex : 76380
THOMSON Books Ltd., 4 Bloomsbury Square, London WC1
    Tel : 01.404 4300
THOMSON Directories Ltd., Thomson House, 296 Farnborough
    Road, Farnborough, Hants. GU14 7NU
    Tel : 0252 44391
THOMSON Publications Ltd., Elm House, 10-16 Elm Street,
    London WC1X 0BP Tel : 01.278 2345 Telex : 21746
    - orders to 93-99 Goswell Road, London EC1V 7QA
    Tel : 01.253 9355
THOR Publ.Co. - c/o TABS
Philip THORN Assoc.Ltd., c/o Guildford Educational Press,
    Belvedere House, 53 Ridgemount, Guildford, Surrey
    GU2 5TH
Stanley THORNES (Publ.)Ltd., Educa House, Liddington Estate
    Leckhampton Road, Cheltenham, Glos. GL53 0DN
    Tel : 0242 42127
THORNHILL Press, 24 Moorend Road, Cheltenham, Glos. GL53
    0EU Tel : 0242 519137
THORNTON Cox, 84-86 Baker Street, London W1N 1DL
    Tel : 01.589 2620 - distributed by Geographia Ltd.
THORNTON & Son, 11 Broad Street, Oxford OX1 3AR
    Tel : 0865 42939
THORSONS Publ.Ltd., Denington Estate, Wellingborough,
    Northants. NN8 2RQ Tel : 0933 76031 Telex : 311072
THREE Candles Ltd., Aston Place, Dublin 2, Republic of Ireland
    Tel : 0001 771429
THREE Cats Press - gone away, 1982
THRESHOLD Books Ltd., 200 Buckingham Palace Road, London
    SW1W 9SR Tel : 01.730 1409
THRESHOLD Foundation Bureau, 7 Regency Terrace, London
    SW7 3QW Tel : 01.370 3651
THROGMORTON Publications - now Financial Times Bus.Publ.Ltd.
THULE Press, The Park, Findhorn, Forres, Morayshire
    Tel : 030 93 2582
THULEPRINT Ltd., 63 Kenneth Street, Stornoway, Isle of Lewis
    PA87 2DS Tel : 0851 4404
THUNDERBIRD Enterprises Ltd., 102 College Road, Harrow,
    Middx.
Charles THURMAN & Sons Ltd., 26-32 Lonsdale Street, Carlisle
    Cumbria Tel : 0228 20222
THURMAN Publ.Ltd., 28 The Mill Trading Estate, Acton Lane,
    London NW10 Tel : 01.961 4477 Telex : 24339 -
    distributed by WHS Distributors
TIETO Ltd., Bank House, 8a Hill Road, Clevedon, Avon BS21
    7HH Tel : 0272 876519

TILNEY & Co., 385 Sefton House, Exchange Buildings, Liverpool
    L2 3RT
TIMBER Research & Development Association - see TRADA
TIME-Life Books, c/o Time-Life International Ltd., 153 New
    Bond Street, London W1Y 0AA Tel : 01.499 4080
    - distributed by WHS Distributors in UK
TIME Magazine, PO Box 71, Croydon, Surrey CR9 9ES
TIMES Books Ltd., 16 Golden Square, London W1R 4BN
    Tel : 01.434 3767 - distributed by TBL Book Service
TIMES Change Press, 27 Clerkenwell Close, London EC1R 0AT
    Tel : 01.251 4976
The TIMES Newspaper Ltd., PO Box 7, New Printing House
    Square, Gray's Inn Road, London WC1X 8EZ
    Tel : 01.837 1234 X7560 Telex : 264971
TIMES Periodicals Pte.Ltd., Times House, 390 Kim Seng Road
    Singapore 9
TIMES Press Ltd., Hill Street, Douglas, Isle of Man
    Tel : 0624 3074
TIN Research Institute, Fraser Road, Perivale, Greenford,Middx.
TINGA Tinga, The Windmill Press, Kingswood Tadworth, Surrey
    KT20 6TG Tel : 0737 833511
TIPTREE Book Services Ltd., Church Road, Tiptree,Colchester
    Essex CO5 0SR Tel : 0621 816362/815706
    Telex : 99487
TO Telephone Europe, 150 Regent Street, London W1
    Tel : 01.734 5351
Marcus TOBIAS & Co., 65 Shakespeare Drive, Shirley, Solihull
    B90 2AN
TOKYO Economic Info.Service Co.Ltd., TASO Building 9-1,
    Takaracito 1-chome, Chuo-ku, Tokyo 104, Japan
TOLLEY Publ.Co.Ltd., 209 High Street, Croydon, Surrey CR0
    1QR Tel : 01.686 9141
C.C.TONSLEY, 46 Queen Street, Geddington, Northants.
    Tel : 0536 742250
TOP Stone Books, 29 Station Road, Harpenden, Herts. AL5 4XB
    Tel : 05827 64510
TOPS'L Books, 13 Wise's Firs, Sulhamstead, Berks RG7 4EH
    Tel : 073 529 2851
Carl TORREY Associates, 100 Weldy Avenue, Oreland, PA19075
    USA Tel : 215 576 0358
TOTHILL Press, 33 Tothill Street, London SW1
TOURISM & Recreation Research Unit, Chisholm House, Dept.of
    Geography, University of Edinburgh, High School
    Yards, Edinburgh EH1 1NR
TOURISM International Press Ltd., 154 Cromwell Road, London
    SW7 Tel : 01.370 4434
TOURISM Planning & Research Assoc., Suite 433, 52 High
    Holborn, London WC1V 6RL Tel : 01.242 3131
TOURISM Publications, Alfred & Sons Ltd., 16-18 Longcauseway
    Farnworth, Bolton BL4 9BG Tel : 0204 73145
TOURRET Publishing, 5 Byron Close, Abingdon, Oxon.OX14
    5PA Tel : 0235 25719
TOUTOUS International Publ., Normandie House, PO Box 75
    'St.Helier, Jersey
TOWN & Country Directory Publ.Ltd., 386 Kenton Road, Kenton
    Harrow, Middx. HA3 9HA
TOWN & Country Planning Association, 27 Clerkenwell Close
    London EC1R 0AT Tel : 01.251 4976
TOWN & County Books Ltd., Terminal House, Shepperton, Middx.
    TW17 8AS Tel : 093 22 28950 Telex : 929806
TOWNE-Oller & Assoc., 200 Madison Avenue, New York 10016,
    USA Tel : 212 684 8060
TOY Libraries Association, Seabrook House, Wyllyolts Manor,
    Darlees Lane, Potters Bar, Herts. EN6 2HL
    Tel : 0707 44571
TRACK & Field News Inc., Box 296, 365 First Street, Los Altos
    CA 94022, USA
TRADE & Technical Press, Crown House, Morden, Surrey
    Tel : 01.540 3897
TRADE & Travel Publ.Ltd., The Mendip Press, Parsonage Lane
    Bath BA1 1EN Tel : 0225 64156
TRADE Counter Ltd., The Airfield, Norwich Road, Mendlesham
    Suffolk Tel : 044 94 629
TRADE Paper Ltd., 902 High Road, London N12 9SB
TRADE Policy Research Centre, 1 Gough Square, Fleet Street
    London EC4A 3DE Tel : 01.353 6371
TRADE Procedures Board, 4-12 Waterloo Place, London SW1Y 4AU
TRADE Research Publications, 6 Beech Hill Court, Berkhamsted
    Herts. HP4 2PR Tel : 044 27 3951
TRADES Union Congress, Congress House, 23-28 Great Russell
    Street, London WC1B 3LS Tel : 01.636 4030
TRAINING Films Intl.Ltd., 14 St.Mary's Street, Whitchurch,
    Shropshire SY13 1QY Tel : 0948 3341
TRANS Tech Publications, PO Box 266, D-3392 Clausthal-
    Zellerfeld, West Germany
TRANS Tech SA, Trans Tech House, CH-4711 Aedermannsdorf,
    W.Germany

TRANSACTION Books, PO Box 978, Edison, New Jersey 08817, USA
TRANSACTION Inc., Rutgers State Univ. - distributed by Holt Saunders
TRANSART Ltd., East Chadley Lane, Godmanchester, Huntingdon, Cambs. PE18 8AU Tel : 0480 51171 Telex : 32170
TRANSATLANTIC Book Service Ltd., Devonshire House, 29 Elmfield Road, Bromley, Kent BR1 1LT Tel : 01.290 6611 Telex : 897948
TRANSCRIPTA Books & Services, Suite 68, 13 Henrietta Street London WC2E 8LH Tel : 01.836 4688
The TRANSNATIONAL Institute, 27 Clerkenwell Close, London EC1R 0AT Tel : 01.251 4976
TRANSPORT & Distribution Press, 118 Ewell Road, Surbiton Surrey KT6 6HA Tel : 01.399 8110
TRANSPORT & Road Research Laboratory, Old Wokingham Road Crowthorne, Berks RG11 6AU Tel : 034 46 3131 Telex : 848272
TRANSPORT Bookman Publ.Ltd., 8 South Street, Isleworth, Middx.TW7 7BG Tel : 01.568 9750
TRANSPORT Publ.Co., 128 Pikes Lane, Glossop, Derbyshire SK13 8EH Tel : 04574 61508
TRANSWORLD Publ.Ltd., Century House, 61-63 Uxbridge Road London W5 5SA Tel : 01.579 2652 Telex : 267974
 - orders to PO Box 17, Wellingborough, Northants. NN8 4BU Tel : 0933 225761 Telex : 311306
J.B.TRATSART Ltd., 154a Greenford Road, Harrow, Middx. HA1 3QT Tel : 01.422 2456.8295 Telex : 8814136
TRAVEL & Transport Ltd., 122 Newgate Street, London EC1A 7AD Tel : 01.606 8465/01.600 8955
TRAVEL Associations' Consultative Council, 55-57 Newman Street, London W1P 4AH Tel : 01.637 2444 Telex : 22254
TRAVEL Information, PO Box 7627, Amsterdam Airport, The Netherlands
TRAVEL Trade Gazette Ltd., Morgan-Grampian House, Calderwood Street, London SE18 6QH Tel : 01.855 7777 Telex : 896284
TRAVELAID Publishing - imprint of Michael Haag Ltd.
TRAVELLING Light Photography Ltd. - gone away, 1982
Charles W.TRAYLEN, Castle House, 49-50 Quarry Street, Guildford, Surrey GU1 3UA Tel : 0483 72424
Nicholas TREADWELL Publications, 36 Chiltern Street, London W1M 1PH Tel : 01.486 1414
TREDOLPHIN Press, 35 Temple Fortune Hill, London NW11 7XL Tel : 01.455 8255
TREFOIL Books, 15 St.John's Hill, London SW11 Tel : 01.223 7037
TRENEAR-Harvey, Bird & Watson Ltd., 7 Langley Street, London WC2H 9JX Tel : 01.379 3555
TRENT Polytechnic, Burton Street, Nottingham NG1 4BU Tel : 0602 48248
TRENTHAM Books, 30 Wenger Crescent, Trentham, Stoke-on-Trent, ST4 8LE Tel : 0782 641234
TRIAD Paperbacks Ltd., 9 Bow Street, London WC2E 7AN Tel : 01.836 9081
TRIBECA Communications Ltd., 401 Broadway, Suite 1907, New York 10013, USA Tel : 212 226 6047 Telex : 238970
TRIBUNE de Geneve, Rue du Stand 42, Geneva, Switzerland
TRIDENT Exhibitions Ltd., Abbey Meed House, 23a Plymouth Road, Tavistock, Devon PL19 8AU Tel : 0822 3694
TRIGON Press, 117 Kent House Road, Beckenham, Kent BR3 1JJ Tel : 01.778 0534
TRIGRAM Press Ltd., 32 Windsor Road, Hebden Bridge, W. Yorks. HX7 8LF Tel : 042 284 3322 - distributed by McBride Bros.& Broadley Ltd.
Robert TRILLO Ltd., High Street, Lymington, Hants. Tel : 0590 75098
TRI-Med Books Ltd., 5 Tudor Cottage, Lovers Walk, Finchley London N3 1JH Tel : 01.346 6001
Vera TRINDER Ltd., 38 Belford Street, Strand, London WC2E 9EU Tel : 01.836 2365/6
TRINITY Lane Press, 40 Aragon Close, Cambridge Tel : 0223 61408
TRIPLEGATE Ltd., 1 Royal Parade, Hindhead, Surrey GU26 6TD Tel : 0428 73 6141 & 6854/5
TRITON Publ.Co.Ltd., 1a Montagu Mews North, London W1H 1AJ Tel : 01.935 8090
TROPICAL Products Institute, 127 Clerkenwell Road, London EC1R 5DB Tel : 01.405 7943
The TRUMAN & Knightley Education Trust Ltd., 76-78 Nottinghill Gate, London W11 3LJ Tel : 01.727 1242

TRUSTEE Savings Bank, PO Box 33, 3 Copthall Avenue, London EC2 Tel : 01.588 9292
J.W.TUCKER Associates, 104 West 40th Street, New York 10018 USA Tel : 212 944 2580
TURF Newspapers Ltd., 55 Curzon Street, London W1Y 7PF Tel : 01.499 4391
Colin TURNER Group, 122 Shaftesbury Avenue, London W1V 8HA Tel : 01.734 3052 Telex : 261140
TURNER Research & Consulting, Seefeldstrasse 71, CH 8008 Zurich, Switzerland Tel : 01 693088
TURNSTILE Press, Great Turnstile, London WC1V 7HJ Tel : 01.405 8471
TURNSTORE Books, Dennington Estate, Wellingborough, Northants. NN8 2RQ Tel : 0933 76031
TURNTABLE Publications, 745 Abbeydale Road, Sheffield S7 2BG Tel : 0742 550602
TUROE Press, 69 Jones Road, Dublin 3, Ireland
TURRET Bookshop, 42 Lamb's Conduit Street, London WC1N 3LJ Tel : 01.405 6058
TURRET Press Ltd., 886 High Road, Finchley, London N12 9SB Tel : 01.446 2411
Charles E.TUTTLE Co.Inc., Rutland, Vermont 05701, USA - distributed by Prentice Hall/IBD
TWELVE by Eight Press, 2 Ratcliffe Road, Leicester LE2 3TB Tel : 0533 703249
TWENTY-First Century Communications - c/o TABS
TWENTY-First Century Security Educ.Ltd., 293 Kingston Road Leatherhead, Surrey KT22 7NJ Tel : 0372 74505
TWO Tree Island Books Ltd., 125 High Street, Brentwood, Essex CM14 4RX Tel : 0277 217798
TYCOOLY Intl.Publ.Ltd., 6 Crofton Terrace, Dun Laoghaire, Co.Dublin, Eire Tel : 800245/6 Telex : 30547
Robert TYNDALL - distributed by Kingsway Publications

U

UBS Publishers Distributors Ltd. - distributed by Bowker
UCCA - see Universities Central Council on Admissions
UCCF Book Centre, Norton Street, Nottingham NG7 3HR Tel : 0602 781054
U.E.G., 6 Storey's Gate, Westminster, London SW1P 3AU Tel : 01.222 8891
UG Books, 202 Barford Street, Birmingham B5 7EP Tel : 021.622 5565
UNESCO, 7 Place de Fontenoy, 75700 Paris, France Tel : 577 1610 - distributed by HMSO in UK
UNIFO Publ.Ltd., PO Box 37, Pleasantville, NY 10570, USA
UNIPUB, 1180 Avenue of the Americas, New York 10036, USA Tel : 212 764 2791
UNISAF Publ.Ltd., UNISAF House, 32-36 Dudley Road, Tunbridge Wells, Kent TN1 1LH Tel : 0892 23184
UOP Johnsen Well Screens Ltd., Salmon Leap, Leixlip, Co. Dublin, Republic of Ireland Tel : 280758
U.S.P.Convention, 12601 Twinbrook Parkway, Rockville, MD 20852, USA
UKRAINIAN Publ.Ltd., 200 Liverpool Road, London N1 1LF Tel : 01.607 6266/7
ULSTER Museum, Botanic Gardens, Belfast BT9 5AB Tel : 0232 668251/5
ULVERSCROFT Large Print Books Ltd., The Green, Bradgate Road, Anstey, Leicester LE7 7FU Tel : 053 721 4325
UMBRELLA Publ.Services Ltd., 131 Trafalgar Road, Greenwich London SE10 9TU
UNDERCURRENTS, 27 Clerkenwell Close, London EC1R 0AT
UNEMPLOYMENT Unit, 9 Poland Street, London W1V 3DG Tel : 01.439 8523/4
UNEVANGELISED Fields Mission, 9 Gunnersbury Avenue, London W5 3NL Tel : 01.992 5232/3
Frederick UNGAR Publ.Co.Inc., 250 Park Avenue South, New York 10003, USA Tel : 212 473 7885
UNIMATIC Engineers Ltd., 122 Granville Road, Cricklewood London NW2 2LN
UNION of Construction & Allied Trades, Winweed House, 64-66 Crossgates Road, Leeds Tel : 0532 646211
UNION of International Associations, 40 rue Washington, 1050 Brussels, Belgium Tel : 640 41 09 / 640 18 08
UNIT for Retail Planning Info.Ltd., Victoria House, 26 Queen Victoria Street, Reading RG1 1TG Tel : 0734 588181
UNIT for the Study of Govt.in Scotland, University of Edinburgh 31 :Buccleuch Place, Edinburgh
UNITED Associations of Professional Engineers, 32 High Street Bookham, Leatherhead, Surrey KT23 4AG Tel : 0372 56471

UNITED Commercial Travellers Association, Bexton Lane, Knutsford, Cheshire
UNITED Kingdom Atomic Energy Authority, 11 Charles II Street, London SW1Y 4QP Tel : 01.930 5454
UNITED Kingdom Committee for the Intl. Institute of Welding, 54 Princes Gate, Exhibition Road, London SW7
UNITED Kingdom International Communications, 63 Long Acre London WC2E 9JH Tel : 01.836 8731
UNITED Kingdom Iron & Steel Statistics Bureau, 12 Addiscombe Road, Croydon CR9 6BS Tel : 01.686 9050 X494
UNITED Kingdom Press Gazette, Cliffords Inn, Fetter Lane, London EC4A 1PJ Tel : 01.242 0935/9
UNITED Kingdom Publications Ltd., 902 High Road, London N12 9SB
UNITED Nations Educational Scientific & Cultural Organisation, 7 Place de Fontenoy, 75700 Paris, France Tel : 577 1610 - distributed by HMSO in UK
UNITED Nations Publications, Palais des Nations, CH-1211 Geneva 10, Switzerland Tel : 022 3460 11 - distributed by HMSO in UK
UNITED Nations University, Tokyo Semei Skyscraper, Tokyo, Japan / United Nations, Stratford Place, London W1 Tel : 01.408 1101
UNITED Publicity Services Ltd., Acorn House, 314-320 Gray's Inn Road, London WC1X 8QS Tel : 01.837 1776
UNITED Society for the Propagation of the Gospel, 15 Tufton Street, London SW1P 3QQ Tel : 01.222 4222
UNITED States Bureau of Reclamation, PO Box 25007, Denver Federal Centre, Denver, Colorado, USA
UNITED States Chamber of Commerce in Ireland, 20 College Green, Dublin 2, Republic of Ireland Tel : 712733/712885 Telex : 25880
UNITED States Dept.of Commerce, National Bureau of Standards Office of Tech.Information & Publ., Washington DC 20234, USA
UNITED States Dept.of Geological Survey, Eastern Distribution Branch, Text Products Section, 604 South Pickett Street, Alexandria V.A. 22304, USA
UNITED States Dept.of the Interior, 1012 Federal Building, Denver, Colorado 80294, USA
UNITED States Pharmacoperial Convention Inc., 12601 Twinbrook Parkway, Rockville, MD 20882, USA
UNITED States Steel Intl.Inc., 606 Grant Street, Pittsburgh, PA 15230, USA
UNITED Trade Press Ltd., 33-35 Bowling Green Lane, London EC1R 0DA Tel : 01.837 1212 Telex : 299049
UNITED Writers Publ.Ltd., Trevail Mill, Zennor, St.Ives, Cornwall TR26 3BW Tel : 0736 796038
UNITEX-Verlag, Landbergerstrasse 439, D-8000 Munchen 60, West Germany
UNIVERSAL Books Ltd., The Grange, Grange Yard, Bermondsey London SE1 3AG Tel : 01.232 0565 Telex : 8952022
UNIVERSAL-Tandem Publ.Co.Ltd. - now Tandem Publ.Ltd.
UNIVERSAL Technology Corp., 1616 Mardon Drive, Dayton, Ohio 45432, USA
The UNIVERSE (Associated Catholic Publ.Ltd.), 33-39 Bowling Green Lane, London EC1R 0AB Tel : 01.278 7321 Telex : 25604
UNIVERSE Books - c/o TABS
L'UNIVERSITE de Lille 111 - distributed by Colin Smythe Ltd.
UNIVERSITETSFORLAGET, PO Box 307, Blindern, Oslo 3, Norway - distributed by IBD
UNIVERSITIES Central Council on Admissions, PO Box 28, Cheltenham, Glos. GL50 1HY Tel : 0242 519091
UNIVERSITIES Federation for Animal Welfare (UFAW), 8 Hamilton Close, Potters Bar, Herts. EN6 3QD Tel : 0707 58202
UNIVERSITY Associates, 8517 Production Avenue, PO Box 26240 San Diego, CA 92126, USA
UNIVERSITY Associates Intl.Ltd., Challenge House, 45-47 Victoria Street, Mansfield, Notts. NG18 5SU Tel : 0623 640203
UNIVERSITY Associates Publ., PO Box 615, Iowa City, Iowa 52240, USA - distributed by People at Work
UNIVERSITY College Cardiff Press, PO Box 78, Cardiff CF1 1XL Tel : 0222 44211
UNIVERSITY College of Swansea, Publications Office, The Registry, Singleton Park, Swansea SA2 8PP Tel : 0792 25678
UNIVERSITY College of Wales, Dept.of Agricultural Economics Penglais, Aberystwyth, Dyfed SY23 3DD Tel : 0970 3111
UNIVERSITY Education Press, Newton, PO Box 96, Singapore 11
UNIVERSITY Microfilms International - represented by Information Publications Intl.Ltd., 30-32 Mortimer Street, London W1N 7RA Tel : 01.631 5030

UNIVERSITY of Aberdeen, Dept.of Political Economy, Edward Wright Building, Dunbar Street, Old Aberdeen AB9 2TY Tel : 0224 40241 X 5304
UNIVERSITY of Alabama Press - distributed by IBD
UNIVERSITY of Alberta Press, c/o A.R.Hodges, Lea Valley Books, 10 Linton Road, Hastings, E.Sussex TN34 1TN Tel : 0424 434455
UNIVERSITY of Aston in Birmingham, Information Office, Gosta Green, Birmingham B4 7ET
UNIVERSITY of Bath, Claverton Down, Bath BA2 7AY Tel : 0225 61244 X705
UNIVERSITY of Birmingham, Information Office, PO Box 363 Birmingham B15 2TT Tel : 021.472 1301 X2549
UNIVERSITY of Birmingham, Centre for Contemporary Cultural Studies, PO Box 363, Birmingham B15 2TT Tel : 021.472 1301 X3549
UNIVERSITY of Birmingham, Joint Centre for Regional Urban & Local Govt.Studies, PO Box 363, Birmingham B15 2TT Tel : 021.472 1301 X2742
UNIVERSITY of Bradford, Management Centre, Emm Lane, Bradford, W.Yorks BD9 4JL Tel : 0274 42299
UNIVERSITY of Bristol, 1-9 Old Park Hill, Bristol BS2 8BB
UNIVERSITY of Bristol, Dept.of Extra Mural Studies, 32 Tyndalls Park Road, Bristol BS8 1HR Tel : 0272 24161
UNIVERSITY of Bristol, School of Education, Helen Wodenhouse Building, 35 Berkeley Square, Bristol BS8 1JA
UNIVERSITY of British Columbia Press - distributed by Eurospan
UNIVERSITY of California Press - distributed by IBD
UNIVERSITY of Cambridge, Dept.of Applied Economics, Sidgwick Avenue, Cambridge CB3 9DE Tel : 0223 358944
UNIVERSITY of Cambridge, Dept.of Architecture, 1 Scroope Terrace, Cambridge CB2 1PX
UNIVERSITY of Cambridge, Institute of Criminology, 7 West Road, Cambridge CB3 9DT Tel : 0223 68511
UNIVERSITY of Chicago Press Ltd., 126 Buckingham Palace Road, London SW1W 9SD Tel : 01.730 9208 Telex : 23933 - distributed by IBD
UNIVERSITY of Colorado State, Fort Collins, Colorado 80523, USA
UNIVERSITY of Durham, Old Shire Hall, Old Elvet, Durham DH1 3HP Tel : 0385 64466
UNIVERSITY of Durham, Dept.of Geography, Science Labs., South Road, Durham DH1 3LE
UNIVERSITY of Durham, Library, Palace Green, Durham DH1 3RN Tel : 0385 61262/3 Telex : 537351
UNIVERSITY of East Anglia, University Plain, Norwich NR4 7TJ
UNIVERSITY of Edinburgh, Dept.of Electrical Engineering, Kings Buildings, Edinburgh EH9 3JL
UNIVERSITY of Edinburgh, Dept.of Forestry & Natural Resources Darwin Building, The Kings Buildings, Mayfield Road Edinburgh EH9 3JU Tel : 031.667 1081
UNIVERSITY of Edinburgh Unit for the Study of Government in Scotland, 31 Buccleuch Place, Edinburgh EH8 9JT Tel : 031.667 1011 X6355
UNIVERSITY of Essex, Wivenhoe Park, Colchester, Essex CO4 3SQ Tel : 0206 862286
UNIVERSITY of Exeter Publications, Northcote House, The Queen's Drive, Exeter EX4 4QJ Tel : 0392 77911
UNIVERSITY of Exeter, Agricultural Economics Unit, Lafrowda House, St.German's Road, Exeter EX4 6TL Tel : 0392 73025
UNIVERSITY of Exeter, School of Education, Heavitree Road Exeter EX1 2LU Tel : 0392 52221
UNIVERSITY of Glasgow Press, The University, Glasgow G12 8QG Tel : 041.339 8855 - Publications Office now closed : order individual publications from relevant departments
UNIVERSITY of Hull, Publications Committee, The Brynmor Jones Library, The University, Hull HU6 7RX Tel : 0482 46311 Telex : 52530
UNIVERSITY of Hull, Institute of Education, 173 Cottingham Road Hull HU5 2EH Tel : 0482 46311 X7402
UNIVERSITY of Illinois Press - distributed by IBD
UNIVERSITY of Keele, Sociological Review Monographs, Keele, Staffs. ST5 5BC Tel : 0782 621111 Telex : 36113
UNIVERSITY of Kent, Canterbury, Kent CT2 7NZ
UNIVERSITY of Lancaster, University House, Bailrigg, Lancaster LA1 4YW
UNIVERSITY of Lancaster, Dept.of Marketing, Gillow House, Lancaster LA1 4TX
UNIVERSITY of Leeds, The University, Leeds LS2 9JT Tel : 0532 31751
UNIVERSITY of Leeds, Industrial Services Ltd., The University Leeds LS2 9JT Tel : 0532 31751/454084

UNIVERSITY of Leeds, Nuffield Centre for Health Services Studies, Clarendon Road, Leeds LS2 9PL
UNIVERSITY of Leicester, Centre for Mass Communication Research, 104 Regent Road, Leicester LE1 7LT
UNIVERSITY of Leicester, Dept.of Adult Education, University Road, Leicester LE1 7RH Tel : 0533 554455
UNIVERSITY of Liverpool, Senate House, Abercromby Square, PO Box 147, Liverpool L69 3BX Tel : 051.709 6022
UNIVERSITY of London, Publication Office, 52 Gordon Square London WC1H 0PJ Tel : 01.636 8000
UNIVERSITY of London, Goldsmith's College, Publications Service, Lewisham Way, New Cross, London SE14 6NW Tel : 01.692 7171
UNIVERSITY of London, Institute of Advanced Legal Studies, Charles Clore House, 17 Russell Square, London WC1B 5DR Tel : 01.637 1731
UNIVERSITY of London Institute of Education, 20 Bedford Way, London WC1H 0AL - distributed by NFER Publ.Co.Ltd.
UNIVERSITY of London, Institute of Education Library, 11-13 Ridgmount Street, London WC1E 7AH Tel : 01.637 0846
UNIVERSITY of London, Institute of Germanic Studies, 29 Russell Square, London WC1B 5DP Tel : 01.580 2711
UNIVERSITY of London, Institute of Historical Research, Senate House, Malet Street, London WC1E 7HU Tel : 01.636 0272/3 - distributed by Wm.Dawson & Sons
UNIVERSITY of London Press Ltd. - now Hodder & Stoughton Educational
UNIVERSITY of London, School of Oriental & African Studies, Malet Street, London WC1E 7HP Tel : 01.637 2388
UNIVERSITY of London, Teaching Methods Unit, 55 Garden Square, London WC1H 0NT Tel : 01.636 1500
UNIVERSITY of London, The Warburg Institute, Woburn Square London WC1H 0AB Tel : 01.580 9663
UNIVERSITY of Malaysia, Publications Committee, Minden, Pulau Pinang, Malaysia Telex : USMLIB MA 40254
UNIVERSITY of Manchester, Publications Secretary, Dept.of Adult & Higher Education, Manchester M13 9PL
UNIVERSITY of Manchester, Institute of Science & Technology, PO Box 88, Manchester M60 1QD Tel : 061.236 3311
UNIVERSITY of Maryland, College Park, Maryland 20742, USA
UNIVERSITY of Massachusetts, Room 285, Hills South, Amhurst Mass.01002, USA
UNIVERSITY of Michigan, Ann Arbor, Michigan 48106, USA - distributed by TABS
UNIVERSITY of Michigan, Michigan Technological University, Houghton, Michigan 49931, USA - distributed by TABS
UNIVERSITY of Minnesota Press - c/o TABS
UNIVERSITY of Missouri Press - distributed by IBD
UNIVERSITY of Natal Press, PO Box 375, Pietermaritzburg, 3200 South Africa Tel : 0331 63320 Telex : 63719 SA
UNIVERSITY of Nebraska Press, USA - distributed by IBD
UNIVERSITY of Newcastle upon Tyne, Publications, 6 Kensington Terrace, Newcastle upon Tyne NE1 7RU Tel : 0632 28511
UNIVERSITY of Newcastle upon Tyne, British Geotechnical Society, c/o Dept.of Mining Engineering, Drummond Building, Newcastle upon Tyne NE1 7RU
UNIVERSITY of Newcastle upon Tyne, Dept.of Agricultural Economics, Newcastle upon Tyne NE1 7RU
UNIVERSITY of New England Publ., University of New England Unit, Armidale, NSW 2351, Australia
UNIVERSITY of New South Wales, PO Box 1, Kensington NSW 2033, Australia
UNIVERSITY of North Carolina Press, PO Box 2288, Chapel Hill NC 27514, USA - distributed by Academic & Univ. Publishers Group
UNIVERSITY of Notre Dame Press - distributed by IBD
UNIVERSITY of Nottingham Dept.of Adult Education, C Block, Cherry Tree Buildings, University Park, Nottingham NG7 2RD Tel : 0602 56101 X2717
UNIVERSITY of Nottingham, Dept.of Agriculture & Horticulture (Farm Management), Sutton Bonington, Loughborough Leics. LE12 5RD Tel : 050 97 2386
UNIVERSITY of Nottingham, Dept.of Geography & School of Education, University Park, Nottingham NG7 2RD Tel : 0602 56101
UNIVERSITY of Oklahoma Press - distributed by Bailey Bros. & Swinfen Ltd.
UNIVERSITY of Queensland Press - distributed by Prentice Hall
UNIVERSITY of Reading, Library, Whiteknights, Reading RG6 2AH Tel : 0734 85123/84331

UNIVERSITY of Reading, Dept.of Agricultural Economics & Management, 4 Earley Gate, Whiteknights Road Reading RG6 2AR Tel : 0734 875123 X6296
UNIVERSITY of St.Andrews, Library, St.Andrews, Fife KY16 9TR Tel : 0334 76161 Telex : 76213
UNIVERSITY of Sheffield, Sheffield S10 2TN Tel : 0742 78555 Telex : 54348
UNIVERSITY of Southampton, Publications Dept., Highfield Southampton SO9 5NH Tel : 0703 559122 Telex : 47661
UNIVERSITY of Stanford, Stanford, CA 94305, USA
UNIVERSITY of Stirling, Stirling FK9 4LA
UNIVERSITY of Stockholm - distributed by Almqvist & Wiksell
UNIVERSITY of Strathclyde, George Street, Glasgow Tel : 041.552 7141
UNIVERSITY of Surrey, Guildford, Surrey GU2 5XH Tel : 0483 71281
UNIVERSITY of Surrey Press - see Surrey University Press
UNIVERSITY of Sussex Press, Sussex House, Falmer, Brighton BN1 9QL Tel : 0273 606755 - orders to Chatto & Cape Services Ltd.
UNIVERSITY of Technology, Loughborough, Leics. LE11 3TU Tel : 0509 63171 X217
UNIVERSITY of Texas Press - distributed by IBD
UNIVERSITY of the West Indies, Institute of Social & Economic Research, Mona, Kingston 7, Jamaica
UNIVERSITY of the Witwatersrand Library, Private Bag 31550 Braamfontein, 2017 South Africa Tel : 011 716 1111 Telex : 54 22460 SA
UNIVERSITY of Tokyo - distributed by IBD
UNIVERSITY of Toronto Press - distributed by IBD
UNIVERSITY of Wales Press, 6 Gwennyth Street, Cathays, Cardiff CF2 4YD Tel : 0222 31919
UNIVERSITY of Warwick Library, Coventry CV4 7AL
UNIVERSITY of Warwick, Manpower Research Group, Coventry CV4 7AL
UNIVERSITY of West Virginia, Morgan Town, West Virginia 26506 USA
UNIVERSITY of York, Heslington, York YO1 5DD Tel : 0904 59861
UNIVERSITY of York Language Materials Development Unit, Micklegate House, Micklegate, York YO1 1JZ Tel : 0904 27844/8
UNIVERSITY Press Arabia & Africa, 1 West Street, Tavistock Devon Tel : 0822 3577
UNIVERSITY Press of Kansas, 303 Carruth, Lawrence, KS66045 USA Tel : 913 864 4154
UNIVERSITY Presses of Columbia & Princeton, c/o 15a Epsom Road, Guildford, Surrey GU1 3JT Tel : 0483 68364
UNIVERSITY Publications, University of New England, Armidale New South Wales, 2351 Australia
UNIVERSITY Publ.Projects, 28 Hana Tyiv, Tel Aviv, Israel
UNIVERSITY Science Books, USA - distributed by J.Wiley & Sons
UNIVERSITY Tutorial Press Ltd., 842 Yeovil Road, Trading Estate, Slough, Berks SL1 4JQ Tel : 0753 29844
UNIWORLD Business Publ.Inc., 50 E 42nd Street, New York NY 10017, USA
UNKNOWN Publisher, PO Box 66, Warwick CV34 4XE Tel : 0926 499497
UNWIM Bros. Ltd., The Gresham Press, Old Woking, Surrey GU22 6LH Tel : 048 62 61971
UNWIN Paperbacks, 40 Museum Street, London WC1A 1LU Tel : 01.405 8577 - orders to PO Box 18, Park Lane Hemel Hempstead, Herts. HP2 4TE Tel : 0442 3244
UPDATE Publications Ltd., 33-34 Alfred Place, London WC1E 7DP Tel : 01.637 4544
UPLANDS Press, 2 Woodstock Road, Croydon, Surrey CR9 1LB Tel : 01.686 6330/9
URBAN & Economic Dev.Group, 12-13 Henrietta Street, Covent Garden, London WC2E 8LH Tel : 01.836 1894
URBAN & Schwarzenberg - distributed by Pitman Books Ltd.
URBAN Institute Publications, 2100 M Street NW, Washington DC20037, USA
URBAN Publishing Co., 17 The Green, Richmond, Surrey TW9 1PX Tel : 01.948 5721
URWICK Nexos, Safebarrow Ltd., Clove House, The Broadway Farnham Common, Slough, Berks SL2 3PQ Tel : 02814 5123 Telex : 849826
USBORNE Publ.Ltd., 20 Garrick Street, London WC2 9BJ Tel : 01.379 3535 Telex : 8953589 - distributed by WHS Distributors

V

VDE-Verlag, Bismarckstrasse 33, 1000 Berlin 12, West Germany Tel : 030 3 41 30 41
VNU Business Publ.Ltd., 53-55 Frith Street, London W1A 2HG Tel : 01.439 4242
VACATION Work, 9 Park End Street, Oxford OX1 1HJ Tel : 0865 41978/43311
VACHERS Publ., Leeder House, Erskine Road, London NW3 3AJ Tel : 01.586 0135
VALLANCEY International, PO Box 280, Guernsey Tel : 0481 21673
VALLENTINE, Mitchell & Co.Ltd., Gainsborough House, 11 Gainsborough Road, London E11 1RS Tel : 01.530 4226 Telex : 897719 - distributed by Macdonald & Evans Ltd.
VALVE Manufacturers Assoc., 3 Pannells Court, Chertsey Street, Guildford, Surrey GU1 4EU Tel : 0483 37379
VAN Dusen Aircraft Supplies, Murdock Road, Bicester, Oxon OX6 7RB Tel : 08692 43381
VAN GORCUM, PO Box 43, 9400 AA Assen, The Netherlands Tel : 05920 46846
VAN Nostrand Reinhold Co.Ltd., Molly Millars Lane, Wokingham Berks RG11 2PY Tel : 0734 789456 Telex : 847798
VANTAGE Press Inc., 516 West 34th Street, New York 10001 USA Tel : 212 736 1767/9
VARIAN Associates Ltd., 28 Manor Road, Walton on Thames, Surrey KT12 2QF Tel : 093 22 43741
VARIORUM, 20-21a Pembridge Mews, London W11 3EQ Tel : 01.727 5492 Telex : 261234
VEGETARIAN Society of the UK Ltd., Parkdale, Durham Road, Altrincham, Cheshire WA14 4QG Tel : 061.928 0793 / 53 Marloes Road, London W8 6LA Tel : 01.937 7739 - distributed by C.W.Daniel & Co.Ltd.
VEHICLE Builders & Repairers Assoc., Belmont House, Finkle Lane, Gildersome, Leeds LS27 7TW Tel : 0532 538333
Colin VENTON Ltd., The Uffington Press, 24 High Street, Melksham, Wilts. SN12 6LA Tel : 0225 703424
VENTON Educational Ltd., The Uffington Press, 24 High Street Melksham, Wilts. SN12 6LA Tel : 0225 703424
VENTURA Publ.Ltd., 44 Uxbridge Street, London W8 7TG Tel : 01.221 6395
VENTURE Development Corp., One Washington Street, Wellesley, Mass.02181, USA Tel : 617 237 5080
VERACITY Ventures Ltd., 6 Temple Gardens, Rickmansworth Herts. WD3 1QJ Tel : 092 74 25757
VERITAS Foundation Publ.Centre, 4-12 Praed Mews, London W2 1QZ Tel : 01.723 1368/9734
VERITAS Publications, Veritas House, 7-8 Lower Abbey Street, Dublin 1, Republic of Ireland Tel : 0001 788177 Telex : 32238
VERKERKE Ltd., Braintree, Essex CM7 6YL Tel : 0376 21120 Telex : 987717
VERLAG Chemie, Germany - distributed by Royal Society of Chemistry
VERLAG Dokumentation - now K.G.Saur Verlag, Munich
VERLAG Ernest Battenburg, Kaustneweg 12, Postfach 710260, D-6000 Munchen 71, W.Germany
VERLAG Eugen Ulmer, Postfach 700561, Wollgrasweg 41, D-7000 Stuttgart 70, W.Germany Tel : 0711 4507-0 Telex : 7 23634
VERLAG Fuer Deutsch, Schillerstrasse 5, D-8000 Munchen 2, W.Germany Tel : 089 557825 Telex : 5213212
VERLAG Hoppenstadt & Co., Postfach 40 06, Havelstrasse 9, D-6100 Darmstadt 1, W.Germany
VERLAG Otto Harrassowitz, Postfach 2929, 6200 Wiesbaden 1 W.Germany Tel : 06121 521046 Telex : 04186135
VERSO Editions, 15 Greek Street, London W1V 5LF Tel : 01.437 3546 - distributed by IBD
VICTORIA House Publ.Ltd., Paulton, Bristol BS18 5LQ Tel : 0761 413301
VICTORY Press, Lottbridge Drive, Eastbourne, E.Sussex BN23 6NT
VIDEO Arts Ltd., Dumbarton House, 2nd Floor, 68 Oxford Street, London W1N 9LA Tel : 01.637 7288 Telex : 298838
VIDEOSPACE Ltd., 272 London Road, Wallington, Surrey SM6 7DJ Tel : 01.773 0921 Telex : 943763
VIENNA House Inc., 347 Madison Avenue, New York 10019, USA
VIKAS Publ.House Ltd., India - c/o UBS Publ.Distributors Ltd. 71 Mount Drive, N.Harrow, Middx. - non fiction titles distributed by Croom Helm Ltd.
VIKING Press Inc.Publ. - c/o TABS
VIKING Publications Ltd., 1 Hope Street, Douglas, Isle of Man Tel : 0624 22601
VIKING Publicity, 3a Hailes Street, Winchcombe, Glos. Tel : 0242 603333
VILLA Books Ltd., 55 Dame Street, Dublin 2, Republic of Ireland Tel : 0001 775138
VILLIERS Publ.Ltd., Ingestre Road, London NW5 1UL Tel : 01.485 8404
VINE Books, Whitefield House, 186 Kennington Park Road, London SE11 4BT
VINTAGE Aviation Publ.Ltd., VAP House, Station Field Industrial Estate, Kidlington, Oxford OX5 1LL
VINTAGE Books, Flevolaan 36-38, PO Box 124, 1380 K Weesp, The Netherlands
VIRAGO Press, Ely House, 37 Dover Street, London W1X 4HS Tel : 01.499 9716
VIRGIN Books, 61-63 Portobello Road, London W11 3DD Tel : 01.221 7535 Telex : 22542
VIRTUE & Co.Ltd., 25 Breakfield, Coulsdon, Surrey CR3 2UE Tel : 01.668 4632/5 Telex : 261507
VISAGE Press, 2333 N Vernon Street, Arlington, VA 22207 USA
VISAPHONE Co.Ltd., 17 Middleton Road, London NW11 Tel : 01.450 7712
VISION Press Ltd., 30 Museum Street, London WC1 Tel : 01.636 9516
VISUAL Publ.Ltd., 82a The Street, Rustington, W.Sussex BN16 3NR
VITALOGRAPH, Maids Morton House, Buckingham MK18 1SW
VIVASH-Jones Consultants Ltd., 36 Belgrave Mews North, Belgrave Square, London SW1X 8RS Tel : 01.235 9071
VOLTAIRE Foundation at the Taylor Institution, St.Giles, Oxford OX1 3NA
VOLTURNA & Marsland Press, 52 Ormonde Road, Hythe, Kent CT21 6DW Tel : 0303 69465
VOLUNTEERS in Asia - distributed by Intermediate Technology Publ.Ltd.
George VYNER (Distribution)Ltd., PO Box 1, Holmfirth, Huddersfield HD7 2RP Tel : 048 489 5221

W

W.H.O. (World Health Organisation) - distributed by HMSO
WHS Distributors Ltd., St.John's House, East Street, Leicester LE1 6NE Tel : 0533 551196 Telex : 341415
W.I.Books Ltd., 39 Eccleston Street, Victoria, London SW1W 9NT Tel : 01.730 7212
WIRA (Wood Industries Research Assoc.), WIRA House, West Park Ring Road, Leeds LS16 6QL Tel : 0532 781381 Telex : 557189
WADSWORTH, USA - distributed by Proost & Brandt, 85 Strijkviertel, 2543-De Maarn, Utrecht, The Netherlands / UK Office : 53 Bloomsbury Street, London WC1B 3QT Tel : 01.631 0864
John WAITE, 14 Hartington Villas, Hove, Brighton, Sussex Tel : 0273 779970
WALES Tourist Board, Davis Street, Cardiff CF1 2FU Tel : 0222 372685 Telex : 497269
WALKER Books, 17-19 Hanway House, Hanway Place, London W1 Tel : 01.636 0374
WALL St.Journal, c/o Specialised Distribution Services, 218 Feltham Road, Ashford, Middx.
WALLCOVERING Manufacturers Assoc., Alembic House, 93 Albert Embankment, London SE1 7TY Tel : 01.582 1185
H.G.WALTERS Ltd., Tenby, Dyfed
Henry E.WALTER Ltd., 26 Grafton Road, Worthing, W.Sussex BN11 1QU Tel : 0903 204567
J.WALTERS, Technical Formulae, 10 Northern Drive, Fareham Hants. PO16 7PY
WALTHAMSTOW Antiquarian Society, Hon.Secretary, 43 Dale View Avenue, Chingford, London E4 6PJ
WALTHUS Noordorft, PO Box 58, Groningren, The Netherlands
WALTON Press, Benedict Street, Glastonbury, Somerset BA6 9NN Tel : 0458 32829
WARBURG Institute, University of London, Woburn Square, London WC1H 0AB Tel : 01.580 9663
WARD Lock Ltd., 82 Gower Street, London WC1E 6EQ Tel : 01.637 9472 Telex : 262364
Frederick WARNE (Publ.)Ltd., 40 Bedford Square, London WC1B 3HE Tel : 01.580 9622 Telex : 25963
WARNER Book Services, PO Box 690, New York 10019, USA
WARREN-Gash, 247 Molesey Avenue, West Molesey, Surrey Tel : 01.979 5593
WARREN Gorham & Lamont Inc., 210 South Street, Boston, Mass.02111, USA

WARREN House Press, 12 New Road, North Walsham, Norfolk
    NR28 9DF   Tel : 069 24 5277
WARREN Point Ltd., Prospect Place, Welwyn, Herts. AL6 9FW
WARREN Spring Laboratory, PO Box 20, Gunnels Wood Road,
    Stevenage, Herts. SG1 2BX   Tel : 0438 3388
    Telex : 82250
Keith WARTON Consultants Ltd., 11 Beaumont Avenue, Richmond
    Surrey TW9 2HE   Tel : 01.948 1814
WARWICK Publications, 8 Moore Street, Queensway, Birmingham
    B4 7UH
WASHINGTON Information Directory, c/o Congressional
    Quarterly Inc., 1414 22nd Street NW, Washington
    DC 20037, USA   Tel : 202 887 8500
WASHINGTON Researchers, 1120 Connecticut Avenue, Washington
    DC 20036, USA
WASHINGTON University Press - no longer in operation
WATCH Tower Bible & Tract Society, Watch Tower House, The
    Ridgeway, London NW7 1RN   Tel : 01.906 2211
WATER Information Center Inc., 7 High Street, Huntingdon,
    New York 11743, USA
WATER Research Centre, Stevenage Laboratory, Elder Way,
    Stevenage, Herts. SG1 1TH   Tel : 0438 2444
WATER Resources Publications, PO Box 2841, Littleton,
    Colorado 80161, USA   Tel : 303 779 6685
WATERLOW (London)Ltd., Holywell House, Worship Street,
    London EC2A 2EN   Tel : 01.377 4600   Telex : 888804
    - distributed by Pergamon Press
WATMOUGHS Ltd., High Street, Idle, Bradford, W.Yorks BD10
    8NL   Tel : 0274 612111 - distributed by Independent
    Magazines (Publ.)Ltd.
Peter WATSON Ltd., 92 High Street, Henley-in-Arden, Solihull
    B95 5AN   Tel : 056 42 3816
W.WATSON & Co., St.Ann's Hill, Carlisle, Cumbria
WATT Committee on Energy Ltd., The London Science Centre,
    18 Adam Street, London WC2N 6AH   Tel : 01.930 7637
WATT Publ.Co., Mount Morris, Ill. 61054, USA
Franklin WATTS Ltd. - distributed by J.M.Dent & Sons Ltd.
Peter WATTS Publishing, 13-19 Stroud Road, Gloucester GL1
    5AA   Tel : 0452 411860
WAYLAND (Publ.)Ltd., 49 Lansdowne Place, Hove, E.Sussex
    BN3 1HF   Tel : 0273 722561
J.P.WAYNE Borg, Postfach 646, D-5300 Bonn, W.Germany
WEALD Publishing Agency - now Weald UK Ltd.
WEALD UK Ltd., 43 High Street, Tunbridge Wells, Kent TN1
    1XU   Tel : 0892 45355   Telex : 95625
WEALDEN Press Ltd., South Park Lodge, Mayfield Lane,
    Wadhurst, Sussex TN5 6JE   Tel : 089 288 2366
WEATHER, James Glaister House, Grenville Place, Bracknell,
    Berks RG12 1BX   Tel : 0344 22957/8
WEATHERALL Green & Smith, 22 Chancery Lane, London WC2A
    1LT   Tel : 01.405 6944
WEATHERILL Inc. - see Pall Mall Press Ltd.
A.C.M.WEBB (Publ.)Ltd., 33 West Street, Brighton, Sussex
    BN1 2RE   Tel : 0273 27365
WEBB & Bower (Publ.)Ltd., 9 Colleton Crescent, Exeter
    Devon EX2 4BY   Tel : 0392 35362   Telex : 42544
John WEBBER & Co., 606 Grenville House, Dolphin Square
    London SW1V 3LR   Tel : 01.821 6736
C.G.WEDGEWOOD & Co., 14 Kings Road, Wimbledon, London
    SW19 8QN   Tel : 01.540 6224   Telex : 8954665
WEED Research Organisation, Begbroke Hill, Kidlington, Oxford
Grosso Hans WEGNER, Postfach 102540, D-2000 Hamburg 1,
    West Germany
WEIDENFELD & Nicolson, 91 Clapham High Street, London SW4
    9TA   Tel : 01.622 9933 - distributed by Heinemann
    Group
WELDING Institute, Abington Hall, Abington, Cambridge CB1
    6AL   Tel : 0223 891162   Telex : 81183
WELDING Research Council, 345 East 47th Street, New York
    10017, USA   Tel : 212 705 7956
WELLBEING Books, c/o Open Marketing Group, Box 735 -
    Brookline Village, Boston, Mass., USA
    Tel : 617 277 5226
WELLENS Publishing, High Street, Gullsborough, Northampton
    NN6 8PY   Tel : 060 122 379
P.& G.WELLS Ltd., 11 College Street, Winchester, Hants. SO23
    9LZ   Tel : 0962 2016
WELLS Gardner, Darton & Co.Ltd., Faygate, Horsham, W.
    Sussex   Tel : 029 383 444
Owen WELLS Publ.Co., 66 The Grove, Ilkley, W.Yorks LS29
    9PA   Tel : 0943 608394
WELSH Books Centre, Industrial Estate, Llanbadarn, Aberystwyth
    Dyfed
WELSH Dragon Books, County Press Buildings, Bala, Gwynedd
    LL23 7PG   Tel : 0678 520262

WELSH Folk Museum, St.Fagans, Cardiff CF5 6XB
    Tel : 0222 569441
WELSH Plant Breeding Station, Plas Gogerddan, Aberystwyth
    Dyfed SY23 3EB   Tel : 0970 828255
WELSH Soils Discussion Group - Dr D.A.Jenkins, Publications
    Manager, Dept.of Biochemistry & Soil Science,
    Univ.College of N.Wales, Bangor, Gwynedd LL57 2UW
WENSUM Press, 4 Farmers Avenue, Norwich, Norfolk
    Tel : 0603 619745
WENTWORTH Book Co.Ltd., Pinder Road, Hoddesdon, Herts.
    EN11 0HF   Tel : 0992 67864   Telex : 27236
WERNER Management Consultants, 111 W.40th Street, New
    York 10018, USA   Tel : 212 730 1280
P.C.WERTH Ltd., Audiology House, 45 Nightingale Lane,
    Balham, London SW12 8SU   Tel : 01.675 5151
WESLEY Historical Society, Bankhead Press, Broxton, Chester
    Tel : 082 925 206
WESSEX (Electronic)Publ.Ltd., Beaminster, Dorset DT8 3BU
    Tel : 0308 862314
WEST Highland Publ.Co.Ltd., Old School, Breakish, Isle of
    Skye   Tel : 047 12 464
WEST Publ.Co.Inc., 170 Old Country Road, Mineola, NY 11501
    USA - distributed by Castle House Publ.Ltd.
WEST Sussex County Council, County Hall, Chichester, W.
    Sussex PO19 1RQ   Tel : 0243 785100   Telex : 86279
WEST Sussex Record Office, County Hall, Chichester, W.Sussex
    PO19 1RQ   Tel : 0243 785100   Telex ; 86279
WESTERHAM Press Ltd., London Road, Westerham, Kent TN16
    1BX
WESTERN Electric Co.Ltd., 222 Broadway, New York 10038
    USA
WESTGATE Educational Pub.Co., Digswell Place, Welwyn Garden
    City, Herts. AL8 7SX
WESTHALL Books, Westhall Place, Westhall Hill, Fulbrook,
    Oxon.
WESTMINSTER City Libraries, Marylebone Road, London NW1
    5PS   Tel : 01.828 8076   Telex : 263305
WESTMINSTER Productions Ltd., Westminster Theatre, Palace
    Street, Buckingham Palace Road, London SW1E 5JB
    Tel : 01.834 7882 - distributed by Grosvenor Books
    (The Good Road Ltd.)
WESTMORLAND Gazette, 22 Stricklandgate, Kendal, Cumbria
    LA9 4NE   Tel : 0539 20555
M.J.WESTON, The Stables, Monkton, Andover, Hants.
    Tel : 026 471 216
WESTPORT Publ.Ltd. - distributed by Eurospan Ltd.
WESTVIEW Press, USA - distributed by Bowker Publ.Co. in UK
WEYENBORGH Verlag, 5300 Bonn 2, Postfach 200646, West
    Germany
Keith WHARTON Consultants Ltd., 11 Beaumont Avenue,
    Richmond, Surrey TW9 2HE
WHEATLAND Journals, Penn House, Penn Place, Rickmansworth
    WD3 1SN   Tel : 0923 774262
A.WHEATON & Co., Hennock Road, Exeter EX2 8RP
    Tel : 0392 74121/5 - distributed by Pergamon Press
WHEATSHEAF Books Ltd. - distributed by Harvester Press
WHEELER Associates Inc., 120 N.Mulberry Street, Elizabethtown
    KY 42701, USA   Tel : 502 765 6773
WHEELPLAN Ltd., Stanley House, Smarden, Ashford, Kent
WHEELPLAN(Tourism) in Europe Ltd., Stanley House, Smarden
    Ashford, Kent TN27 8NH   Tel : 023 377 516
WHELDON & Wesley Ltd., Lytton Lodge, Codicote, Hitchin,
    Herts. SG4 8TE   Tel : 0438 820370
WHERE To Buy Ltd., Queensway House, 2 Queensway, Redhill
    Surrey RH1 1QZ   Tel : 0737 68611
WHICH Computer, 2 Duncan Terrace, London N1
    Tel : 01.278 9517
WHIRLWIND Books - c/o TABS
J.WHITAKER & Sons Ltd., 12 Dyott Street, London WC1A 1DF
    Tel : 01.836 8911
WHITCOULLS Ltd., 3 Addle Hill, Carter Lane, London EC4V
    5BB   Tel : 01.248 7204 - distributed by IBD
Don WHITE Consultants Inc., Circle House South, 65-67 Wembley
    Hill Road, Wembley, Middx. HA9 8DF
    Tel : 01.902 7580
WHITE Crescent Press Ltd., Crescent Road, Luton LU2 0AG
    Tel : 0582 23122
WHITE Eagle Publ.Trust, New Lands, Brewells Lane, Rake, Liss
    Hants. GU33 7HY   Tel : 073 082 3300
WHITE Fish Authority, Sea Fisheries House, 10 Young Street,
    Edinburgh EH2 4JQ   Tel : 031.225 2515
WHITE Horse Books, Dene House, Bridge Street, Kineton,
    Warwicks. CV35 0HP   Tel : 0926 640504
WHITE House Books, Carlisle Place, London SW1
    Tel : 01.834 1174

WHITECHAPEL Art Gallery, Whitechapel High Street, London
    E1 7QX Tel : 01.377 0107
WHITEHALL Press Ltd., Earl House, 27 Earl Street, Maidstone
    Kent ME14 1PE Tel : 0622 59841
WHITEKNIGHTS Press, Dept.of Typography & Graphic
    Communication, University of Reading, 2 Earley
    Gate, Whiteknights, Reading RG6 2AU
    Tel : 0734 85123
WHITTET Books Ltd., The Oil Mills, Weybridge, Surrey KT13
    8LD Tel : 0932 42274
WHITTINGTON Press, Manor Farm, Andoversford, Cheltenham,
    Glos. GL54 4HP Tel : 024 282 615
WHIZZARD Publ.Ltd., 11a Camden High Street, London NW1
    7JE Tel : 01.388 7411/2 - distributed to Heinemann
    Group
WHO Owns Whom Ltd., 6-8 Bonhill Street, London EC2A 4BU
    Tel : 01.628 3691 - now part of Dun & Bradstreet Ltd.
WHO's Who in America - see Marquis Publications
WHO's Who in Europe, Servi-tech Sprl, Rue de Livourne 75,
    B-1050 Brussels, Belgium
WHO's Who in France - see Editions Jacques Lafitte
WHO's Who in the Arab World - now International Who's Who in
    the Arab World, 2 South Audley Street, London
    W1X 5DQ Tel : 01.409 1525
WHO's Who of Southern Africa, Argus Printing & Publ.Co.Ltd.
    5th Floor, Star Building, 47 Sauer Street,
    Johannesburg, South Africa
WHO's Who Verlag - distributed by Bowker Publ.Co.
WILD Hawthorne Press, Stonypath, Dunsyre, Carnwath, Lanark.
    Tel : 089 981 252
WILDFOWL Trust, Slimbridge, Gloucester GL2 7BT
    Tel : 045 389 333
WILDINGS of Shrewsbury Ltd., Windsor Place, Shrewsbury
    SY1 2DB Tel : 0743 51278
WILDWOOD House, Jubilee House, Chapel Road, Hounslow, Middx.
    TW3 1TX Tel : 01.572 6525
WILDY & Son Ltd., Lincoln's Inn Archway, Carey Street, London
    WC2A 2JD Tel : 01.242 5778
John WILEY & Sons Ltd., Baffins Lane, Chichester, W.Sussex
    PO19 1UD Tel : 0243 784531 Telex : 86290 - orders
    to Distribution Centre, Southern Cross Trading
    Estate, Olands Way, Shripney, Bognor Regis, W.
    Sussex PO22 9SA Tel : 02433 29121
Roger WILLIAMS Technical & Economic Services Inc., 34
    Washington Road, PO Box 426, Princeton, NJ 08540
    USA Tel : 609 799 1200 Telex : 843455
Stewart WILLIAMS Intl.Ltd., Carlton Chambers, Station Road,
    Shortlands, Bromley, Kent BR2 0EY Tel : 01.464 5418
Stewart WILLIAMS Publishers, Bryn Awel, Buttrills Road, Barry
    S.Glamorgan CF6 6AD Tel : 044 62 735667
WILLIAMS & Wilkins, London House, 266 Fulham Road, London
    SW10 9EL Tel : 01.351 1138/3822 Telex : 8954102
John WILLIAMSON, Kennet Cottage, Bathampton, Bath BA2
    6TP Avon
WILLOW Books, 8 Grafton Street, London W1X 3LA
    Tel : 01.493 7070
G.F.WILSON & Co.Ltd., Eastgate Printing Works Town Quay
    Southampton SO9 5TN Tel : 0703 28881
H.W.WILSON Co., 950 University Avenue, Bronx, New York
    10452, USA
Philip WILSON Publ.Ltd., Russell Chambers, Covent Garden
    London WC2E 8AA Tel : 01.240 1091/2
    Telex : 22158
WILSTOW Ltd., Prince Rupert House, 64 Queen Street, London
    EC4R 1AD Tel : 01.248 0654
WILTON House Publ. - distributed by Gower Publ.Co.Ltd.
WILTSHIRE Studio Designs Ltd., 122 Bath Road, Cheltenham
    Glos. Tel : 0242 584520
WINCHMORE Publishing, 40 Triton Square, London NW1 3HG
    Tel : 01.387 4549 Telex : 261967
The WINDMILL Press (Heinemann Group), Kingswood,
    Tadworth, Surrey KT20 6TG Tel : 073 783 3511
    Telex : 947458
WINE Warehouses Publ.Co.Ltd., 34-36 The Highway, London
    E1 9BG Tel : 01.488 0100
Allan WINGATE (Publ.)Ltd., 44 Hill Street, London W1X 8LB
    Tel : 01.493 6777 - distributed by W.H.Allen & Co.
WINSOR & Newton, Wealdstone, Harrow, Middx.HA3 5RH
    Tel : 01.427 4343
WINSTON, Washington, USA - distributed by J.Wiley & Sons
R.WINSTONE, 23 Hyland Grove, Henbury Hill, Bristol 9
    Tel : 0272 503646
David WINTER & Son Ltd., PO Box 99, 15 Shore Terrace, Dundee
    DD1 9QU Tel : 0382 22146
WINTHROP Laboratories, Winthrop House, Surbiton-on-Thames
    Surrey KT6 4PH Tel : 01.399 5252

WINTHROP Publ.Co., 17 Dunster Street, Cambridge, Mass.
    USA - distributed by Prentice Hall Intl.
WISE Books, 82 Chart Lane, Reigate, Surrey RH2 7EA
    Tel : 073 72 42586
H.F.& G.WITHERBY Ltd., 32 Aylesbury Street, London EC1R
    0ET Tel : 01.251 5750
George WITTENBORN Inc., 1018 Madison Avenue, New York
    10021, USA
WITWATERSRAND University Press, 1 Jan Smuts Avenue, 2001
    Johannesburg, South Africa Tel : 011 716 2023
WITZSTROCK Verlag Gerhard GmbH, Postfach 509, Bismarck-
    strasse 9, 7570 Baden-Baden, W.Germany
WOBURN Press, Gainsborough House, 11 Gainsborough Road
    London E11 1RS Tel : 01.530 4226 Telex : 897719
WOLFE Medical Publ.Ltd., Wolfe House, 3-5 Conway Street,
    London W1P 6HE Tel : 01.636 4622 Telex : 8814230
Oswald WOLFF (Publ.)Ltd., 9 Park Lorne, Park Road, London
    NW8 7JL Tel : 01.258 0401
WOLFF-Ingham Co., Tintagel, Western Road, Cheltenham, Glos.
    Tel : 0242 37702
WOLFHOUND Press, 68 Mountjoy Square, Dublin 1
    Tel : 0001 740354
WOLPERT & Jones Studios Ltd., 24 St.John's Road, Golders
    Green, London NW11 Tel : 01.455 9343
WOLTERS-Noordhoff BV, Oude Boteringestraat 22, Postbus 58
    9700 MB Groningen, The Netherlands
WOMEN in Distribution Inc., PO Box 8858, Washington DC 20003
    USA
WOMEN in Media, 37 Brondesbury Road, London NW6
WOMEN's Engineering Society, 25 Fouberts Place, London W1V
    2AL Tel : 01.437 5212
The WOMEN's Press Ltd., 124 Shoreditch High Street, London
    E1 6JE Tel : 01.729 5257 Telex : 919034
WOMEN's Research & Resources Centre, 190 Upper Street,
    London N1 Tel : 01.359 5773
WOOD Bridgedale & Co.Ltd., Kent House, Market Place, London
    W1N 7AJ Tel : 01.636 3152
WOOD Mackenzie & Co., Erskine House, 68-73 Queen Street,
    Edinburgh EH2 4NS Tel : 031.226 4141
A.J.WOOD Research, 1405 Locust Street, Philadelphia, PA 19102
    USA Tel : 215 546 6100
Henry WOODFIELD & Stanley Ltd., Broad Lane, Moldgreen,
    Huddersfield HD5 8DD Tel : 0484 21467
WOODHEAD Faulkner, Fitzwilliam House, 32 Trumpington Street
    Cambridge CB2 1QY Tel : 0223 66733
Barbara WOODHOUSE, Campions, Croxley Green, Rickmansworth
    Herts. WD3 3JD Tel : 0923 74499
WOODMANSTERNE Ltd., Greenhill Crescent, Holywell Industrial
    Estate, Watford, Herts. Tel : 0923 28236/45788
WOODS of Colchester Ltd., Tufnell Way, Colchester, Essex
    CO4 5AR Tel : 0206 44122
WOODVILLE Press, PO Box 6, Gerrards Cross, Bucks SL9 8EL
    Tel : 0753 86000
WOOL Industries Research Association, Wira House, West Park
    Ring Road, Leeds LS16 6QL Tel : 0532 781381
    Telex : 557189
WOOLLEN Yarn Spinners Federation, Hudcar Mills, Hudcar Lane
    Bury, BO9 6HD
Cecil WOOLF, 1 Mornington Place, London NW1 7RP
    Tel : 01.387 2394
WORD Books (UK)Ltd., Northbridge Road, Berkhamsted, Herts.
    HP4 1EH Tel : 04427 74711/5
WORKER Writers & Community Publishers, 69 Heaton Road,
    Newcastle upon Tyne NE6 1SA Tel : 0632 761351
WORKERS' Educational Association, Temple House, 2 Upper
    Berkeley Street, London W1H 8BY Tel : 01.402 5608
WORKING Together Campaign Ltd., 128 Marsham Court,
    Marsham Street, London SW1P 4LB Tel : 01.828 4815
WORKSHOP Press, Thatch Cottage, Tarrant Monston, Blandford
    Forum, Dorset Tel : 025 889 381
WORKSHOP Press Ltd., 2 Culham Court, Granville Road,
    London N4 4JB Tel : 01.348 4054
WORLD Almanac, USA - distributed by Seymour Press Ltd.
WORLD Association of Girl Guides & Girl Scouts, 132 Ebury
    Street, London SW1W 9QQ Tel : 01.730 6226
WORLD Aviation Directory, 26 East Holm, London NW11
WORLD Bank (IBEG), 2-4 Brook Street, London W1Y 1AA
    Tel : 01.493 5061 - distributed by IBD
WORLD Bank, 66 Avenue d'Iena, 75116 Paris, France
    Tel : 1 723 54 21 Telex : 842 620628
WORLD Book - Childcraft Intl.Inc., Canterbury House,
    Sydenham Road, Croydon, Surrey CR9 2LR
    Tel : 01.686 6421 Telex : 946314
WORLD Coal, 500 Howard Street, San Francisco, California
    94105, USA
WORLD Council of Churches, Publications Office, PO Box 66
    1211 Geneva 20, Switzerland

WORLD Economics Ltd., 500 Chesham House, 150 Regent Street London W1R 5FA Tel : 01.439 6288
WORLD Energy Conference, 34 St.James's Street, London SW1A 1HD Tel : 01.930 3966
WORLD Hospitals, International Hospital Federation, 126 Albert Street, London NW1 7NF Tel : 01.267 5176
WORLD International Publ.Ltd., PO Box 111, Great Ducie Street Manchester M60 3BL Tel : 061.834 3110
WORLD Market Perspective, PO Box 23, Hounslow, Middx. TW3 1LN
WORLD Meteorological Organization, 41 Avenue Giuseppe-Motta CH-1211 Geneva 20, Switzerland
WORLD Microfilms Publications, 62 Queens Grove, London NW8 6ER Tel : 01.586 3092
WORLD of Information, 21 Gold Street, Saffron Walden, Essex CB10 1EJ Tel : 0799 21150 Telex : 817197
WORLD of Islam Festival Publ.Co.Ltd. - distributed by Thorsons Publ.Ltd.
WORLD Publ.Co. - distributed by Collins Sons & Co.Ltd.
WORLD Review, Milburn House, Dean Street, Newcastle upon Tyne Tel : 0632 21402
WORLD Ship Society, 32 Church Lane, Merton Park, London SW19 3HQ Tel : 01.542 1276
WORLD Telex Directory - published by Telex Verlag Jaeger & Waldman, 15-20 Crossway House, High Street Bracknell, Berks RG12 1DA
WORLD University Library, 91 Clapham High Street, London SW4 9TA Tel : 01.622 9933 Telex : 918066
WORLD Wide Information Services Inc., 660 First Avenue, New York 10016, USA Tel : 212 679 7240 Telex : 223377
WORLDELM Ltd., 194 Heath Road, Twickenham, Middx.TW2 5TX Tel : 01.894 1113 Telex : 8954667
WORLD's Fair Ltd., PO Box 57, 2 Daltry Street, off Shaw Road Oldham OL1 4BB Tel : 061.624 3687
WORLD's Work Ltd., The Windmill Press, Kingswood, Tadworth Surrey KT20 6TG Tel : 0737 833511 Telex : 947458
WORLDWATCH Institute, 1776 Massachusetts Ave. NW, Washington DC 20036, USA Tel : 202 452 1999
WORLDWATCH Papers - c/o Third World Publ.
WRIGHT Allen, USA - distributed by J.Wiley & Sons Ltd.
Gordon WRIGHT Publishing, 55 Marchmont Road, Edinburgh EH9 1HT Tel : 031.229 8566
John WRIGHT & Sons Ltd., 823-825 Bath Road, Bristol BS4 5NU Tel : 0272 775375 Telex : 449907
WRITERS & Readers Publishing Co-operative, 144 Camden High Street, London NW1 0NE Tel : 01.267 0511 - distributed by Macdonald & Evans Ltd.
WRITERS & Scholars Intl.Ltd., 21 Russell Street, Covent Garden London WC2B 5HP Tel : 01.836 0024
WRITERS Digest Books, 9933 Alliance Road, Cincinnati, Ohio 45242, USA
WYE College, Wye, Ashfort, Kent TN25 5AH Tel : 0233 812401
WYKEHAM Publications Ltd., 4 John Street, London WC1N 2ET
WYNDHAM Publications Ltd., 44 Hill Street, London W1X 8LB Tel : 01.493 6777 Telex : 28117 - distributed by Tiptree Book Services Ltd.
WYNKYN de Worde Society, 26 Litchfield Street, London WC2H 9NJ

X

X-S Books International, 92-104 Carnwath Road, London SW6 3SZ Tel : 01.731 4010
XEPHON, Publications Division, King's House, King Street, Maidenhead, Berks SL6 1EF Tel : 0628 74922 Telex : 837225

Y

Y.H.A., 14 Southampton Street, London WC2E 7HY Tel : 01.836 8541/7 Telex : 269330
YALE University Press, 13 Bedford Square, London WC1B 3JF Tel : 01.580 2693 - distributed by IBD
YAMADA Shoin, c/o Dai-2-Sky Building, 5-10-1 Shinjuku, Shinjuku-ku, Tokyo 160, Japan
YANKEE Group, Regal House, Lower Road, Chorleywood, Rickmansworth, Herts. WD3 5LQ Tel : 9278 4119
YANKELOVICH Skelly & White, 575 Madison Avenue, New York 10022, USA Tel : 212 752 7500
YARE Valley Publishers, 20 Bluebell Road, Norwich, Norfolk Tel : 0603 55329
YEARBOOK Medical Publ.Ltd., Barnard's Inn, Holborn, London EC1N 2JA Tel : 01.242 9613 Telex : 268633
YEOMAN Publications Ltd., 17 Prince Albert Road, Regent's Park, London NW1 7ST Tel : 01.586 1056
YORK Publishing Co., 64 Brunswick Centre, Marchmont Street London WC1N 1AE Tel : 01.278 4299
YORKSHIRE Geological Society, Institute of Geological Sciences Ring Road, Halton, Leeds LS15 8TQ
Thomas YOSELOFF Ltd., Magdalen House, 136-148 Tooley Street London SE1 2TT Tel : 01.407 7566
YOUNG & Rubicam Ltd., Greater London House, Hampstead Road London NW1 7QD Tel : 01.387 9366
YOUNG Library, International Press Centre, 76 Shoe Lane, London EC4A 3JB Tel : 01.353 0186 Telex : 23862
YOURDON Press, 1133 Avenue of the Americas, New York 10036, USA / 15-17 Ridgmount Street, London WC1E 7BH Tel : 01.637 2182/9 Telex : 24973
YOUTHAID, Tress House, 3 Stamford Street, London SE1 9NT Tel : 01.928 6424/5
YUCCA Publishers, 71 Rosehill Park West, Sutton, Surrey SM1 3LA Tel : 01.644 9642

Z

ZAEHNSDORF Ltd., 175 Bermondsey Street, London SE1 3UW Tel : 01.407 1244
ZED Press, 57 Caledonian Road, London N1 9DN Tel : 01.837 4014 - distributed by IBD
Mary ZEICHNER, Room P3/17P, 2 Marsham Street, London SW1P 5GB
Hans ZELL Publishers Ltd., PO Box 56, 14a St.Giles, Oxford OX1 3EL Tel : 0865 512934
ZENO Booksellers & Publishers, 6 Denmark Street, London WC2H 8LP Tel : 01.836 2522
ZEUS Press, 18 Church Street, Bishops Castle, Shropshire Tel : 05883 665
ZIMBABWE Information Group - see Third World Publications
ZINC Development Association, 34 Berkeley Square, London W1X 6AJ Tel : 01.499 6636 Telex : 261286
ZIONIST Federation of G.B.& Ireland, 731 High Road, London N12 0BQ
ZODIAC Press - distributed by Bookcentre
ZOMBA Books, 165-167 Willesden High Road, London NW10 2SG Tel : 01.451 3044 Telex : 919884
ZOOLOGICAL Society of London, Regent's Park, London NW1 4RY Tel : 01.722 3333
Charles ZUB Associates Ltd., Tilling Road, London NW2 1LJ Tel : 01.450 9411 Telex : 924550
A.ZWEMMER Ltd., 26 Litchifield Street, London WC2H 9NJ Tel : 01.836 1749